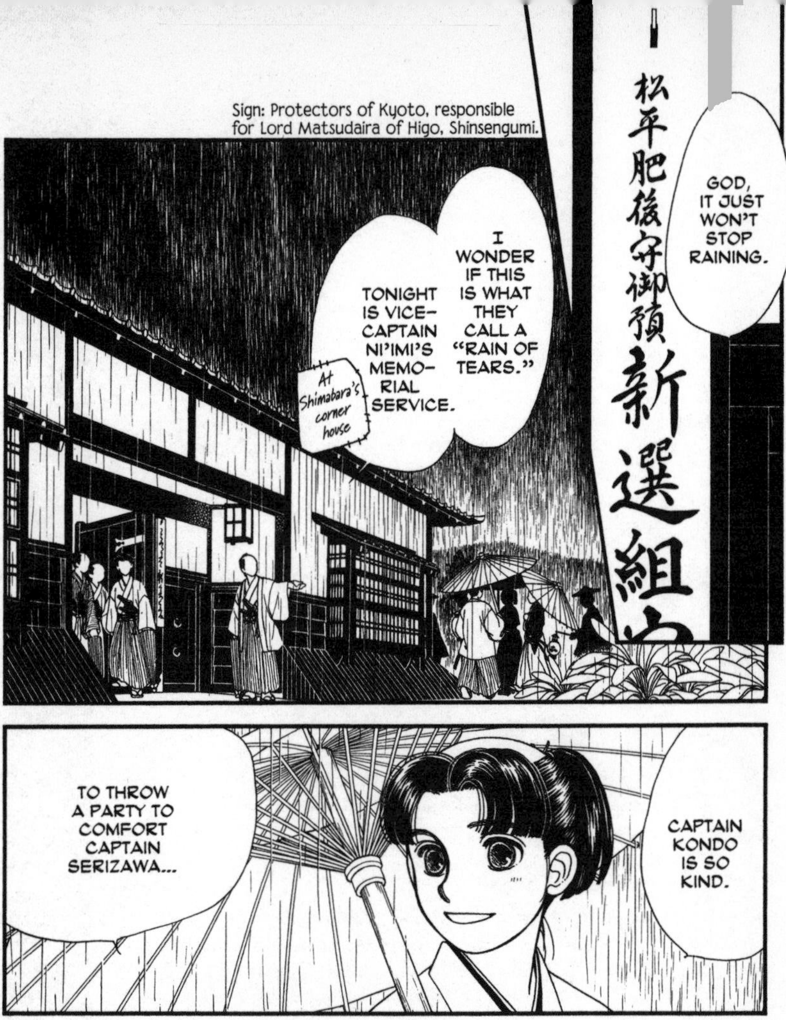
Sign: Protectors of Kyoto, responsible for Lord Matsudaira of Higo, Shinsengumi.
松平肥後守御預新選組
GOD, IT JUST WON'T STOP RAINING.
I WONDER IF THIS IS WHAT THEY CALL A "RAIN OF TEARS."
TONIGHT IS VICE-CAPTAIN NI'IMI'S MEMORIAL SERVICE.
At Shimabara's corner house
CAPTAIN KONDO IS SO KIND.
TO THROW A PARTY TO COMFORT CAPTAIN SERIZAWA...

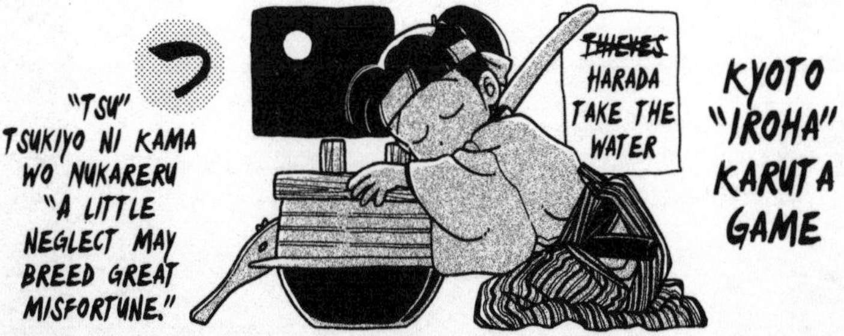
KYOTO "IROHA" KARUTA GAME
~~THIEVES~~ HARADA TAKE THE WATER
つ
"TSU" TSUKIYO NI KAMA WO NUKARERU "A LITTLE NEGLECT MAY BREED GREAT MISFORTUNE."

Characters

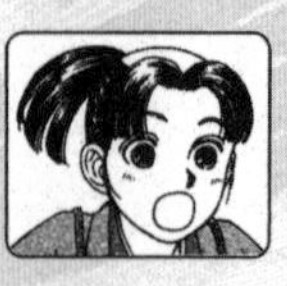

Tominaga Sei
She disguises herself as a boy to enter the Mibu-Roshi. Sei wants to become a warrior so she can avenge her father and brother. She trains under Soji, aspiring to become a true bushi.

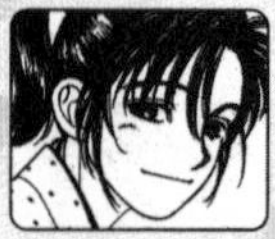

Okita Soji
Assistant vice captain of the Mibu-Roshi and the selected successor of the Ten'nen Rishin-ryu school of sword fighting. He is the only member of the Mibu-Roshi who knows Sei's secret.

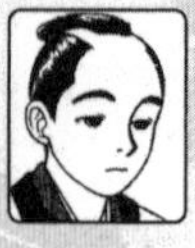

Saito Hajime
Assistant vice captain. He was a friend of Sei's older brother, Yuma, to whom he bears a striking resemblance.

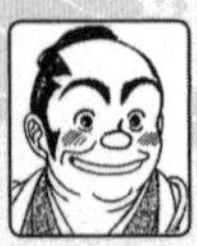

Serizawa Kamo
Captain of the Mibu-Roshi. Captain Serizawa of the Mito clan has a lackadaisical—and often inebriated—facade that belies his cunning and calculating mind.

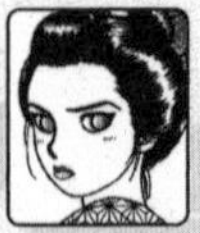

Oume
Captain Serizawa's lover. She was originally a merchant's mistress but then came to the pushy and passionate Serizawa.

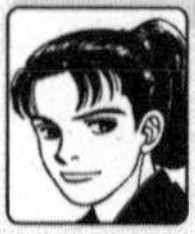

Hijikata Toshizo
Vice captain of the Mibu-Roshi. He commands the Mibu-Roshi with strict authority.

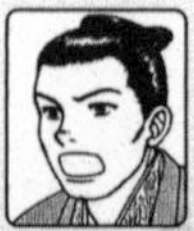

Kondo Isami
Captain of the Mibu-Roshi and fourth master of the Ten'nen Rishin-ryu. Has a very calm temperament and is highly respected.

Contents

Story Thus Far

It is the end of the Bakumatsu era, in the third year of Bunkyu (1863), in Kyoto. The Mibu-Roshi (later to become the Shinsengumi) is created to protect the shogun in this chaotic time.

Both Tominaga Sei's father and brother are killed by anti-Shogunate rebels. Sei then joins the Mibu-Roshi Party disguised as a boy with the name Kamiya Seizaburo to avenge her family. She comes to regard Okita Soji as her mentor after he saves her from being attacked. Sei aspires to become a true bushi, but she finds herself surrounded by "animals." Further, Soji soon discovers Sei is a girl and keeps her secret while watching over her. Sei considers leaving the troop but stays in order to protect Soji.

The Mibu-Roshi are credited for their efforts and the name "Shinsengumi" is bestowed upon them. At the same time, a secret order is given to eliminate Serizawa for his debauchery. Soji volunteers to carry out those orders.

Shojo Beat

4

Story & Art by
Taeko Watanabe

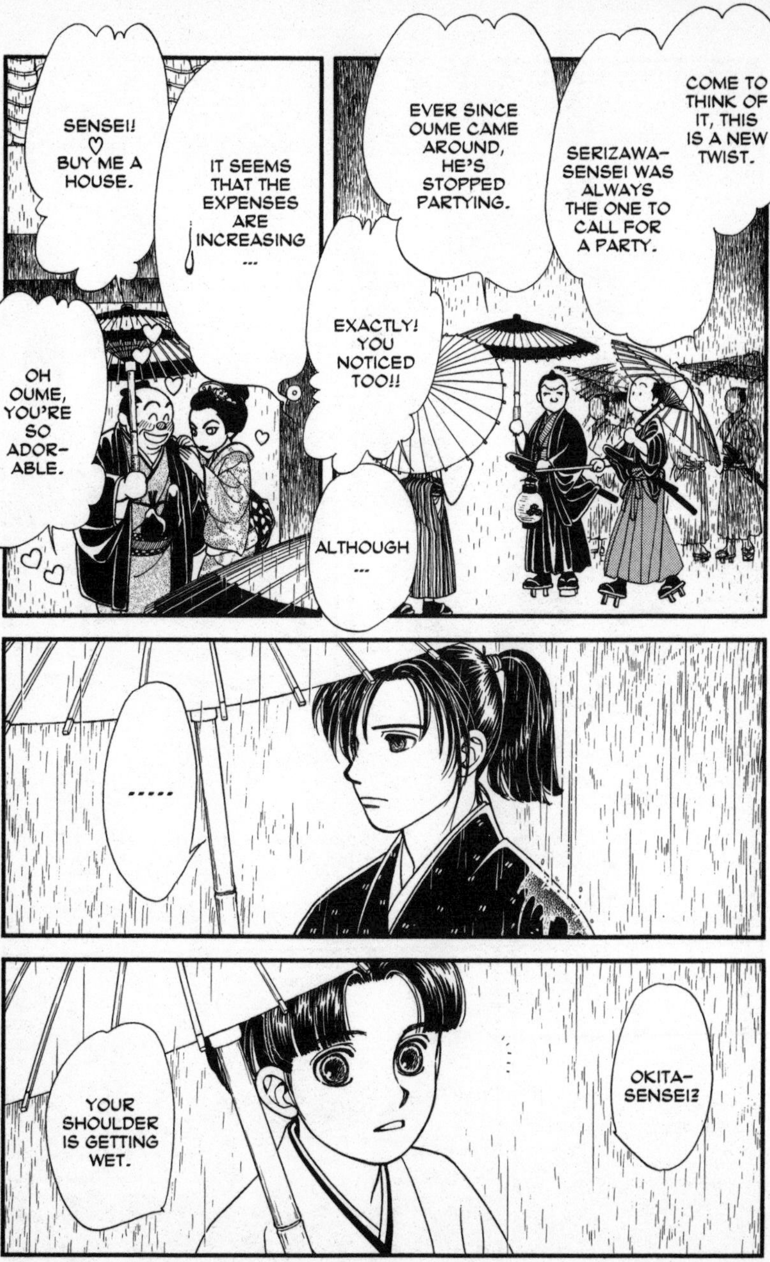
COME TO THINK OF IT, THIS IS A NEW TWIST.
SERIZAWA-SENSEI WAS ALWAYS THE ONE TO CALL FOR A PARTY.
EVER SINCE OUME CAME AROUND, HE'S STOPPED PARTYING.
EXACTLY! YOU NOTICED TOO!!
ALTHOUGH...
IT SEEMS THAT THE EXPENSES ARE INCREASING...
SENSEI! ♡ BUY ME A HOUSE.
OH OUME, YOU'RE SO ADORABLE.
.....
OKITA-SENSEI?
YOUR SHOULDER IS GETTING WET.

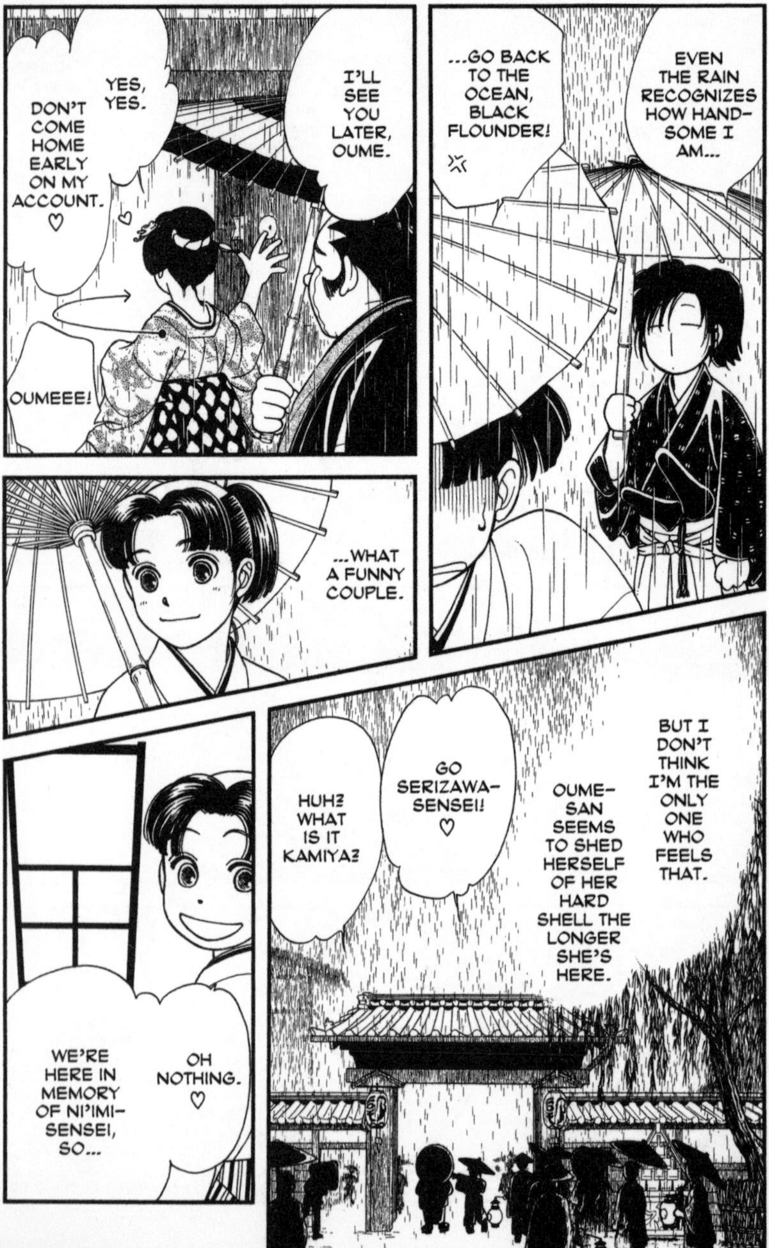
EVEN THE RAIN RECOGNIZES HOW HAND-SOME I AM...
...GO BACK TO THE OCEAN, BLACK FLOUNDER!
I'LL SEE YOU LATER, OUME.
YES, YES.
DON'T COME HOME EARLY ON MY ACCOUNT. ♡
OUMEEE!
...WHAT A FUNNY COUPLE.
BUT I DON'T THINK I'M THE ONLY ONE WHO FEELS THAT.
OUME-SAN SEEMS TO SHED HERSELF OF HER HARD SHELL THE LONGER SHE'S HERE.
GO SERIZAWA-SENSEI! ♡
HUH? WHAT IS IT KAMIYA?
OH NOTHING. ♡
WE'RE HERE IN MEMORY OF NI'IMI-SENSEI, SO...

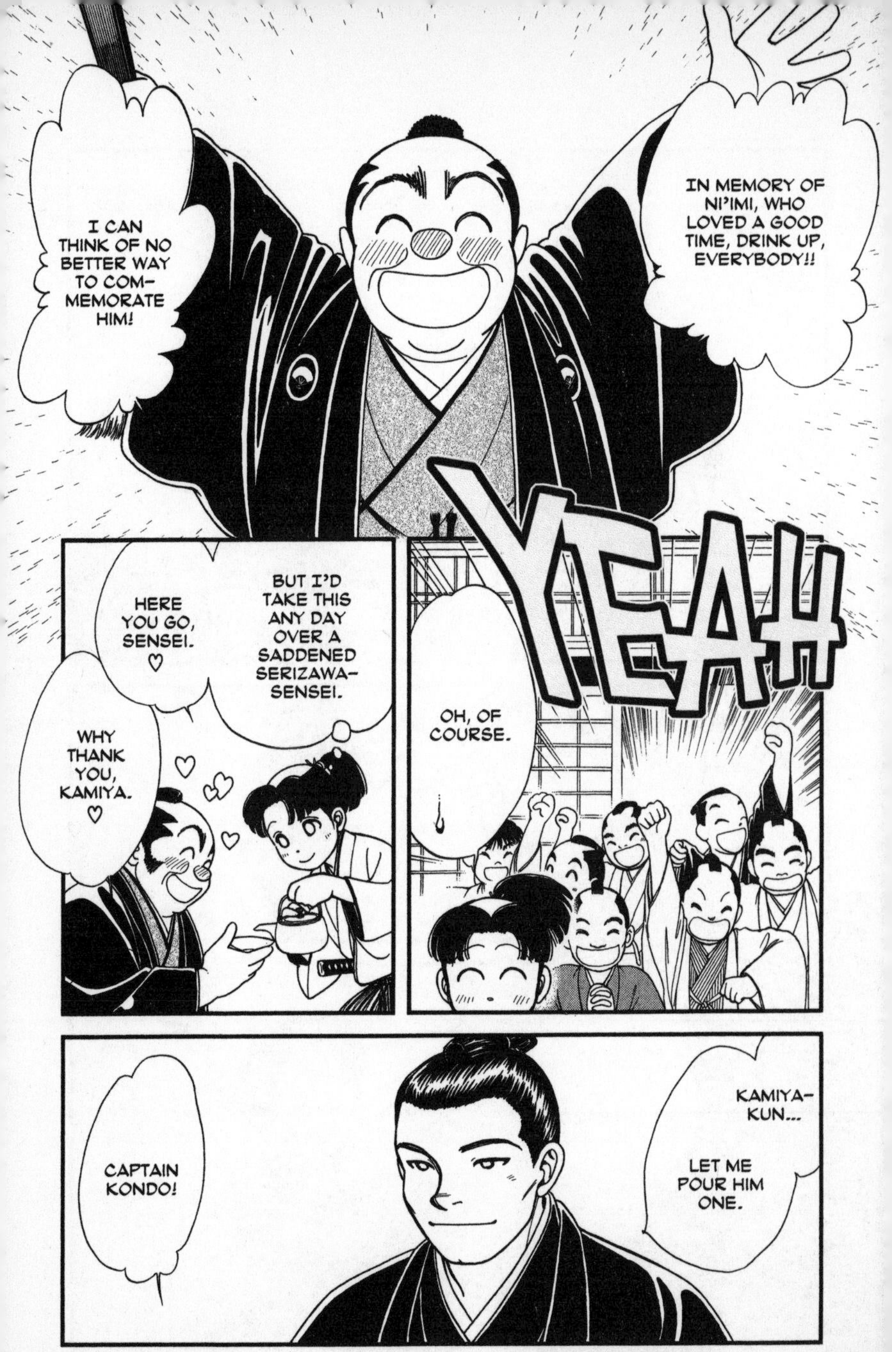
IN MEMORY OF NI'IMI, WHO LOVED A GOOD TIME, DRINK UP, EVERYBODY!!
I CAN THINK OF NO BETTER WAY TO COM-MEMORATE HIM!
YEAH
OH, OF COURSE.
BUT I'D TAKE THIS ANY DAY OVER A SADDENED SERIZAWA-SENSEI.
HERE YOU GO, SENSEI. ♡
WHY THANK YOU, KAMIYA. ♡
KAMIYA-KUN...
LET ME POUR HIM ONE.
CAPTAIN KONDO!

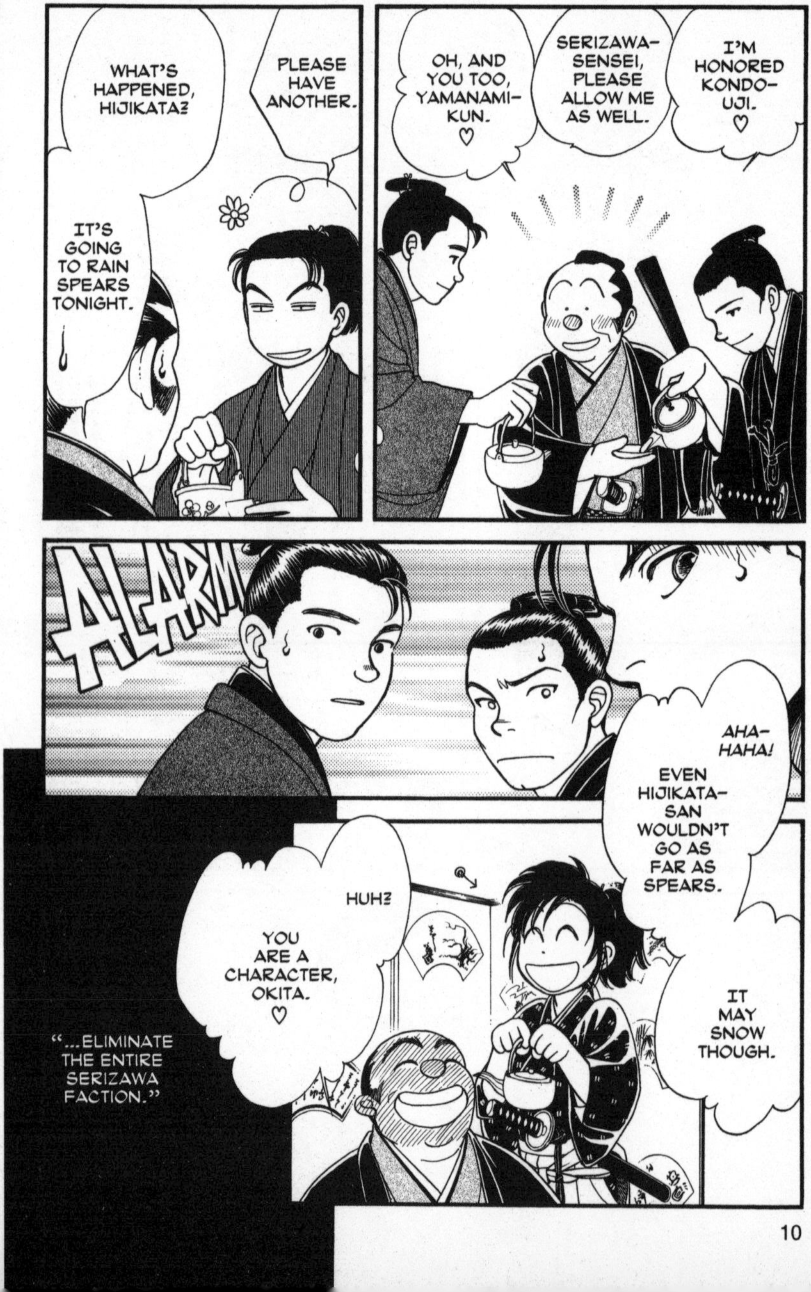
I'M HONORED KONDOU-UJI. ♡
SERIZAWA-SENSEI, PLEASE ALLOW ME AS WELL.
OH, AND YOU TOO, YAMANAMI-KUN. ♡
PLEASE HAVE ANOTHER.
WHAT'S HAPPENED, HIJIKATA?
IT'S GOING TO RAIN SPEARS TONIGHT.
ALARM
AHA-HAHA! EVEN HIJIKATA-SAN WOULDN'T GO AS FAR AS SPEARS.
IT MAY SNOW THOUGH.
HUH?
YOU ARE A CHARACTER, OKITA. ♡
"...ELIMINATE THE ENTIRE SERIZAWA FACTION."

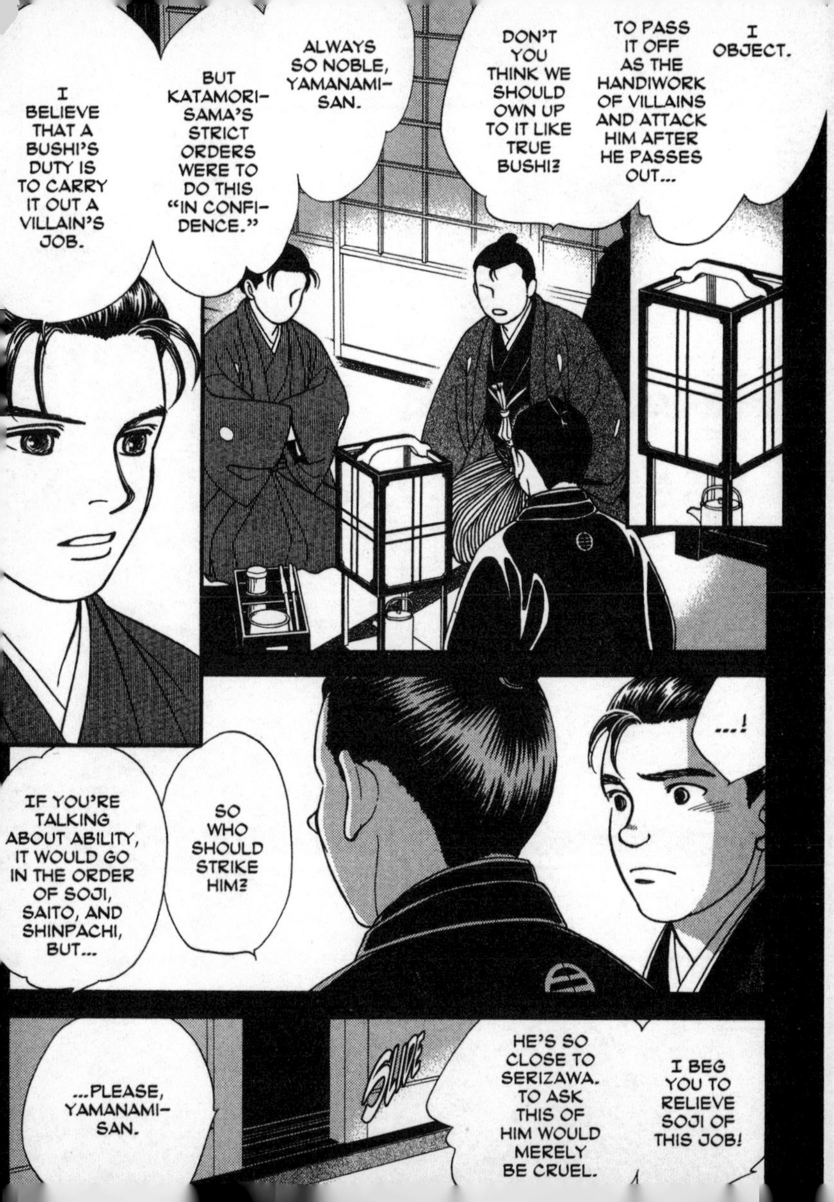
I OBJECT.
TO PASS IT OFF AS THE HANDIWORK OF VILLAINS AND ATTACK HIM AFTER HE PASSES OUT...
DON'T YOU THINK WE SHOULD OWN UP TO IT LIKE TRUE BUSHI?
ALWAYS SO NOBLE, YAMANAMI-SAN.
BUT KATAMORI-SAMA'S STRICT ORDERS WERE TO DO THIS "IN CONFIDENCE."
I BELIEVE THAT A BUSHI'S DUTY IS TO CARRY IT OUT A VILLAIN'S JOB.
...!
SO WHO SHOULD STRIKE HIM?
IF YOU'RE TALKING ABOUT ABILITY, IT WOULD GO IN THE ORDER OF SOJI, SAITO, AND SHINPACHI, BUT...
I BEG YOU TO RELIEVE SOJI OF THIS JOB!
HE'S SO CLOSE TO SERIZAWA. TO ASK THIS OF HIM WOULD MERELY BE CRUEL.
SLIDE
...PLEASE, YAMANAMI-SAN.

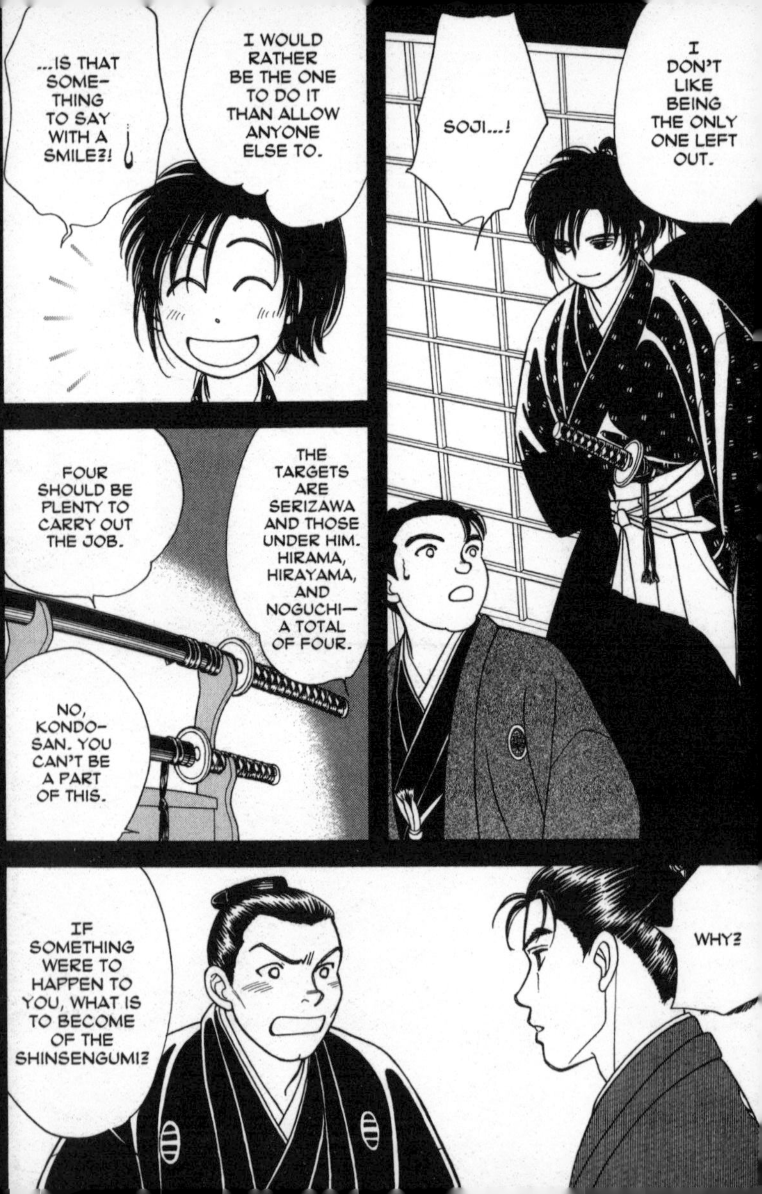
I DON'T LIKE BEING THE ONLY ONE LEFT OUT.
SOJI...!
I WOULD RATHER BE THE ONE TO DO IT THAN ALLOW ANYONE ELSE TO.
...IS THAT SOME-THING TO SAY WITH A SMILE?!
THE TARGETS ARE SERIZAWA AND THOSE UNDER HIM. HIRAMA, HIRAYAMA, AND NOGUCHI— A TOTAL OF FOUR.
FOUR SHOULD BE PLENTY TO CARRY OUT THE JOB.
NO, KONDO-SAN. YOU CAN'T BE A PART OF THIS.
WHY?
IF SOMETHING WERE TO HAPPEN TO YOU, WHAT IS TO BECOME OF THE SHINSENGUMI?

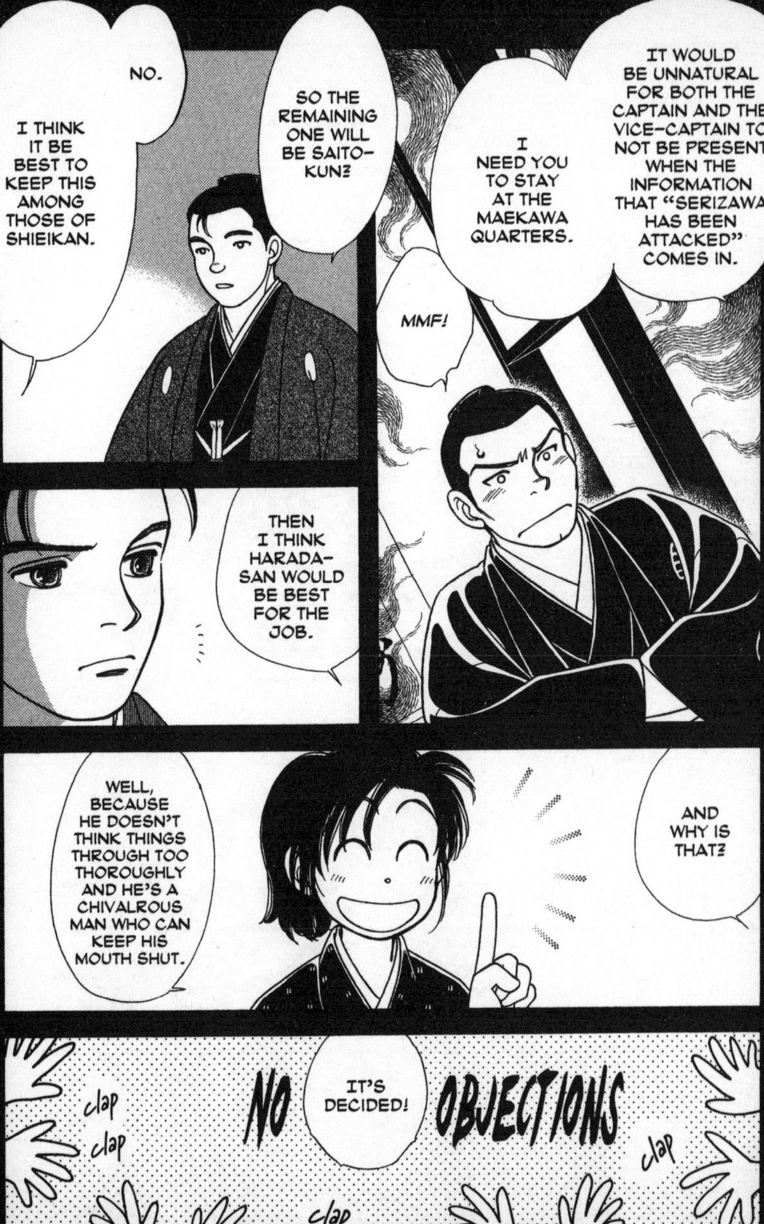
IT WOULD BE UNNATURAL FOR BOTH THE CAPTAIN AND THE VICE-CAPTAIN TO NOT BE PRESENT WHEN THE INFORMATION THAT "SERIZAWA HAS BEEN ATTACKED" COMES IN.
I NEED YOU TO STAY AT THE MAEKAWA QUARTERS.
MMF!
SO THE REMAINING ONE WILL BE SAITO-KUN?
NO.
I THINK IT BE BEST TO KEEP THIS AMONG THOSE OF SHIEIKAN.
THEN I THINK HARADA-SAN WOULD BE BEST FOR THE JOB.
AND WHY IS THAT?
WELL, BECAUSE HE DOESN'T THINK THINGS THROUGH TOO THOROUGHLY AND HE'S A CHIVALROUS MAN WHO CAN KEEP HIS MOUTH SHUT.
clap
IT'S DECIDED!
NO OBJECTIONS
clap
clap
clap

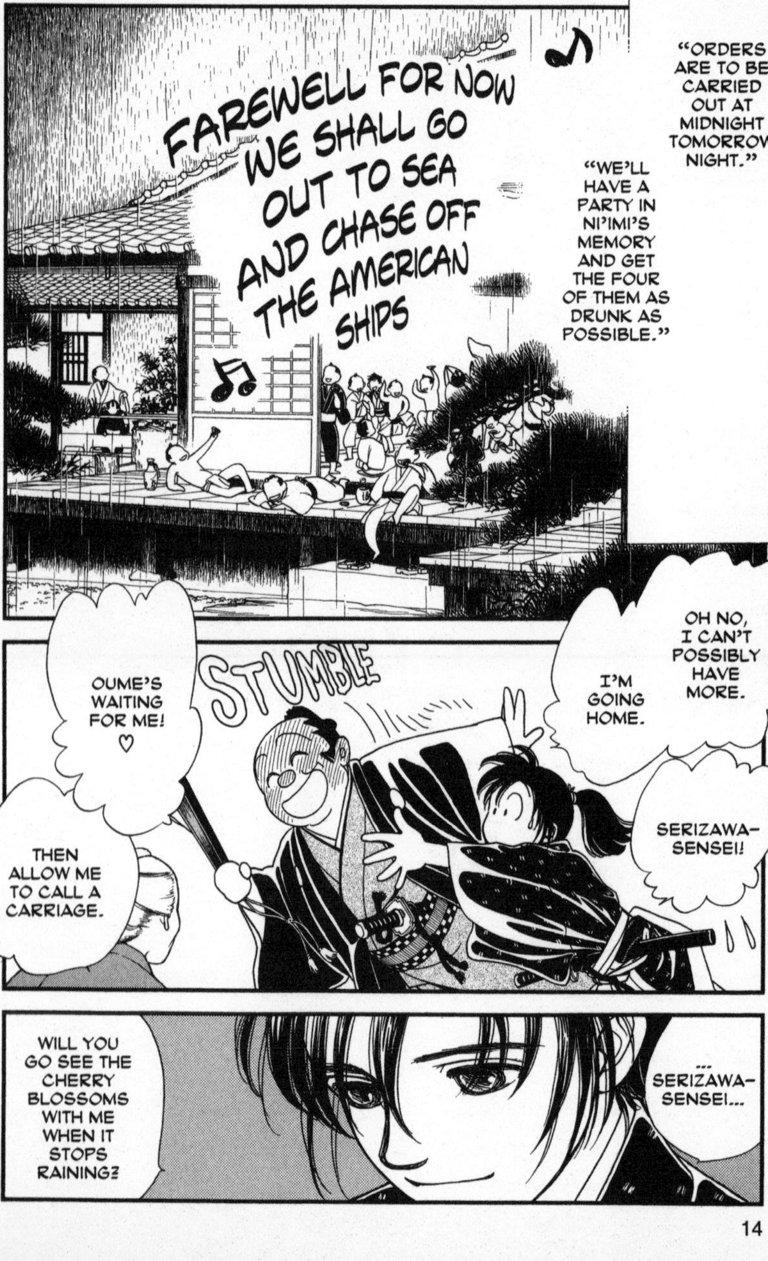
"ORDERS ARE TO BE CARRIED OUT AT MIDNIGHT TOMORROW NIGHT."
"WE'LL HAVE A PARTY IN NI'IMI'S MEMORY AND GET THE FOUR OF THEM AS DRUNK AS POSSIBLE."
FAREWELL FOR NOW WE SHALL GO OUT TO SEA AND CHASE OFF THE AMERICAN SHIPS
OH NO, I CAN'T POSSIBLY HAVE MORE.
I'M GOING HOME.
SERIZAWA-SENSEI!
STUMBLE
OUME'S WAITING FOR ME! ♡
THEN ALLOW ME TO CALL A CARRIAGE.
...SERIZAWA-SENSEI...
WILL YOU GO SEE THE CHERRY BLOSSOMS WITH ME WHEN IT STOPS RAINING?

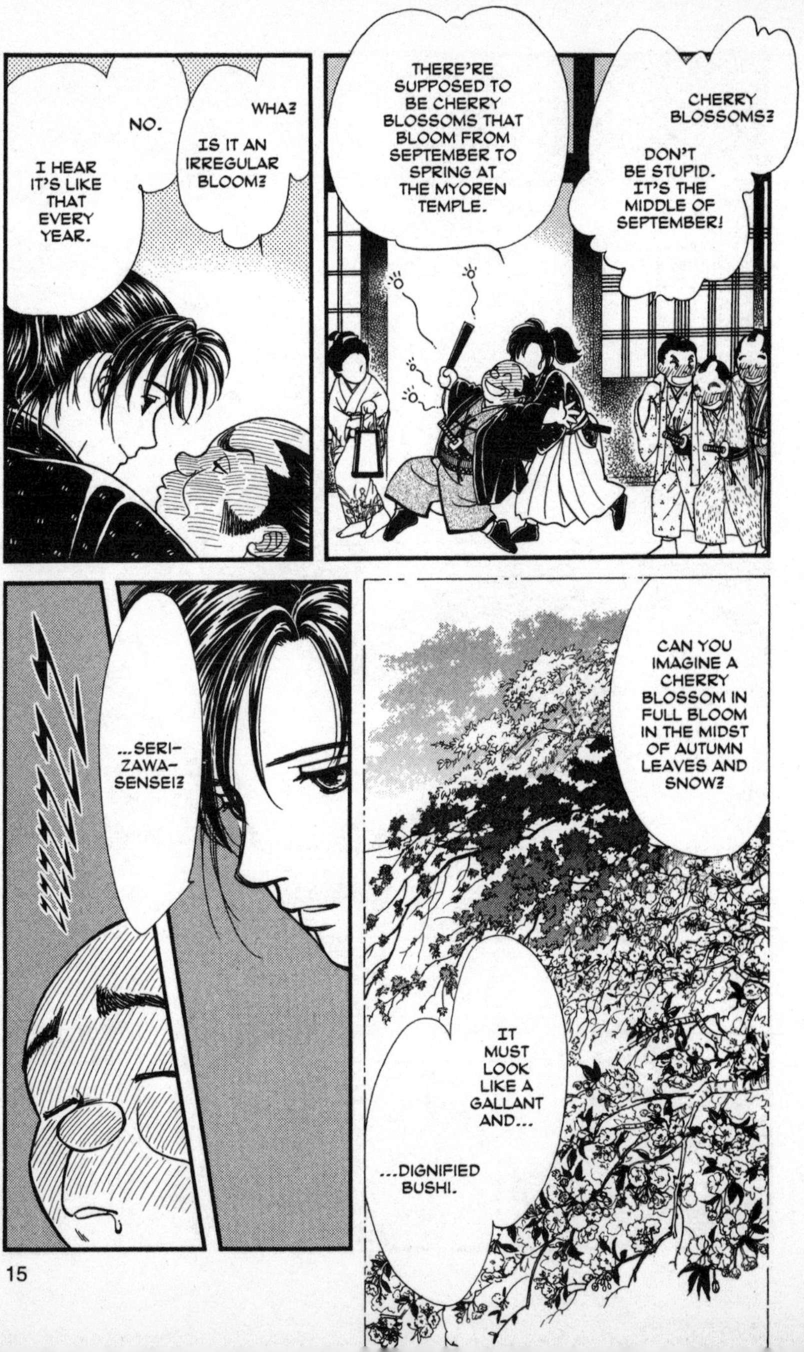
CHERRY BLOSSOMS?
DON'T BE STUPID. IT'S THE MIDDLE OF SEPTEMBER!
THERE'RE SUPPOSED TO BE CHERRY BLOSSOMS THAT BLOOM FROM SEPTEMBER TO SPRING AT THE MYOREN TEMPLE.
WHA?
IS IT AN IRREGULAR BLOOM?
NO.
I HEAR IT'S LIKE THAT EVERY YEAR.
CAN YOU IMAGINE A CHERRY BLOSSOM IN FULL BLOOM IN THE MIDST OF AUTUMN LEAVES AND SNOW?
IT MUST LOOK LIKE A GALLANT AND...
...DIGNIFIED BUSHI.
...SERI-ZAWA-SENSEI?

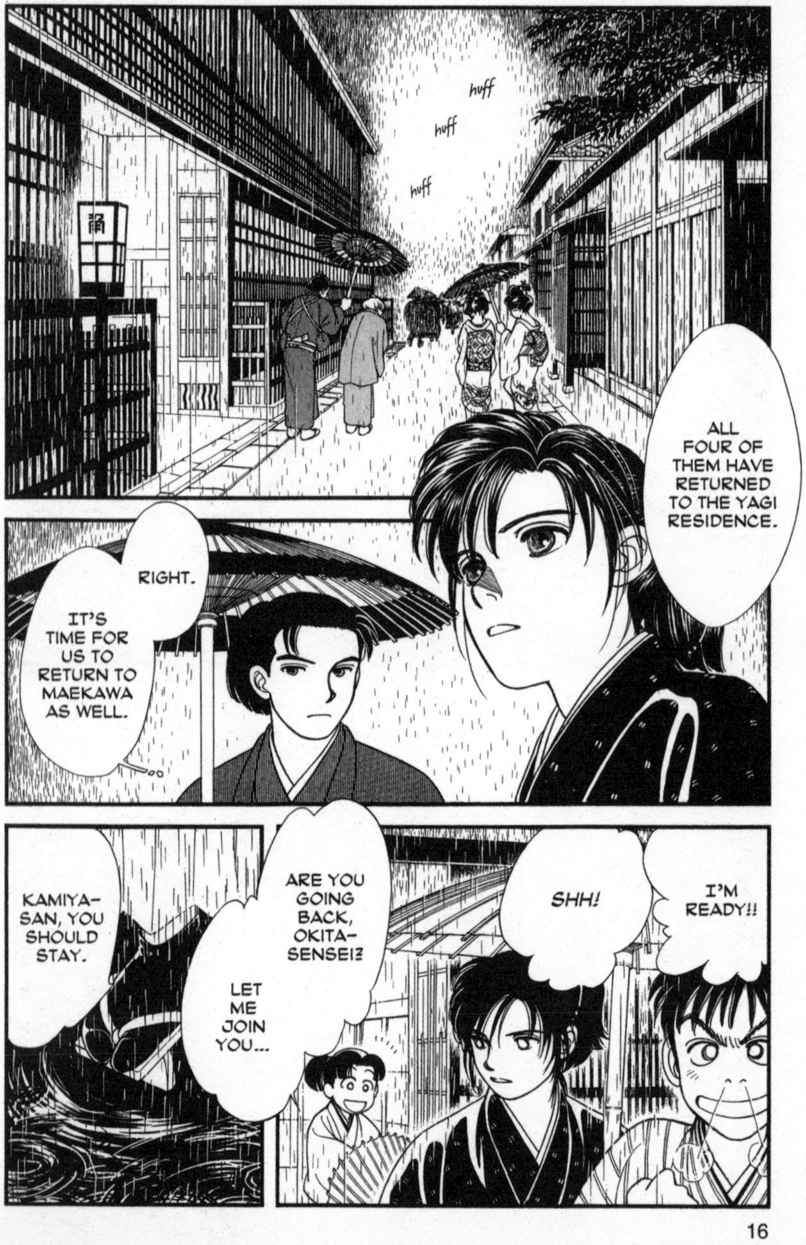
huff
huff
huff
ALL FOUR OF THEM HAVE RETURNED TO THE YAGI RESIDENCE.
RIGHT.
IT'S TIME FOR US TO RETURN TO MAEKAWA AS WELL.
I'M READY!!
SHH!
ARE YOU GOING BACK, OKITA-SENSEI!?
LET ME JOIN YOU...
KAMIYA-SAN, YOU SHOULD STAY.

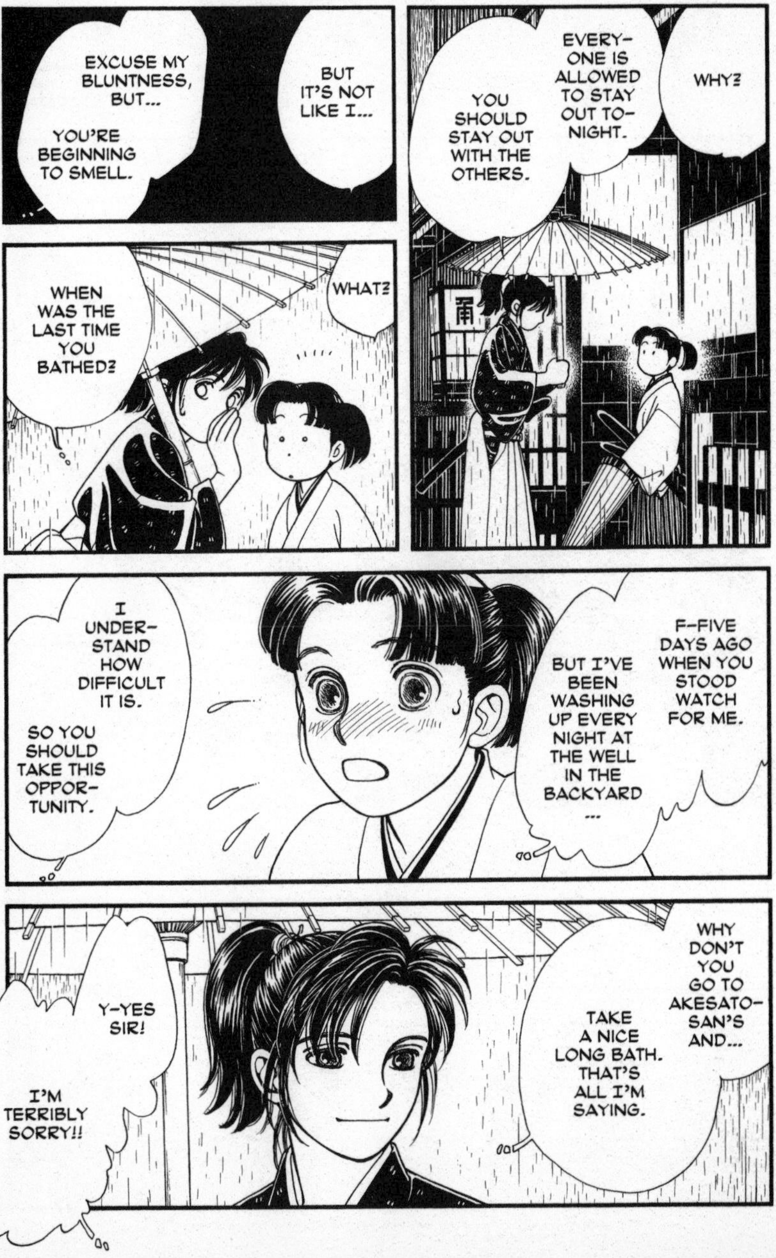
WHY?
EVERYONE IS ALLOWED TO STAY OUT TONIGHT.
YOU SHOULD STAY OUT WITH THE OTHERS.
BUT IT'S NOT LIKE I...
EXCUSE MY BLUNTNESS, BUT...
YOU'RE BEGINNING TO SMELL.
WHAT?
WHEN WAS THE LAST TIME YOU BATHED?
F-FIVE DAYS AGO WHEN YOU STOOD WATCH FOR ME.
BUT I'VE BEEN WASHING UP EVERY NIGHT AT THE WELL IN THE BACKYARD ...
I UNDERSTAND HOW DIFFICULT IT IS.
SO YOU SHOULD TAKE THIS OPPORTUNITY.
WHY DON'T YOU GO TO AKESATO-SAN'S AND...
TAKE A NICE LONG BATH. THAT'S ALL I'M SAYING.
Y-YES SIR!
I'M TERRIBLY SORRY!!

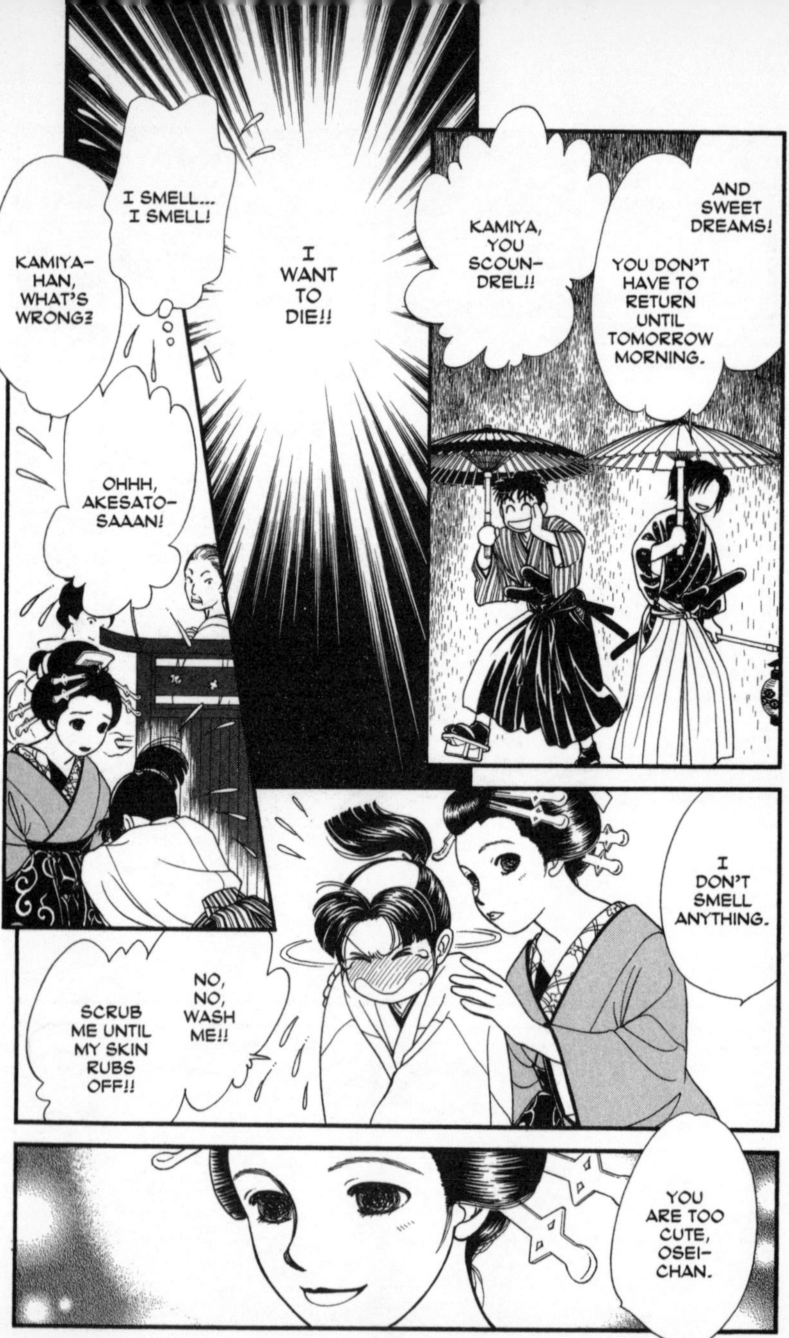
AND SWEET DREAMS!
YOU DON'T HAVE TO RETURN UNTIL TOMORROW MORNING.
KAMIYA, YOU SCOUNDREL!!
I WANT TO DIE!!
I SMELL... I SMELL!
KAMIYA-HAN, WHAT'S WRONG?
OHHH, AKESATO-SAAAN!
I DON'T SMELL ANYTHING.
NO, NO, WASH ME!!
SCRUB ME UNTIL MY SKIN RUBS OFF!!
YOU ARE TOO CUTE, OSEI-CHAN.

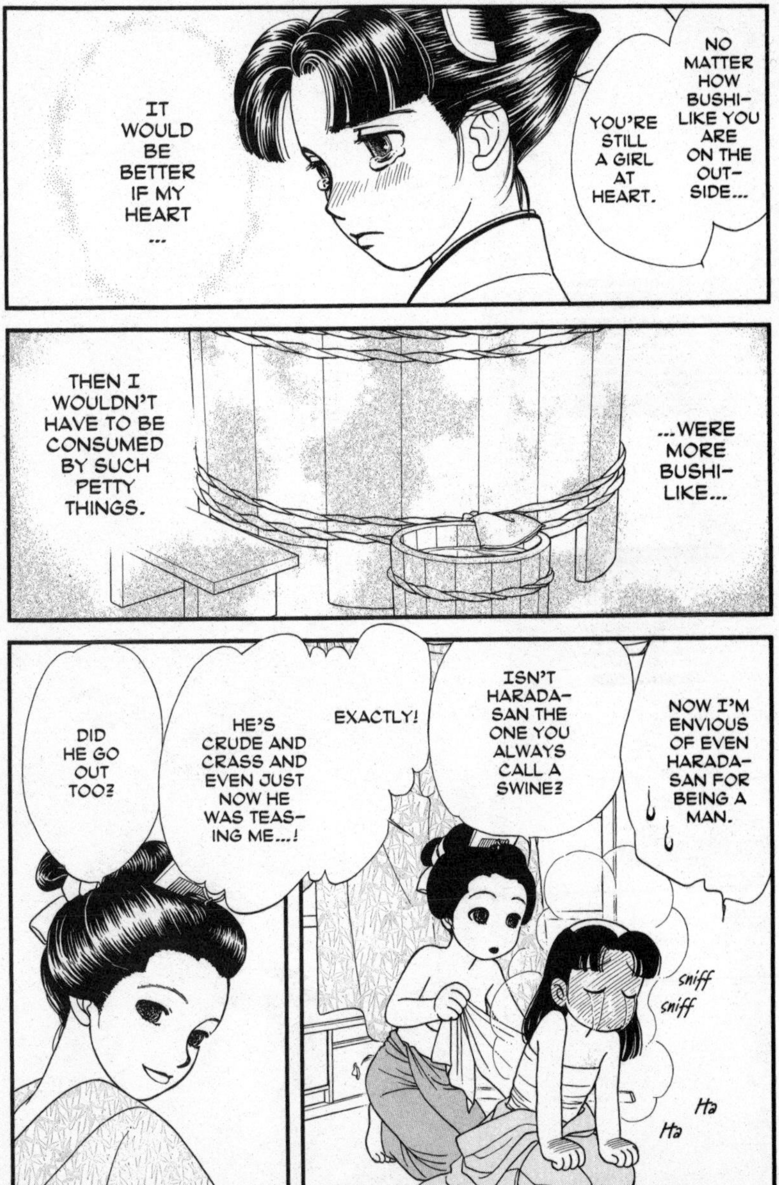
NO MATTER HOW BUSHI-LIKE YOU ARE ON THE OUTSIDE...
YOU'RE STILL A GIRL AT HEART.
IT WOULD BE BETTER IF MY HEART ...
...WERE MORE BUSHI-LIKE...
THEN I WOULDN'T HAVE TO BE CONSUMED BY SUCH PETTY THINGS.
NOW I'M ENVIOUS OF EVEN HARADA-SAN FOR BEING A MAN.
ISN'T HARADA-SAN THE ONE YOU ALWAYS CALL A SWINE?
EXACTLY!
HE'S CRUDE AND CRASS AND EVEN JUST NOW HE WAS TEASING ME...!
sniff sniff
Ha Ha
DID HE GO OUT TOO?

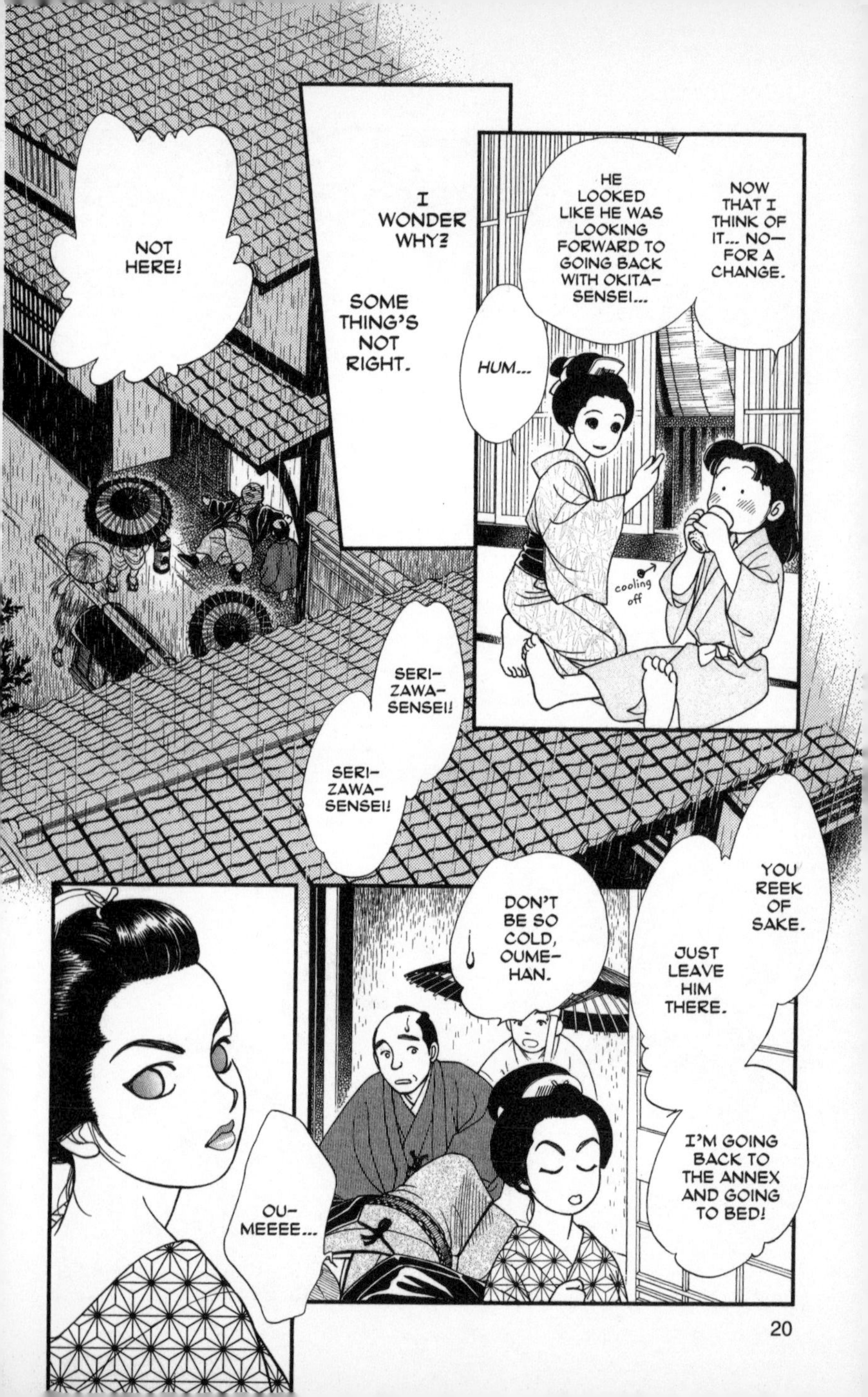
NOW THAT I THINK OF IT... NO— FOR A CHANGE.
HE LOOKED LIKE HE WAS LOOKING FORWARD TO GOING BACK WITH OKITA-SENSEI...
HUM...
cooling off
I WONDER WHY?
SOME THING'S NOT RIGHT.
NOT HERE!
SERI-ZAWA-SENSEI!
SERI-ZAWA-SENSEI!
YOU REEK OF SAKE.
JUST LEAVE HIM THERE.
DON'T BE SO COLD, OUME-HAN.
I'M GOING BACK TO THE ANNEX AND GOING TO BED!
OU-MEEEE...

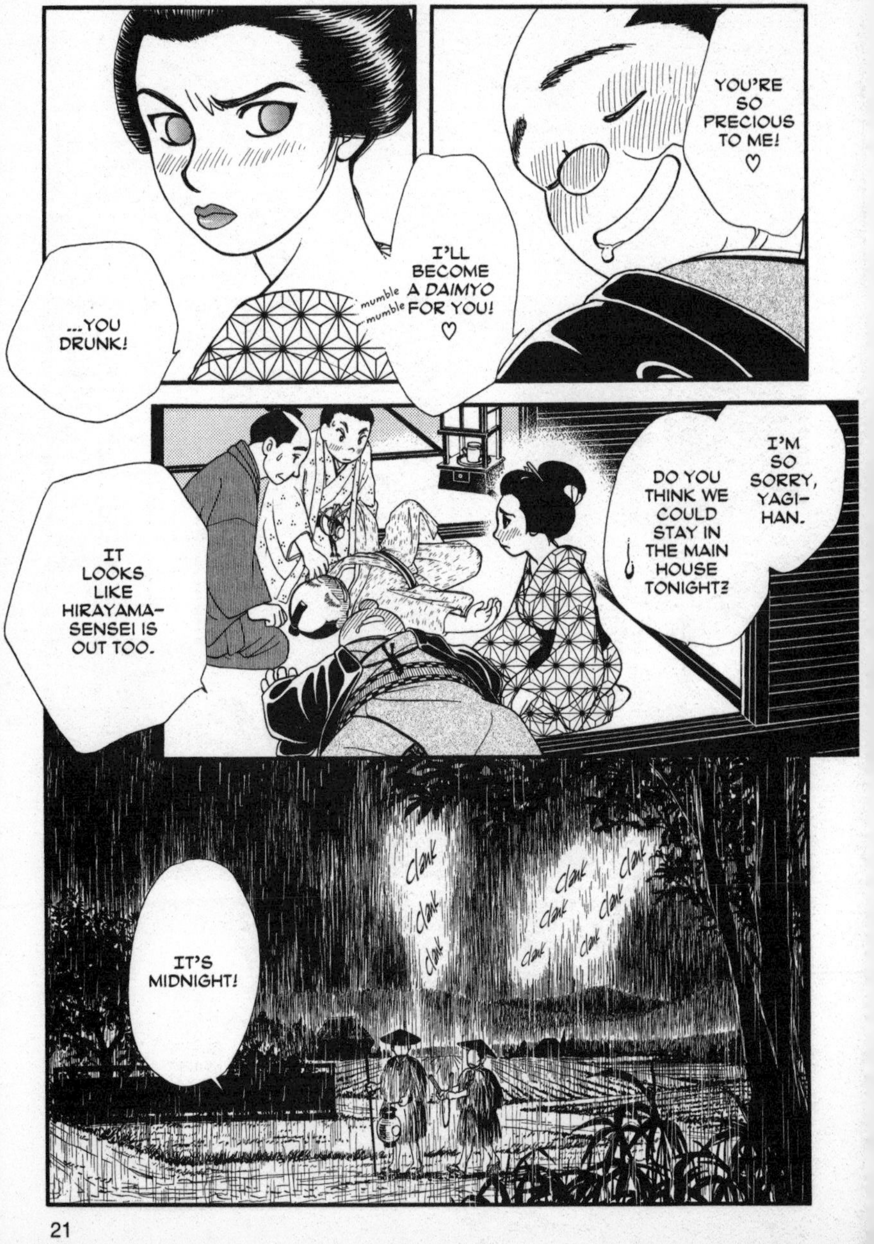
YOU'RE SO PRECIOUS TO ME! ♡
I'LL BECOME A *DAIMYO* FOR YOU! ♡
mumble mumble
...YOU DRUNK!
I'M SO SORRY, YAGI-HAN.
DO YOU THINK WE COULD STAY IN THE MAIN HOUSE TONIGHT?
IT LOOKS LIKE HIRAYAMA-SENSEI IS OUT TOO.
clank clank clank clank
clank clank clank clank
clank clank clank
IT'S MIDNIGHT!

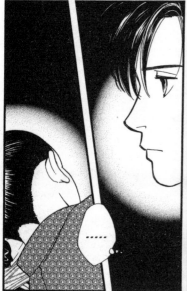

. . . . .

ACK

...I'LL GO IF YOU DON'T WANT TO.

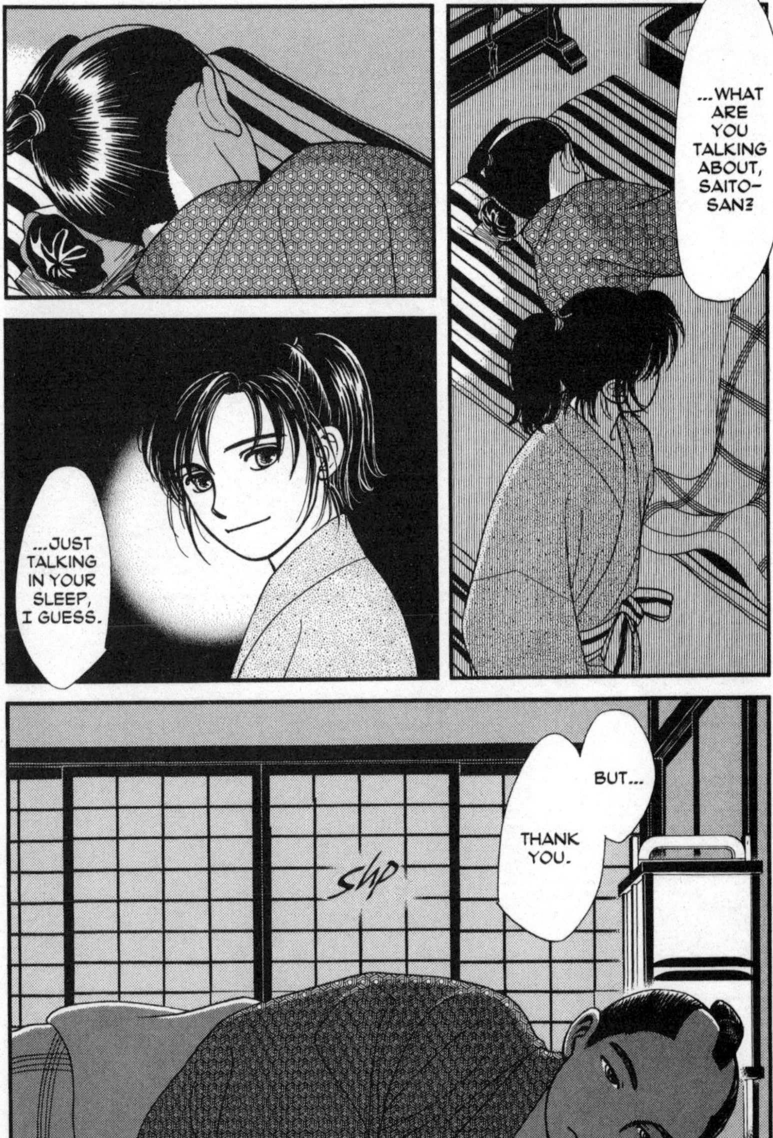
...WHAT ARE YOU TALKING ABOUT, SAITO-SAN?
...JUST TALKING IN YOUR SLEEP, I GUESS.
BUT...
THANK YOU.
SLAP

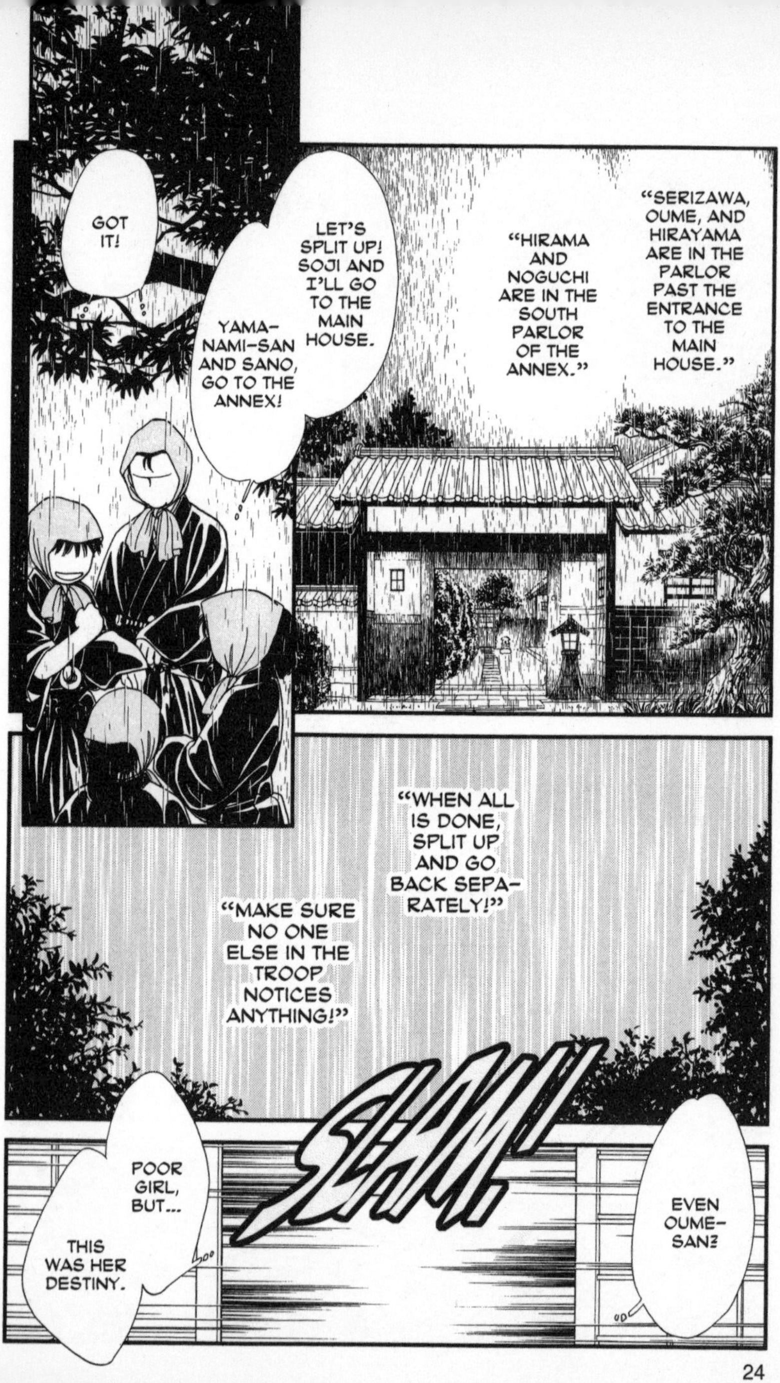
"SERIZAWA, OUME, AND HIRAYAMA ARE IN THE PARLOR PAST THE ENTRANCE TO THE MAIN HOUSE."
"HIRAMA AND NOGUCHI ARE IN THE SOUTH PARLOR OF THE ANNEX."
LET'S SPLIT UP! SOJI AND I'LL GO TO THE MAIN HOUSE.
YAMA-NAMI-SAN AND SANO, GO TO THE ANNEX!
GOT IT!
"WHEN ALL IS DONE, SPLIT UP AND GO BACK SEPA-RATELY!"
"MAKE SURE NO ONE ELSE IN THE TROOP NOTICES ANYTHING!"
EVEN OUME-SAN?
SLAM
POOR GIRL, BUT...
THIS WAS HER DESTINY.

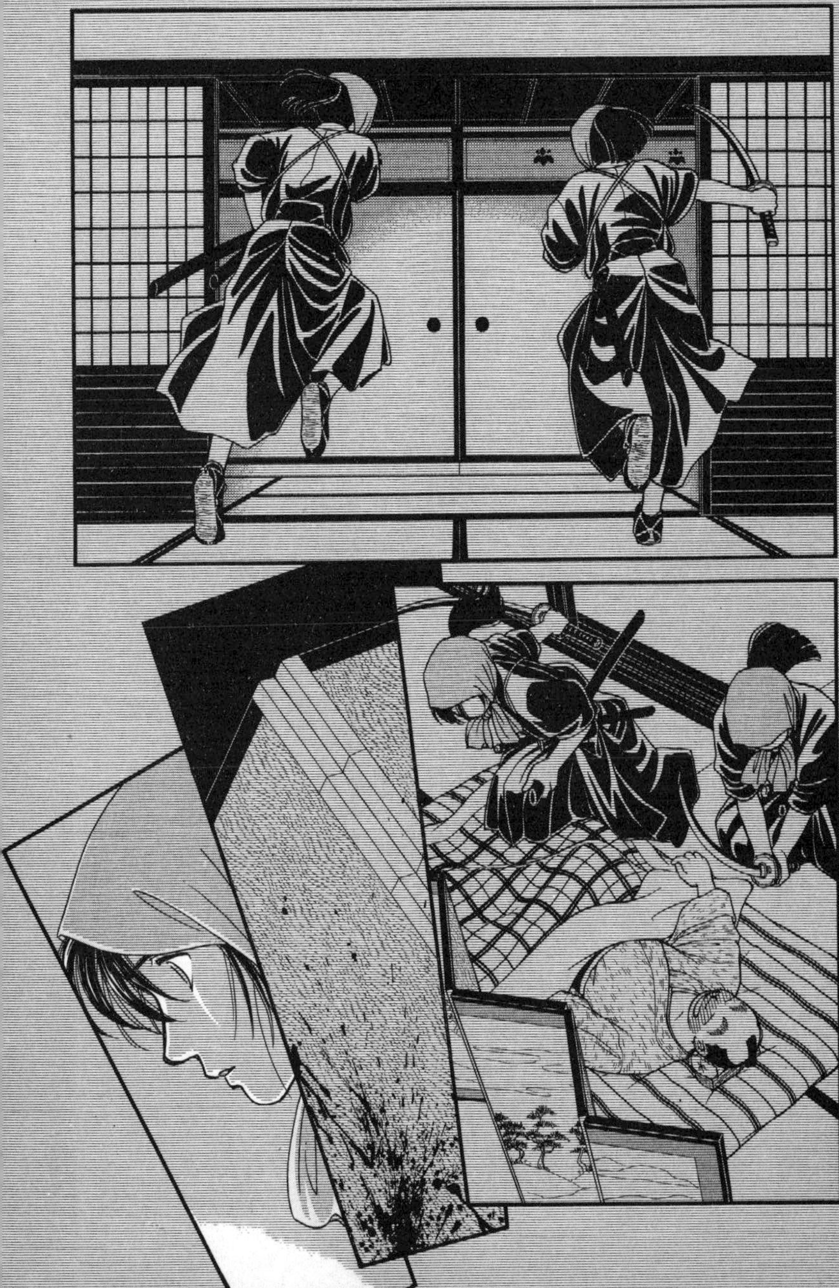

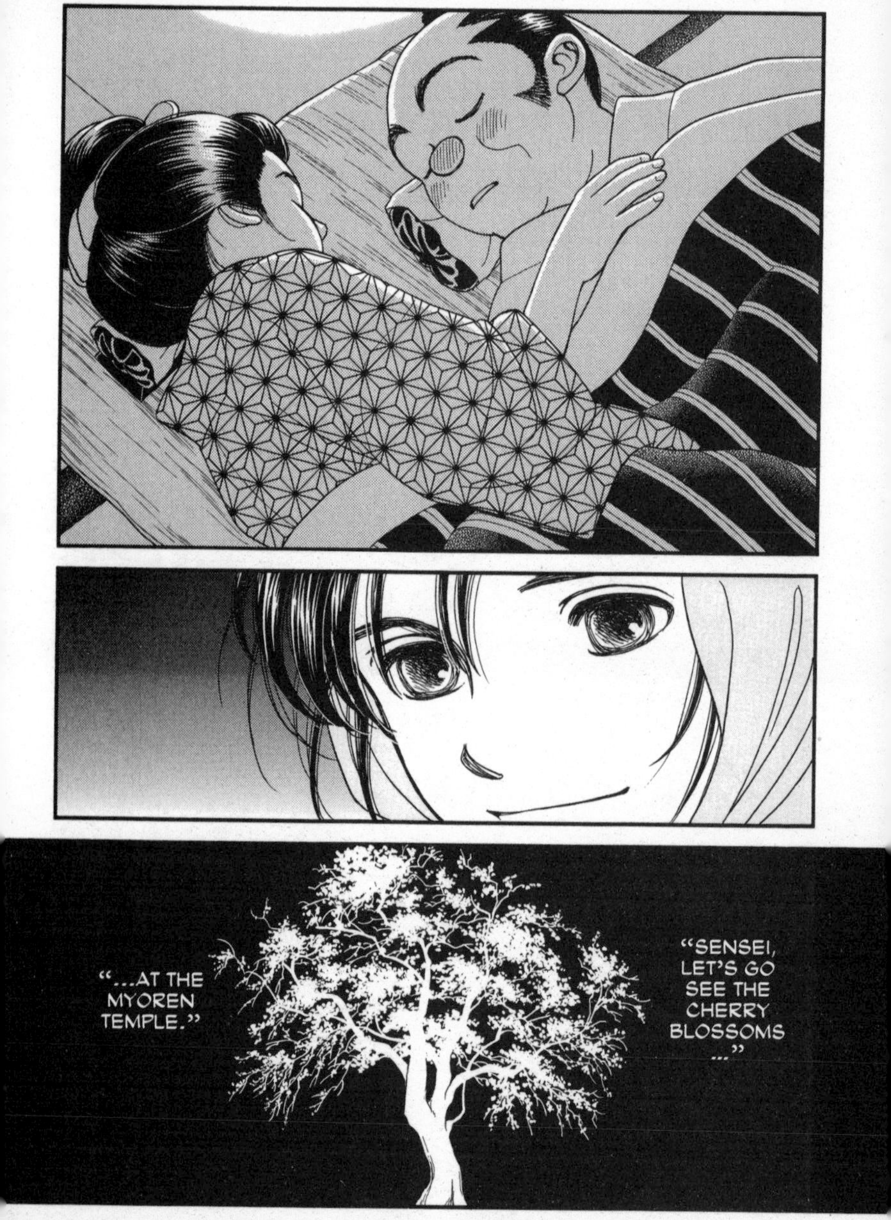
"SENSEI, LET'S GO SEE THE CHERRY BLOSSOMS ..."
"...AT THE MYOREN TEMPLE."

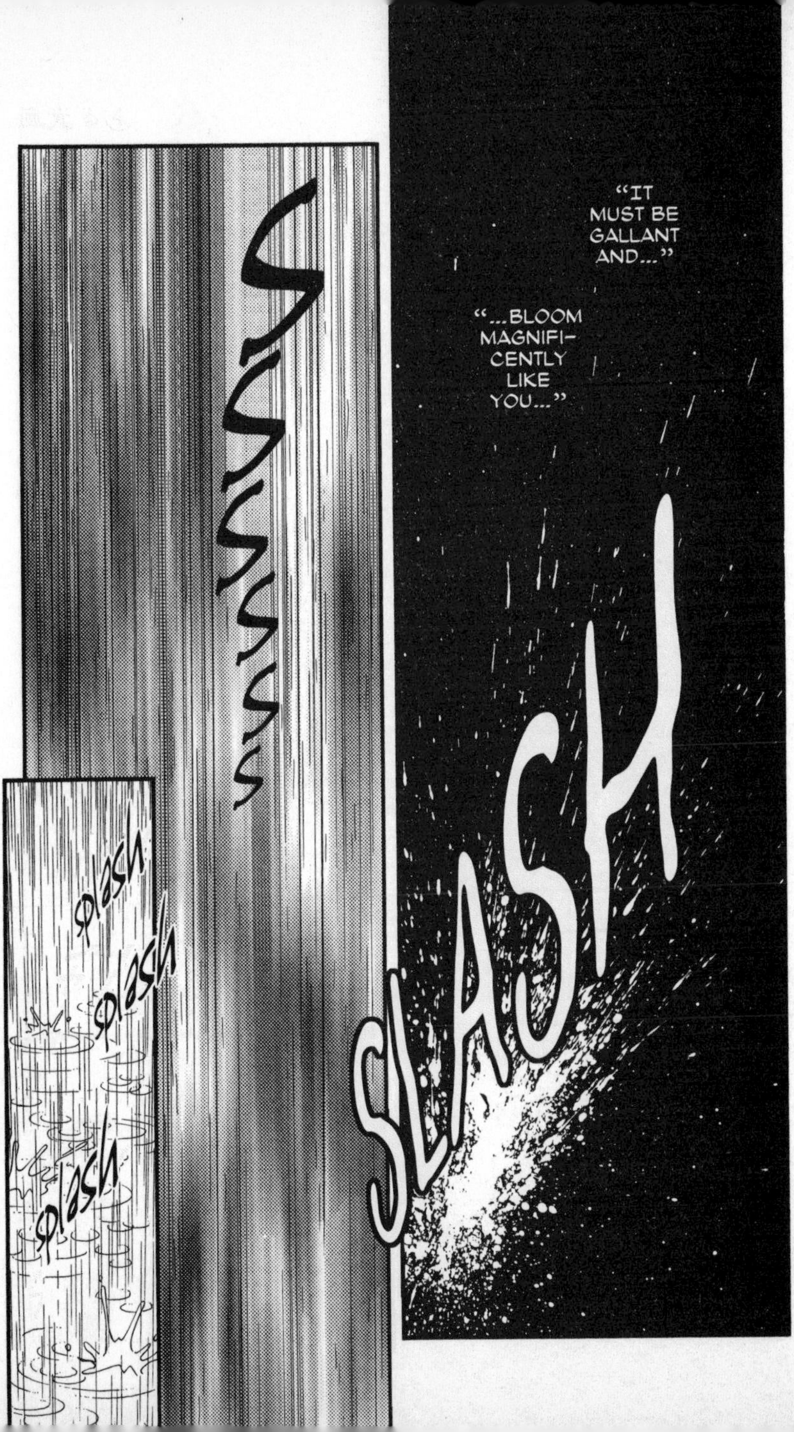
"IT MUST BE GALLANT AND..."
"...BLOOM MAGNIFI- CENTLY LIKE YOU..."
SLASH
SSSSSS
splash
splash
splash

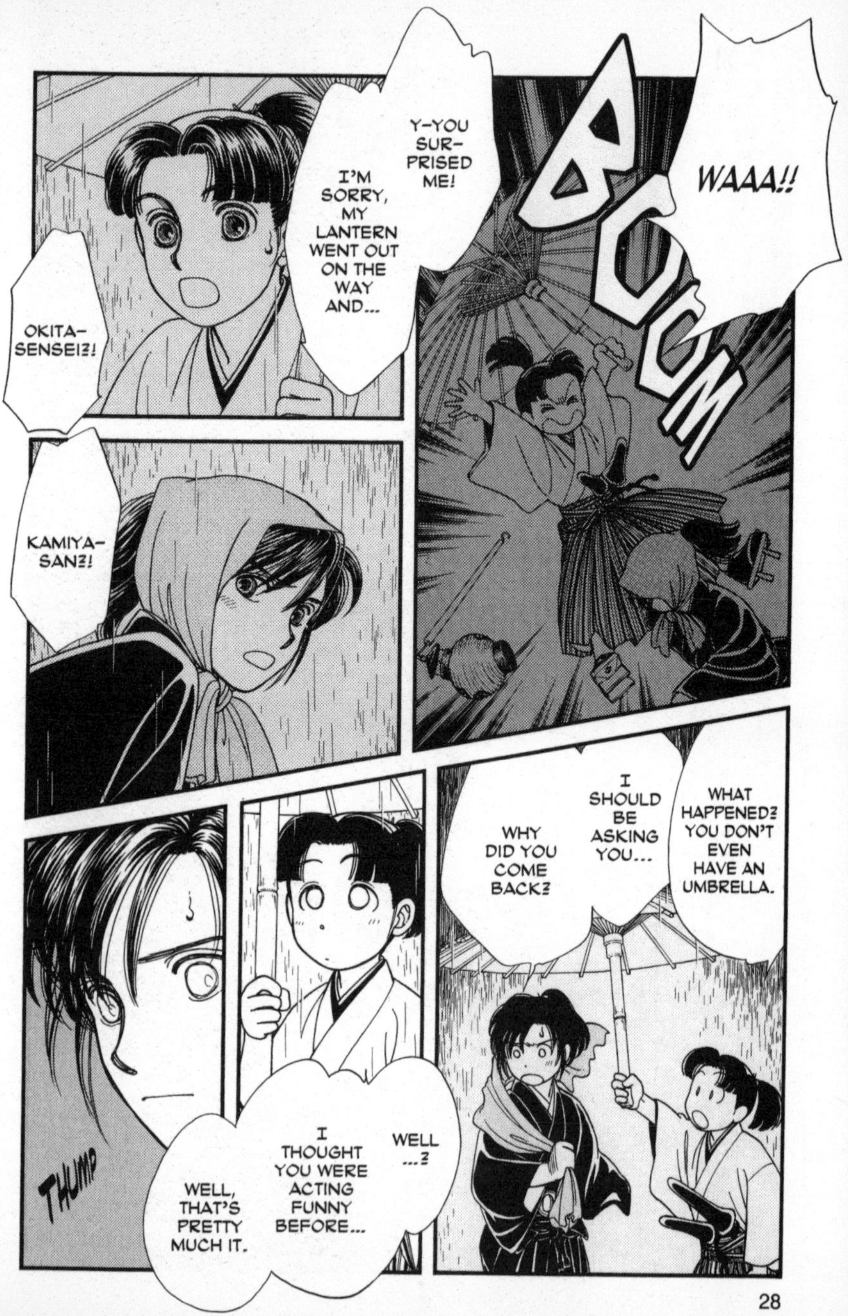
WAAA!!
BOOM
Y-YOU SUR-PRISED ME!
I'M SORRY, MY LANTERN WENT OUT ON THE WAY AND...
OKITA-SENSEI?!
KAMIYA-SAN?!
WHAT HAPPENED? YOU DON'T EVEN HAVE AN UMBRELLA.
I SHOULD BE ASKING YOU...
WHY DID YOU COME BACK?
WELL ...?
I THOUGHT YOU WERE ACTING FUNNY BEFORE...
WELL, THAT'S PRETTY MUCH IT.
THUMP

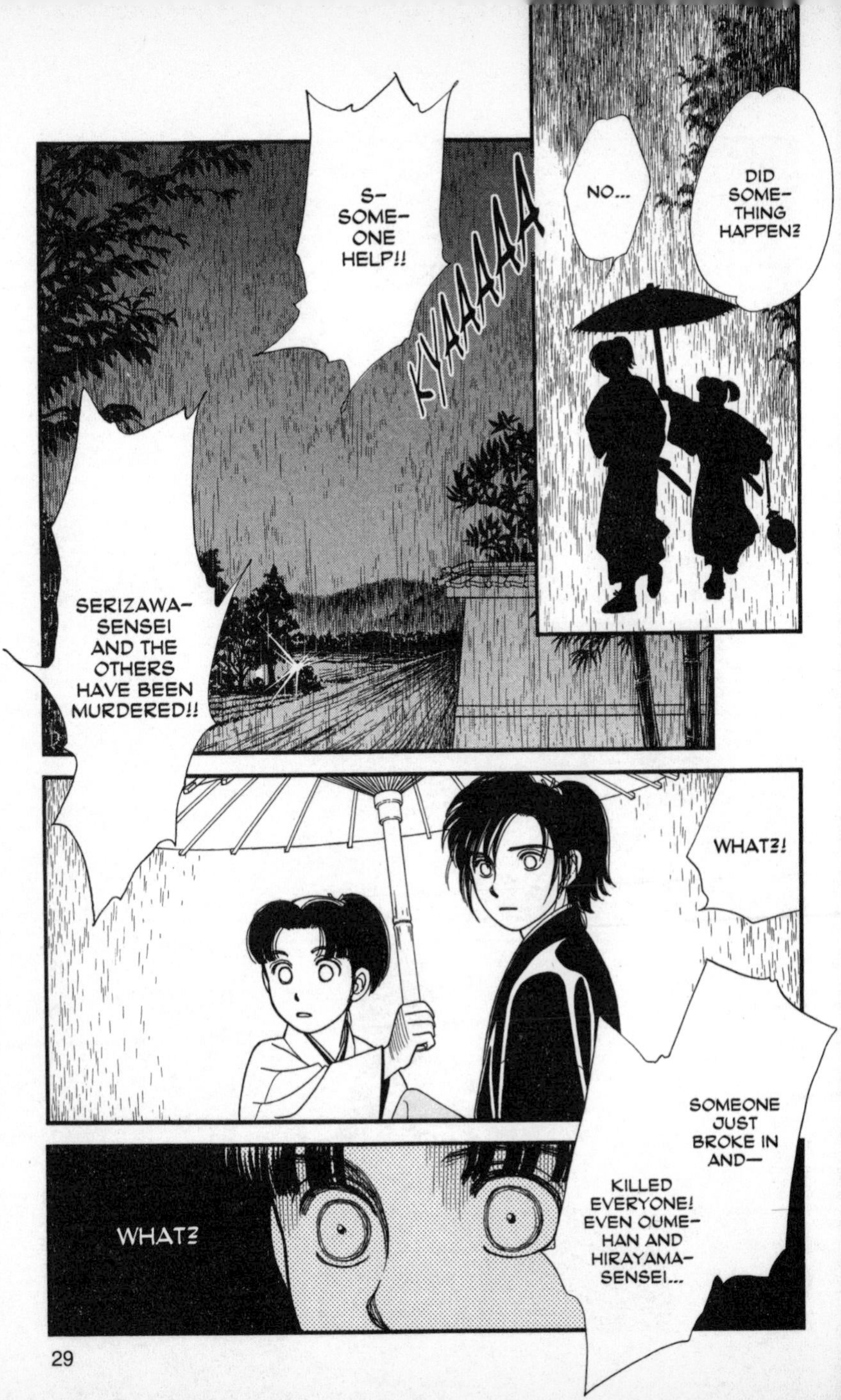
DID SOMETHING HAPPEN?
NO...
S-SOMEONE HELP!!
KYAAAAA
SERIZAWA-SENSEI AND THE OTHERS HAVE BEEN MURDERED!!
WHAT?!
SOMEONE JUST BROKE IN AND—
KILLED EVERYONE! EVEN OUME-HAN AND HIRAYAMA-SENSEI...
WHAT?

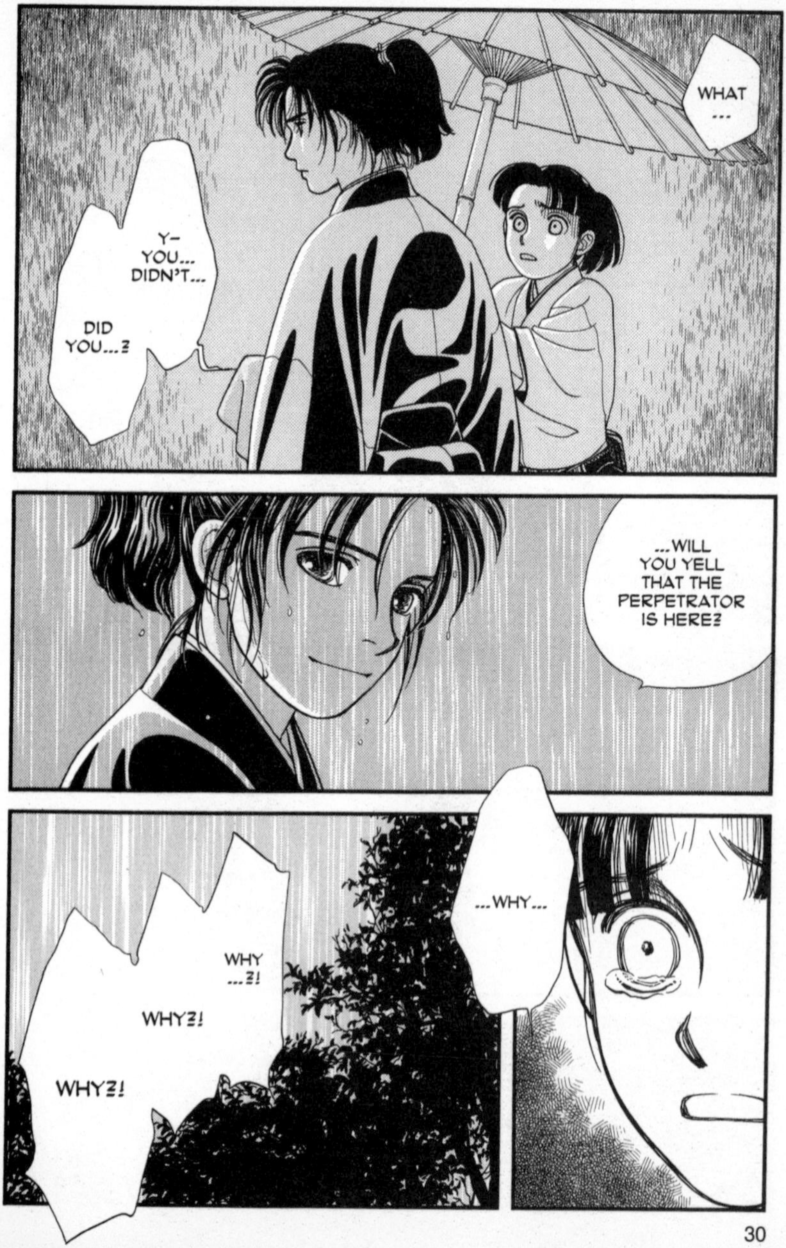
WHAT ...
Y– YOU... DIDN'T...
DID YOU...?
...WILL YOU YELL THAT THE PERPETRATOR IS HERE?
...WHY...
WHY ...?!
WHY?!
WHY?!

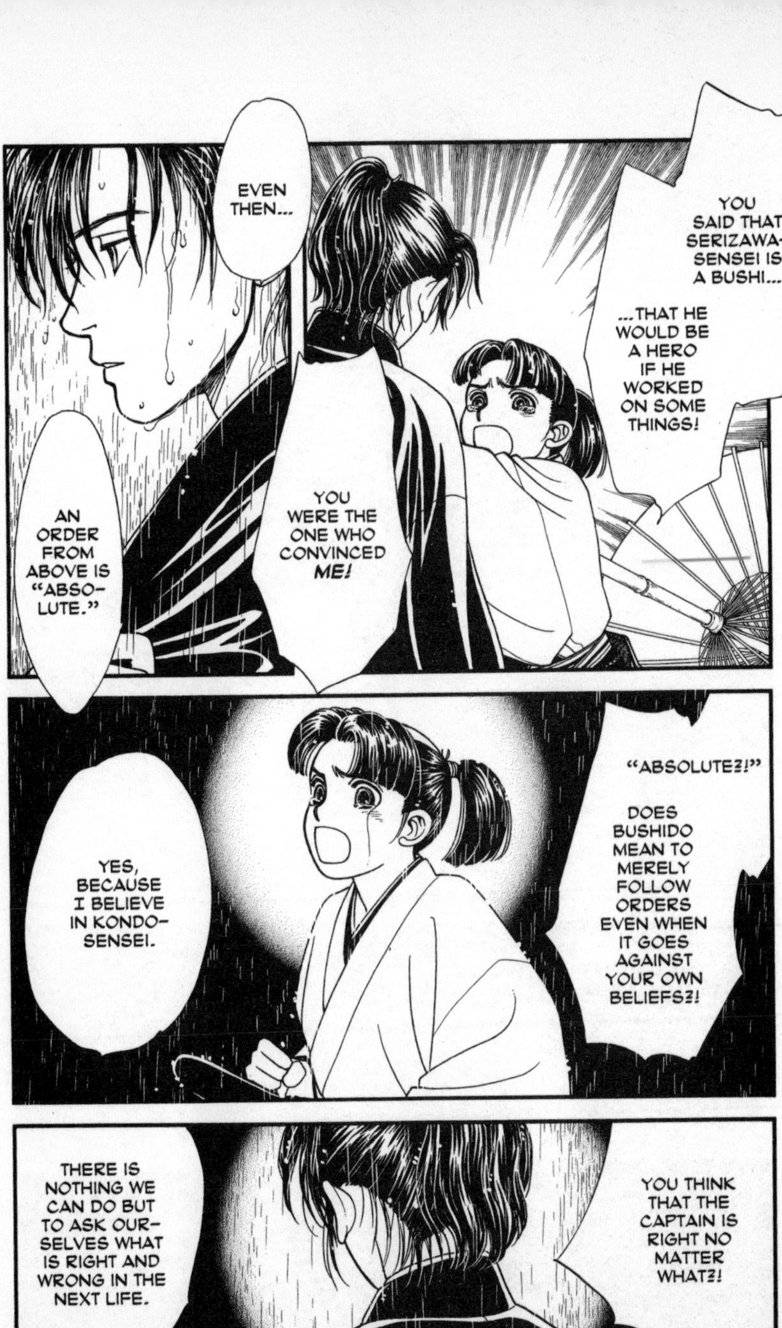
YOU SAID THAT SERIZAWA-SENSEI IS A BUSHI...
...THAT HE WOULD BE A HERO IF HE WORKED ON SOME THINGS!
YOU WERE THE ONE WHO CONVINCED ME!
EVEN THEN...
AN ORDER FROM ABOVE IS "ABSOLUTE."
"ABSOLUTE?!"
DOES BUSHIDO MEAN TO MERELY FOLLOW ORDERS EVEN WHEN IT GOES AGAINST YOUR OWN BELIEFS?!
YES, BECAUSE I BELIEVE IN KONDO-SENSEI.
YOU THINK THAT THE CAPTAIN IS RIGHT NO MATTER WHAT?!
THERE IS NOTHING WE CAN DO BUT TO ASK OURSELVES WHAT IS RIGHT AND WRONG IN THE NEXT LIFE.

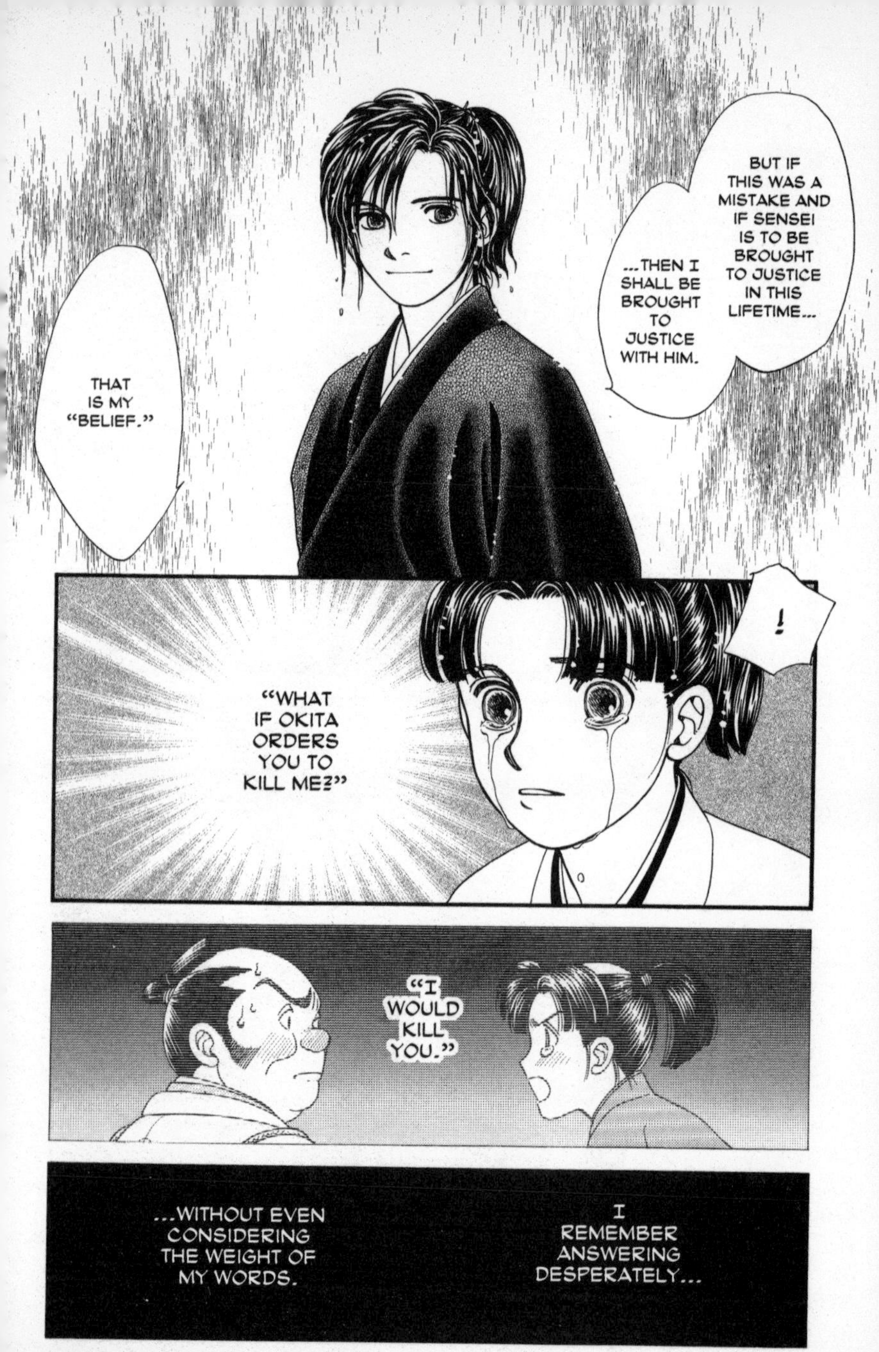
BUT IF THIS WAS A MISTAKE AND IF SENSEI IS TO BE BROUGHT TO JUSTICE IN THIS LIFETIME...
...THEN I SHALL BE BROUGHT TO JUSTICE WITH HIM.
THAT IS MY "BELIEF."
!
"WHAT IF OKITA ORDERS YOU TO KILL ME?"
"I WOULD KILL YOU."
I REMEMBER ANSWERING DESPERATELY...
...WITHOUT EVEN CONSIDERING THE WEIGHT OF MY WORDS.

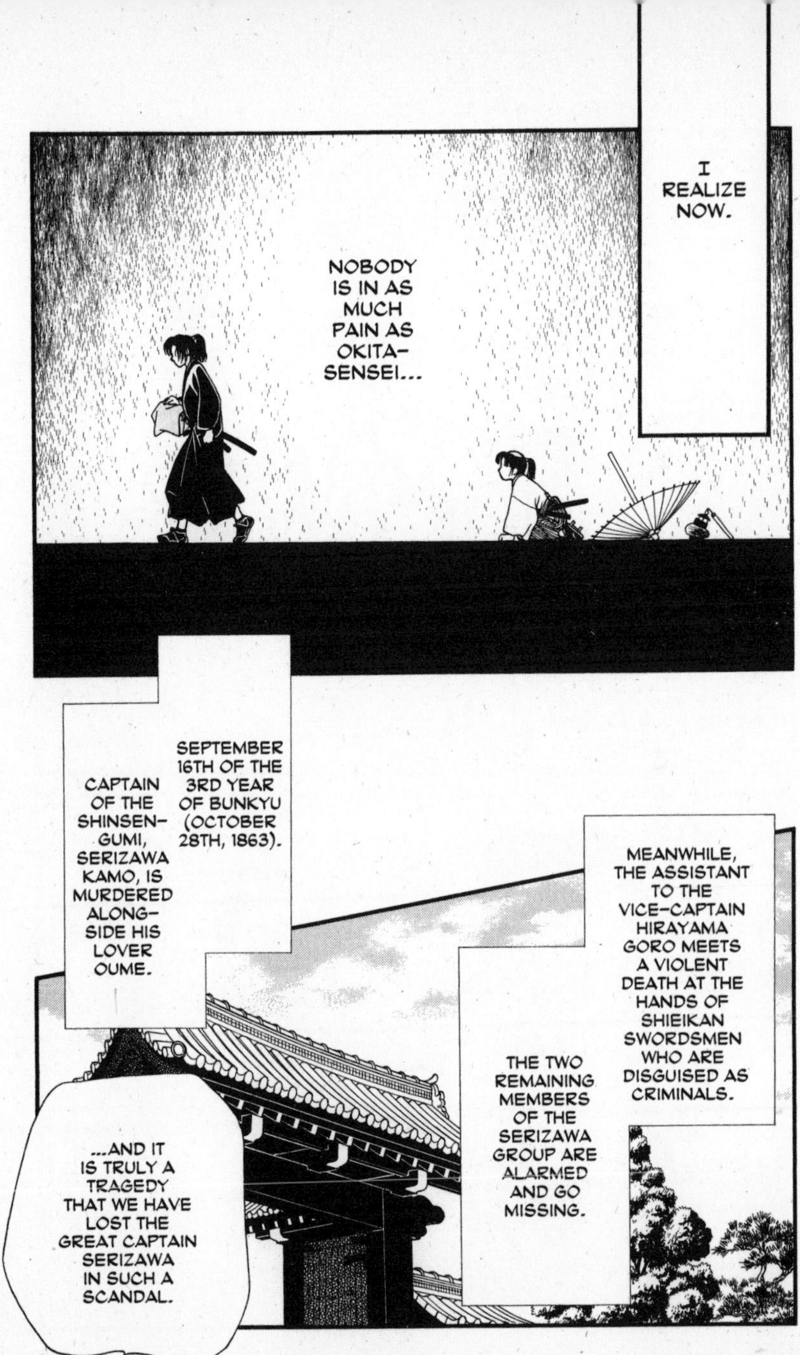
I REALIZE NOW.
NOBODY IS IN AS MUCH PAIN AS OKITA-SENSEI...
SEPTEMBER 16TH OF THE 3RD YEAR OF BUNKYU (OCTOBER 28TH, 1863).
CAPTAIN OF THE SHINSEN-GUMI, SERIZAWA KAMO, IS MURDERED ALONG-SIDE HIS LOVER OUME.
MEANWHILE, THE ASSISTANT TO THE VICE-CAPTAIN HIRAYAMA GORO MEETS A VIOLENT DEATH AT THE HANDS OF SHIEIKAN SWORDSMEN WHO ARE DISGUISED AS CRIMINALS.
THE TWO REMAINING MEMBERS OF THE SERIZAWA GROUP ARE ALARMED AND GO MISSING.
...AND IT IS TRULY A TRAGEDY THAT WE HAVE LOST THE GREAT CAPTAIN SERIZAWA IN SUCH A SCANDAL.

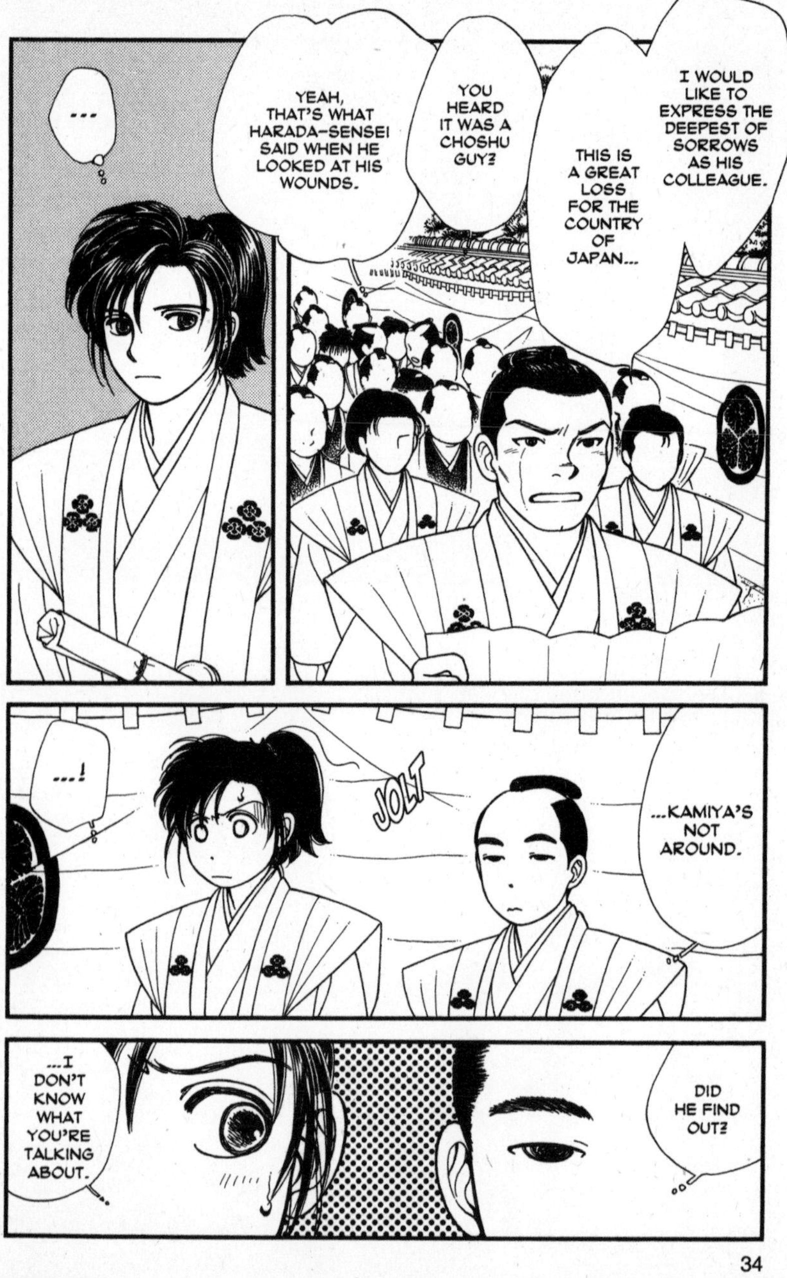
I WOULD LIKE TO EXPRESS THE DEEPEST OF SORROWS AS HIS COLLEAGUE.
THIS IS A GREAT LOSS FOR THE COUNTRY OF JAPAN...
YOU HEARD IT WAS A CHOSHU GUY?
YEAH, THAT'S WHAT HARADA-SENSEI SAID WHEN HE LOOKED AT HIS WOUNDS.
...
...KAMIYA'S NOT AROUND.
JOLT
...!
DID HE FIND OUT?
...I DON'T KNOW WHAT YOU'RE TALKING ABOUT.

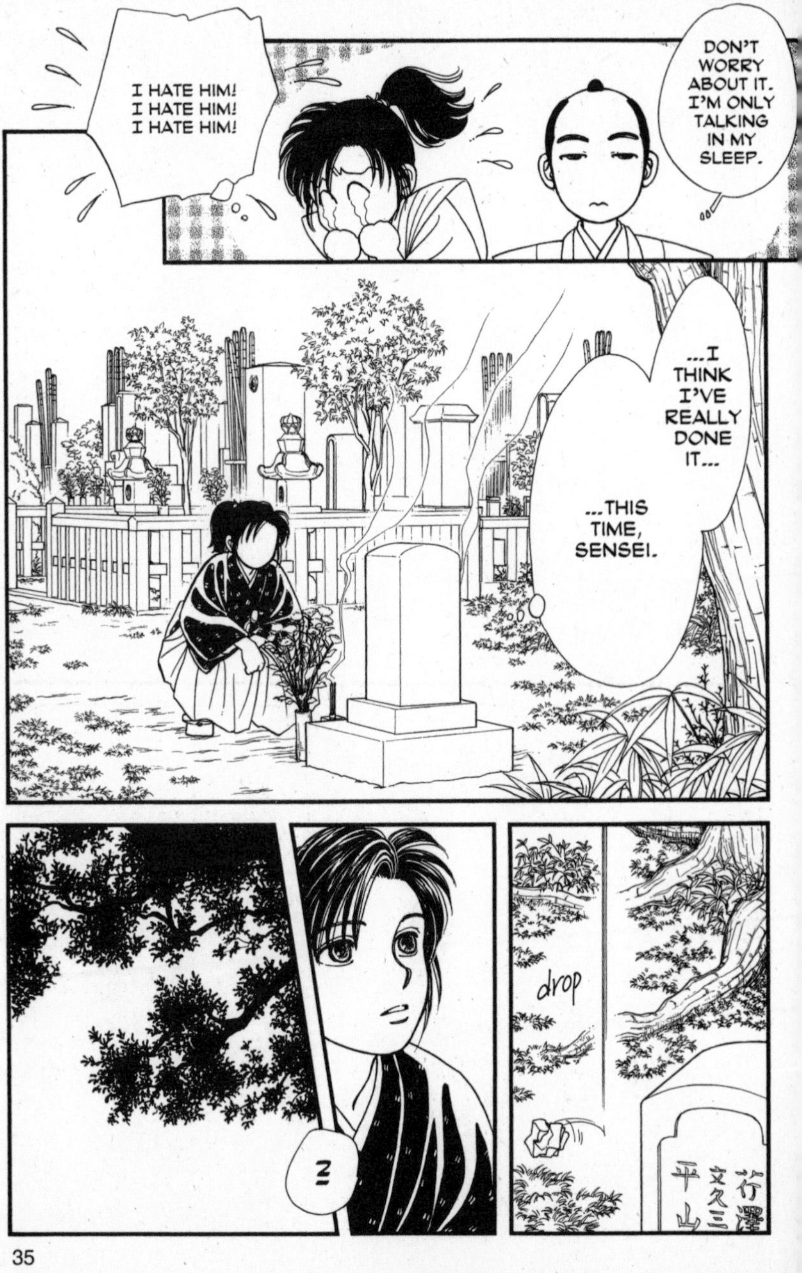
DON'T WORRY ABOUT IT. I'M ONLY TALKING IN MY SLEEP.
I HATE HIM! I HATE HIM! I HATE HIM!
...I THINK I'VE REALLY DONE IT...
...THIS TIME, SENSEI.
drop
行澤
文久三
平山

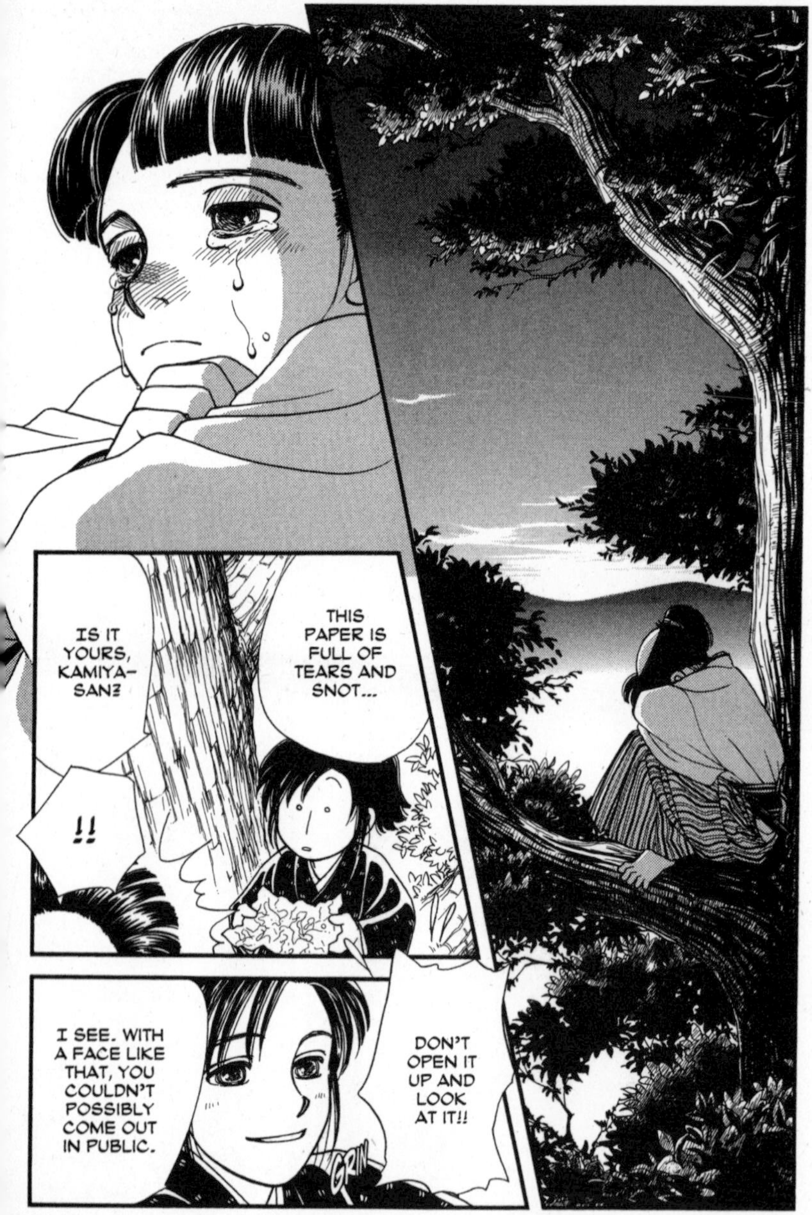
THIS PAPER IS FULL OF TEARS AND SNOT...
IS IT YOURS, KAMIYA-SAN?
!!
DON'T OPEN IT UP AND LOOK AT IT!!
I SEE. WITH A FACE LIKE THAT, YOU COULDN'T POSSIBLY COME OUT IN PUBLIC.
GRIN

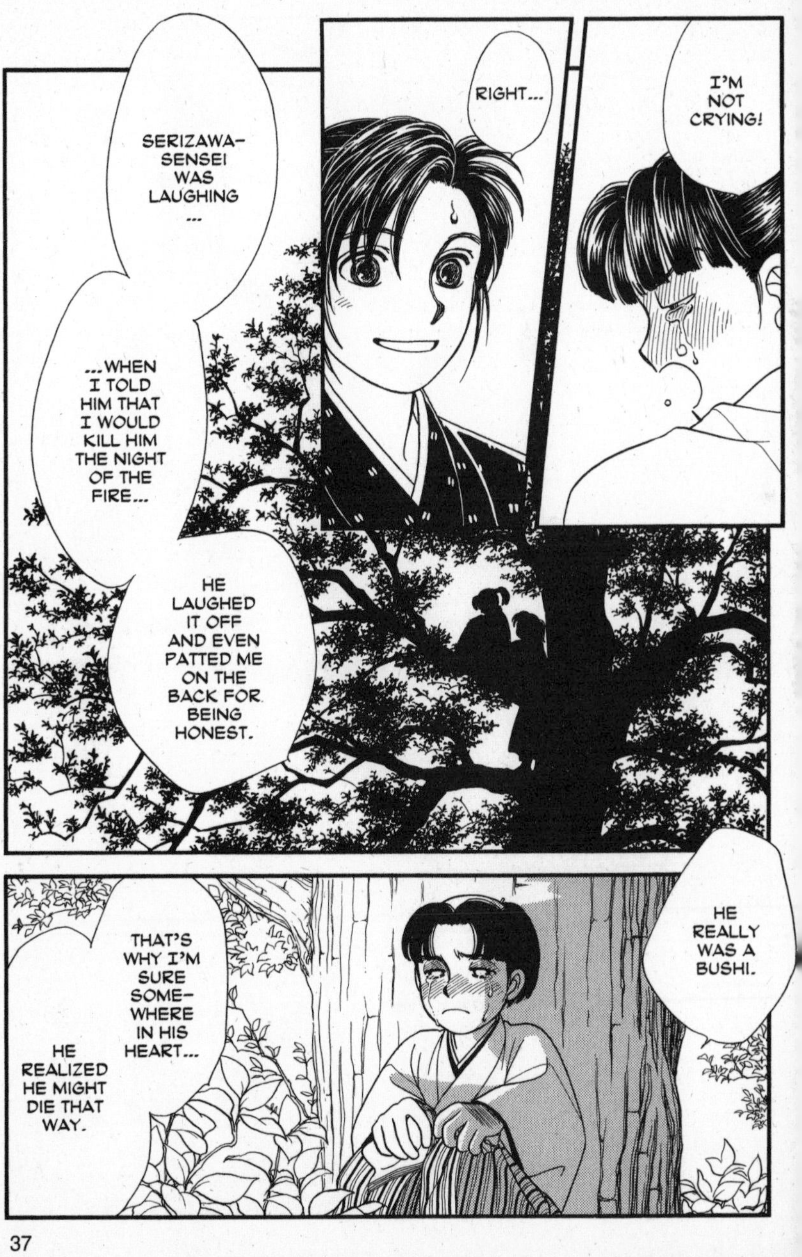
I'M NOT CRYING!
RIGHT...
SERIZAWA-SENSEI WAS LAUGHING...
...WHEN I TOLD HIM THAT I WOULD KILL HIM THE NIGHT OF THE FIRE...
HE LAUGHED IT OFF AND EVEN PATTED ME ON THE BACK FOR BEING HONEST.
HE REALLY WAS A BUSHI.
THAT'S WHY I'M SURE SOMEWHERE IN HIS HEART...
HE REALIZED HE MIGHT DIE THAT WAY.

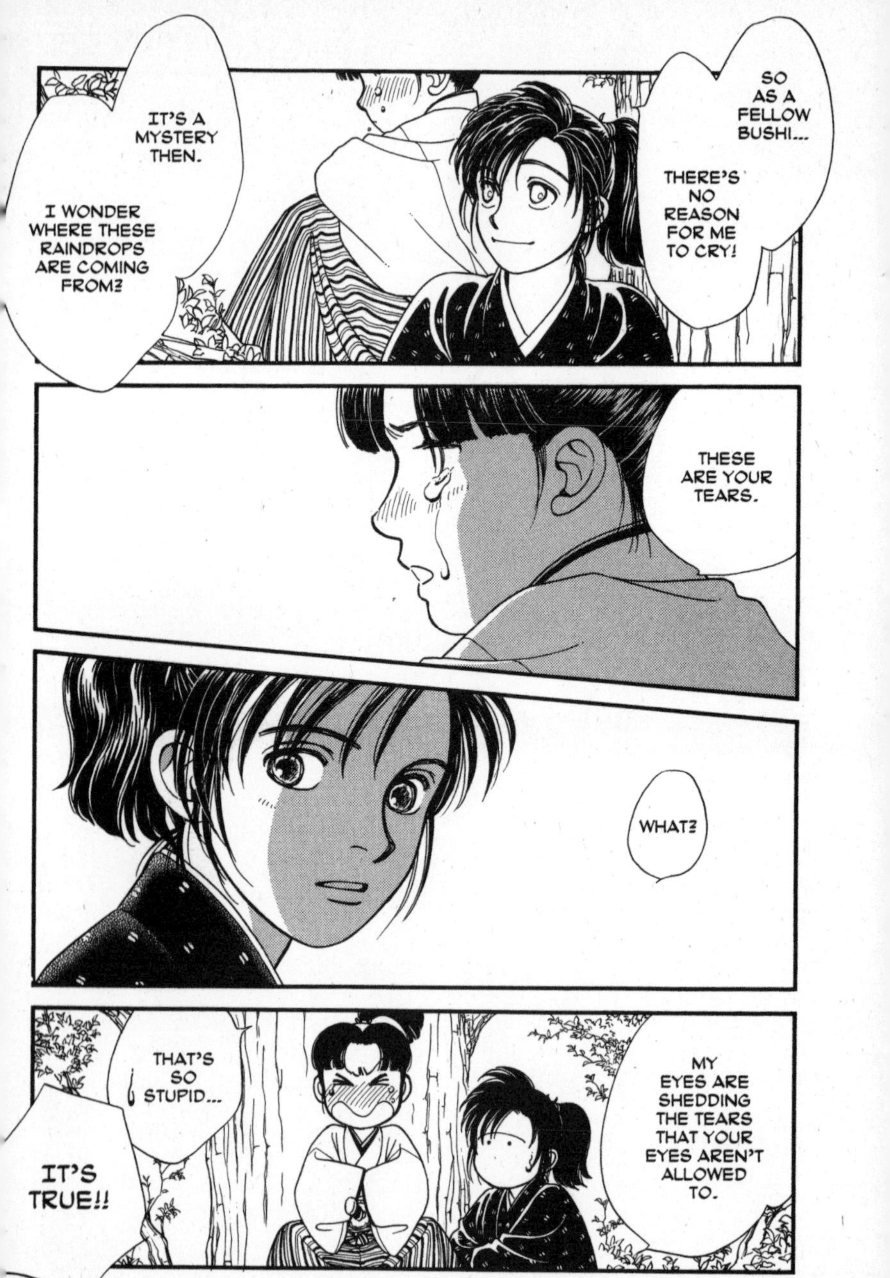
SO AS A FELLOW BUSHI...
THERE'S NO REASON FOR ME TO CRY!
IT'S A MYSTERY THEN.
I WONDER WHERE THESE RAINDROPS ARE COMING FROM?
THESE ARE YOUR TEARS.
WHAT?
MY EYES ARE SHEDDING THE TEARS THAT YOUR EYES AREN'T ALLOWED TO.
THAT'S SO STUPID...
IT'S TRUE!!

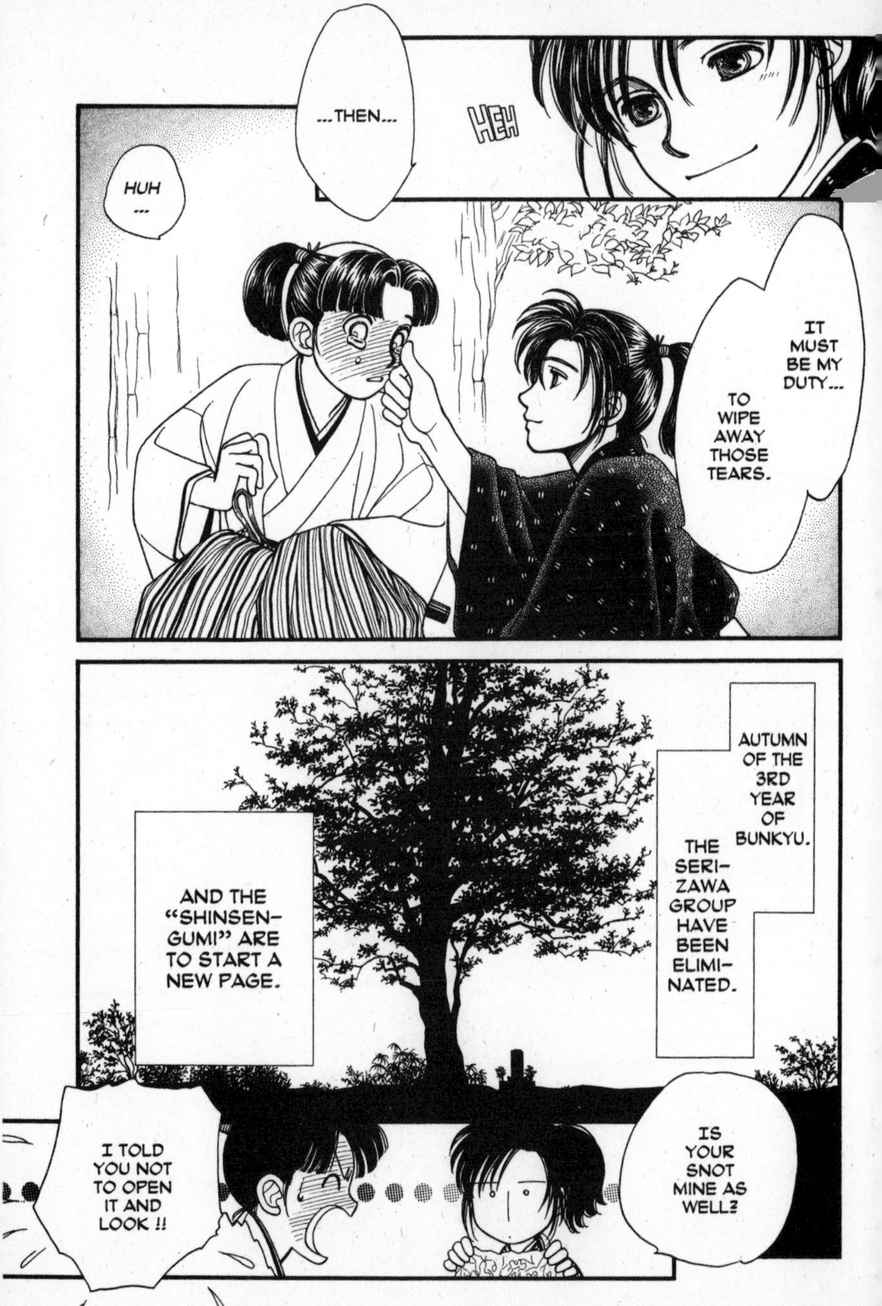
HEH
...THEN...
IT MUST BE MY DUTY...
TO WIPE AWAY THOSE TEARS.
HUH ...
AUTUMN OF THE 3RD YEAR OF BUNKYU.
THE SERI-ZAWA GROUP HAVE BEEN ELIMI-NATED.
AND THE "SHINSEN-GUMI" ARE TO START A NEW PAGE.
IS YOUR SNOT MINE AS WELL?
I TOLD YOU NOT TO OPEN IT AND LOOK !!

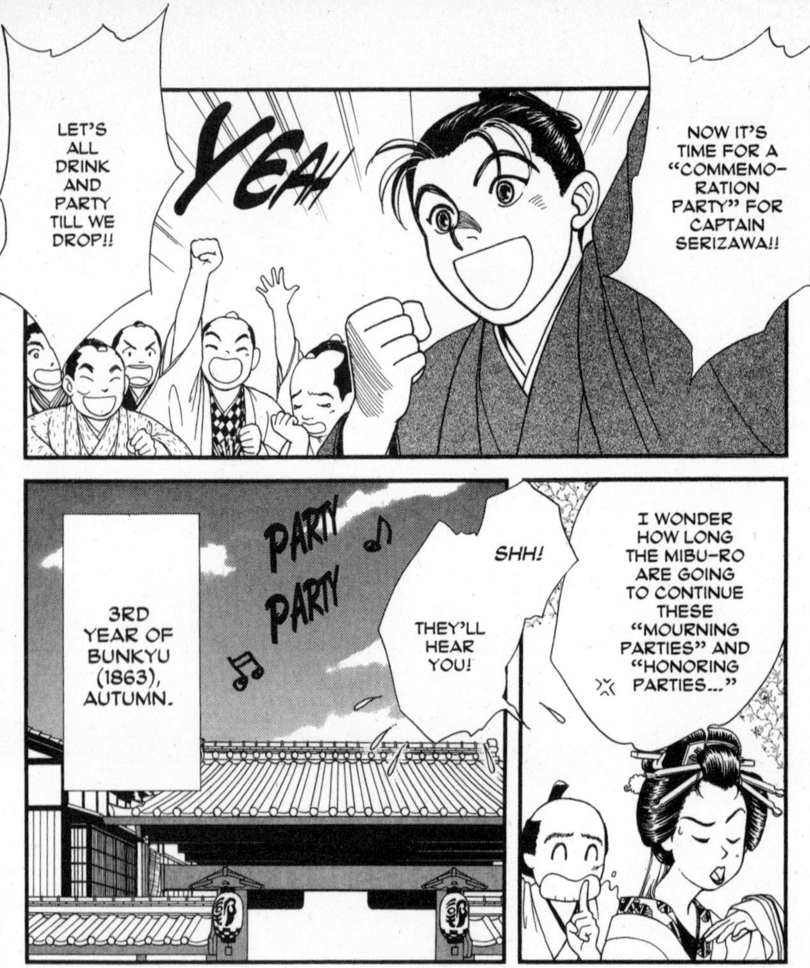
NOW IT'S TIME FOR A "COMMEMORATION PARTY" FOR CAPTAIN SERIZAWA!!
LET'S ALL DRINK AND PARTY TILL WE DROP!!
YEAH
I WONDER HOW LONG THE MIBU-RO ARE GOING TO CONTINUE THESE "MOURNING PARTIES" AND "HONORING PARTIES..."
SHH!
THEY'LL HEAR YOU!
PARTY PARTY
3RD YEAR OF BUNKYU (1863), AUTUMN.

KYOTO "IROHA" KARUTA GAME

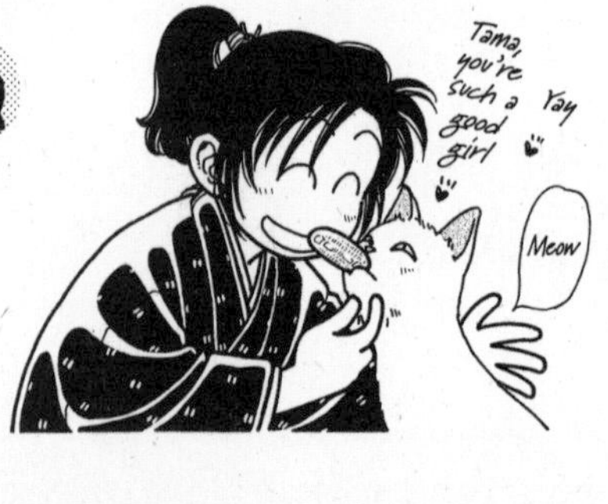
Tama, you're such a good girl
Yay
Meow

ね

"NE" NEKO NI KOBAN "PEARLS BEFORE SWINE."

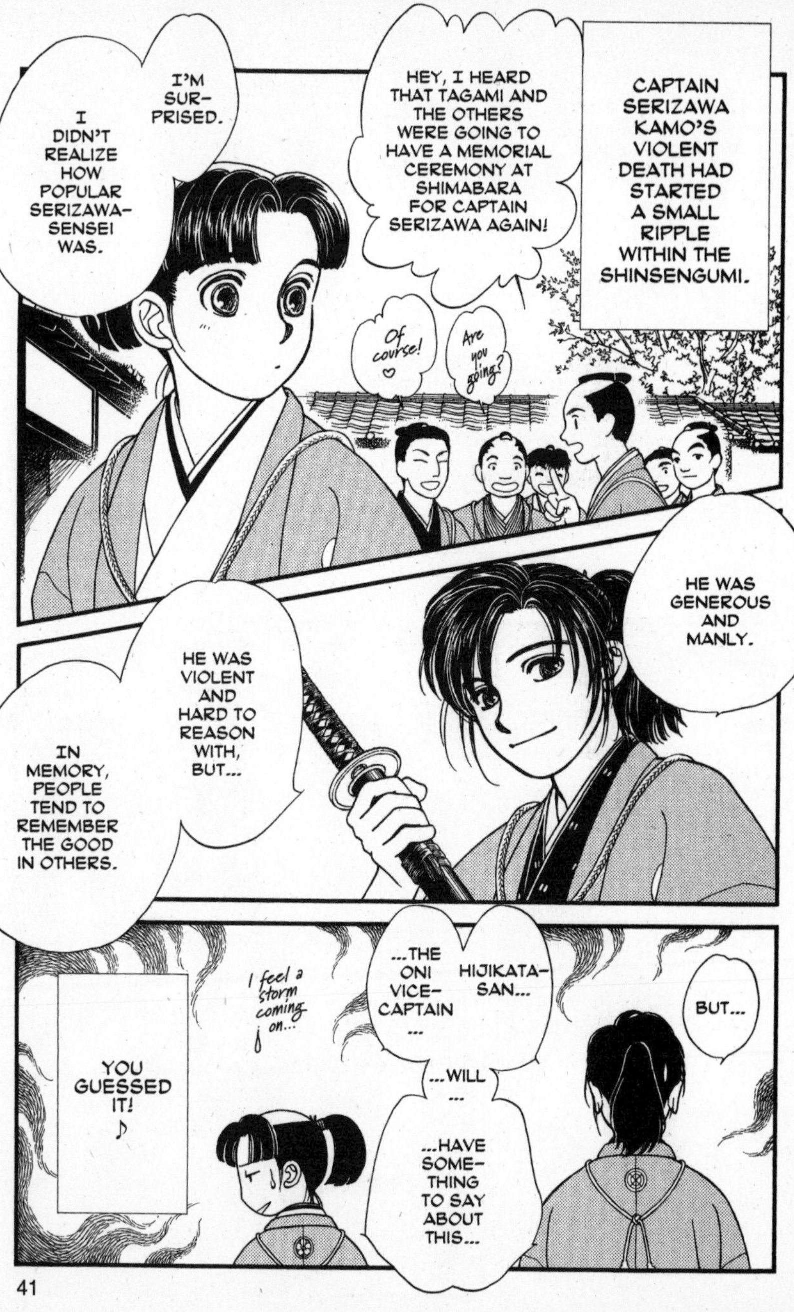
CAPTAIN SERIZAWA KAMO'S VIOLENT DEATH HAD STARTED A SMALL RIPPLE WITHIN THE SHINSENGUMI.
HEY, I HEARD THAT TAGAMI AND THE OTHERS WERE GOING TO HAVE A MEMORIAL CEREMONY AT SHIMABARA FOR CAPTAIN SERIZAWA AGAIN!
Are you going?
Of course! ♡
I'M SUR-PRISED.
I DIDN'T REALIZE HOW POPULAR SERIZAWA-SENSEI WAS.
HE WAS GENEROUS AND MANLY.
HE WAS VIOLENT AND HARD TO REASON WITH, BUT...
IN MEMORY, PEOPLE TEND TO REMEMBER THE GOOD IN OTHERS.
BUT...
HIJIKATA-SAN...
...THE ONI VICE-CAPTAIN...
...WILL...
...HAVE SOME-THING TO SAY ABOUT THIS...
I feel a storm coming on...
YOU GUESSED IT! ♪

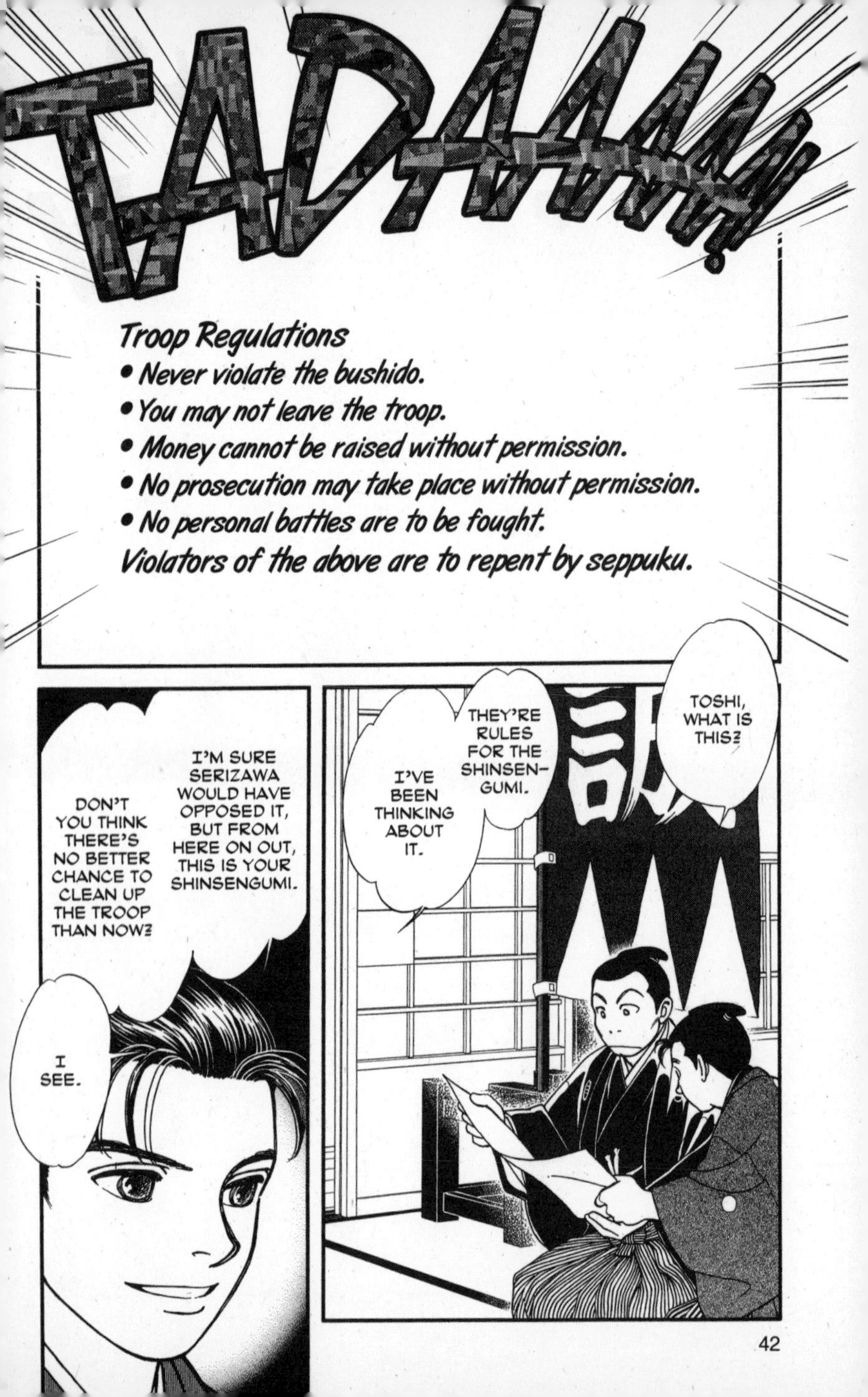
TADAAAM!
Troop Regulations
• Never violate the bushido.
• You may not leave the troop.
• Money cannot be raised without permission.
• No prosecution may take place without permission.
• No personal battles are to be fought.
Violators of the above are to repent by seppuku.
TOSHI, WHAT IS THIS?
THEY'RE RULES FOR THE SHINSENGUMI.
I'VE BEEN THINKING ABOUT IT.
I'M SURE SERIZAWA WOULD HAVE OPPOSED IT, BUT FROM HERE ON OUT, THIS IS YOUR SHINSENGUMI.
DON'T YOU THINK THERE'S NO BETTER CHANCE TO CLEAN UP THE TROOP THAN NOW?
I SEE.

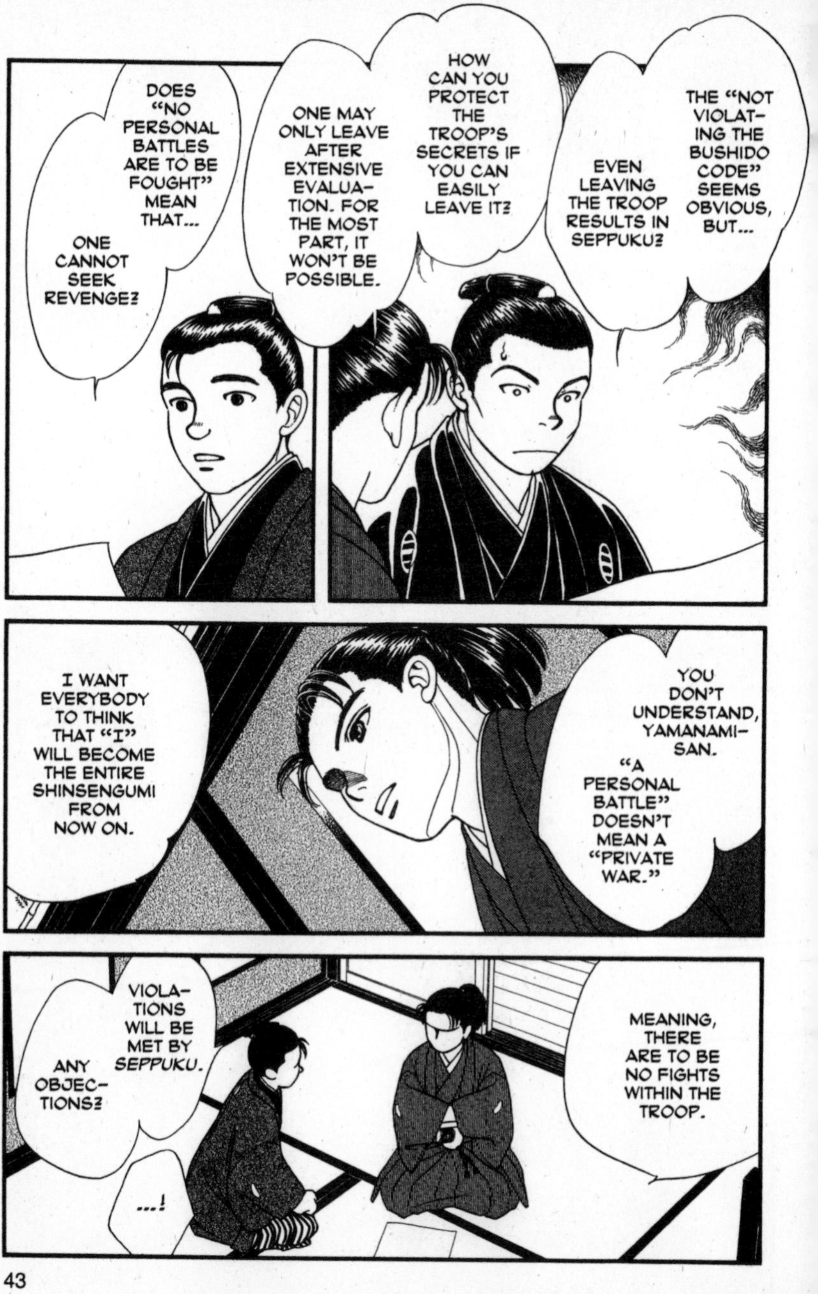

THE "NOT VIOLATING THE BUSHIDO CODE" SEEMS OBVIOUS, BUT...
EVEN LEAVING THE TROOP RESULTS IN SEPPUKU?
HOW CAN YOU PROTECT THE TROOP'S SECRETS IF YOU CAN EASILY LEAVE IT?
ONE MAY ONLY LEAVE AFTER EXTENSIVE EVALUATION. FOR THE MOST PART, IT WON'T BE POSSIBLE.
DOES "NO PERSONAL BATTLES ARE TO BE FOUGHT" MEAN THAT...
ONE CANNOT SEEK REVENGE?
YOU DON'T UNDERSTAND, YAMANAMI-SAN.
"A PERSONAL BATTLE" DOESN'T MEAN A "PRIVATE WAR."
I WANT EVERYBODY TO THINK THAT "I" WILL BECOME THE ENTIRE SHINSENGUMI FROM NOW ON.
MEANING, THERE ARE TO BE NO FIGHTS WITHIN THE TROOP.
VIOLATIONS WILL BE MET BY *SEPPUKU*.
ANY OBJECTIONS?
...!

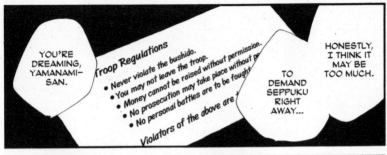

HONESTLY, I THINK IT MAY BE TOO MUCH.
TO DEMAND SEPPUKU RIGHT AWAY...
Troop Regulations
• Never violate the bushido.
• You may not leave the troop.
• Money cannot be raised without permission.
• No prosecution may take place without pe
• No personal battles are to be fought
Violators of the above are
YOU'RE DREAMING, YAMANAMI-SAN.
WE'RE FACING IDIOTS WHO ARE CARRYING OUT SERIZAWA'S LEGACY AT SHIMABARA AND RACKING UP DEBTS.
WHAT KIND OF TROOP DO YOU THINK WE CAN BUILD WITHOUT RULES THAT SMELL OF BLOOD?!
...
HE'S RIGHT!
I'LL SUPPORT THESE RULES!!
WHAT ABOUT YOU, YAMANAMI-SAN?

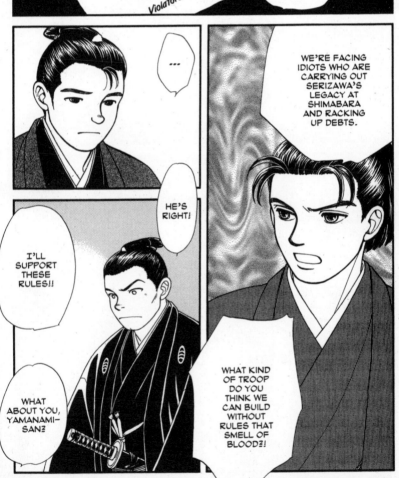

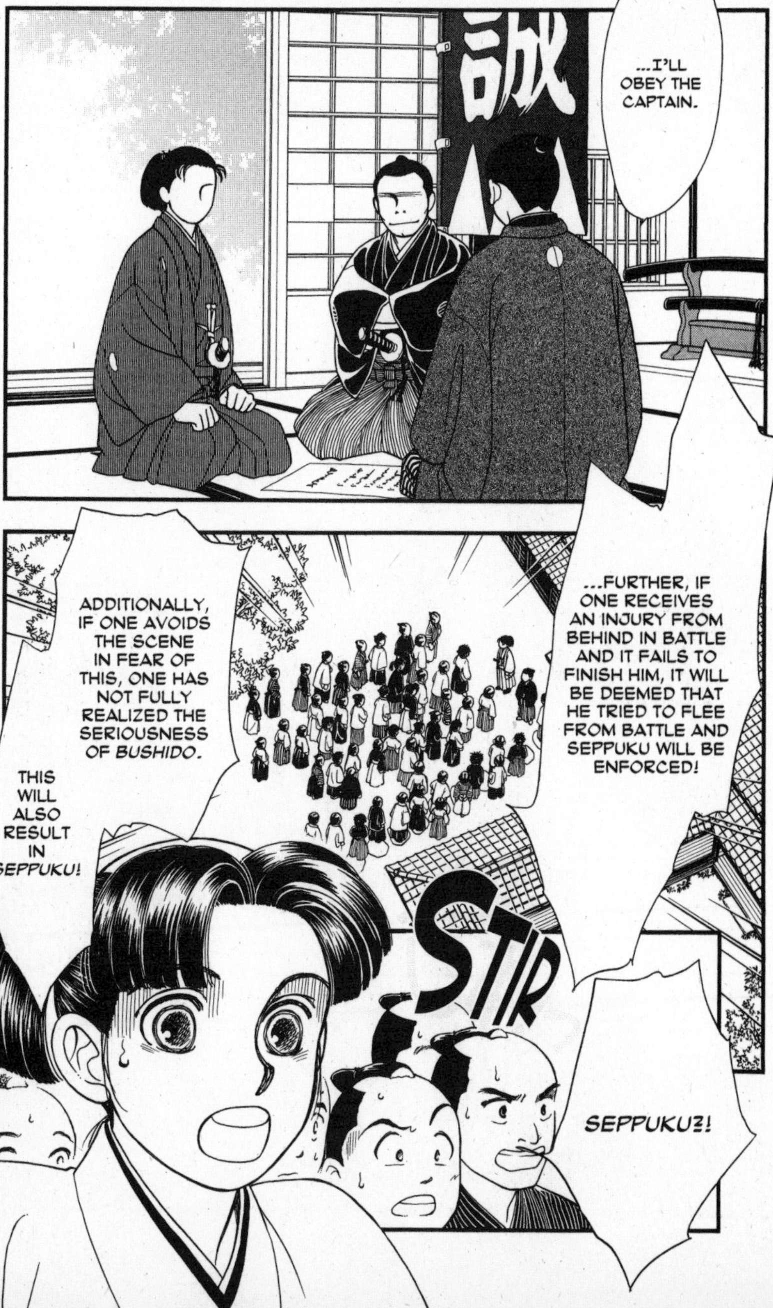
...I'LL OBEY THE CAPTAIN.
...FURTHER, IF ONE RECEIVES AN INJURY FROM BEHIND IN BATTLE AND IT FAILS TO FINISH HIM, IT WILL BE DEEMED THAT HE TRIED TO FLEE FROM BATTLE AND SEPPUKU WILL BE ENFORCED!
ADDITIONALLY, IF ONE AVOIDS THE SCENE IN FEAR OF THIS, ONE HAS NOT FULLY REALIZED THE SERIOUSNESS OF *BUSHIDO*.
THIS WILL ALSO RESULT IN *SEPPUKU*!
STIR
SEPPUKU?!

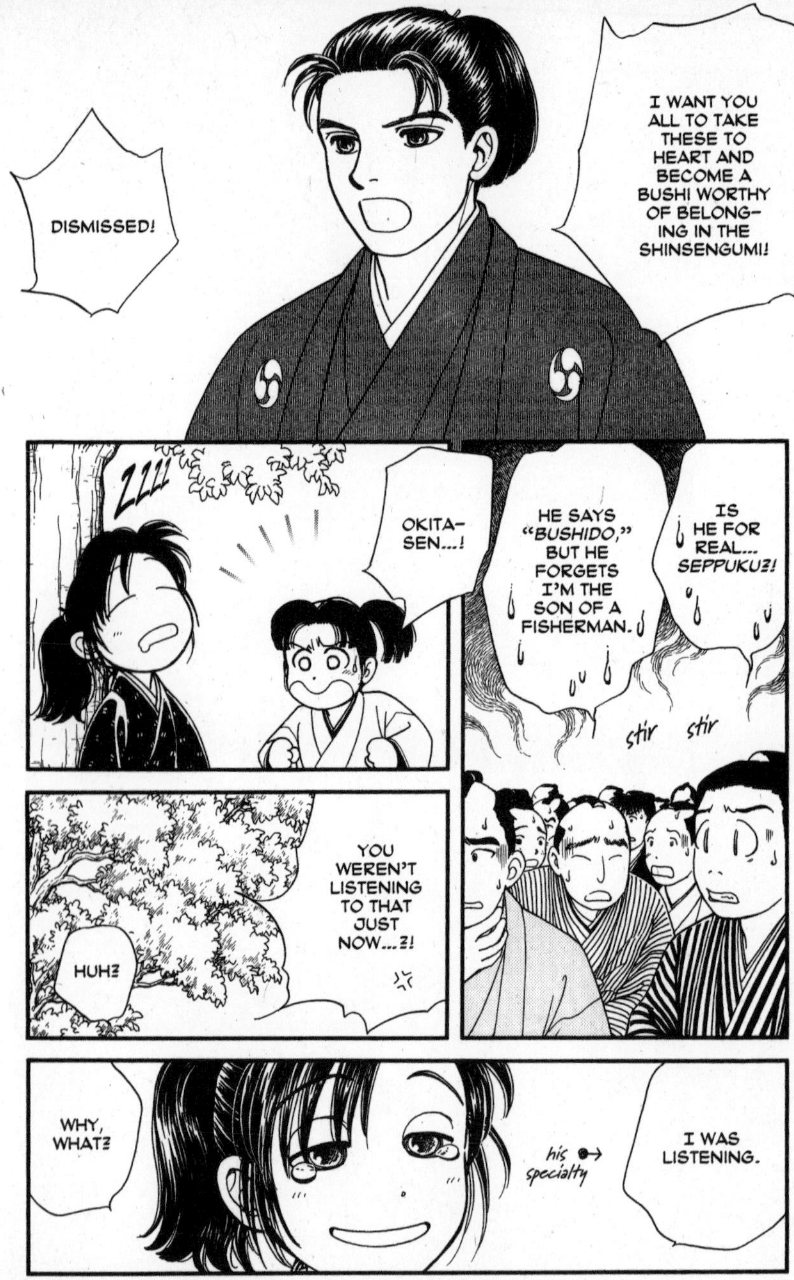
I WANT YOU ALL TO TAKE THESE TO HEART AND BECOME A BUSHI WORTHY OF BELONG-ING IN THE SHINSENGUMI!
DISMISSED!
IS HE FOR REAL... SEPPUKU?!
HE SAYS "BUSHIDO," BUT HE FORGETS I'M THE SON OF A FISHERMAN.
stir stir
OKITA-SEN...!
ZZZZ
YOU WEREN'T LISTENING TO THAT JUST NOW...?!
HUH?
I WAS LISTENING.
his specialty
WHY, WHAT?

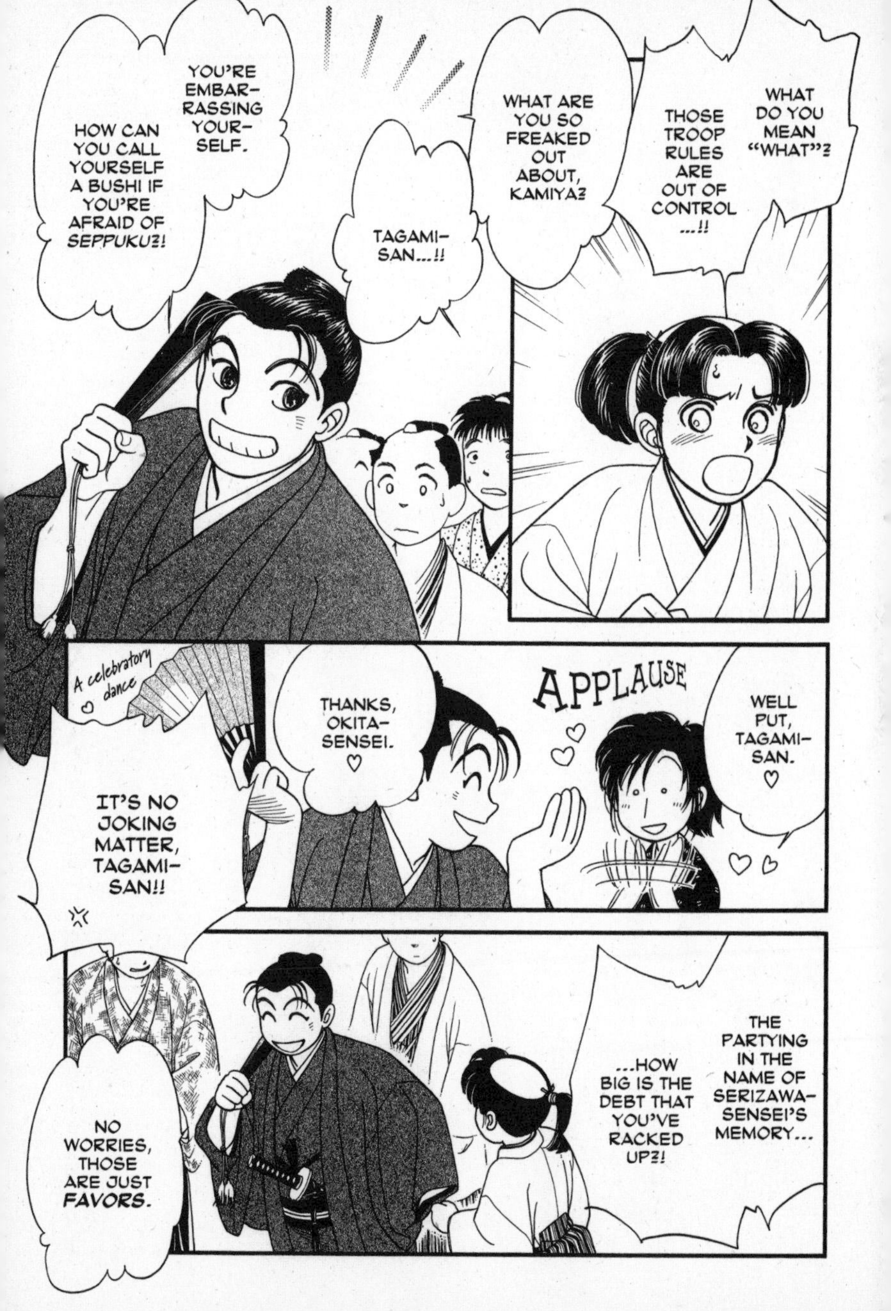
WHAT DO YOU MEAN "WHAT"?
THOSE TROOP RULES ARE OUT OF CONTROL...!!
WHAT ARE YOU SO FREAKED OUT ABOUT, KAMIYA?
TAGAMI-SAN...!!
YOU'RE EMBARRASSING YOURSELF.
HOW CAN YOU CALL YOURSELF A BUSHI IF YOU'RE AFRAID OF SEPPUKU?!
WELL PUT, TAGAMI-SAN. ♡
APPLAUSE
THANKS, OKITA-SENSEI. ♡
A celebratory dance ♡
IT'S NO JOKING MATTER, TAGAMI-SAN!!
THE PARTYING IN THE NAME OF SERIZAWA-SENSEI'S MEMORY...
...HOW BIG IS THE DEBT THAT YOU'VE RACKED UP?!
NO WORRIES, THOSE ARE JUST FAVORS.

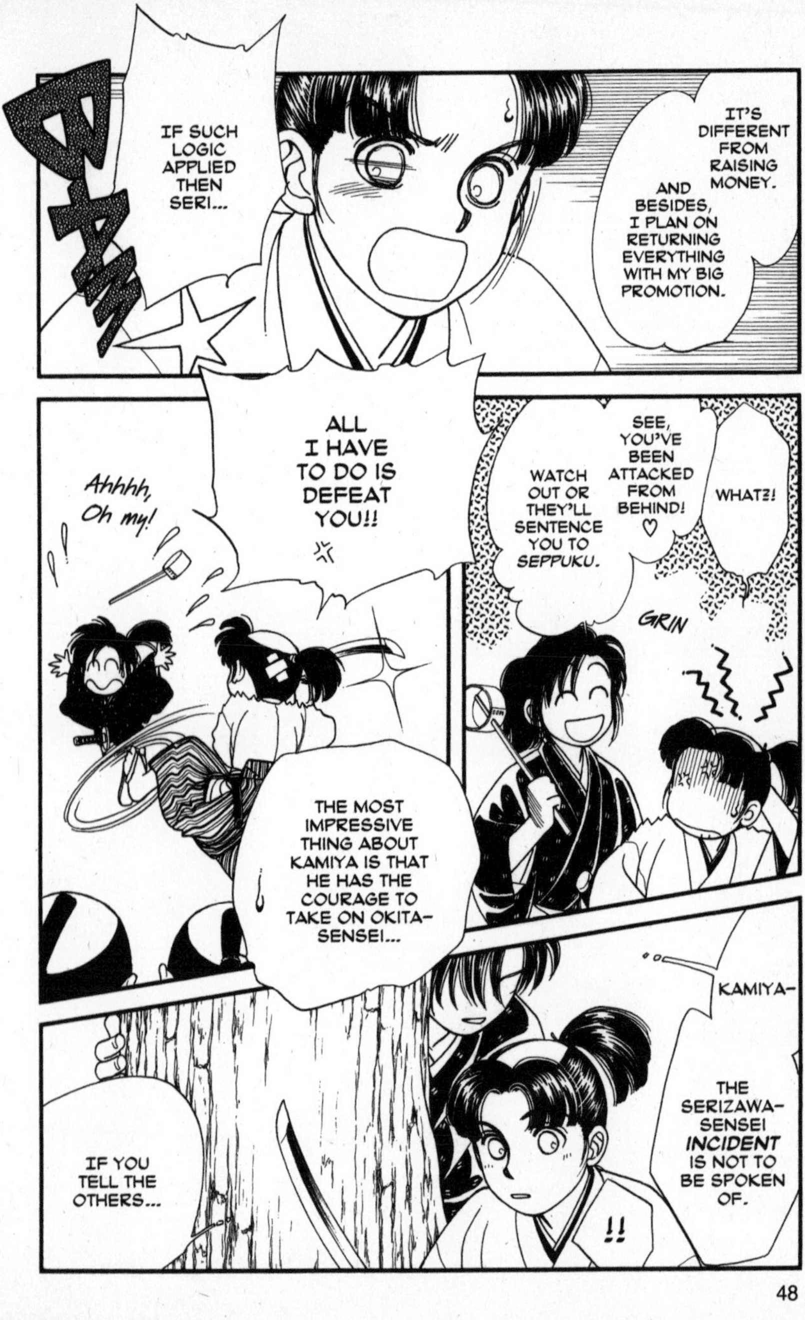
IT'S DIFFERENT FROM RAISING MONEY.
AND BESIDES, I PLAN ON RETURNING EVERYTHING WITH MY BIG PROMOTION.
IF SUCH LOGIC APPLIED THEN SERI...
BAM
WHAT?!
SEE, YOU'VE BEEN ATTACKED FROM BEHIND! ♡
WATCH OUT OR THEY'LL SENTENCE YOU TO *SEPPUKU*.
GRIN
ALL I HAVE TO DO IS DEFEAT YOU!!
Ahhhh, Oh my!
THE MOST IMPRESSIVE THING ABOUT KAMIYA IS THAT HE HAS THE COURAGE TO TAKE ON OKITA-SENSEI...
KAMIYA-
THE SERIZAWA-SENSEI ***INCIDENT*** IS NOT TO BE SPOKEN OF.
!!
IF YOU TELL THE OTHERS...

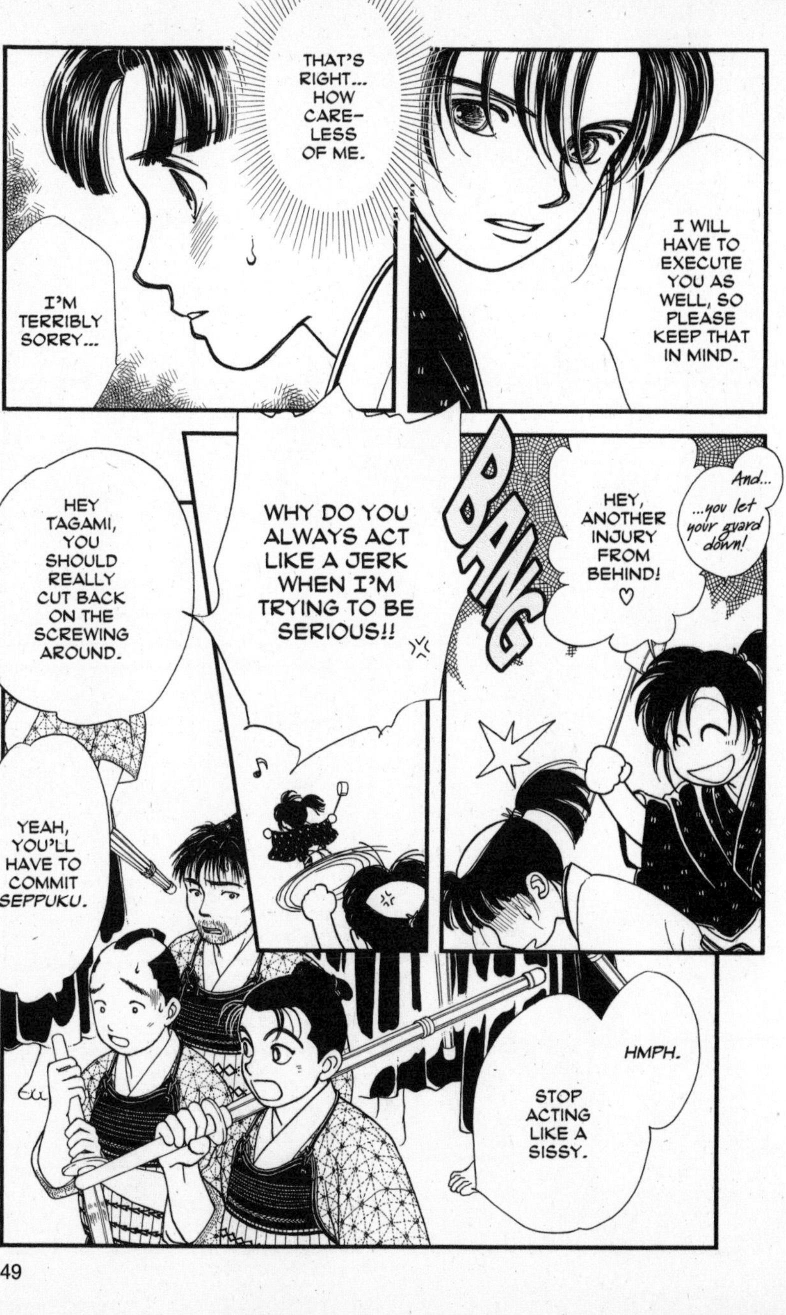
I WILL HAVE TO EXECUTE YOU AS WELL, SO PLEASE KEEP THAT IN MIND.
THAT'S RIGHT... HOW CARE-LESS OF ME.
I'M TERRIBLY SORRY...
And... ...you let your guard down!
HEY, ANOTHER INJURY FROM BEHIND! ♡
BANG
WHY DO YOU ALWAYS ACT LIKE A JERK WHEN I'M TRYING TO BE SERIOUS!!
HEY TAGAMI, YOU SHOULD REALLY CUT BACK ON THE SCREWING AROUND.
YEAH, YOU'LL HAVE TO COMMIT *SEPPUKU*.
HMPH.
STOP ACTING LIKE A SISSY.

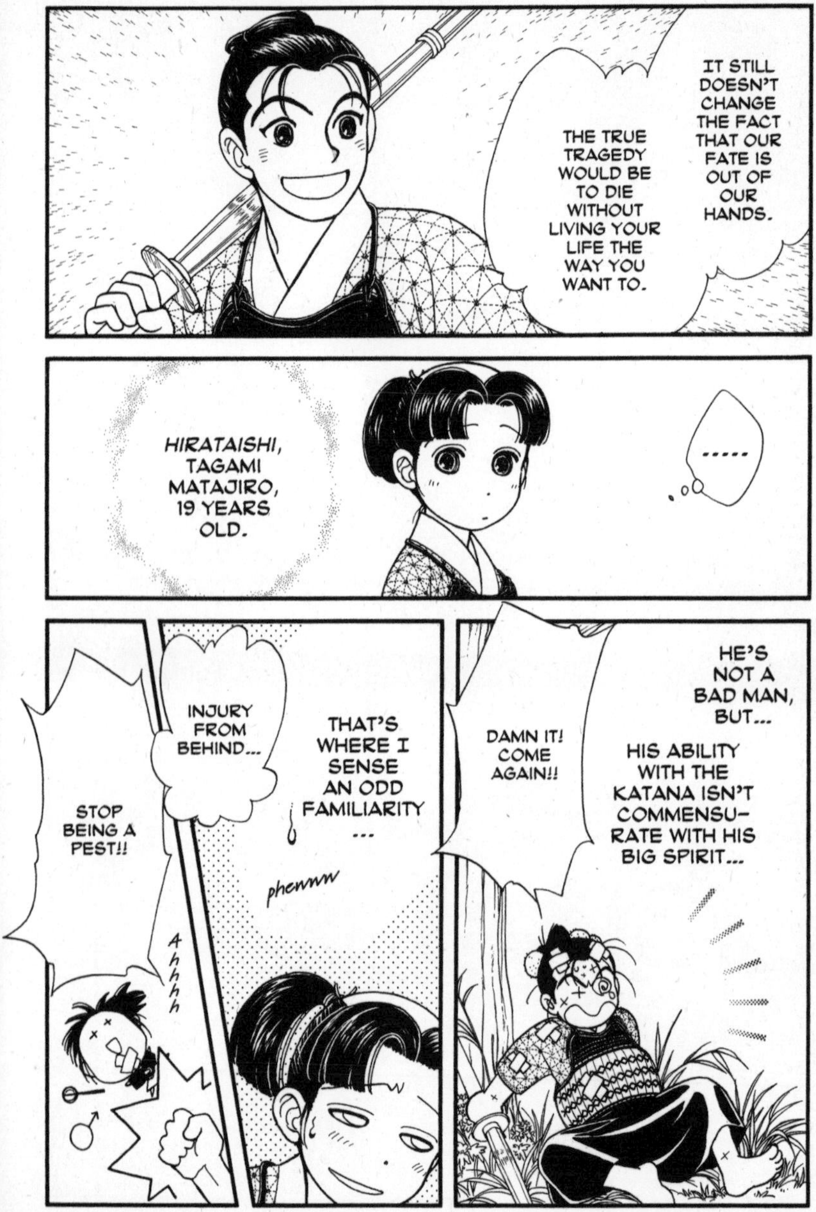
IT STILL DOESN'T CHANGE THE FACT THAT OUR FATE IS OUT OF OUR HANDS.
THE TRUE TRAGEDY WOULD BE TO DIE WITHOUT LIVING YOUR LIFE THE WAY YOU WANT TO.

HIRATAISHI, TAGAMI MATAJIRO, 19 YEARS OLD.
HE'S NOT A BAD MAN, BUT...
HIS ABILITY WITH THE KATANA ISN'T COMMENSU-RATE WITH HIS BIG SPIRIT...
DAMN IT! COME AGAIN!!
THAT'S WHERE I SENSE AN ODD FAMILIARITY ...
INJURY FROM BEHIND...
phewww
STOP BEING A PEST!!
Ahhhh

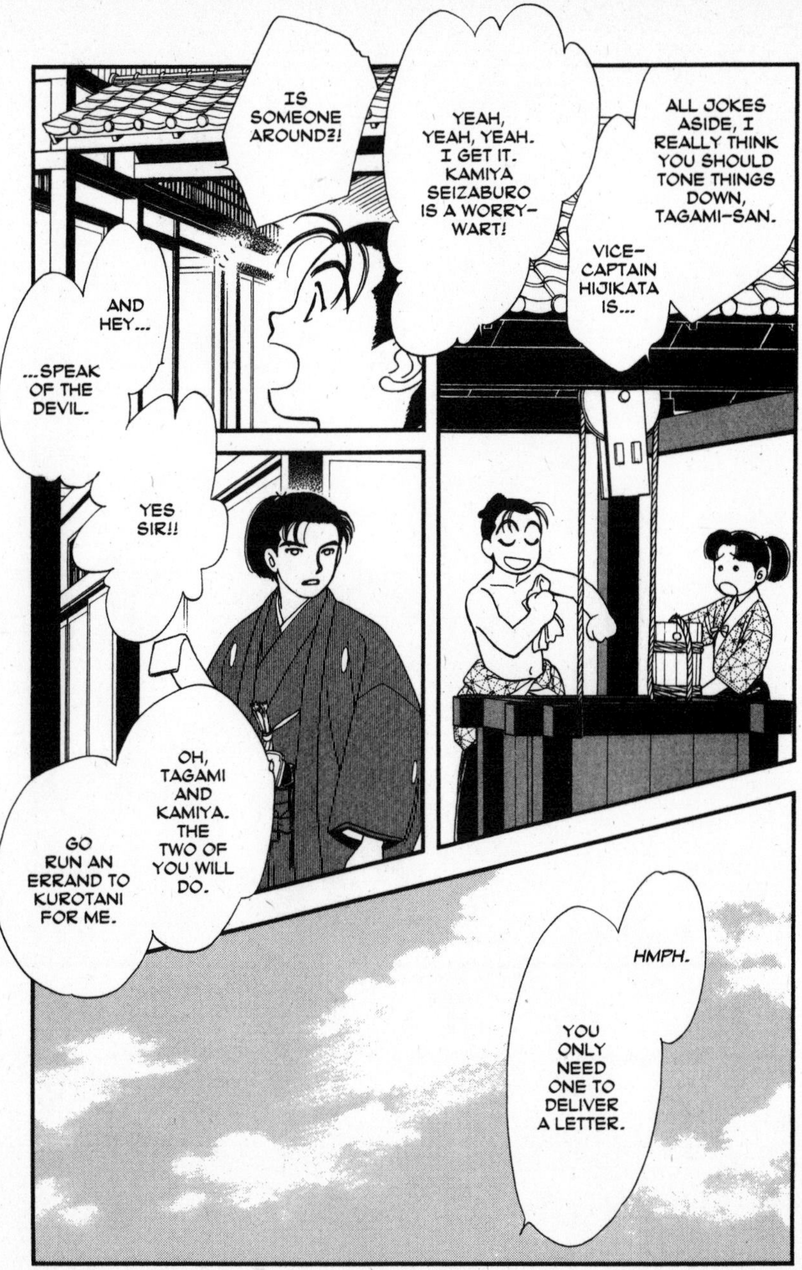
ALL JOKES ASIDE, I REALLY THINK YOU SHOULD TONE THINGS DOWN, TAGAMI-SAN.
VICE-CAPTAIN HIJIKATA IS...
YEAH, YEAH, YEAH. I GET IT. KAMIYA SEIZABURO IS A WORRY-WART!
IS SOMEONE AROUND?!
AND HEY...
...SPEAK OF THE DEVIL.
YES SIR!!
OH, TAGAMI AND KAMIYA. THE TWO OF YOU WILL DO.
GO RUN AN ERRAND TO KUROTANI FOR ME.
HMPH.
YOU ONLY NEED ONE TO DELIVER A LETTER.

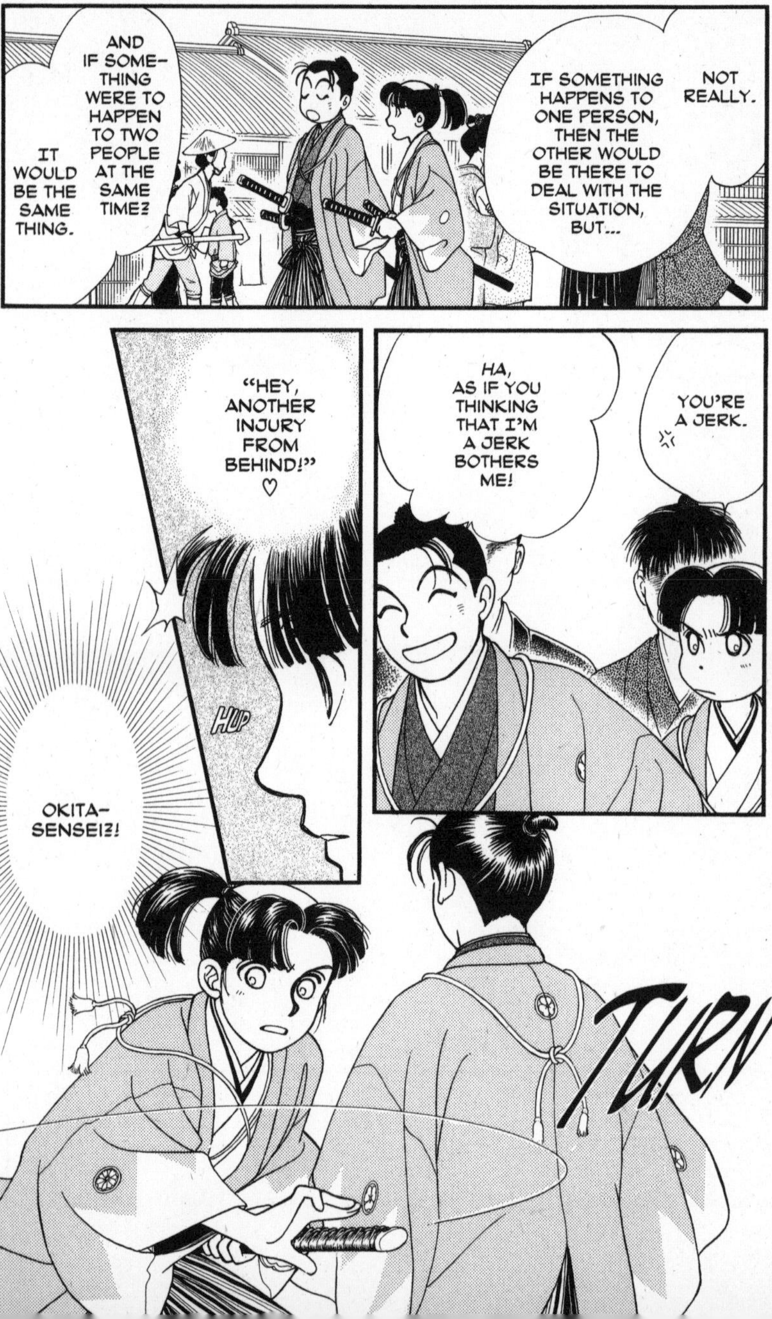
NOT REALLY.
IF SOMETHING HAPPENS TO ONE PERSON, THEN THE OTHER WOULD BE THERE TO DEAL WITH THE SITUATION, BUT...
AND IF SOMETHING WERE TO HAPPEN TO TWO PEOPLE AT THE SAME TIME?
IT WOULD BE THE SAME THING.
YOU'RE A JERK.
HA, AS IF YOU THINKING THAT I'M A JERK BOTHERS ME!
"HEY, ANOTHER INJURY FROM BEHIND!" ♡
HUP
TURN
OKITA-SENSEI?!

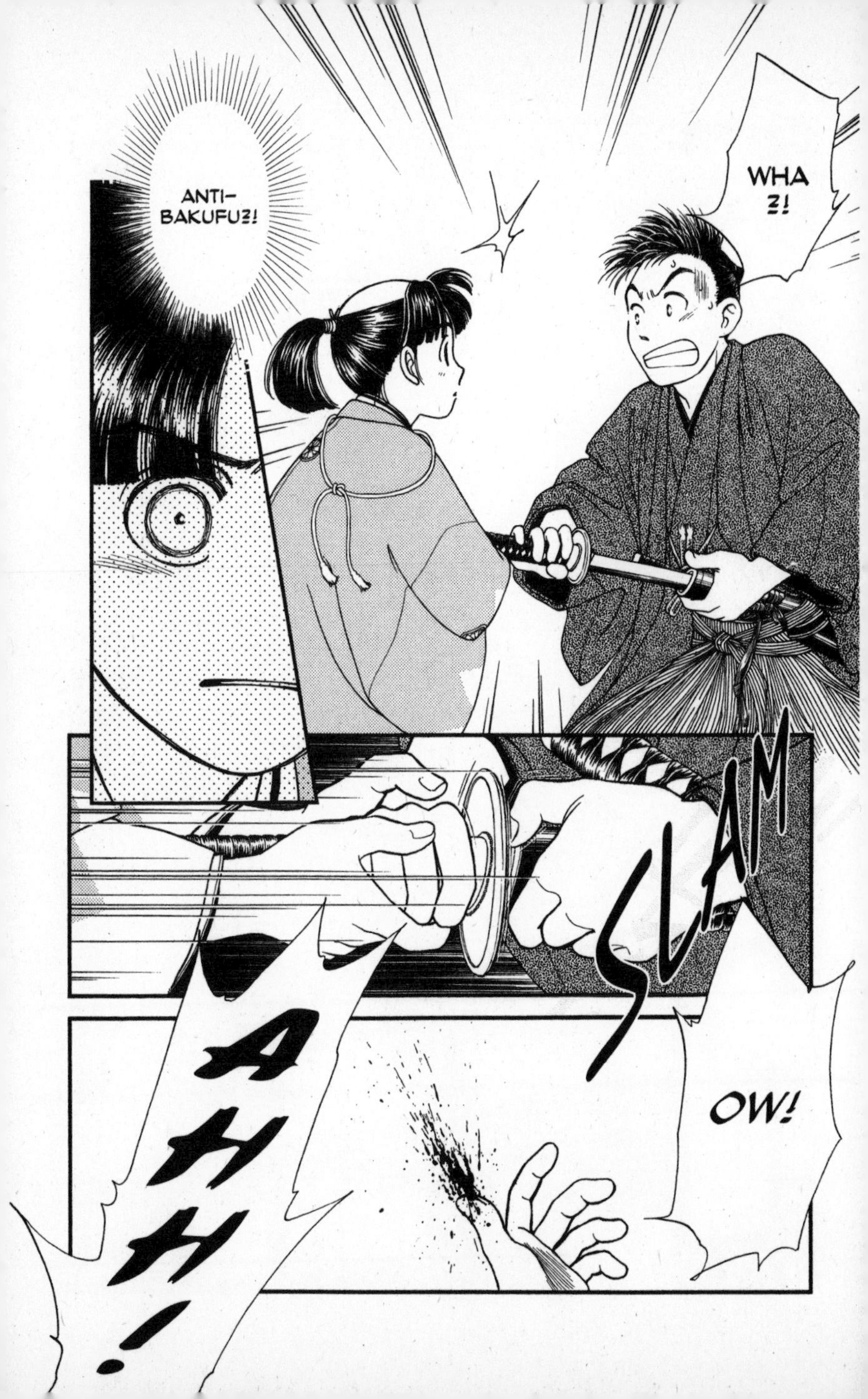
WHA ?!
ANTI-BAKUFU?!
SLAM
OW!
AHHH!

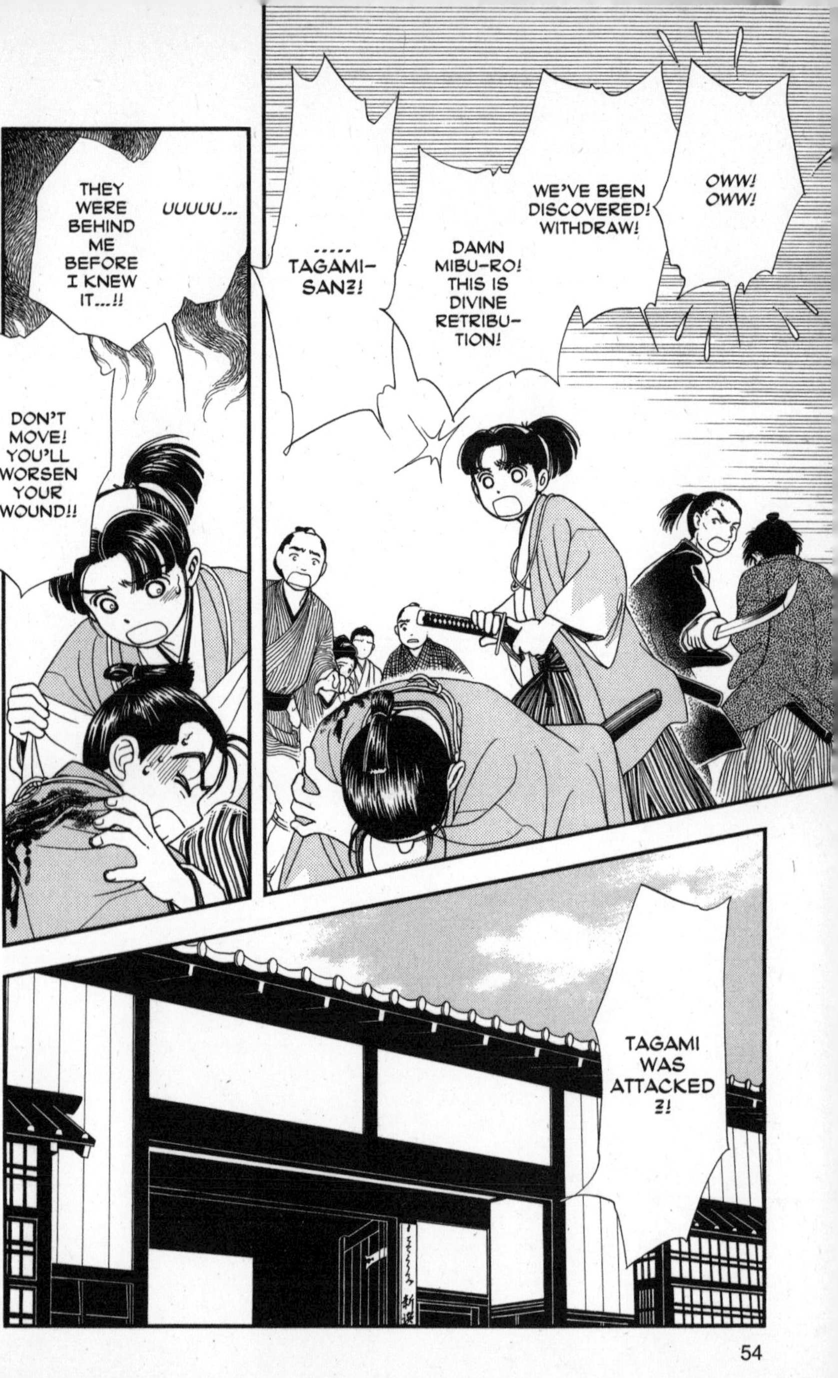
OWW! OWW!
WE'VE BEEN DISCOVERED! WITHDRAW!
DAMN MIBU-RO! THIS IS DIVINE RETRIBUTION!
.....TAGAMI-SAN?!
UUUUU...
THEY WERE BEHIND ME BEFORE I KNEW IT...!!
DON'T MOVE! YOU'LL WORSEN YOUR WOUND!!
TAGAMI WAS ATTACKED?!

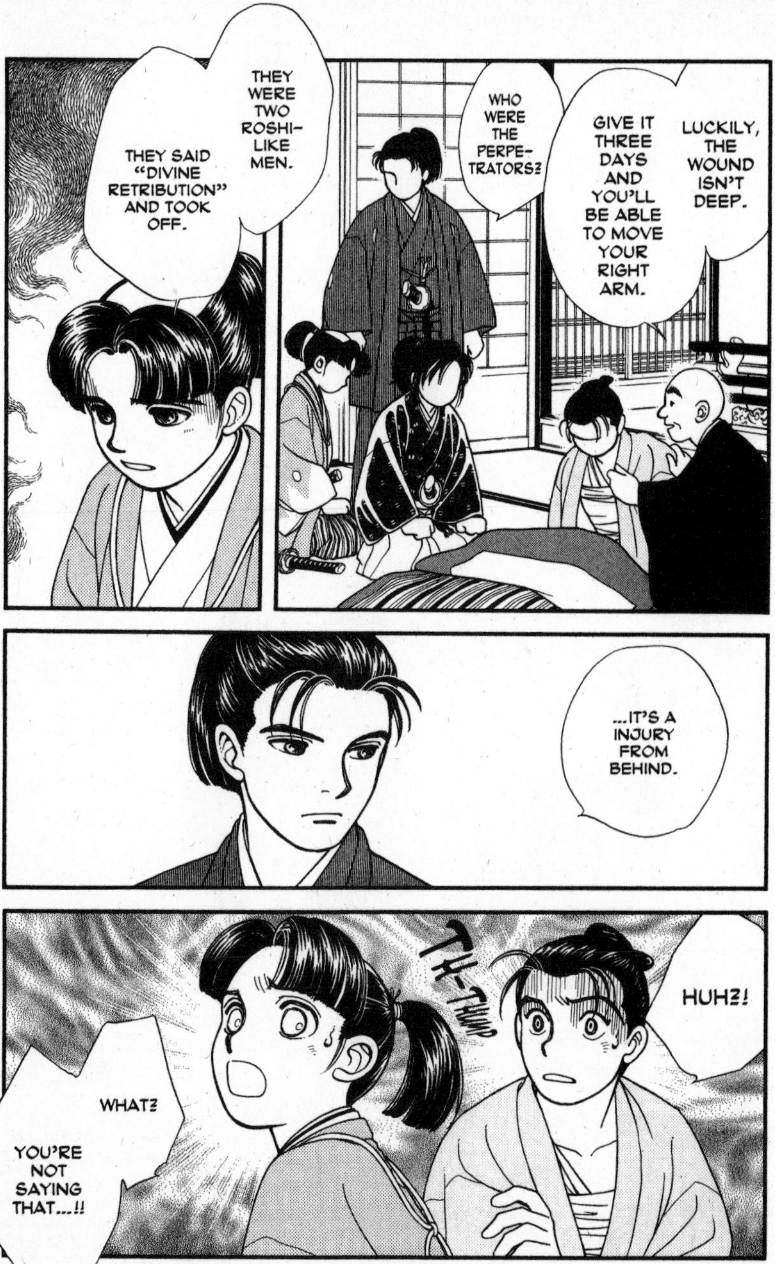
LUCKILY, THE WOUND ISN'T DEEP.
GIVE IT THREE DAYS AND YOU'LL BE ABLE TO MOVE YOUR RIGHT ARM.
WHO WERE THE PERPETRATORS?
THEY WERE TWO ROSHI-LIKE MEN.
THEY SAID "DIVINE RETRIBUTION" AND TOOK OFF.
...IT'S A INJURY FROM BEHIND.
HUH?!
TH-THUMP
WHAT?
YOU'RE NOT SAYING THAT...!!

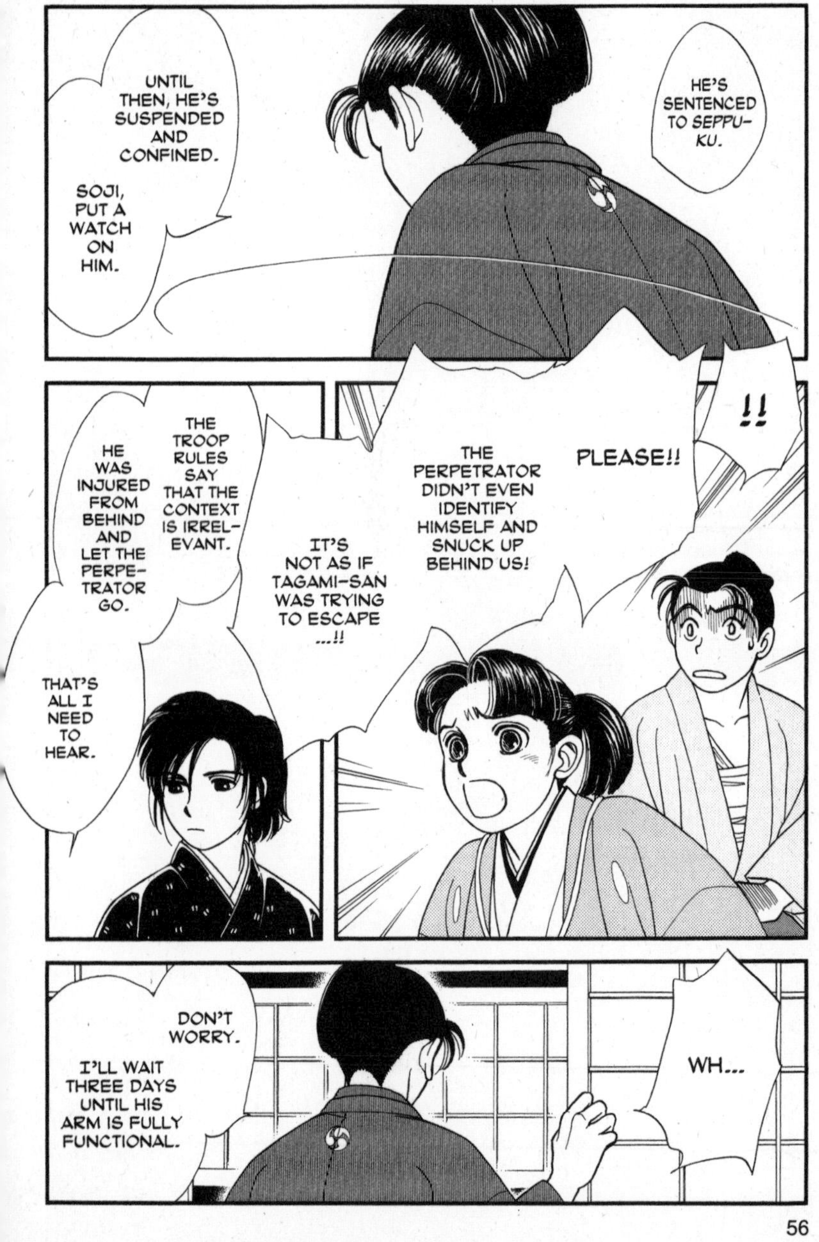
HE'S SENTENCED TO SEPPUKU.
UNTIL THEN, HE'S SUSPENDED AND CONFINED.
SOJI, PUT A WATCH ON HIM.
!!
PLEASE!!
THE PERPETRATOR DIDN'T EVEN IDENTIFY HIMSELF AND SNUCK UP BEHIND US!
IT'S NOT AS IF TAGAMI-SAN WAS TRYING TO ESCAPE ...!!
THE TROOP RULES SAY THAT THE CONTEXT IS IRREL-EVANT.
HE WAS INJURED FROM BEHIND AND LET THE PERPE-TRATOR GO.
THAT'S ALL I NEED TO HEAR.
WH...
DON'T WORRY.
I'LL WAIT THREE DAYS UNTIL HIS ARM IS FULLY FUNCTIONAL.

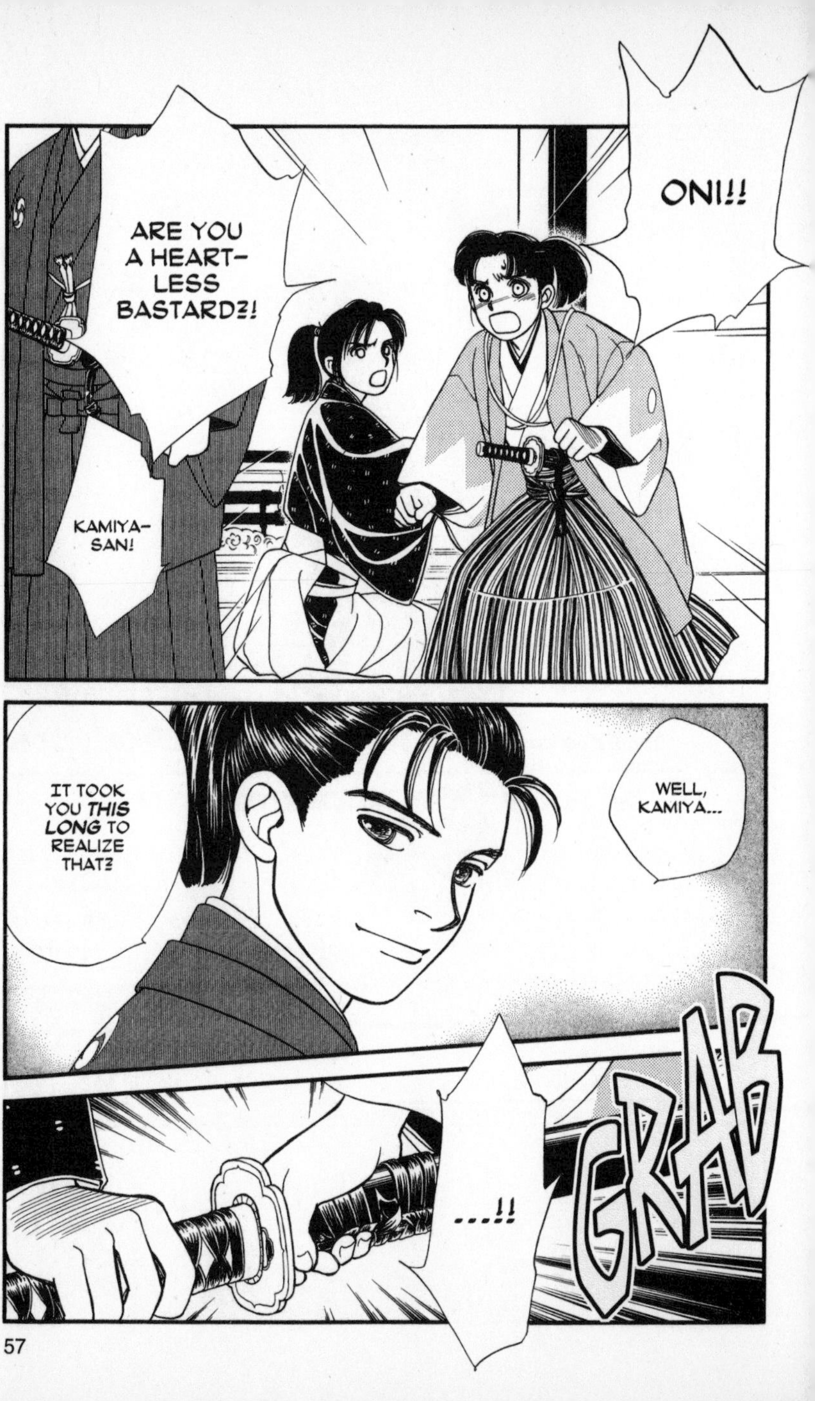
ONI!!
ARE YOU A HEARTLESS BASTARD?!
KAMIYA-SAN!
WELL, KAMIYA...
IT TOOK YOU *THIS LONG* TO REALIZE THAT?
GRAB
...!!

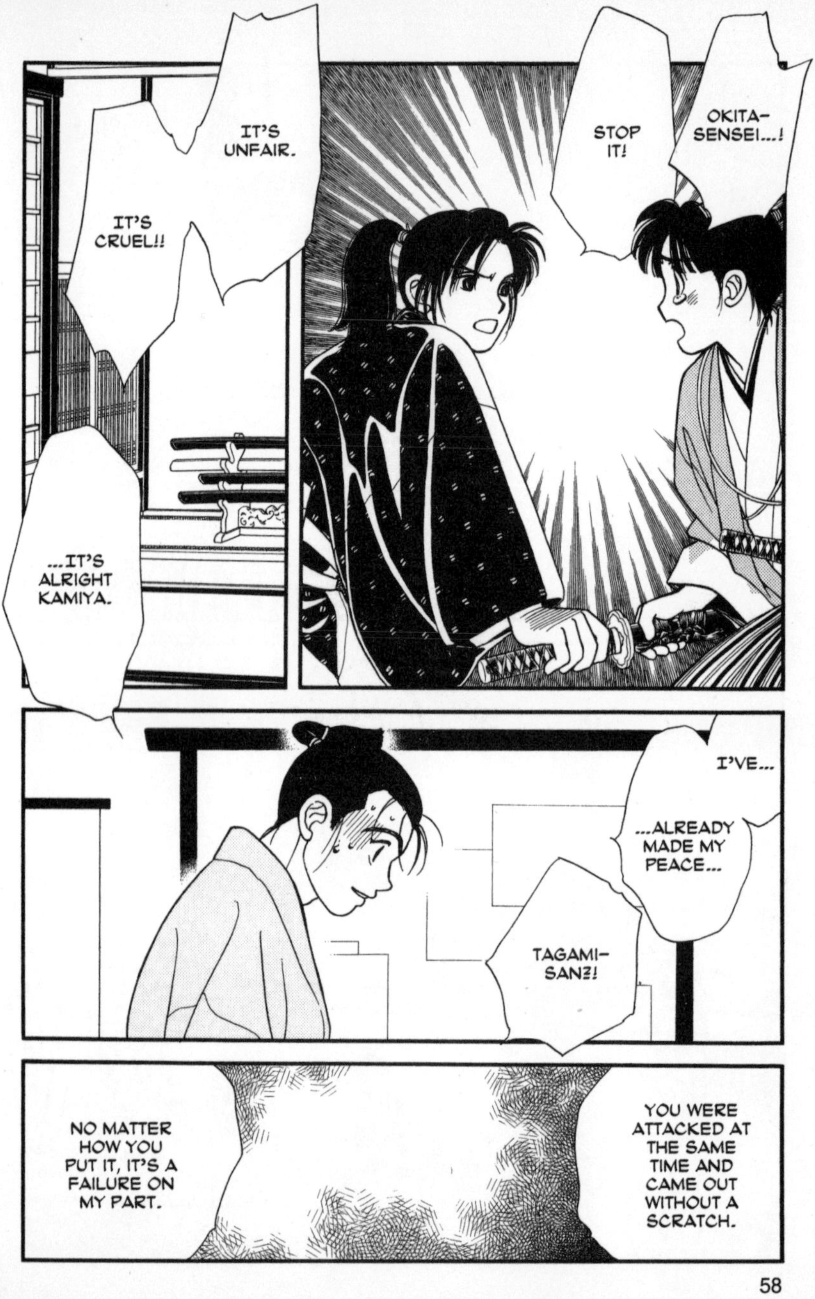
OKITA-SENSEI...!
STOP IT!
IT'S UNFAIR.
IT'S CRUEL!!
...IT'S ALRIGHT KAMIYA.
I'VE...
...ALREADY MADE MY PEACE...
TAGAMI-SAN?!
YOU WERE ATTACKED AT THE SAME TIME AND CAME OUT WITHOUT A SCRATCH.
NO MATTER HOW YOU PUT IT, IT'S A FAILURE ON MY PART.

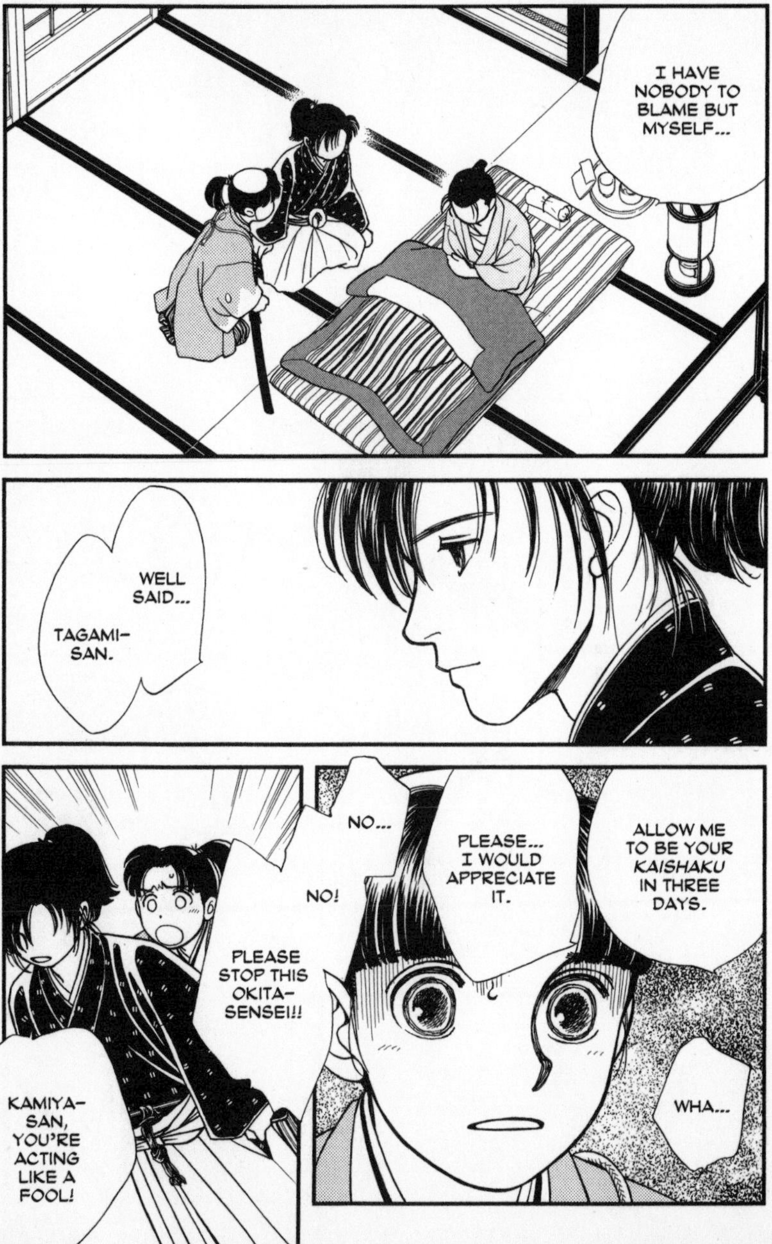
I HAVE NOBODY TO BLAME BUT MYSELF...
WELL SAID...
TAGAMI-SAN.
ALLOW ME TO BE YOUR *KAISHAKU* IN THREE DAYS.
PLEASE... I WOULD APPRECIATE IT.
WHA...
NO...
NO!
PLEASE STOP THIS OKITA-SENSEI!!
KAMIYA-SAN, YOU'RE ACTING LIKE A FOOL!

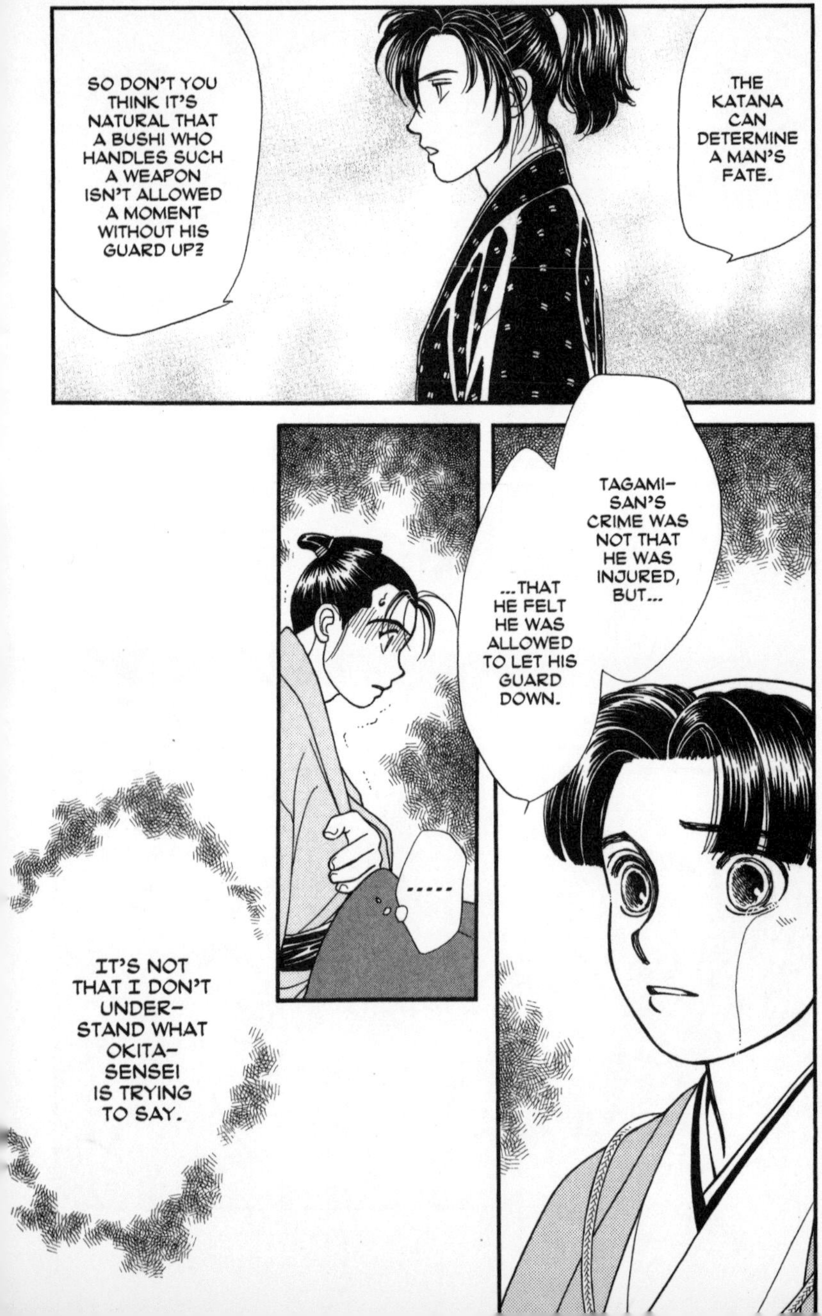
THE KATANA CAN DETERMINE A MAN'S FATE.
SO DON'T YOU THINK IT'S NATURAL THAT A BUSHI WHO HANDLES SUCH A WEAPON ISN'T ALLOWED A MOMENT WITHOUT HIS GUARD UP?
TAGAMI-SAN'S CRIME WAS NOT THAT HE WAS INJURED, BUT...
...THAT HE FELT HE WAS ALLOWED TO LET HIS GUARD DOWN.
.....
IT'S NOT THAT I DON'T UNDER-STAND WHAT OKITA-SENSEI IS TRYING TO SAY.

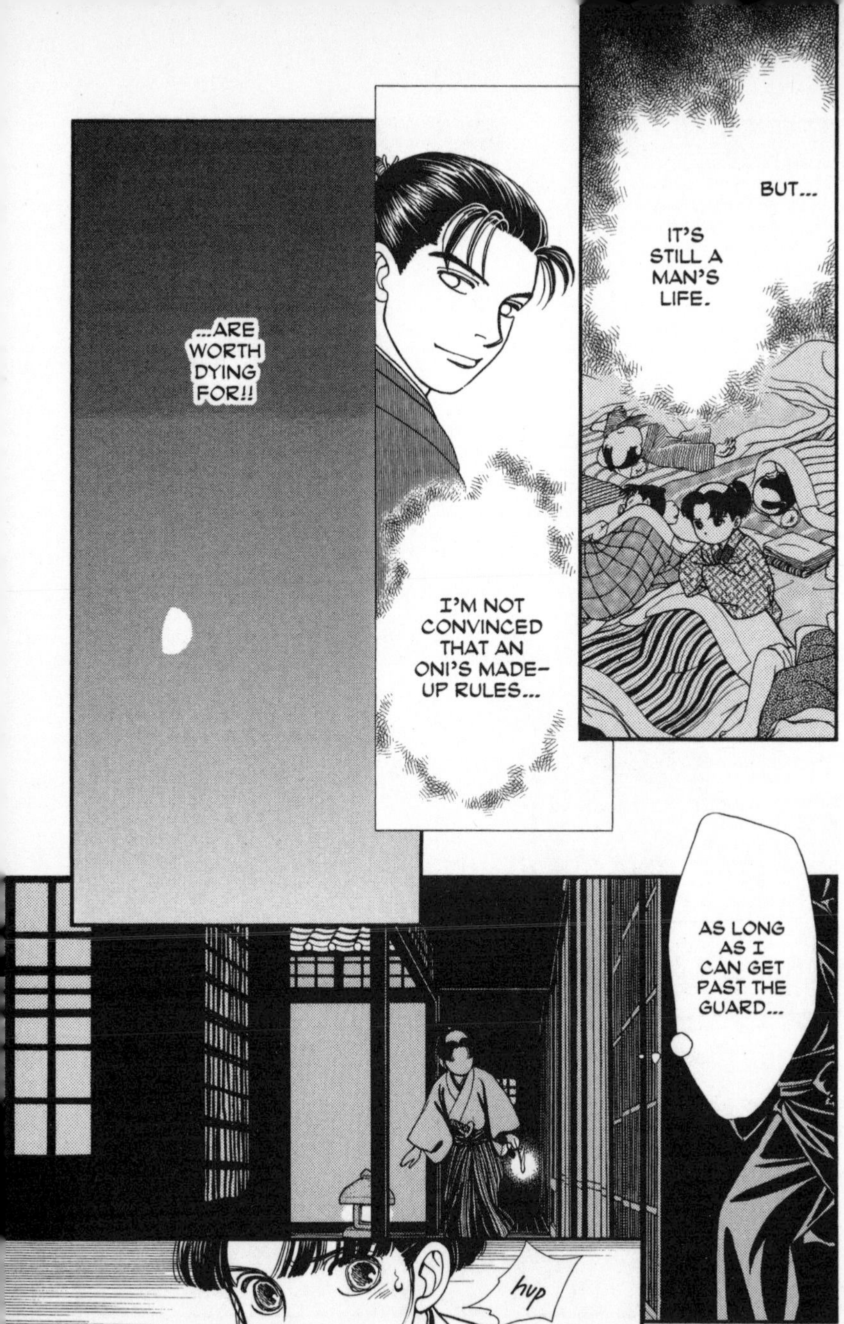
BUT...
IT'S STILL A MAN'S LIFE.
I'M NOT CONVINCED THAT AN ONI'S MADE-UP RULES...
...ARE WORTH DYING FOR!!
AS LONG AS I CAN GET PAST THE GUARD...
hup

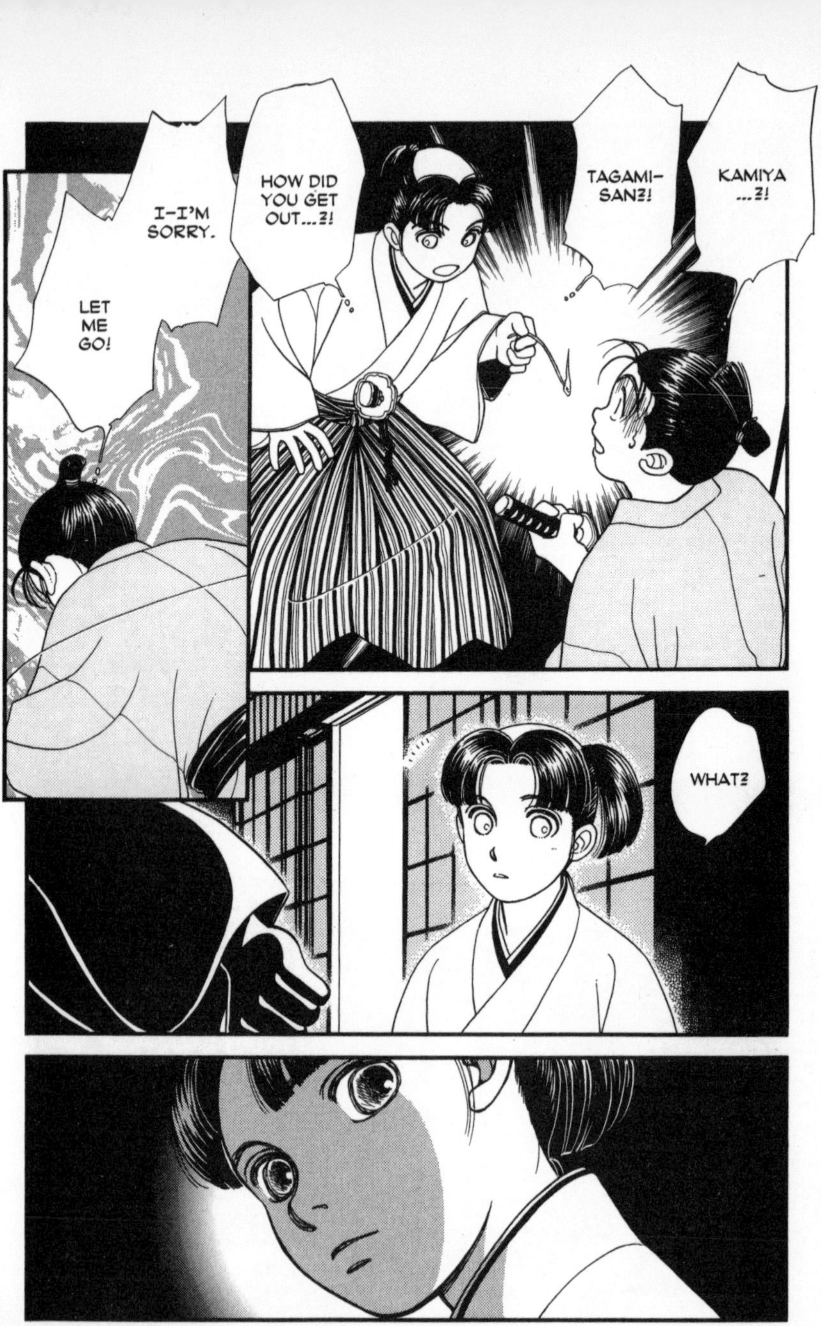
KAMIYA ...?!
TAGAMI-SAN?!
HOW DID YOU GET OUT...?!
I-I'M SORRY.
LET ME GO!
WHAT?

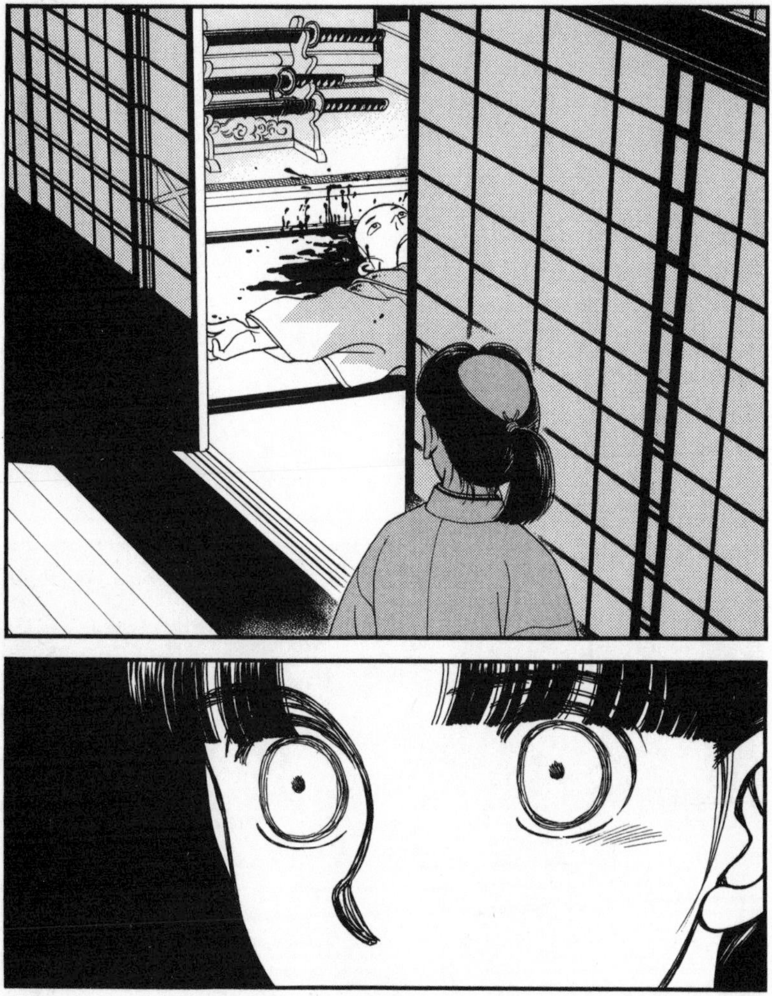

THE KATANA CAN DETERMINE A MAN'S FATE.

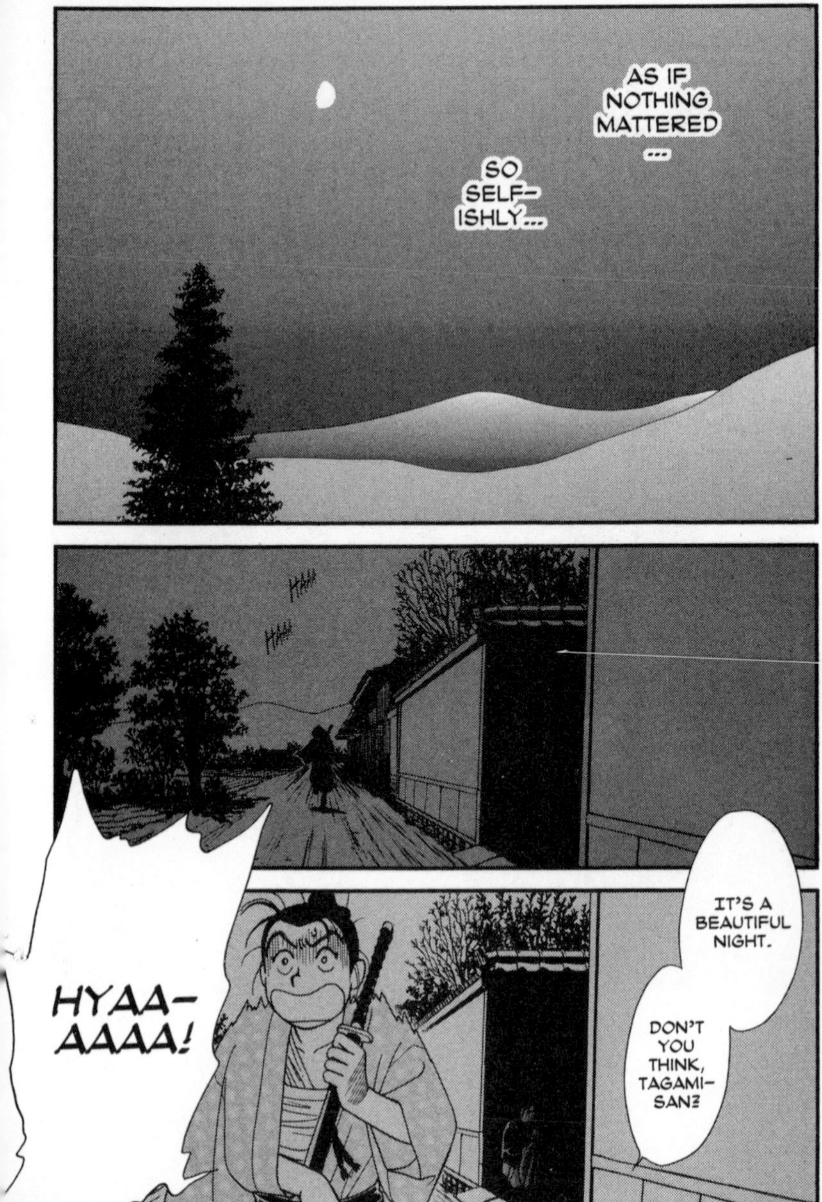
AS IF NOTHING MATTERED ...
SO SELF-ISHLY...
IT'S A BEAUTIFUL NIGHT.
DON'T YOU THINK, TAGAMI-SAN?
HYAA-AAAA!

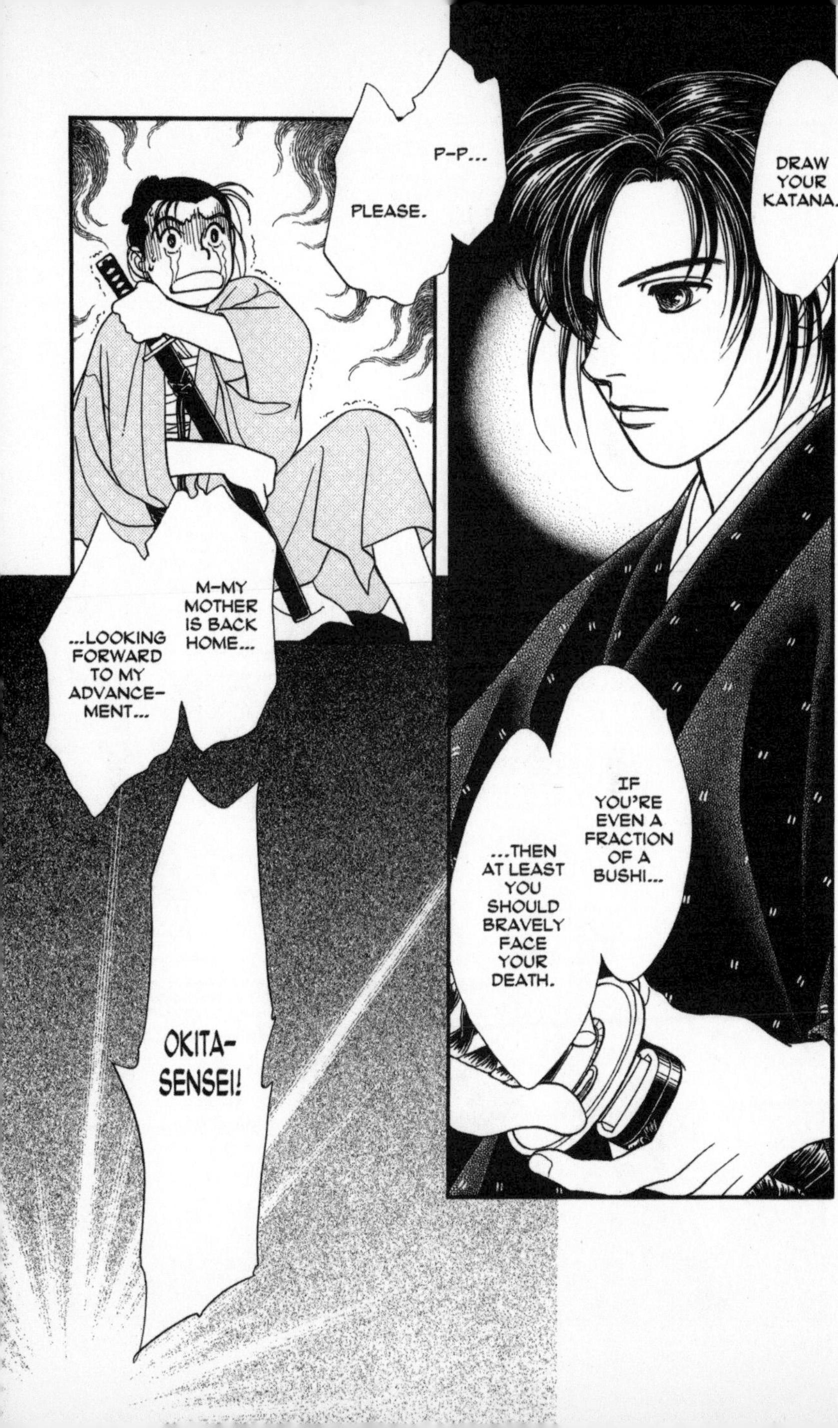
DRAW YOUR KATANA.
IF YOU'RE EVEN A FRACTION OF A BUSHI...
...THEN AT LEAST YOU SHOULD BRAVELY FACE YOUR DEATH.
P-P...
PLEASE.
M-MY MOTHER IS BACK HOME...
...LOOKING FORWARD TO MY ADVANCEMENT...
OKITA-SENSEI!

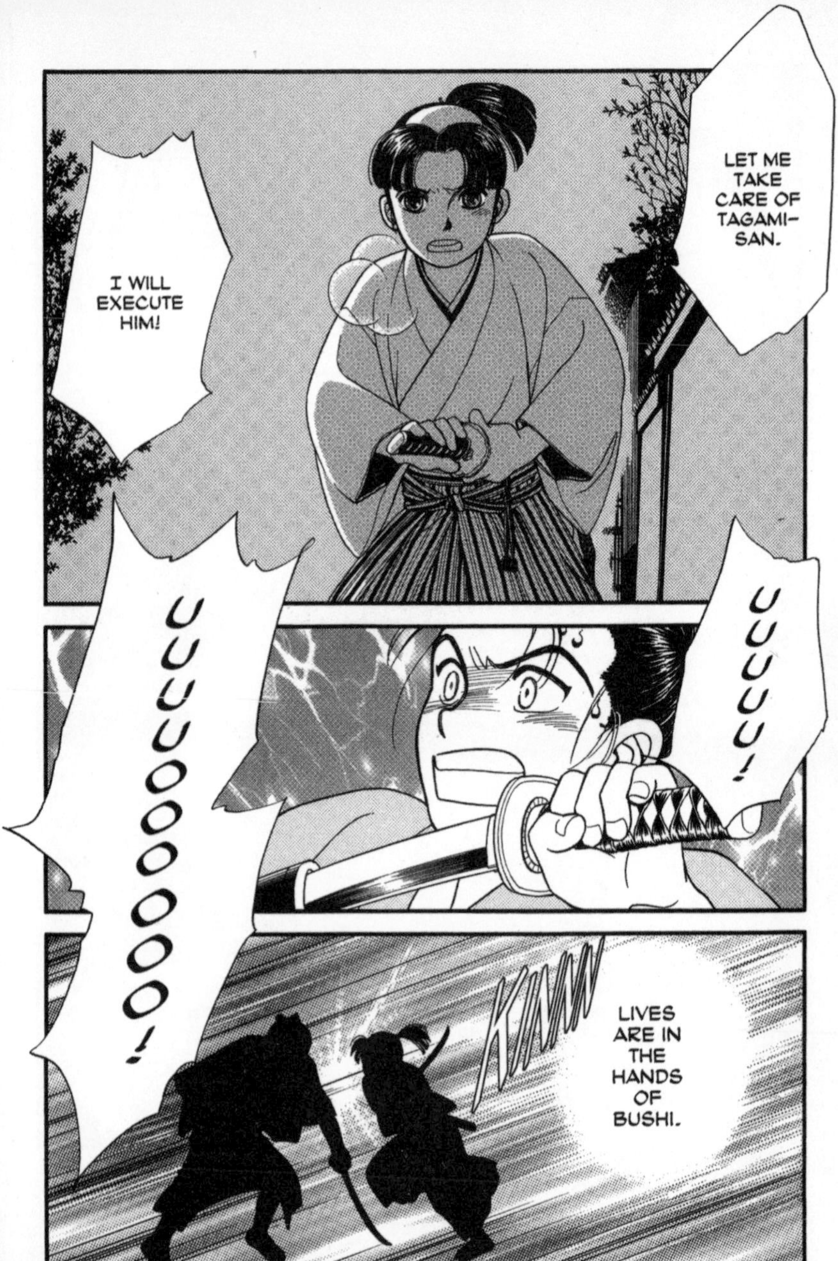
LET ME TAKE CARE OF TAGAMI-SAN.
I WILL EXECUTE HIM!
UUUUUU!
UUUUUOOOOOOOOO!
LIVES ARE IN THE HANDS OF BUSHI.
KINNN

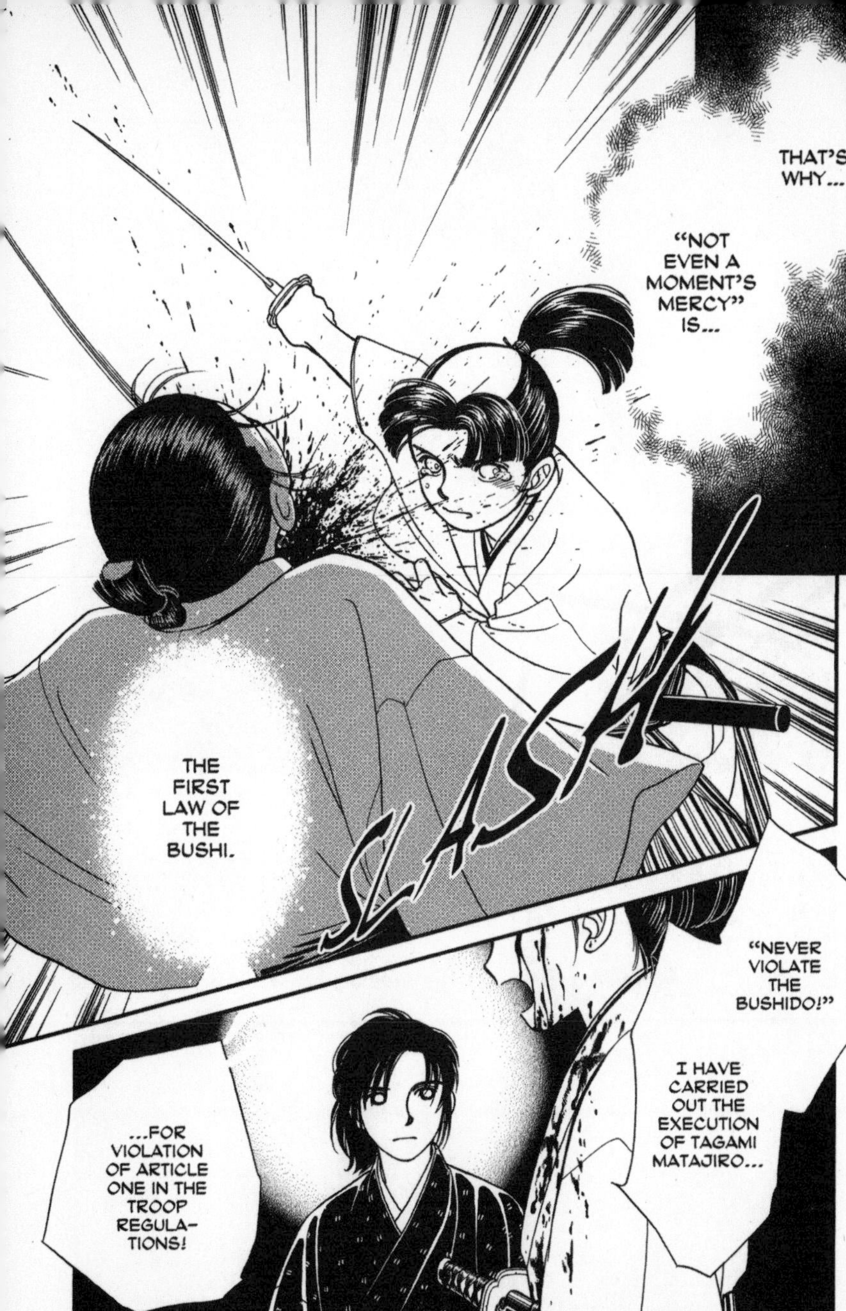
THAT'S WHY...
"NOT EVEN A MOMENT'S MERCY" IS...
THE FIRST LAW OF THE BUSHI.
SLASH
"NEVER VIOLATE THE BUSHIDO!"
I HAVE CARRIED OUT THE EXECUTION OF TAGAMI MATAJIRO...
...FOR VIOLATION OF ARTICLE ONE IN THE TROOP REGULATIONS!

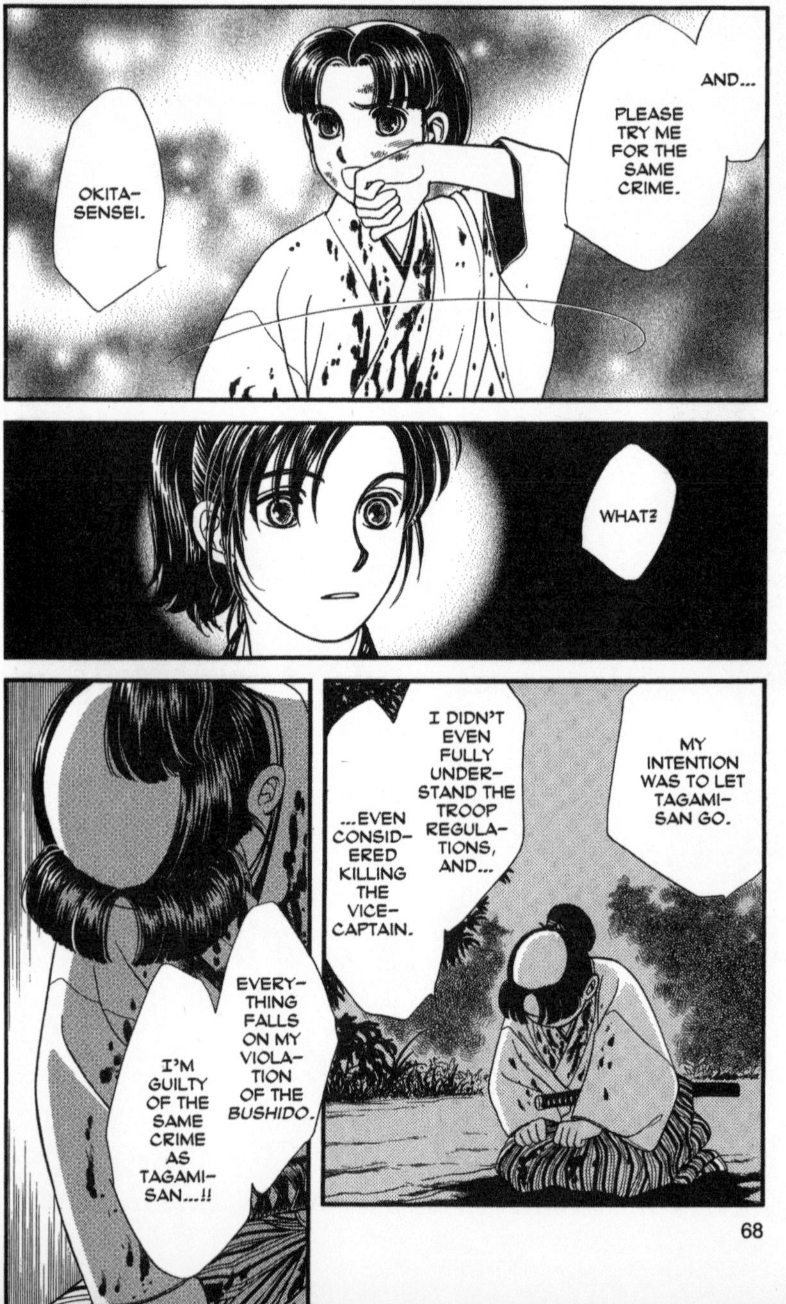
AND... PLEASE TRY ME FOR THE SAME CRIME.
OKITA-SENSEI.
WHAT?
MY INTENTION WAS TO LET TAGAMI-SAN GO.
I DIDN'T EVEN FULLY UNDERSTAND THE TROOP REGULATIONS, AND...
...EVEN CONSIDERED KILLING THE VICE-CAPTAIN.
EVERYTHING FALLS ON MY VIOLATION OF THE *BUSHIDO*.
I'M GUILTY OF THE SAME CRIME AS TAGAMI-SAN...!!

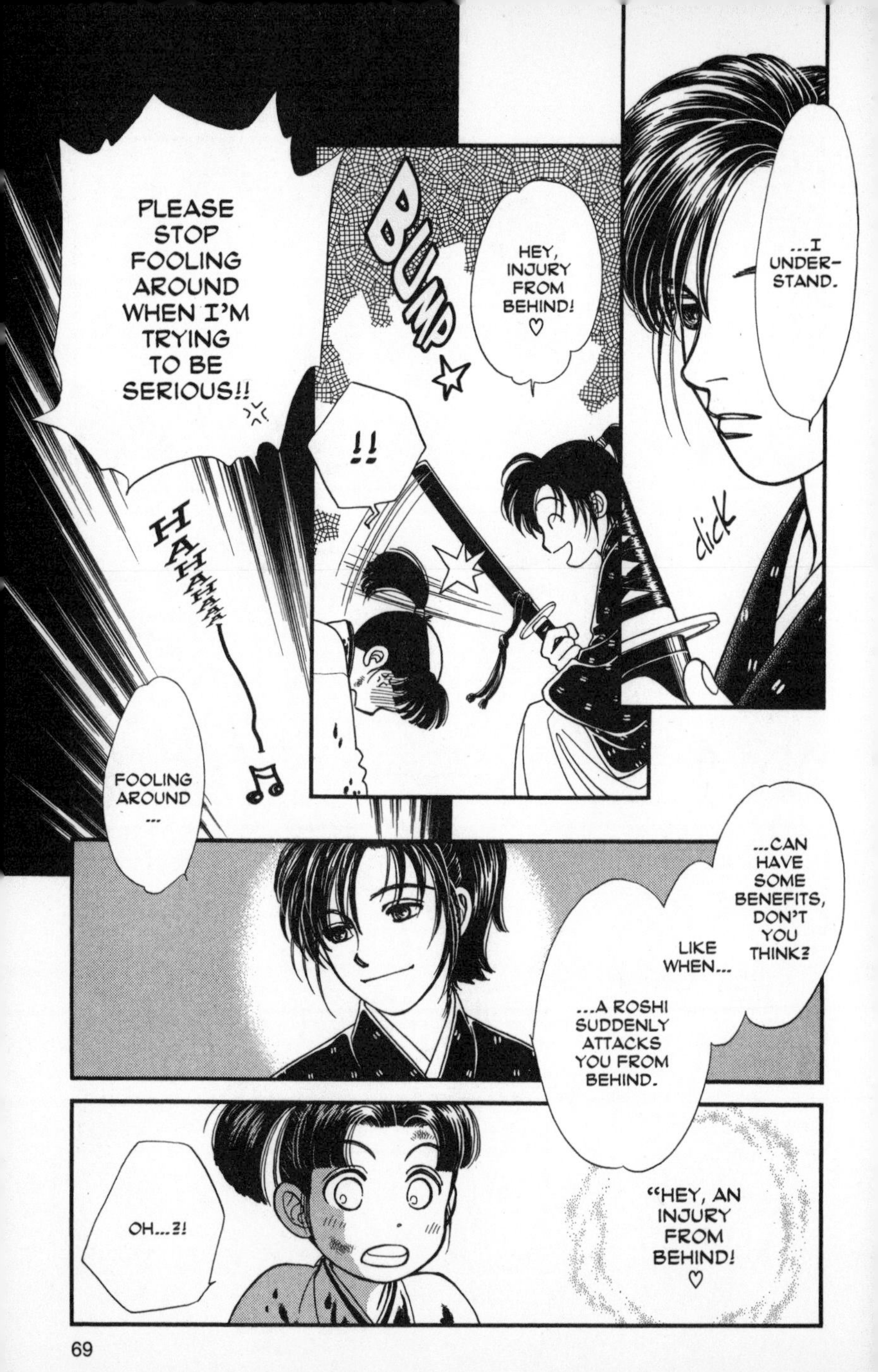
...I UNDERSTAND.
click
HEY, INJURY FROM BEHIND! ♡
BUMP ☆
!!
PLEASE STOP FOOLING AROUND WHEN I'M TRYING TO BE SERIOUS!!
HAHAHAHAHA
FOOLING AROUND ...
...CAN HAVE SOME BENEFITS, DON'T YOU THINK?
LIKE WHEN...
...A ROSHI SUDDENLY ATTACKS YOU FROM BEHIND.
"HEY, AN INJURY FROM BEHIND! ♡
OH...?!

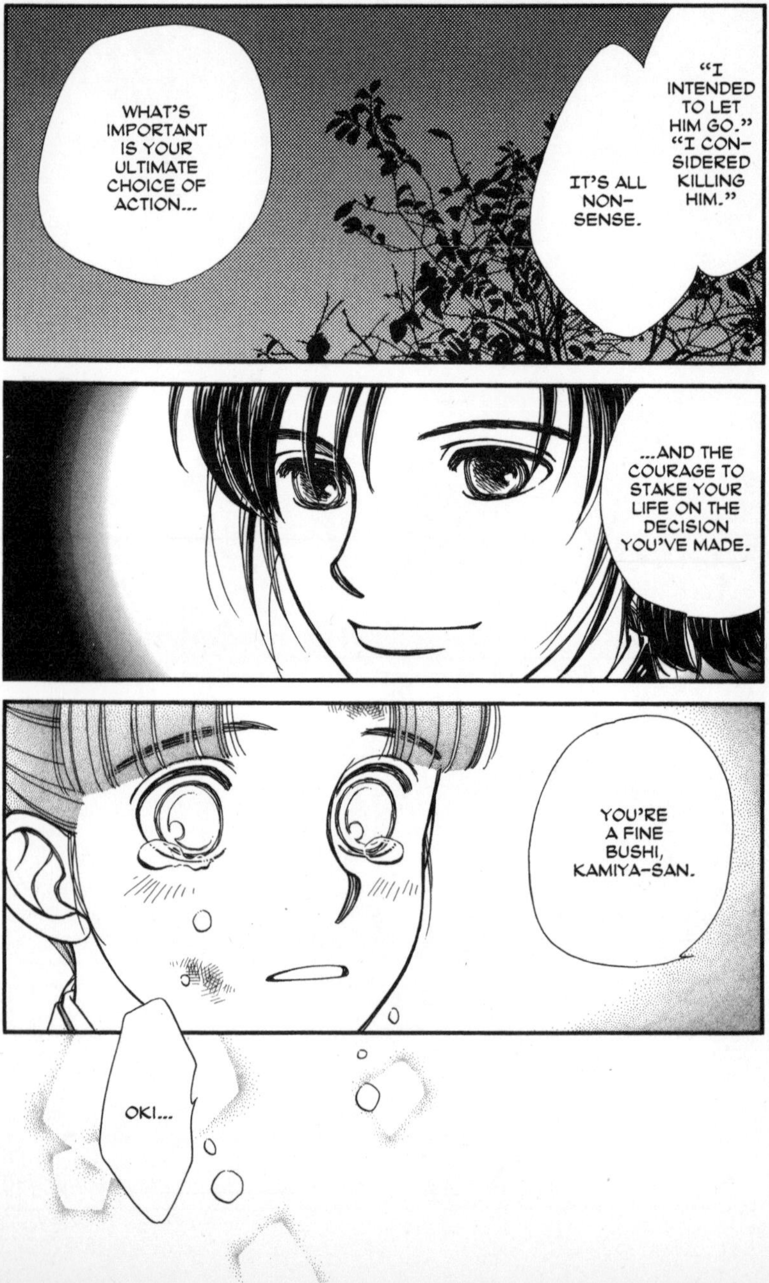
"I INTENDED TO LET HIM GO." "I CONSIDERED KILLING HIM."
IT'S ALL NONSENSE.
WHAT'S IMPORTANT IS YOUR ULTIMATE CHOICE OF ACTION...
...AND THE COURAGE TO STAKE YOUR LIFE ON THE DECISION YOU'VE MADE.
YOU'RE A FINE BUSHI, KAMIYA-SAN.
OKI...

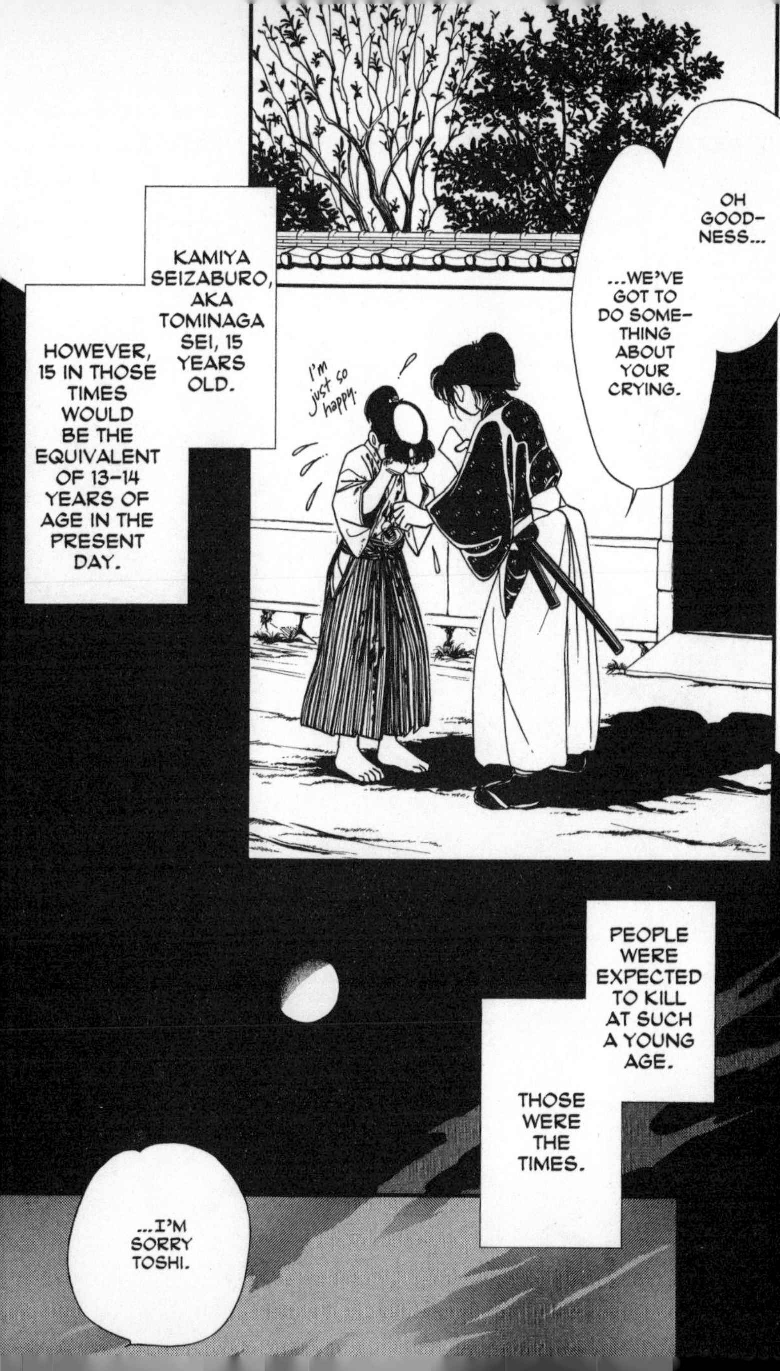
OH GOODNESS...
...WE'VE GOT TO DO SOMETHING ABOUT YOUR CRYING.
I'm just so happy.
KAMIYA SEIZABURO, AKA TOMINAGA SEI, 15 YEARS OLD.
HOWEVER, 15 IN THOSE TIMES WOULD BE THE EQUIVALENT OF 13–14 YEARS OF AGE IN THE PRESENT DAY.
PEOPLE WERE EXPECTED TO KILL AT SUCH A YOUNG AGE.
THOSE WERE THE TIMES.
...I'M SORRY TOSHI.

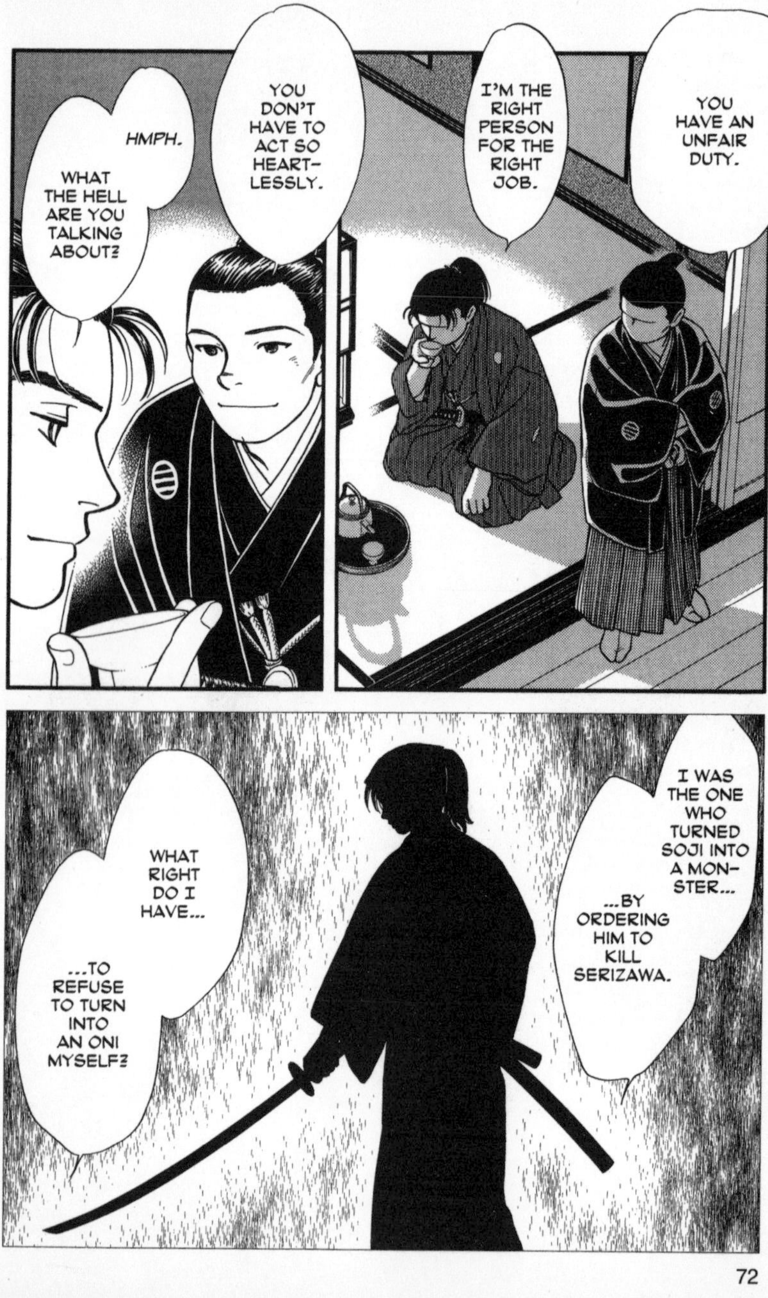
YOU HAVE AN UNFAIR DUTY.
I'M THE RIGHT PERSON FOR THE RIGHT JOB.
YOU DON'T HAVE TO ACT SO HEART-LESSLY.
HMPH.
WHAT THE HELL ARE YOU TALKING ABOUT?
I WAS THE ONE WHO TURNED SOJI INTO A MON-STER...
...BY ORDERING HIM TO KILL SERIZAWA.
WHAT RIGHT DO I HAVE...
...TO REFUSE TO TURN INTO AN ONI MYSELF?

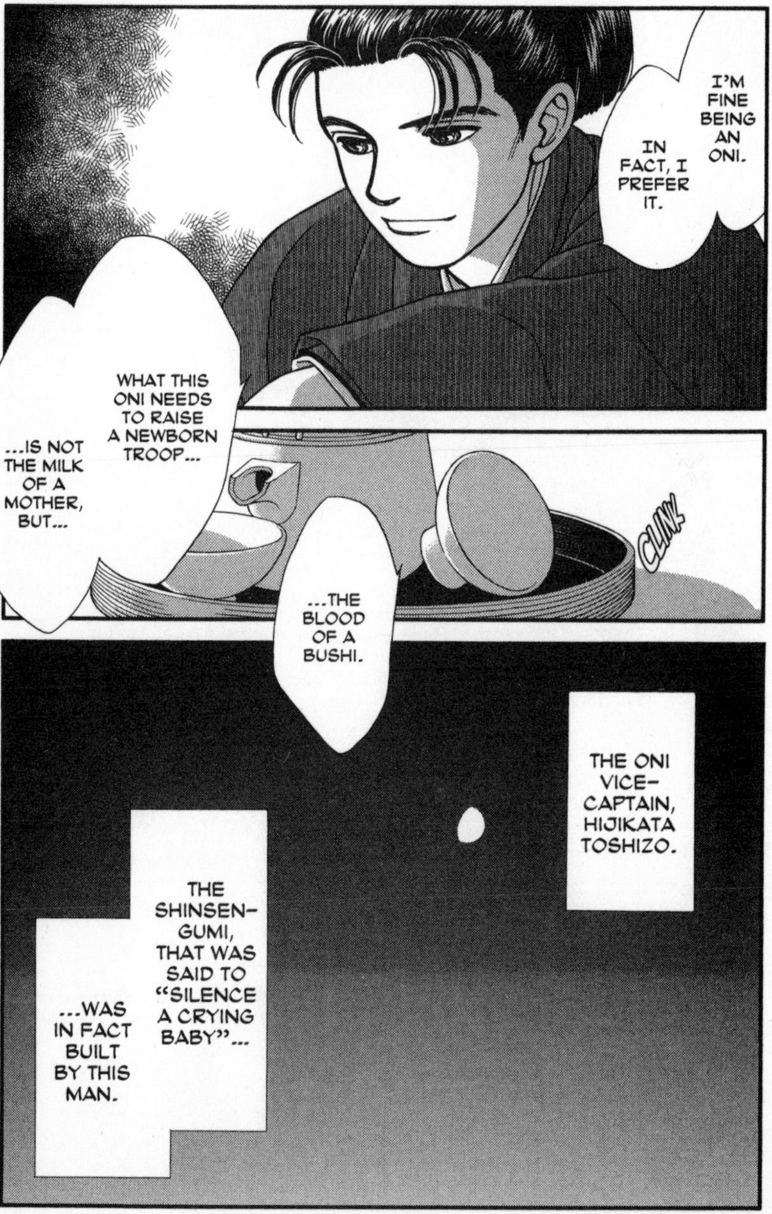
I'M FINE BEING AN ONI.
IN FACT, I PREFER IT.
WHAT THIS ONI NEEDS TO RAISE A NEWBORN TROOP...
...IS NOT THE MILK OF A MOTHER, BUT...
CLINK
...THE BLOOD OF A BUSHI.
THE ONI VICE-CAPTAIN, HIJIKATA TOSHIZO.
THE SHINSEN-GUMI, THAT WAS SAID TO "SILENCE A CRYING BABY"...
...WAS IN FACT BUILT BY THIS MAN.

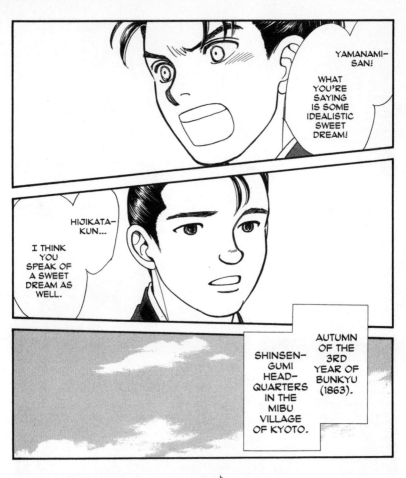

YAMANAMI-SAN!
WHAT YOU'RE SAYING IS SOME IDEALISTIC SWEET DREAM!
HIJIKATA-KUN...
I THINK YOU SPEAK OF A SWEET DREAM AS WELL.
AUTUMN OF THE 3RD YEAR OF BUNKYU (1863).
SHINSEN-GUMI HEAD-QUARTERS IN THE MIBU VILLAGE OF KYOTO.

KYOTO "IROHA" KARUTA GAME
Damn
Now that I've been discovered, I'll give it back.
Saito
I don't want it anymore.
な
"NA" NASUTOKI NO ENMAGAO "MONEY BORROWED IS SOON SORROWED."

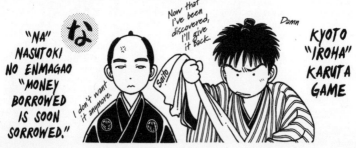

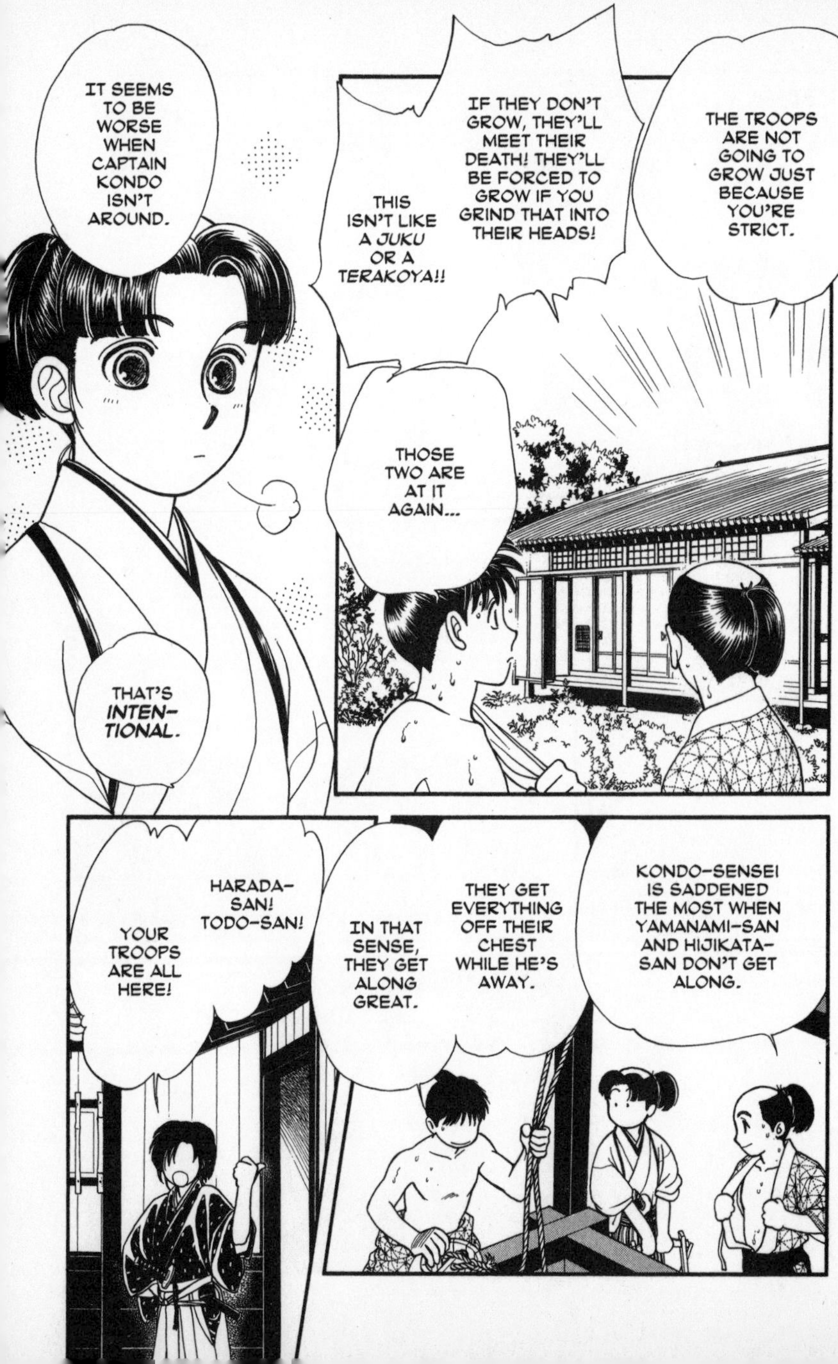
THE TROOPS ARE NOT GOING TO GROW JUST BECAUSE YOU'RE STRICT.
IF THEY DON'T GROW, THEY'LL MEET THEIR DEATH! THEY'LL BE FORCED TO GROW IF YOU GRIND THAT INTO THEIR HEADS!
THIS ISN'T LIKE A *JUKU* OR A *TERAKOYA*!!
THOSE TWO ARE AT IT AGAIN...
IT SEEMS TO BE WORSE WHEN CAPTAIN KONDO ISN'T AROUND.
THAT'S *INTENTIONAL*.
KONDO-SENSEI IS SADDENED THE MOST WHEN YAMANAMI-SAN AND HIJIKATA-SAN DON'T GET ALONG.
THEY GET EVERYTHING OFF THEIR CHEST WHILE HE'S AWAY.
IN THAT SENSE, THEY GET ALONG GREAT.
HARADA-SAN! TODO-SAN!
YOUR TROOPS ARE ALL HERE!

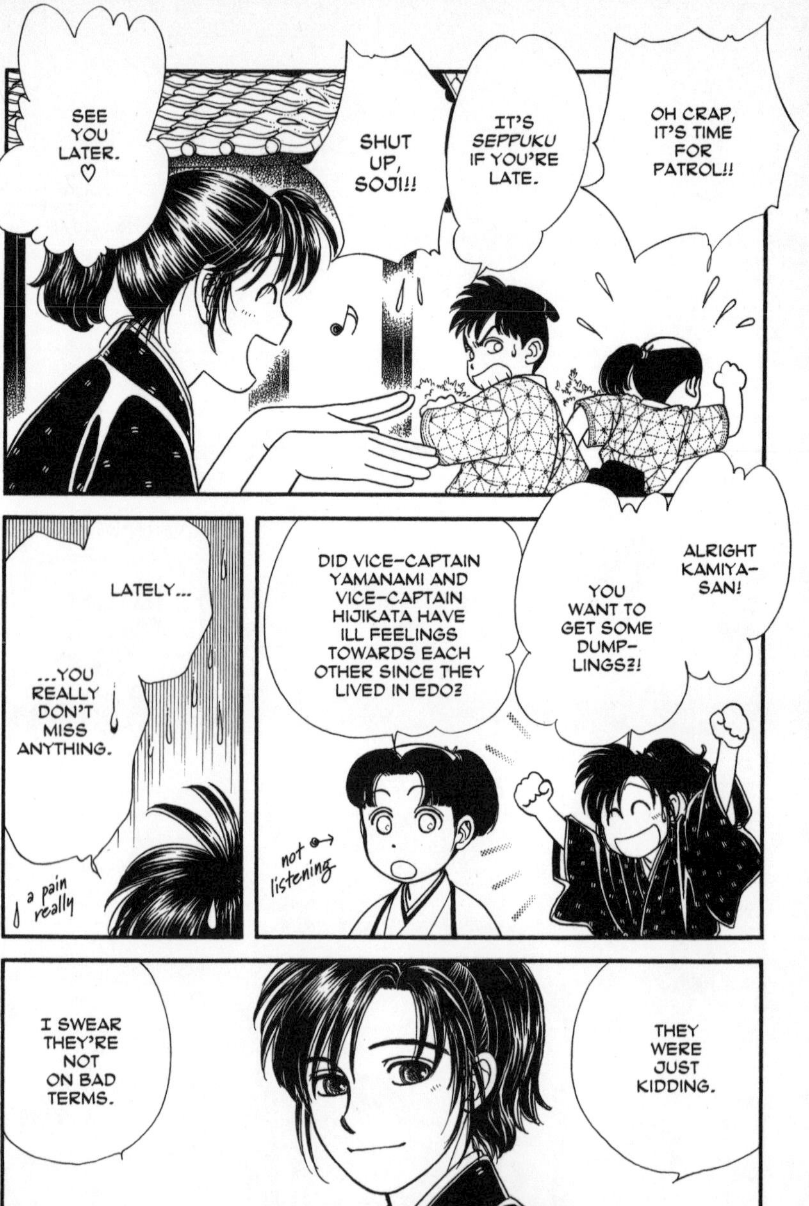
OH CRAP, IT'S TIME FOR PATROL!!
IT'S SEPPUKU IF YOU'RE LATE.
SHUT UP, SOJI!!
SEE YOU LATER. ♡
ALRIGHT KAMIYA-SAN!
YOU WANT TO GET SOME DUMP-LINGS?!
DID VICE-CAPTAIN YAMANAMI AND VICE-CAPTAIN HIJIKATA HAVE ILL FEELINGS TOWARDS EACH OTHER SINCE THEY LIVED IN EDO?
not listening
LATELY...
...YOU REALLY DON'T MISS ANYTHING.
a pain really
THEY WERE JUST KIDDING.
I SWEAR THEY'RE NOT ON BAD TERMS.

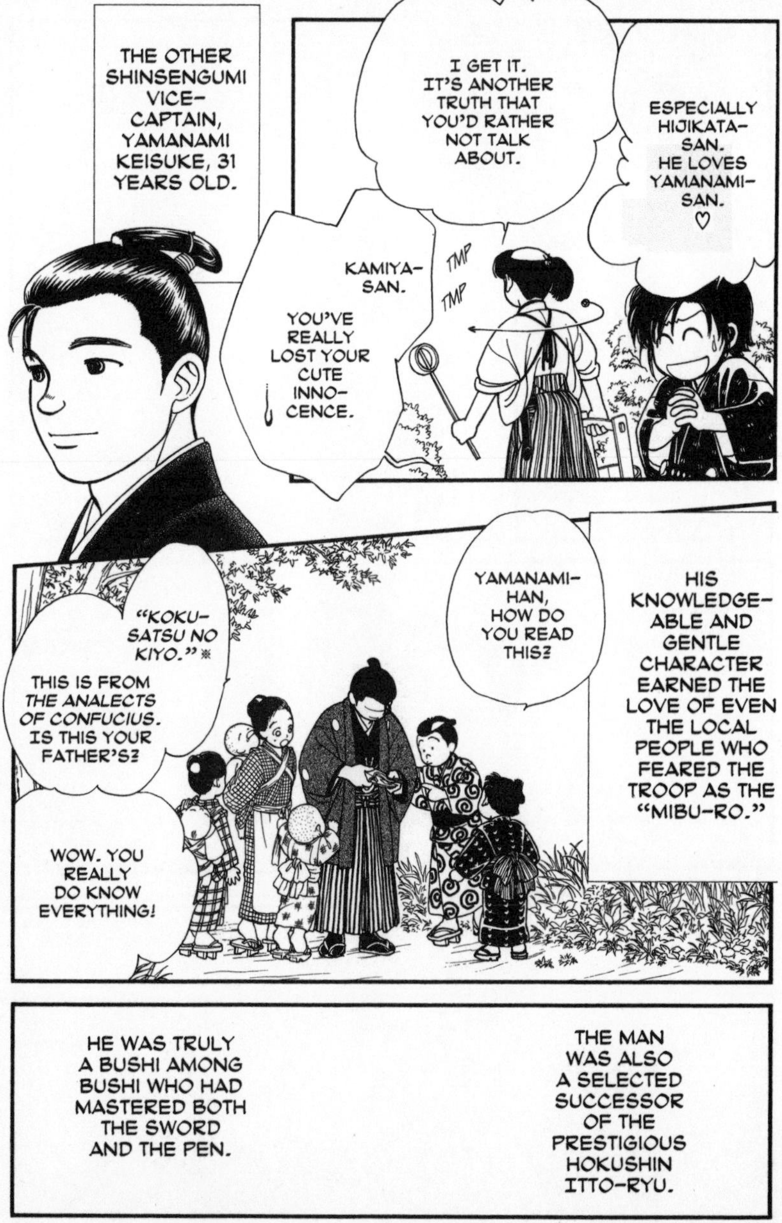
ESPECIALLY HIJIKATA-SAN. HE LOVES YAMANAMI-SAN. ♡
I GET IT. IT'S ANOTHER TRUTH THAT YOU'D RATHER NOT TALK ABOUT.
TMP
TMP
KAMIYA-SAN.
YOU'VE REALLY LOST YOUR CUTE INNOCENCE.
THE OTHER SHINSENGUMI VICE-CAPTAIN, YAMANAMI KEISUKE, 31 YEARS OLD.
HIS KNOWLEDGEABLE AND GENTLE CHARACTER EARNED THE LOVE OF EVEN THE LOCAL PEOPLE WHO FEARED THE TROOP AS THE "MIBU-RO."
YAMANAMI-HAN, HOW DO YOU READ THIS?
"KOKU-SATSU NO KIYO." ※
THIS IS FROM *THE ANALECTS OF CONFUCIUS*. IS THIS YOUR FATHER'S?
WOW. YOU REALLY DO KNOW EVERYTHING!
THE MAN WAS ALSO A SELECTED SUCCESSOR OF THE PRESTIGIOUS HOKUSHIN ITTO-RYU.
HE WAS TRULY A BUSHI AMONG BUSHI WHO HAD MASTERED BOTH THE SWORD AND THE PEN.

※An old metaphor of losing substance and only maintaining form.

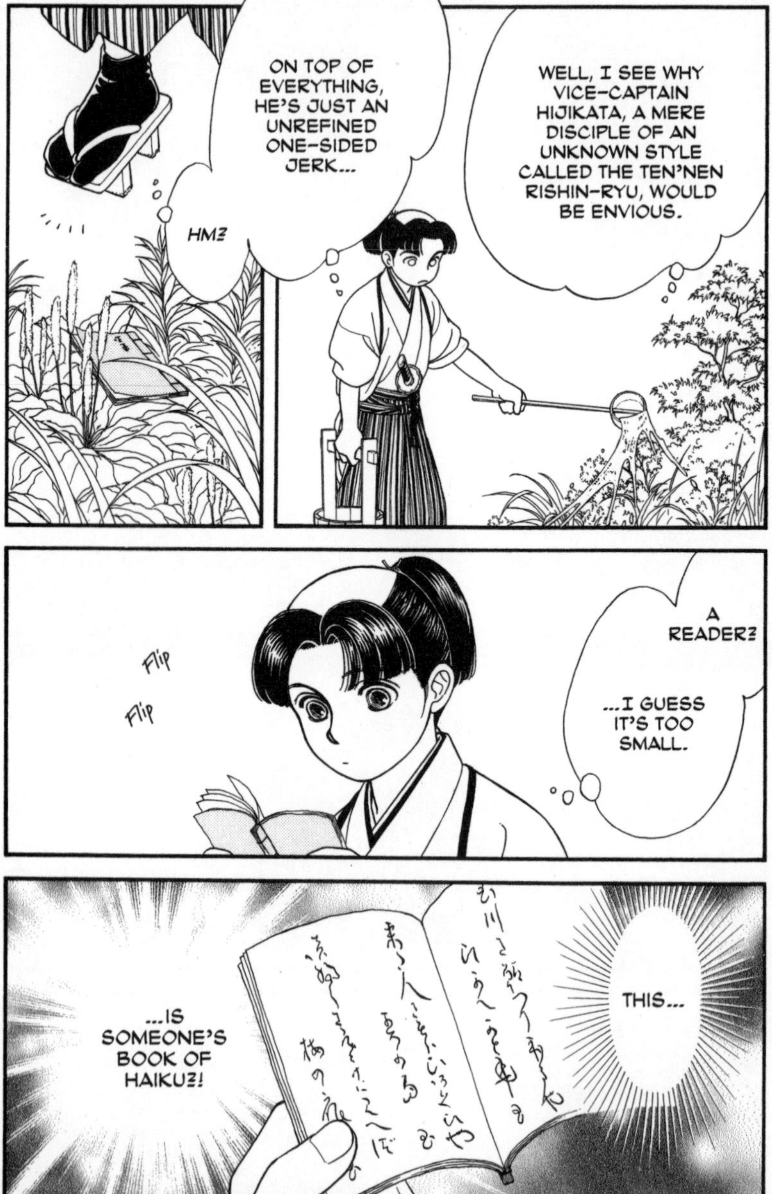
WELL, I SEE WHY VICE-CAPTAIN HIJIKATA, A MERE DISCIPLE OF AN UNKNOWN STYLE CALLED THE TEN'NEN RISHIN-RYU, WOULD BE ENVIOUS.
ON TOP OF EVERYTHING, HE'S JUST AN UNREFINED ONE-SIDED JERK...
HM?
A READER?
...I GUESS IT'S TOO SMALL.
Flip
Flip
THIS...
...IS SOMEONE'S BOOK OF HAIKU?!

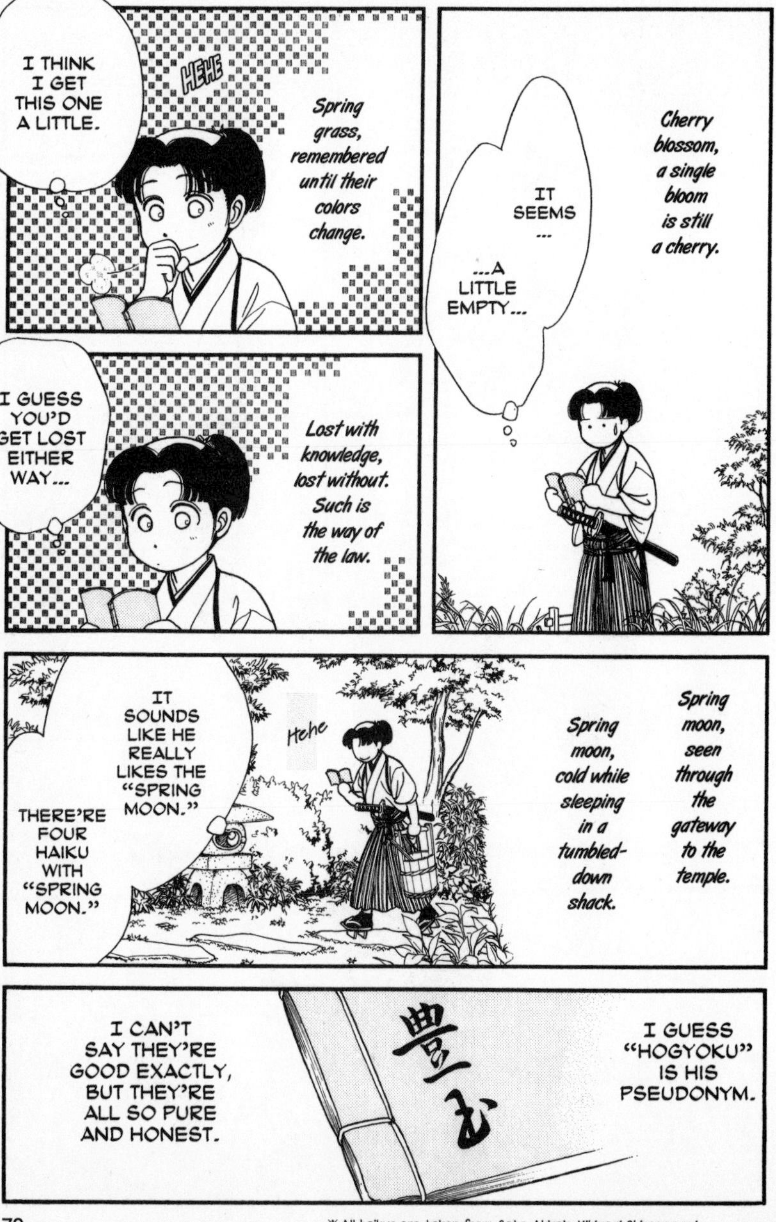
Cherry blossom, a single bloom is still a cherry.
IT SEEMS ...
...A LITTLE EMPTY...
Spring grass, remembered until their colors change.
HEHE
I THINK I GET THIS ONE A LITTLE.
Lost with knowledge, lost without. Such is the way of the law.
I GUESS YOU'D GET LOST EITHER WAY...
Spring moon, seen through the gateway to the temple.
Spring moon, cold while sleeping in a tumbled-down shack.
Hehe
IT SOUNDS LIKE HE REALLY LIKES THE "SPRING MOON."
THERE'RE FOUR HAIKU WITH "SPRING MOON."
I GUESS "HOGYOKU" IS HIS PSEUDONYM.
豊玉
I CAN'T SAY THEY'RE GOOD EXACTLY, BUT THEY'RE ALL SO PURE AND HONEST.

※All haikus are taken from Sato Akira's *Kikigagi Shinsengumi.*

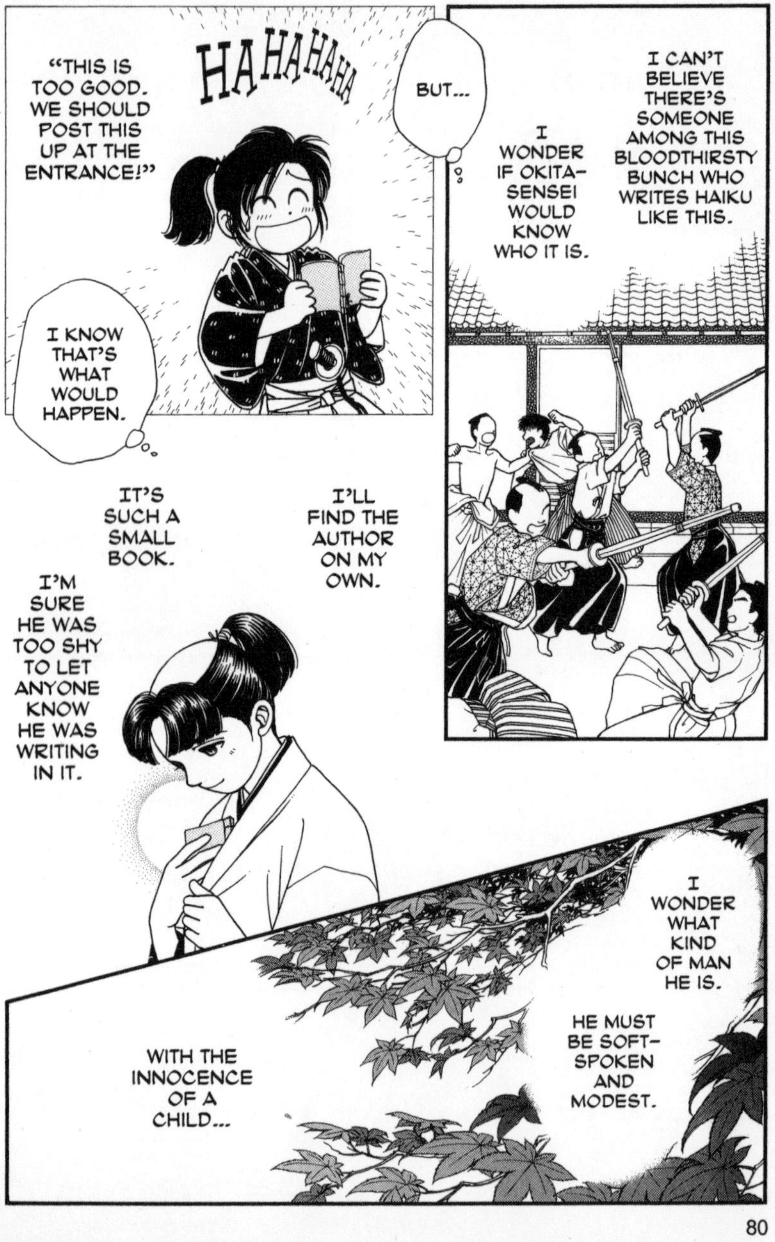
I CAN'T BELIEVE THERE'S SOMEONE AMONG THIS BLOODTHIRSTY BUNCH WHO WRITES HAIKU LIKE THIS.
I WONDER IF OKITA-SENSEI WOULD KNOW WHO IT IS.
BUT...
HAHAHAHA
"THIS IS TOO GOOD. WE SHOULD POST THIS UP AT THE ENTRANCE!"
I KNOW THAT'S WHAT WOULD HAPPEN.
I'LL FIND THE AUTHOR ON MY OWN.
IT'S SUCH A SMALL BOOK.
I'M SURE HE WAS TOO SHY TO LET ANYONE KNOW HE WAS WRITING IN IT.
I WONDER WHAT KIND OF MAN HE IS.
HE MUST BE SOFT-SPOKEN AND MODEST.
WITH THE INNOCENCE OF A CHILD...

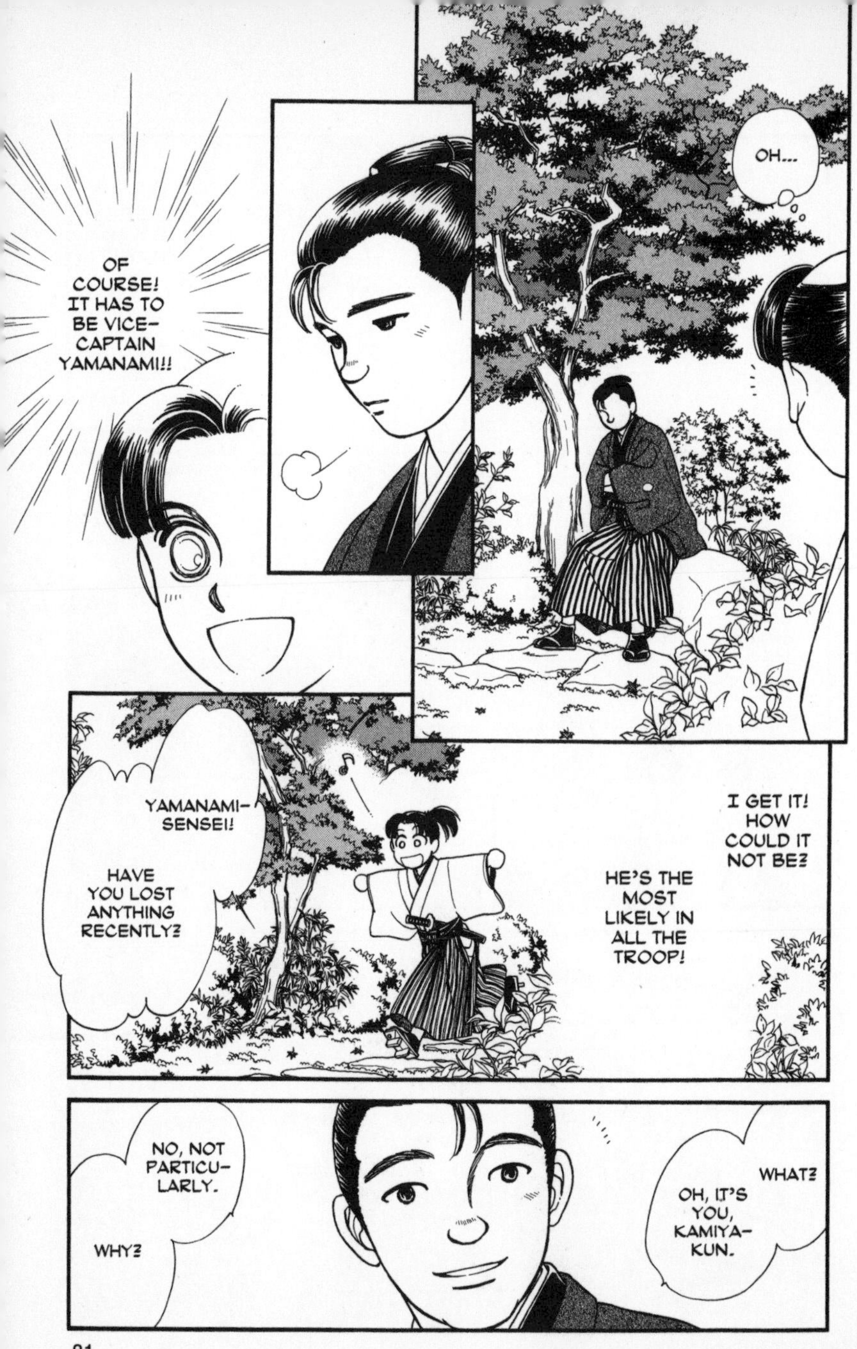
OH...
OF COURSE! IT HAS TO BE VICE-CAPTAIN YAMANAMI!!
I GET IT! HOW COULD IT NOT BE?
HE'S THE MOST LIKELY IN ALL THE TROOP!
YAMANAMI-SENSEI!
HAVE YOU LOST ANYTHING RECENTLY?
WHAT?
OH, IT'S YOU, KAMIYA-KUN.
NO, NOT PARTICULARLY.
WHY?

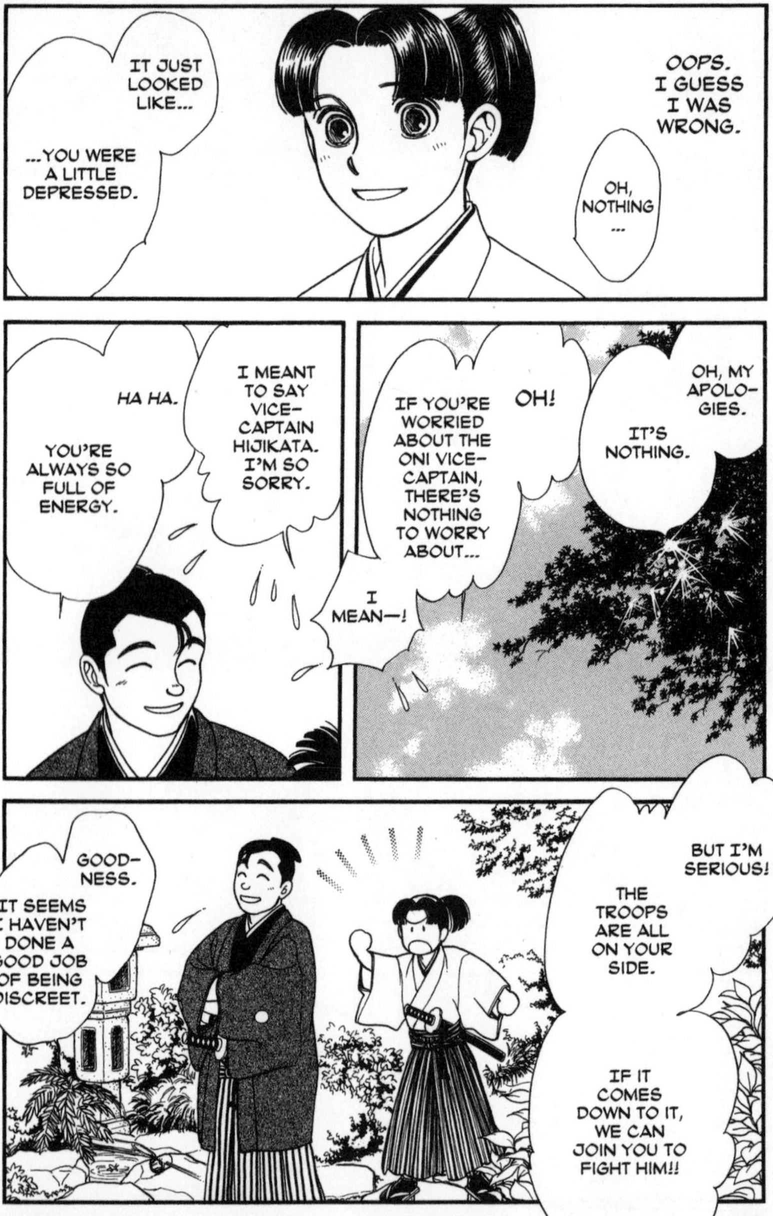
OOPS. I GUESS I WAS WRONG.
OH, NOTHING ...
IT JUST LOOKED LIKE...
...YOU WERE A LITTLE DEPRESSED.
OH, MY APOLOGIES.
IT'S NOTHING.
OH!
IF YOU'RE WORRIED ABOUT THE ONI VICE-CAPTAIN, THERE'S NOTHING TO WORRY ABOUT...
I MEAN—!
I MEANT TO SAY VICE-CAPTAIN HIJIKATA. I'M SO SORRY.
HA HA.
YOU'RE ALWAYS SO FULL OF ENERGY.
BUT I'M SERIOUS!
THE TROOPS ARE ALL ON YOUR SIDE.
IF IT COMES DOWN TO IT, WE CAN JOIN YOU TO FIGHT HIM!!
GOOD-NESS.
IT SEEMS I HAVEN'T DONE A GOOD JOB OF BEING DISCREET.

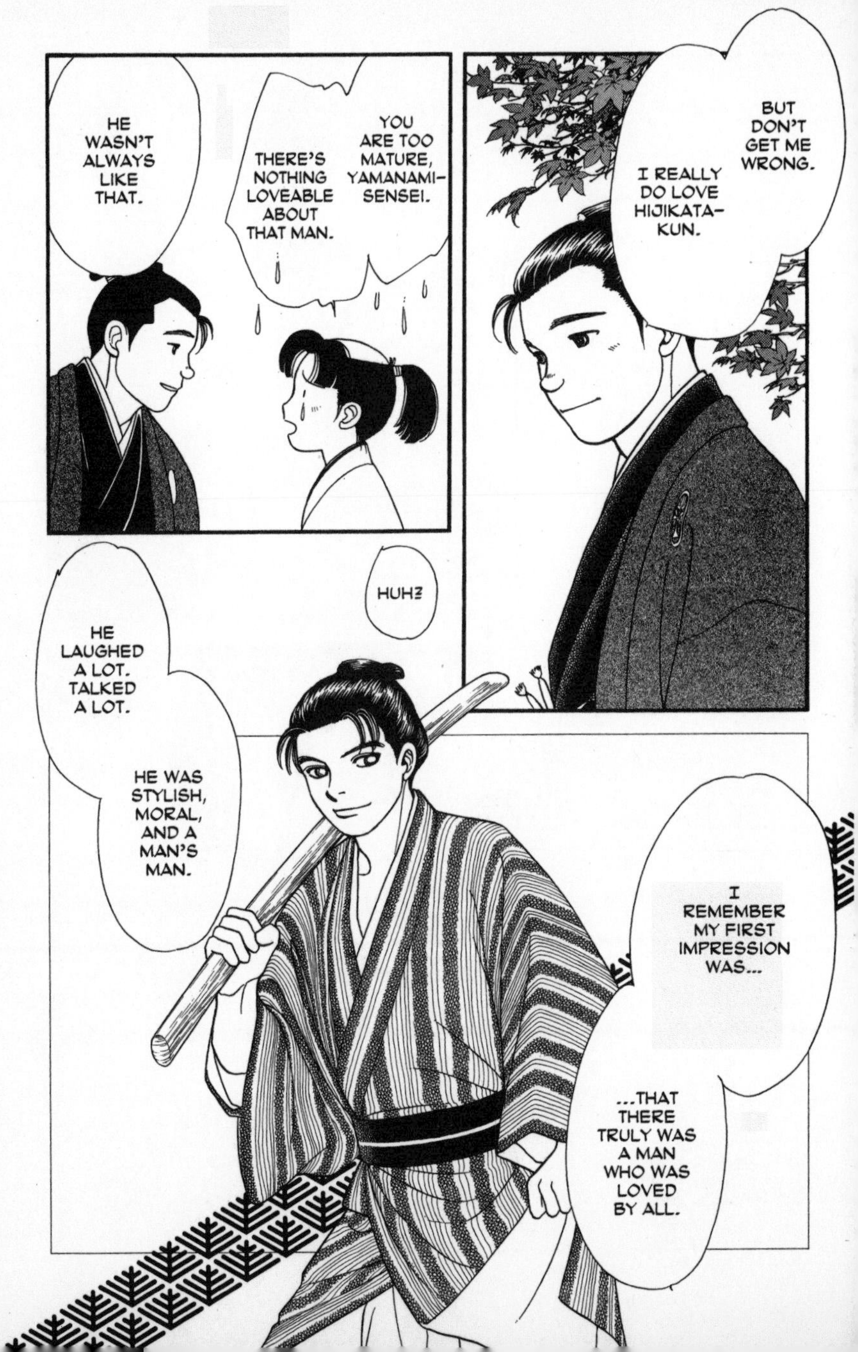
BUT DON'T GET ME WRONG.
I REALLY DO LOVE HIJIKATA-KUN.
YOU ARE TOO MATURE, YAMANAMI-SENSEI.
THERE'S NOTHING LOVEABLE ABOUT THAT MAN.
HE WASN'T ALWAYS LIKE THAT.
HUH?
HE LAUGHED A LOT. TALKED A LOT.
HE WAS STYLISH, MORAL, AND A MAN'S MAN.
I REMEMBER MY FIRST IMPRESSION WAS...
...THAT THERE TRULY WAS A MAN WHO WAS LOVED BY ALL.

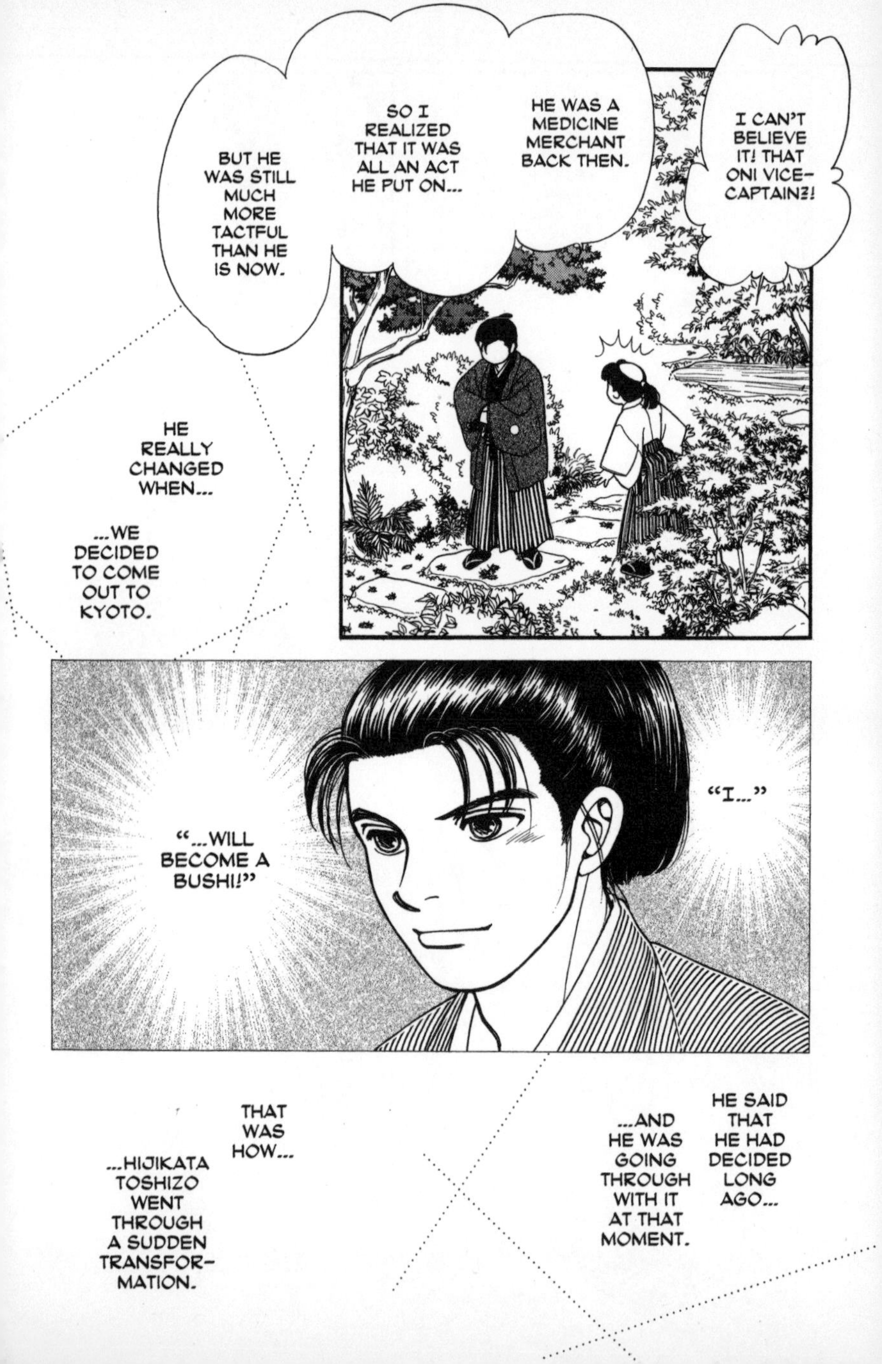
I CAN'T BELIEVE IT! THAT ONI VICE-CAPTAIN?!
HE WAS A MEDICINE MERCHANT BACK THEN.
SO I REALIZED THAT IT WAS ALL AN ACT HE PUT ON...
BUT HE WAS STILL MUCH MORE TACTFUL THAN HE IS NOW.
HE REALLY CHANGED WHEN...
...WE DECIDED TO COME OUT TO KYOTO.
"I..."
"...WILL BECOME A BUSHI!"
HE SAID THAT HE HAD DECIDED LONG AGO...
...AND HE WAS GOING THROUGH WITH IT AT THAT MOMENT.
THAT WAS HOW...
...HIJIKATA TOSHIZO WENT THROUGH A SUDDEN TRANSFORMATION.

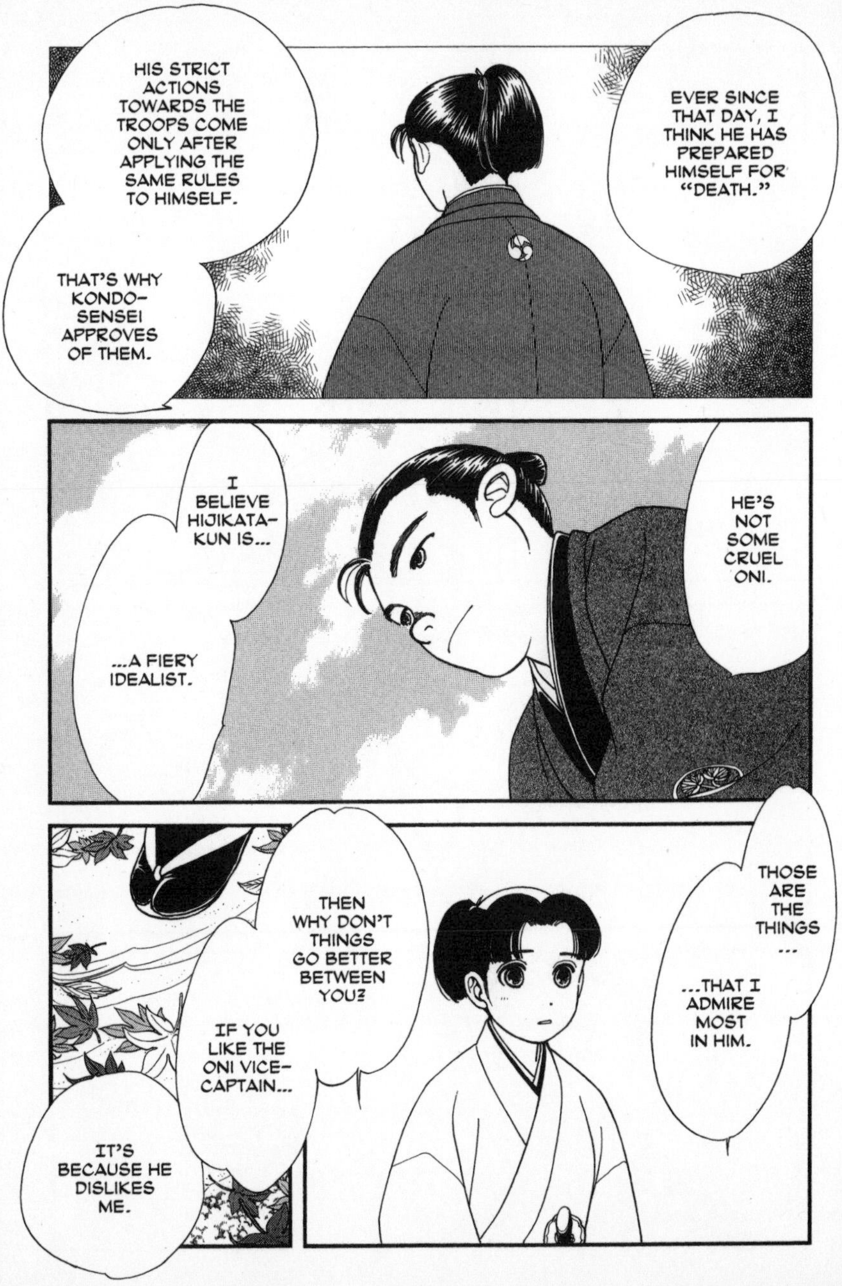
EVER SINCE THAT DAY, I THINK HE HAS PREPARED HIMSELF FOR "DEATH."
HIS STRICT ACTIONS TOWARDS THE TROOPS COME ONLY AFTER APPLYING THE SAME RULES TO HIMSELF.
THAT'S WHY KONDO-SENSEI APPROVES OF THEM.
HE'S NOT SOME CRUEL ONI.
I BELIEVE HIJIKATA-KUN IS...
...A FIERY IDEALIST.
THOSE ARE THE THINGS...
...THAT I ADMIRE MOST IN HIM.
THEN WHY DON'T THINGS GO BETTER BETWEEN YOU?
IF YOU LIKE THE ONI VICE-CAPTAIN...
IT'S BECAUSE HE DISLIKES ME.

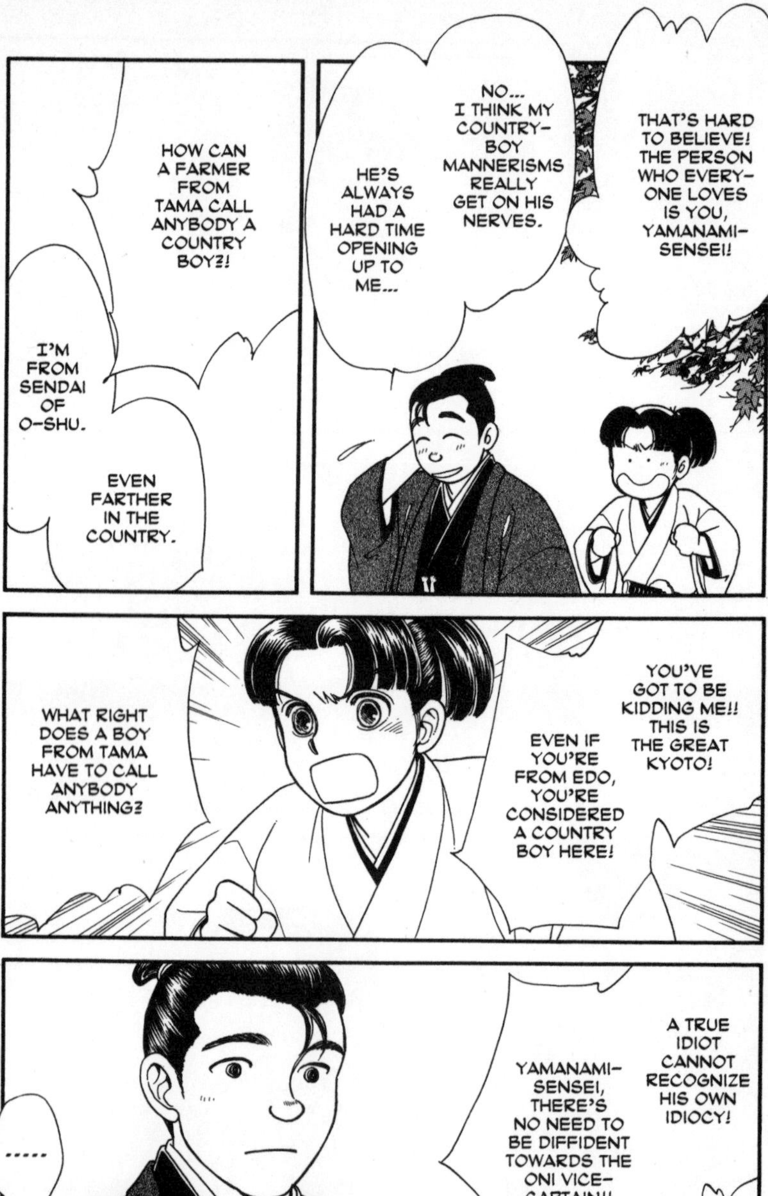
THAT'S HARD TO BELIEVE! THE PERSON WHO EVERYONE LOVES IS YOU, YAMANAMI-SENSEI!
NO... I THINK MY COUNTRY-BOY MANNERISMS REALLY GET ON HIS NERVES.
HE'S ALWAYS HAD A HARD TIME OPENING UP TO ME...
HOW CAN A FARMER FROM TAMA CALL ANYBODY A COUNTRY BOY?!
I'M FROM SENDAI OF O-SHU.
EVEN FARTHER IN THE COUNTRY.
YOU'VE GOT TO BE KIDDING ME!! THIS IS THE GREAT KYOTO!
EVEN IF YOU'RE FROM EDO, YOU'RE CONSIDERED A COUNTRY BOY HERE!
WHAT RIGHT DOES A BOY FROM TAMA HAVE TO CALL ANYBODY ANYTHING?
A TRUE IDIOT CANNOT RECOGNIZE HIS OWN IDIOCY!
YAMANAMI-SENSEI, THERE'S NO NEED TO BE DIFFIDENT TOWARDS THE ONI VICE-CAPTAIN!!
.....

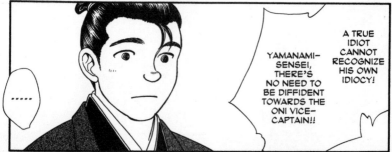

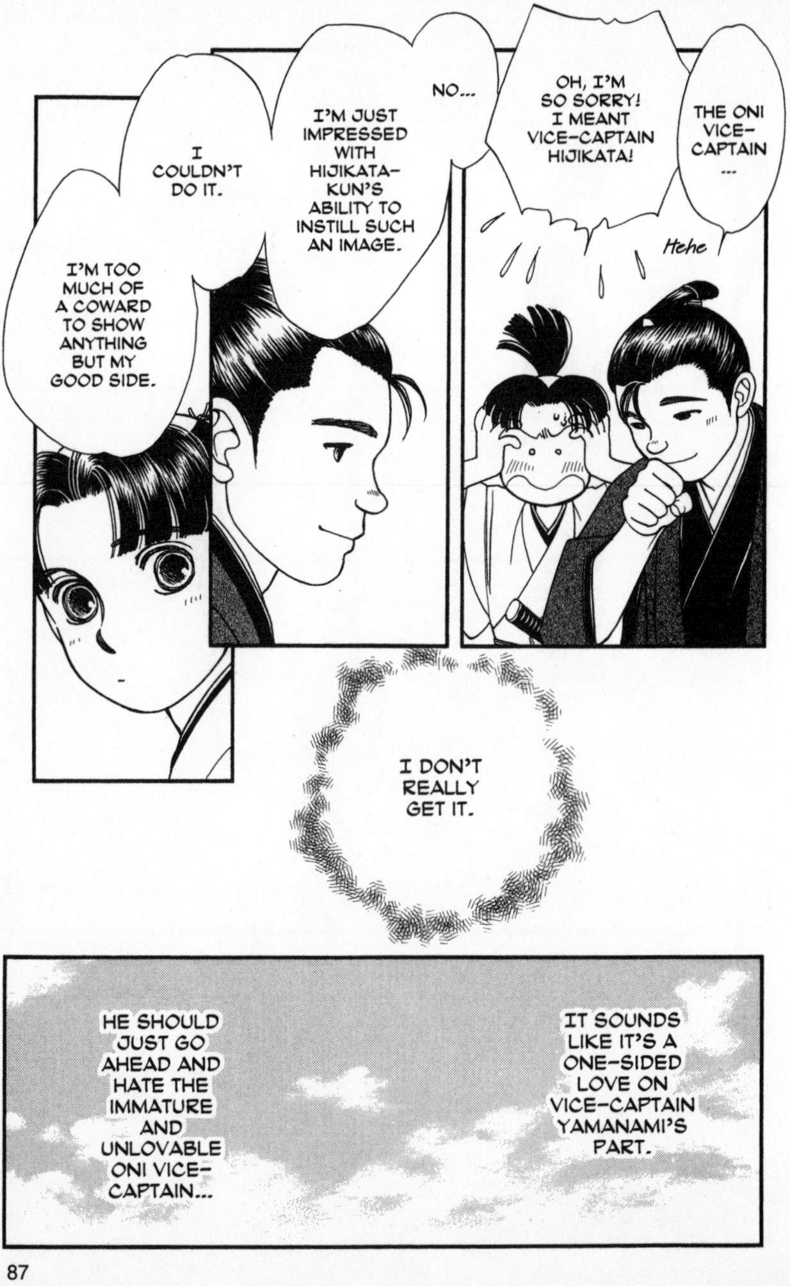
THE ONI VICE-CAPTAIN ...
OH, I'M SO SORRY! I MEANT VICE-CAPTAIN HIJIKATA!
Hehe
NO...
I'M JUST IMPRESSED WITH HIJIKATA-KUN'S ABILITY TO INSTILL SUCH AN IMAGE.
I COULDN'T DO IT.
I'M TOO MUCH OF A COWARD TO SHOW ANYTHING BUT MY GOOD SIDE.
I DON'T REALLY GET IT.
IT SOUNDS LIKE IT'S A ONE-SIDED LOVE ON VICE-CAPTAIN YAMANAMI'S PART.
HE SHOULD JUST GO AHEAD AND HATE THE IMMATURE AND UNLOVABLE ONI VICE-CAPTAIN...

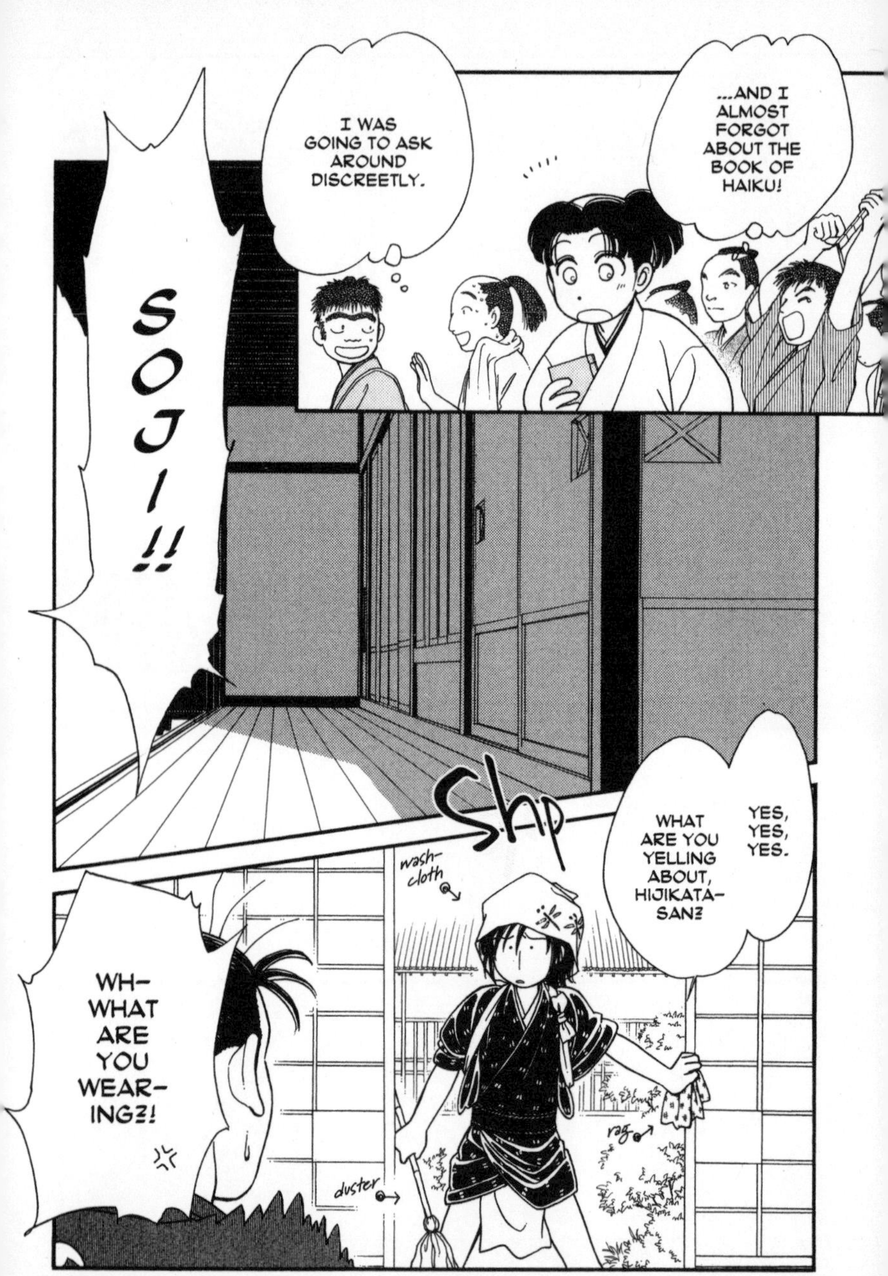
...AND I ALMOST FORGOT ABOUT THE BOOK OF HAIKU!
I WAS GOING TO ASK AROUND DISCREETLY.
SOJI!!
Shp
YES, YES, YES.
WHAT ARE YOU YELLING ABOUT, HIJIKATA-SAN?
wash-cloth
rag
duster
WH-WHAT ARE YOU WEARING?!

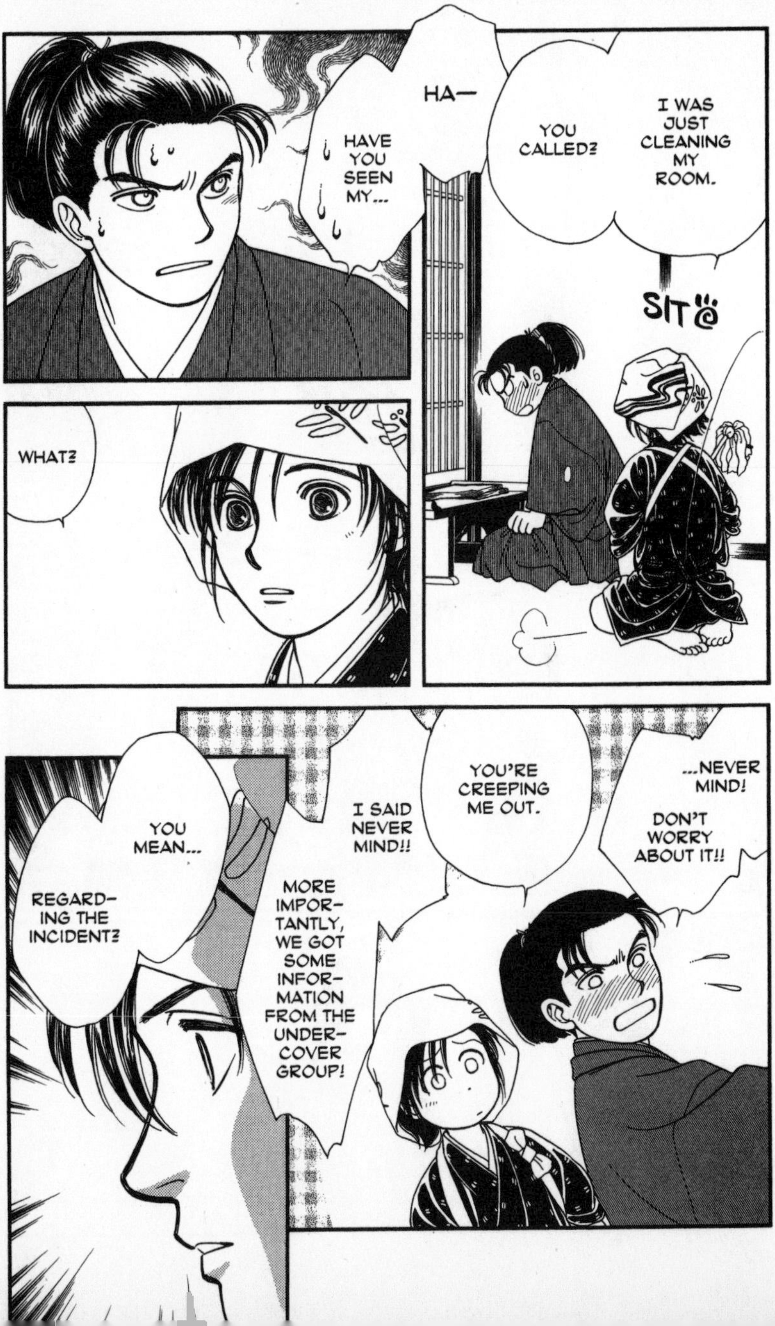
I WAS JUST CLEANING MY ROOM.
YOU CALLED?
SIT
HA—
HAVE YOU SEEN MY...
WHAT?
...NEVER MIND!
DON'T WORRY ABOUT IT!!
YOU'RE CREEPING ME OUT.
I SAID NEVER MIND!!
MORE IMPORTANTLY, WE GOT SOME INFORMATION FROM THE UNDERCOVER GROUP!
YOU MEAN...
REGARDING THE INCIDENT?

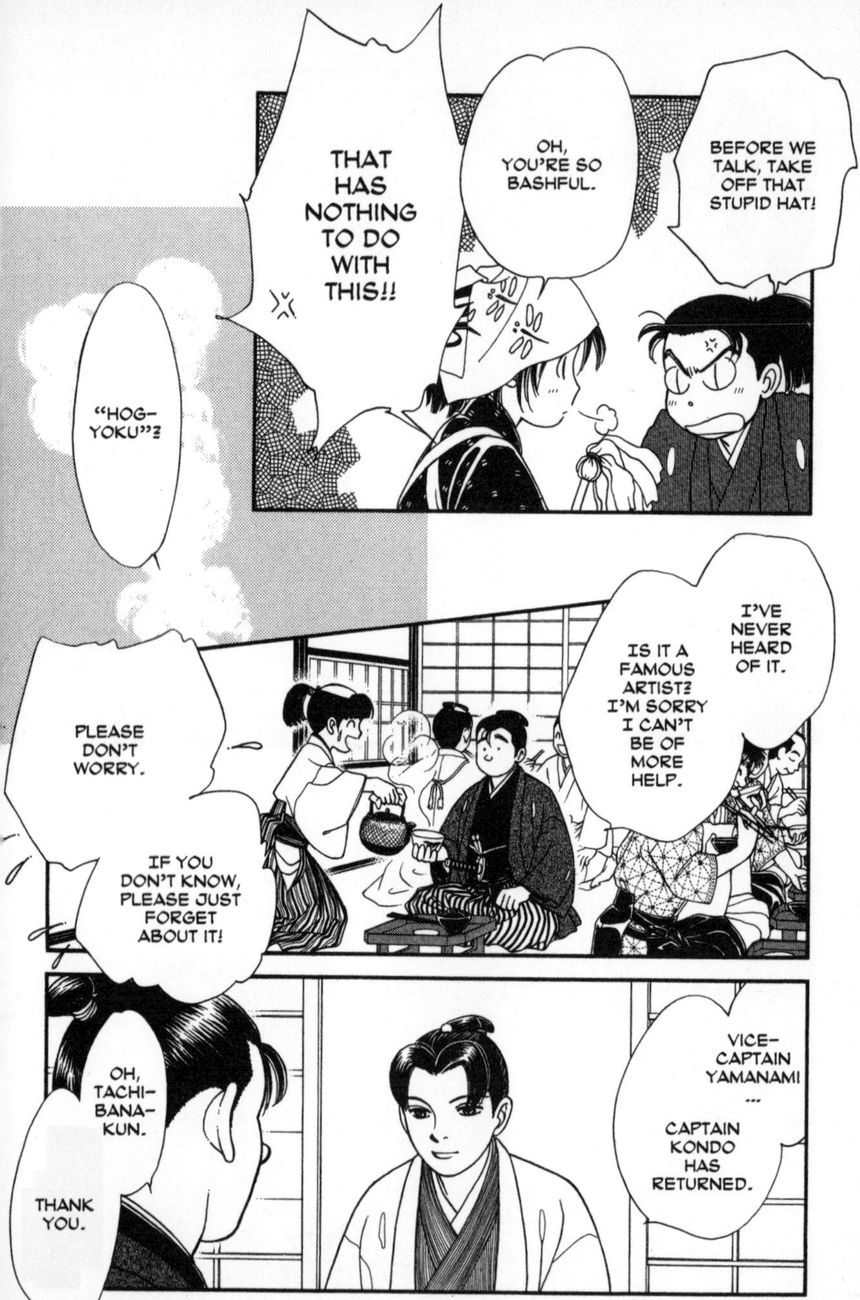
BEFORE WE TALK, TAKE OFF THAT STUPID HAT!
OH, YOU'RE SO BASHFUL.
THAT HAS NOTHING TO DO WITH THIS!!
"HOG-YOKU"?
I'VE NEVER HEARD OF IT.
IS IT A FAMOUS ARTIST? I'M SORRY I CAN'T BE OF MORE HELP.
PLEASE DON'T WORRY.
IF YOU DON'T KNOW, PLEASE JUST FORGET ABOUT IT!
VICE-CAPTAIN YAMANAMI ... CAPTAIN KONDO HAS RETURNED.
OH, TACHIBANA-KUN.
THANK YOU.

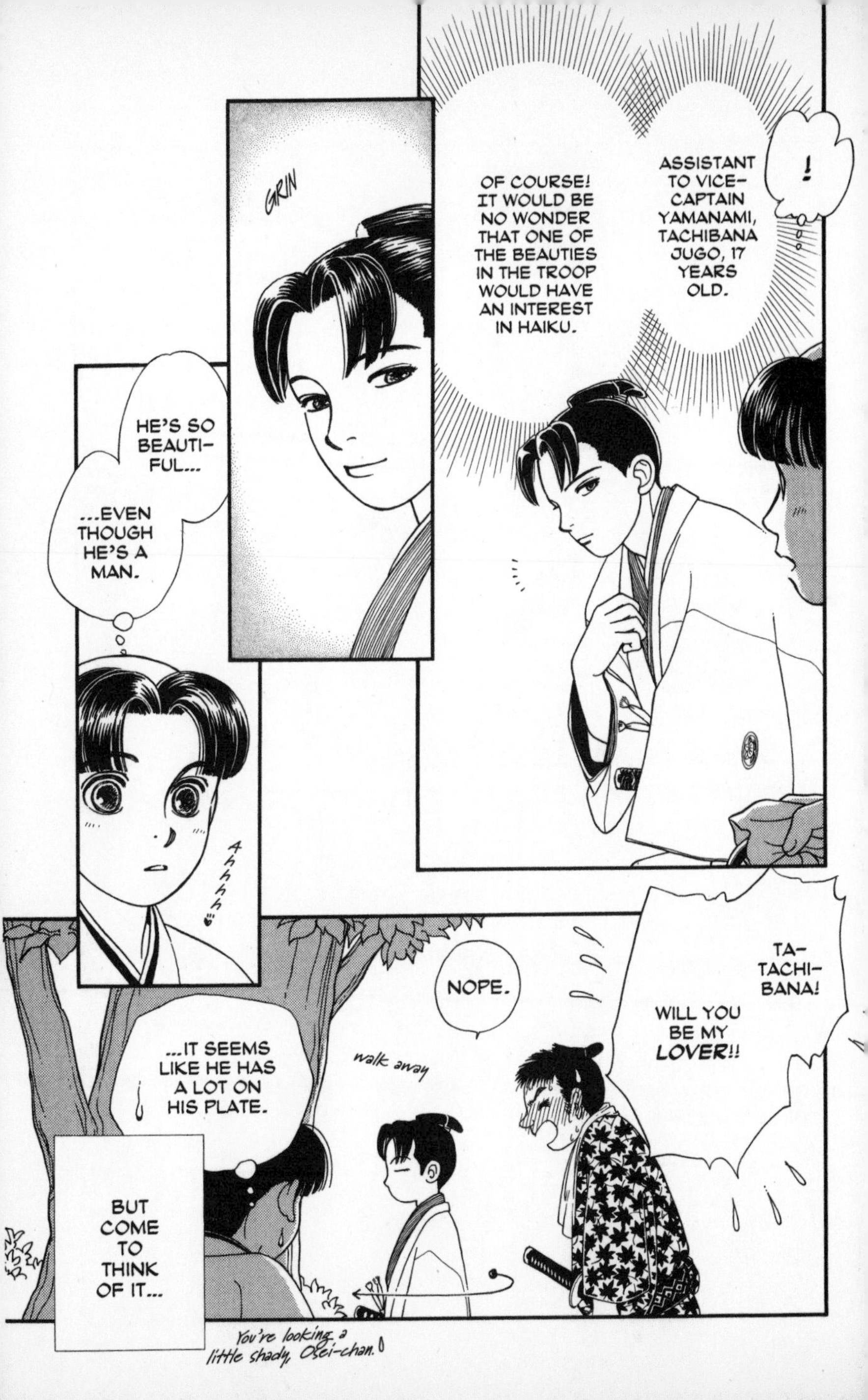
!
ASSISTANT TO VICE-CAPTAIN YAMANAMI, TACHIBANA JUGO, 17 YEARS OLD.
OF COURSE! IT WOULD BE NO WONDER THAT ONE OF THE BEAUTIES IN THE TROOP WOULD HAVE AN INTEREST IN HAIKU.
GRIN
HE'S SO BEAUTI-FUL...
...EVEN THOUGH HE'S A MAN.
Ahhhh
TA-TACHI-BANA!
WILL YOU BE MY LOVER!!
NOPE.
walk away
...IT SEEMS LIKE HE HAS A LOT ON HIS PLATE.
BUT COME TO THINK OF IT...
You're looking a little shady, Osei-chan.

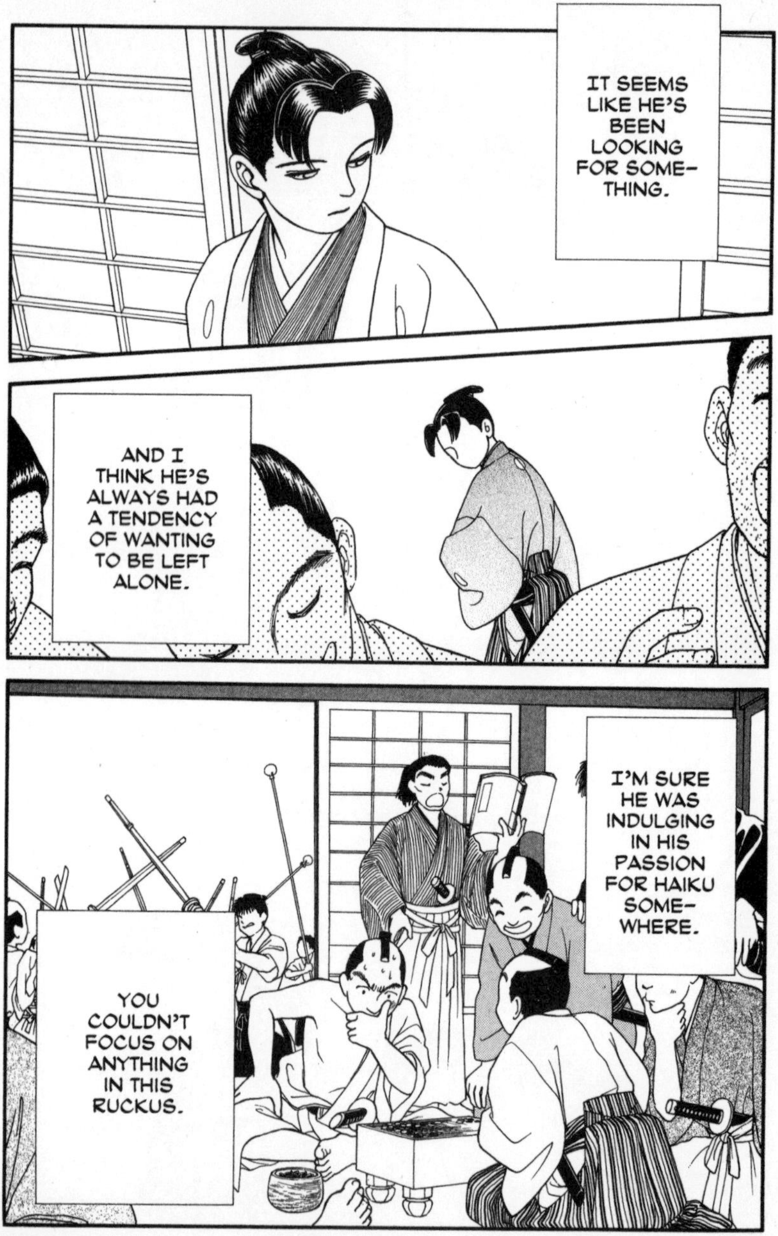
IT SEEMS LIKE HE'S BEEN LOOKING FOR SOME-THING.
AND I THINK HE'S ALWAYS HAD A TENDENCY OF WANTING TO BE LEFT ALONE.
I'M SURE HE WAS INDULGING IN HIS PASSION FOR HAIKU SOME-WHERE.
YOU COULDN'T FOCUS ON ANYTHING IN THIS RUCKUS.

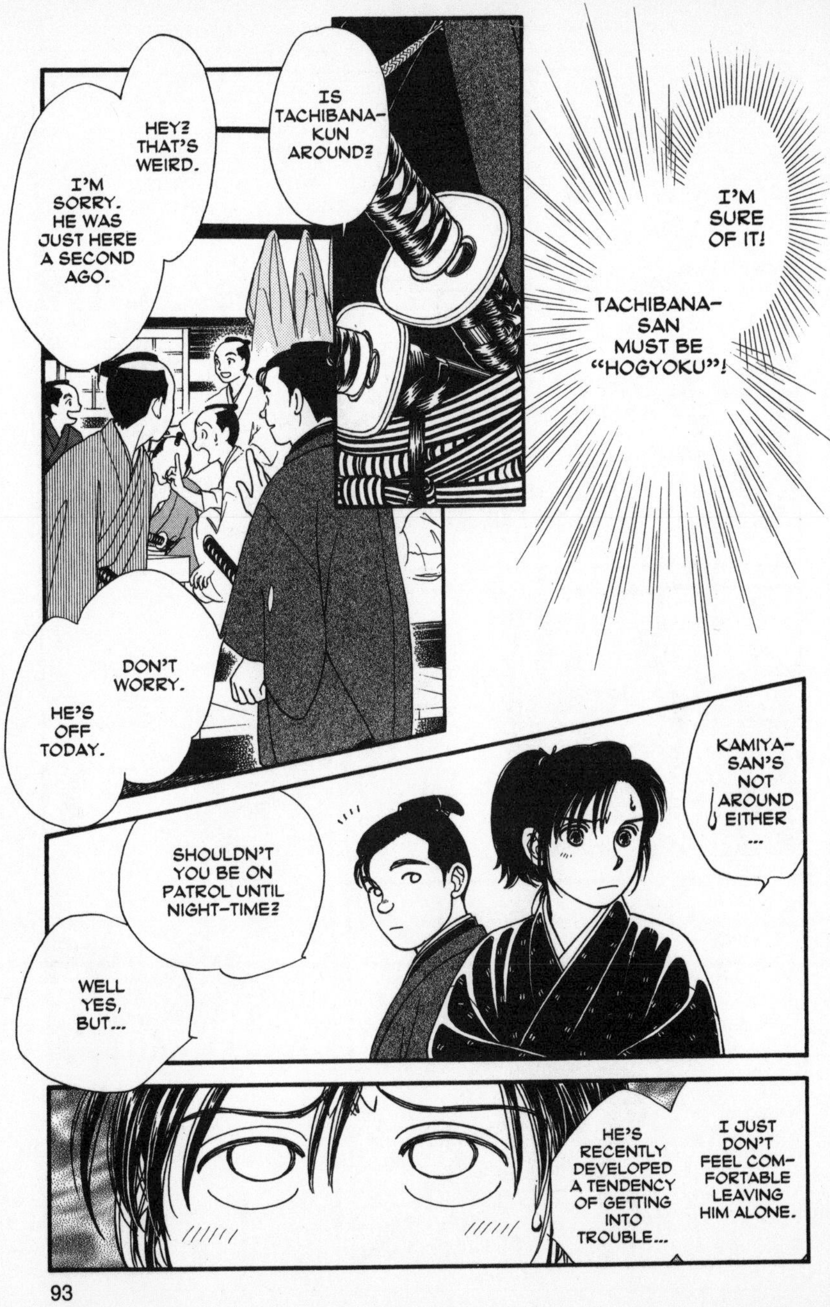
I'M SURE OF IT!
TACHIBANA-SAN MUST BE "HOGYOKU"!
IS TACHIBANA-KUN AROUND?
HEY? THAT'S WEIRD.
I'M SORRY. HE WAS JUST HERE A SECOND AGO.
DON'T WORRY.
HE'S OFF TODAY.
KAMIYA-SAN'S NOT AROUND EITHER ...
SHOULDN'T YOU BE ON PATROL UNTIL NIGHT-TIME?
WELL YES, BUT...
I JUST DON'T FEEL COM-FORTABLE LEAVING HIM ALONE.
HE'S RECENTLY DEVELOPED A TENDENCY OF GETTING INTO TROUBLE...

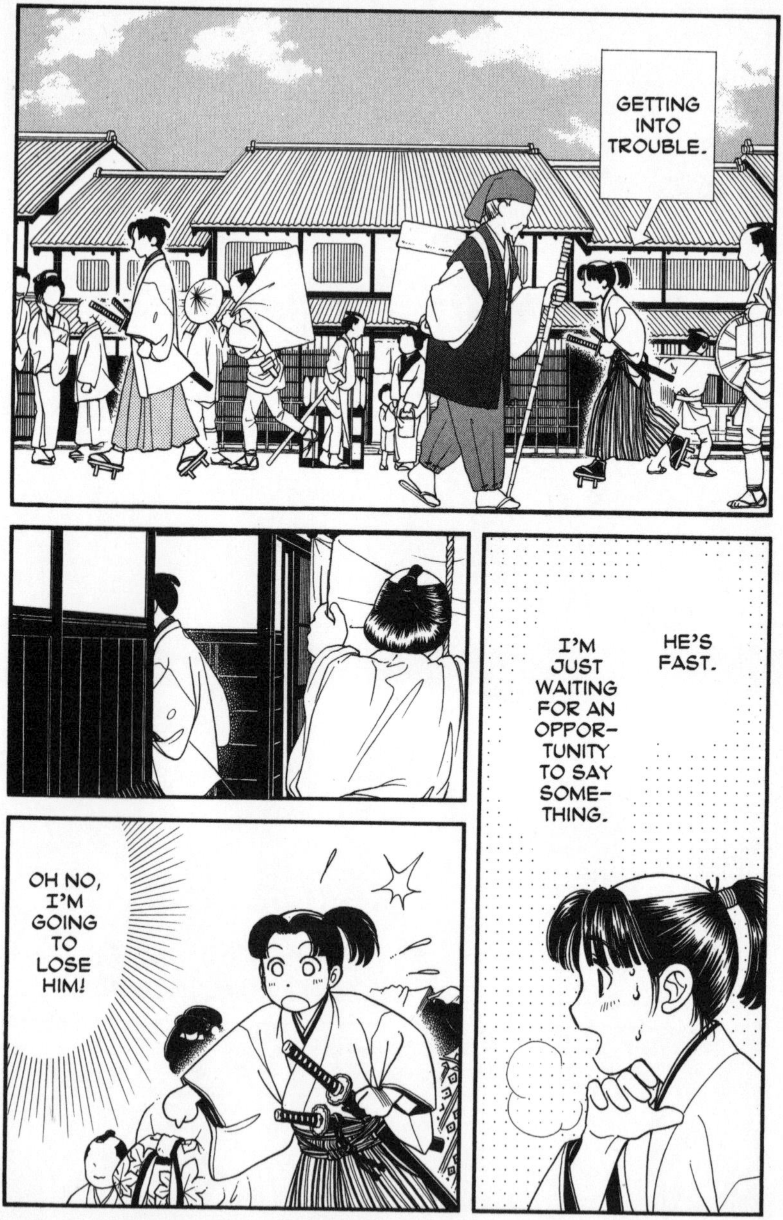
GETTING INTO TROUBLE.
HE'S FAST.
I'M JUST WAITING FOR AN OPPOR-TUNITY TO SAY SOME-THING.
OH NO, I'M GOING TO LOSE HIM!

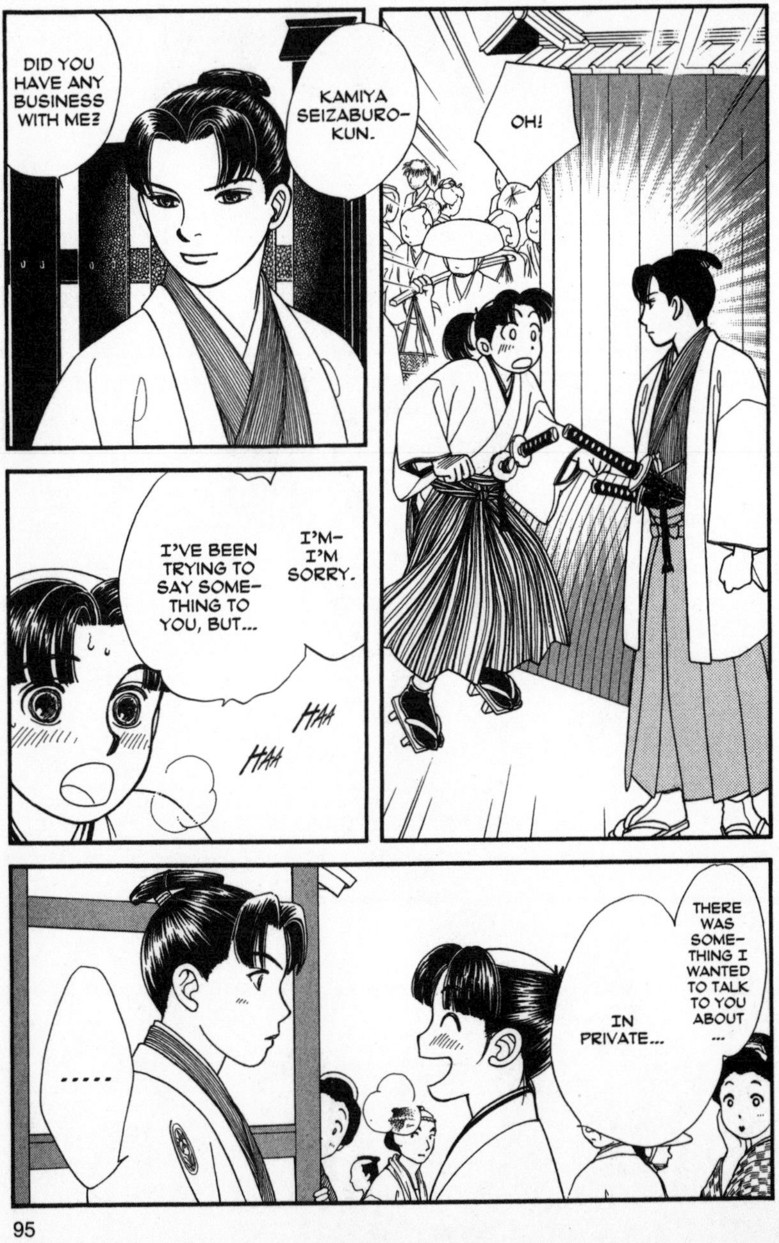
OH!
KAMIYA SEIZABURO-KUN.
DID YOU HAVE ANY BUSINESS WITH ME?
I'M— I'M SORRY.
I'VE BEEN TRYING TO SAY SOME-THING TO YOU, BUT...
HAA
HAA
THERE WAS SOME-THING I WANTED TO TALK TO YOU ABOUT ...
IN PRIVATE...
.....

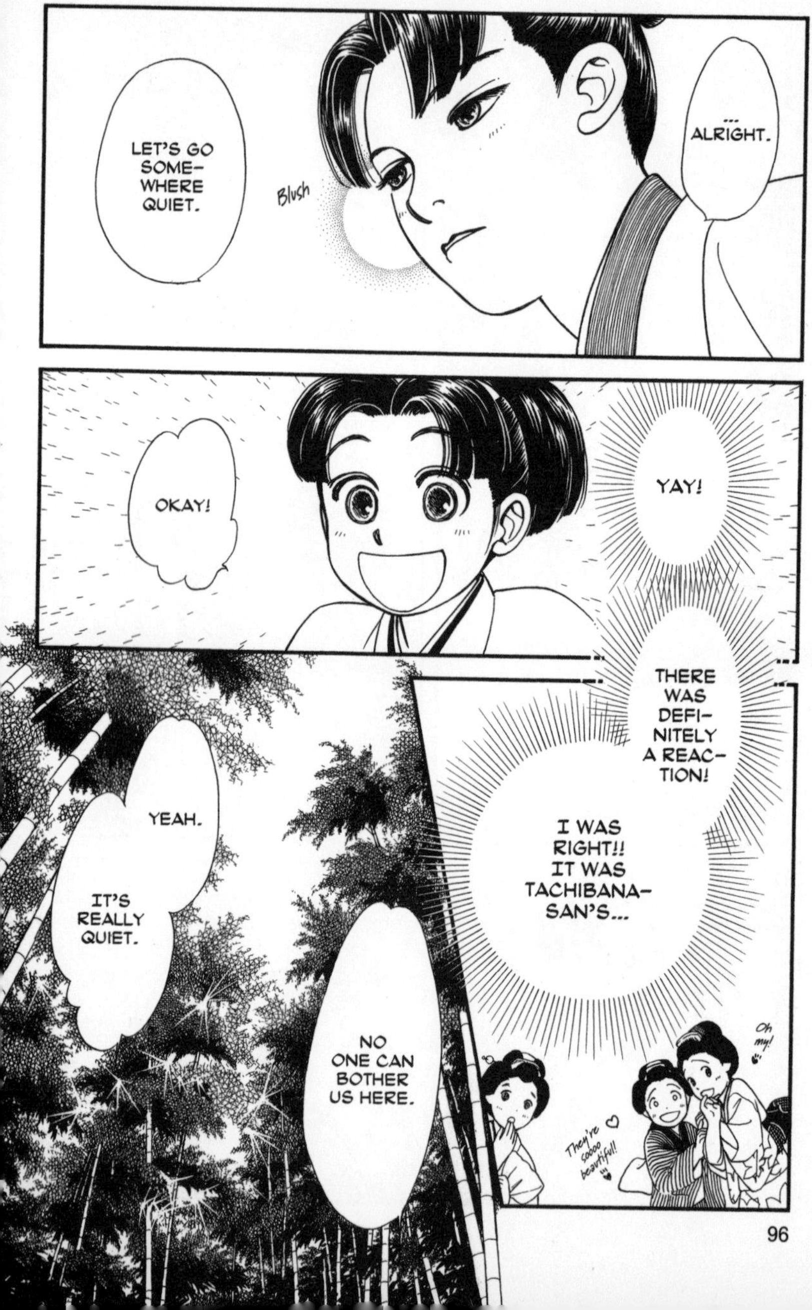
...ALRIGHT.
LET'S GO SOME-WHERE QUIET.
Blush
YAY!
OKAY!
THERE WAS DEFI-NITELY A REAC-TION!
I WAS RIGHT!! IT WAS TACHIBANA-SAN'S...
Oh my!
They're soooo beautiful!
YEAH.
IT'S REALLY QUIET.
NO ONE CAN BOTHER US HERE.

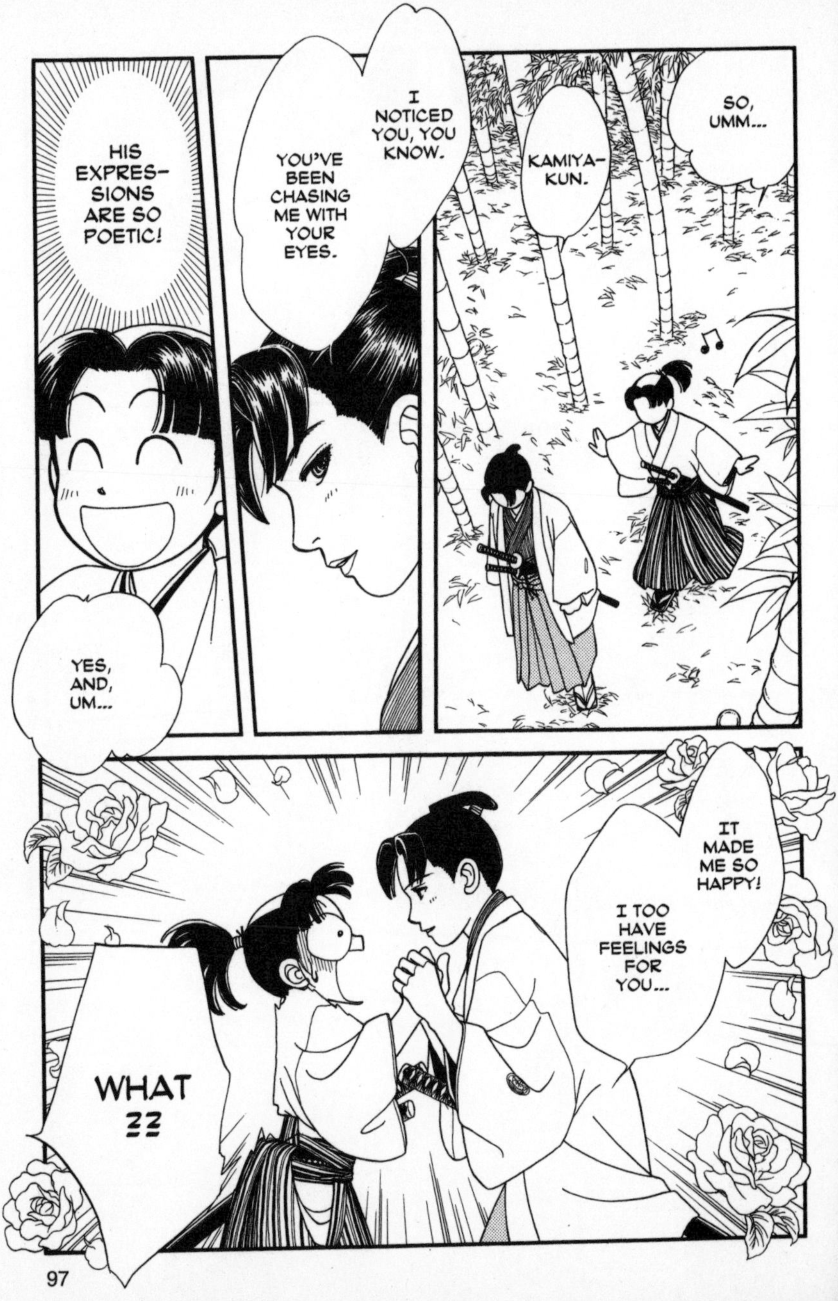
SO, UMM...
KAMIYA-KUN.
I NOTICED YOU, YOU KNOW.
YOU'VE BEEN CHASING ME WITH YOUR EYES.
HIS EXPRES-SIONS ARE SO POETIC!
YES, AND, UM...
IT MADE ME SO HAPPY!
I TOO HAVE FEELINGS FOR YOU...
WHAT ??

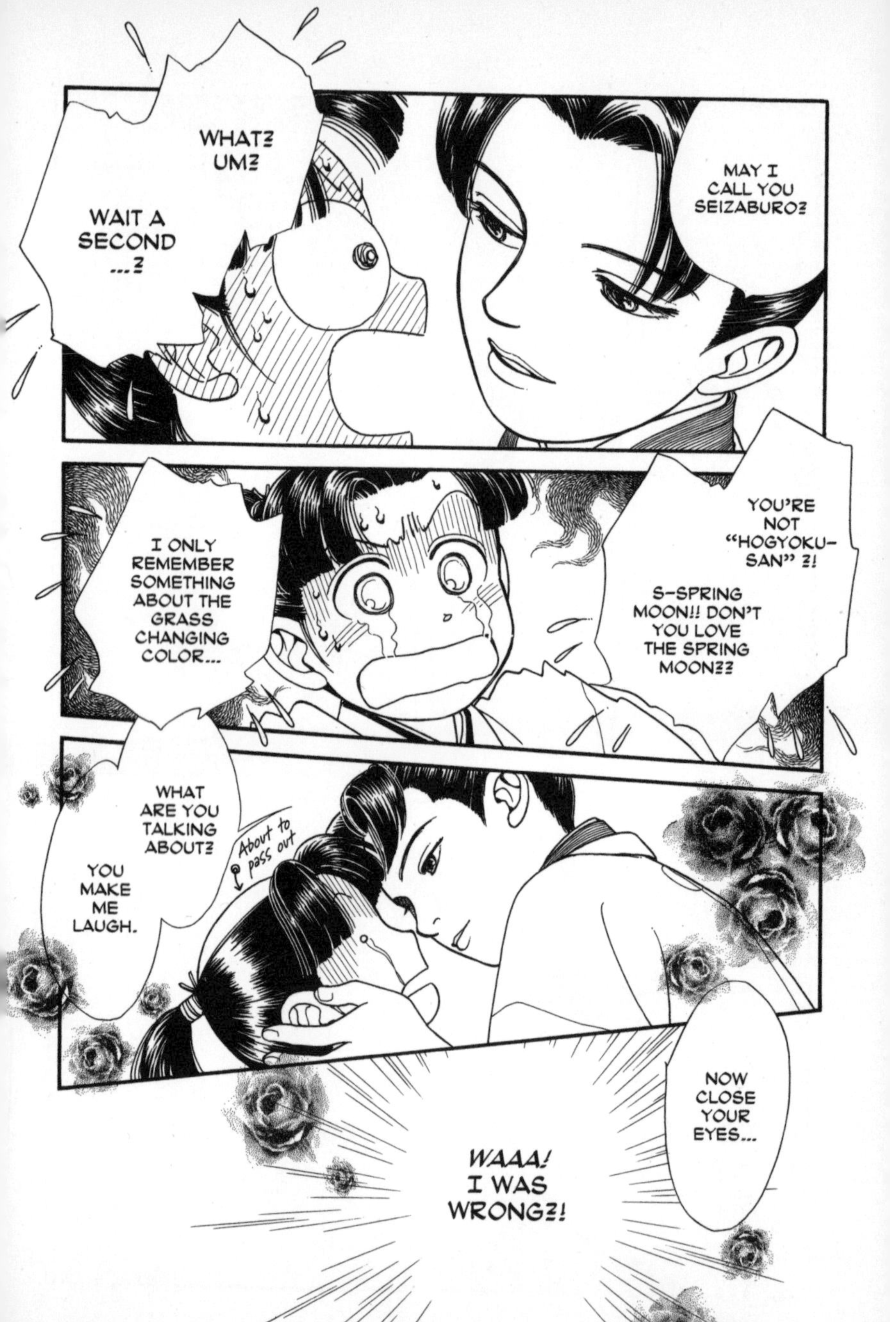
MAY I CALL YOU SEIZABURO?
WHAT? UM?
WAIT A SECOND ...?
YOU'RE NOT "HOGYOKU-SAN"?!
S-SPRING MOON!! DON'T YOU LOVE THE SPRING MOON??
I ONLY REMEMBER SOMETHING ABOUT THE GRASS CHANGING COLOR...
WHAT ARE YOU TALKING ABOUT?
YOU MAKE ME LAUGH.
About to pass out
NOW CLOSE YOUR EYES...
WAAA! I WAS WRONG?!

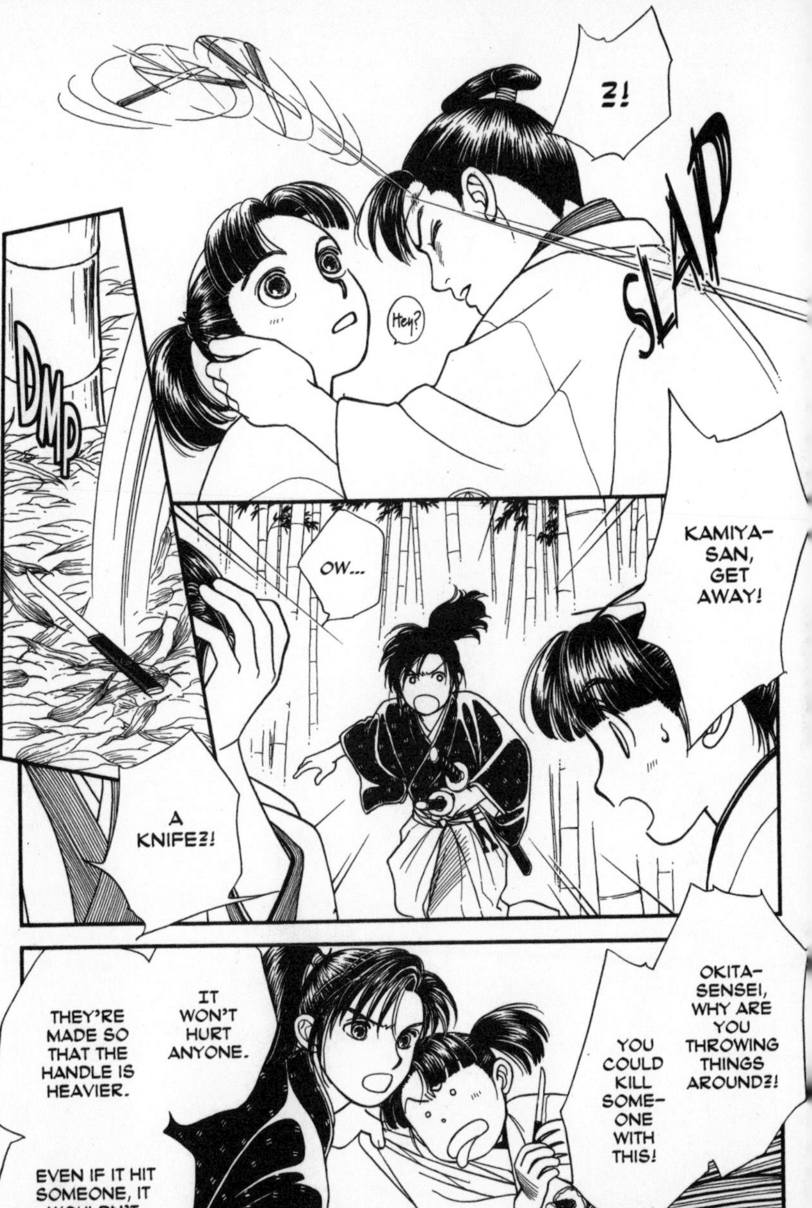
?!
SLAP
Hey?
KAMIYA-SAN, GET AWAY!
OW...
A KNIFE?!
DMP
OKITA-SENSEI, WHY ARE YOU THROWING THINGS AROUND?!
YOU COULD KILL SOMEONE WITH THIS!
IT WON'T HURT ANYONE.
THEY'RE MADE SO THAT THE HANDLE IS HEAVIER.
EVEN IF IT HIT SOMEONE, IT WOULDN'T SERIOUSLY INJURE THEM.

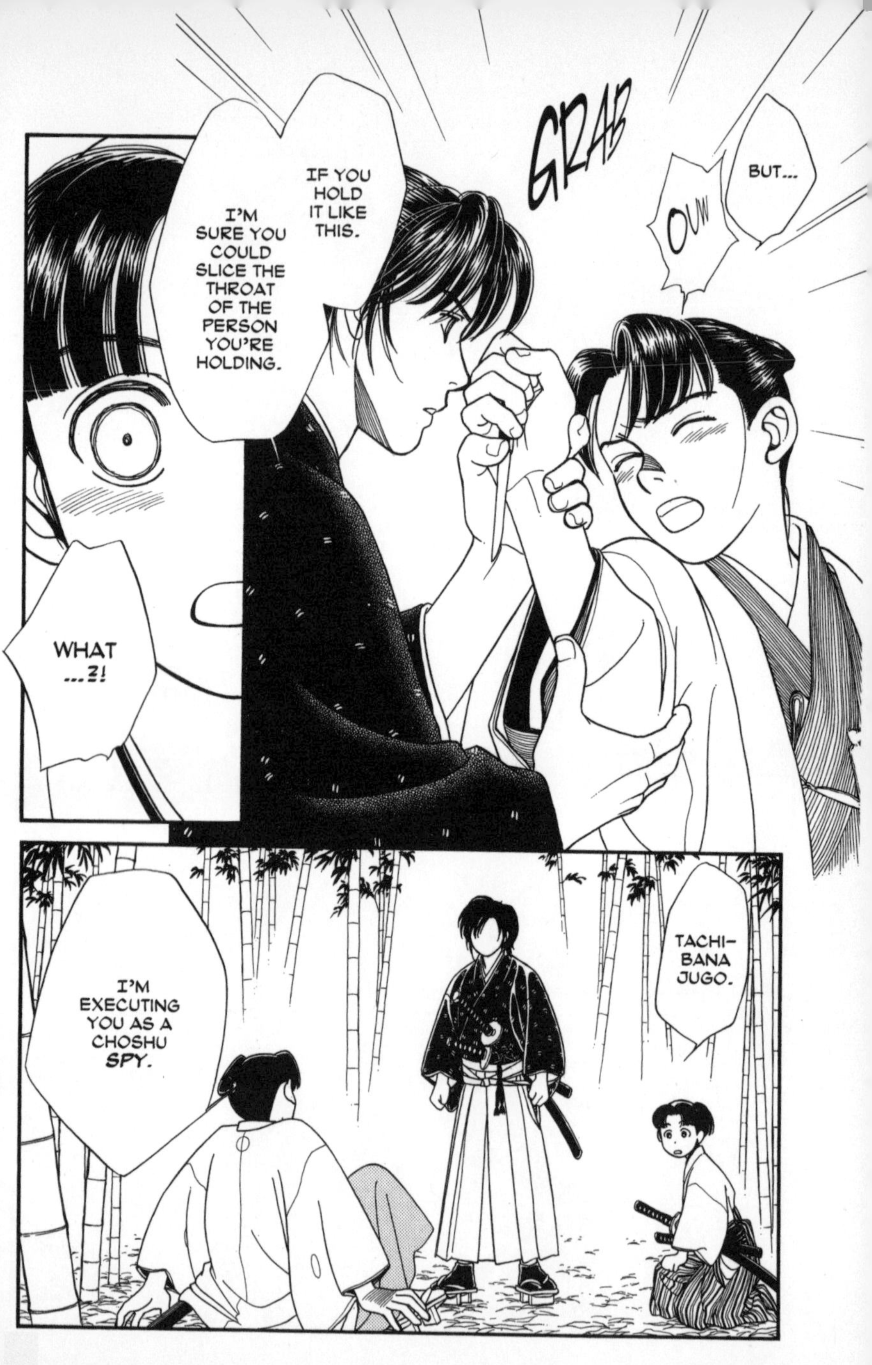
BUT...
OUW
GRAB
IF YOU HOLD IT LIKE THIS.
I'M SURE YOU COULD SLICE THE THROAT OF THE PERSON YOU'RE HOLDING.
WHAT ...?!
TACHI-BANA JUGO.
I'M EXECUTING YOU AS A CHOSHU SPY.

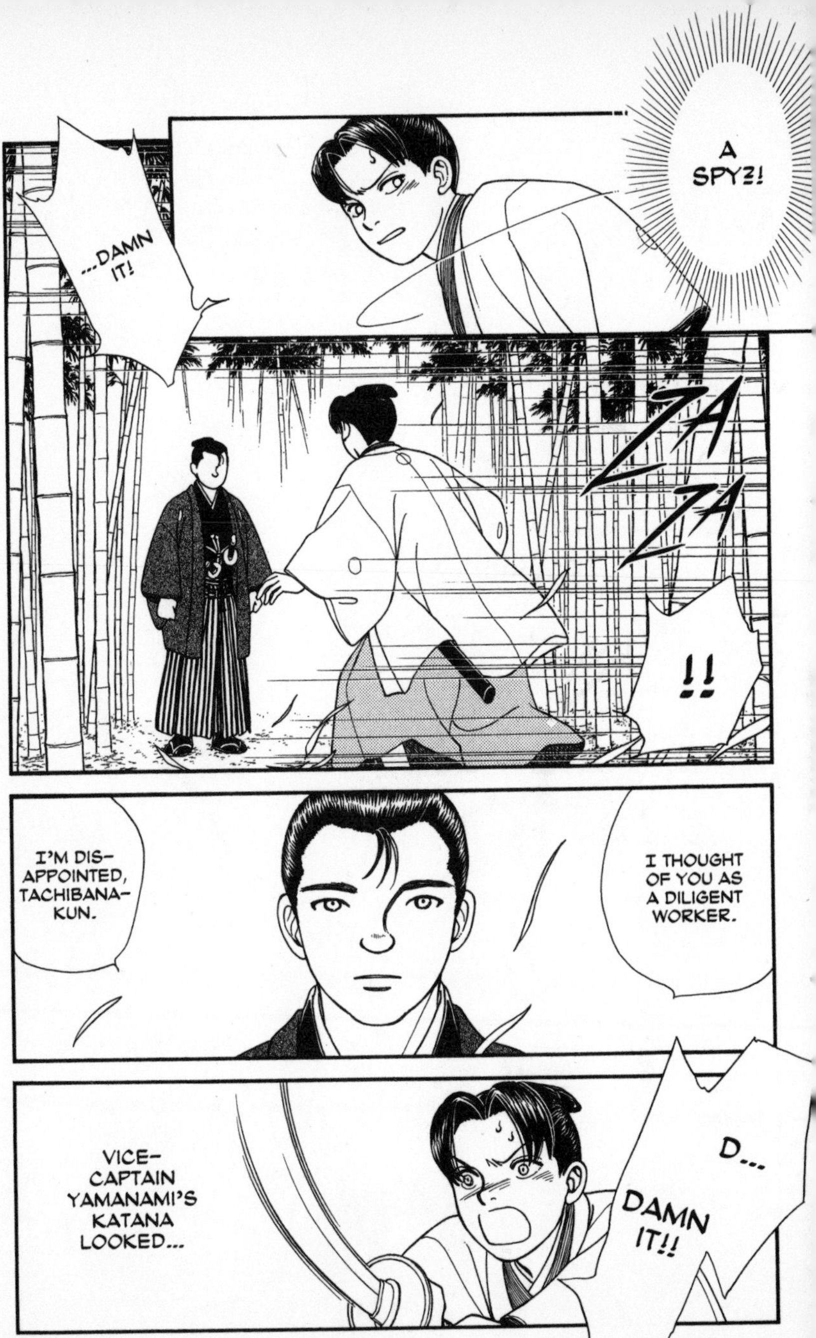
A SPY?!
...DAMN IT!
ZA ZA ZA
!!
I THOUGHT OF YOU AS A DILIGENT WORKER.
I'M DIS-APPOINTED, TACHIBANA-KUN.
D... DAMN IT!!
VICE-CAPTAIN YAMANAMI'S KATANA LOOKED...

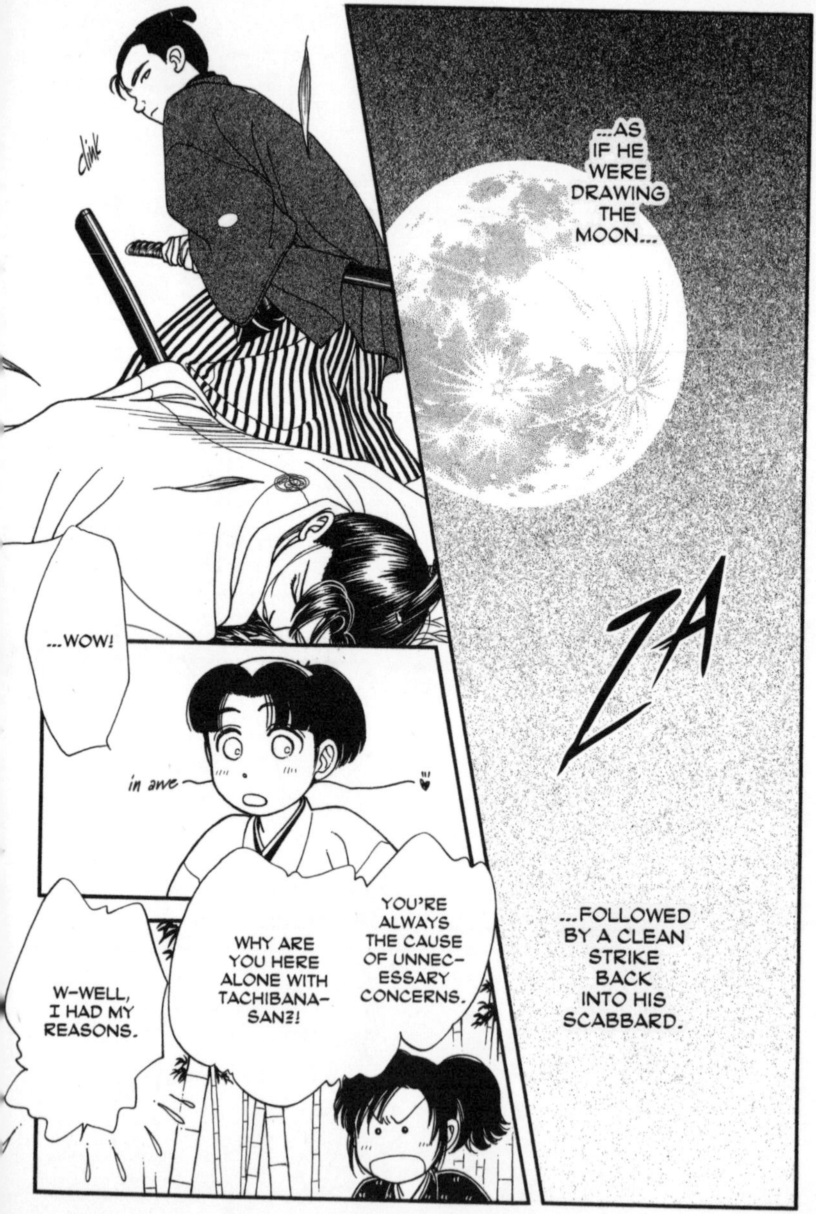
...AS IF HE WERE DRAWING THE MOON...
ZA
...FOLLOWED BY A CLEAN STRIKE BACK INTO HIS SCABBARD.
clink
...WOW!
in awe
YOU'RE ALWAYS THE CAUSE OF UNNEC-ESSARY CONCERNS.
WHY ARE YOU HERE ALONE WITH TACHIBANA-SAN?!
W-WELL, I HAD MY REASONS.

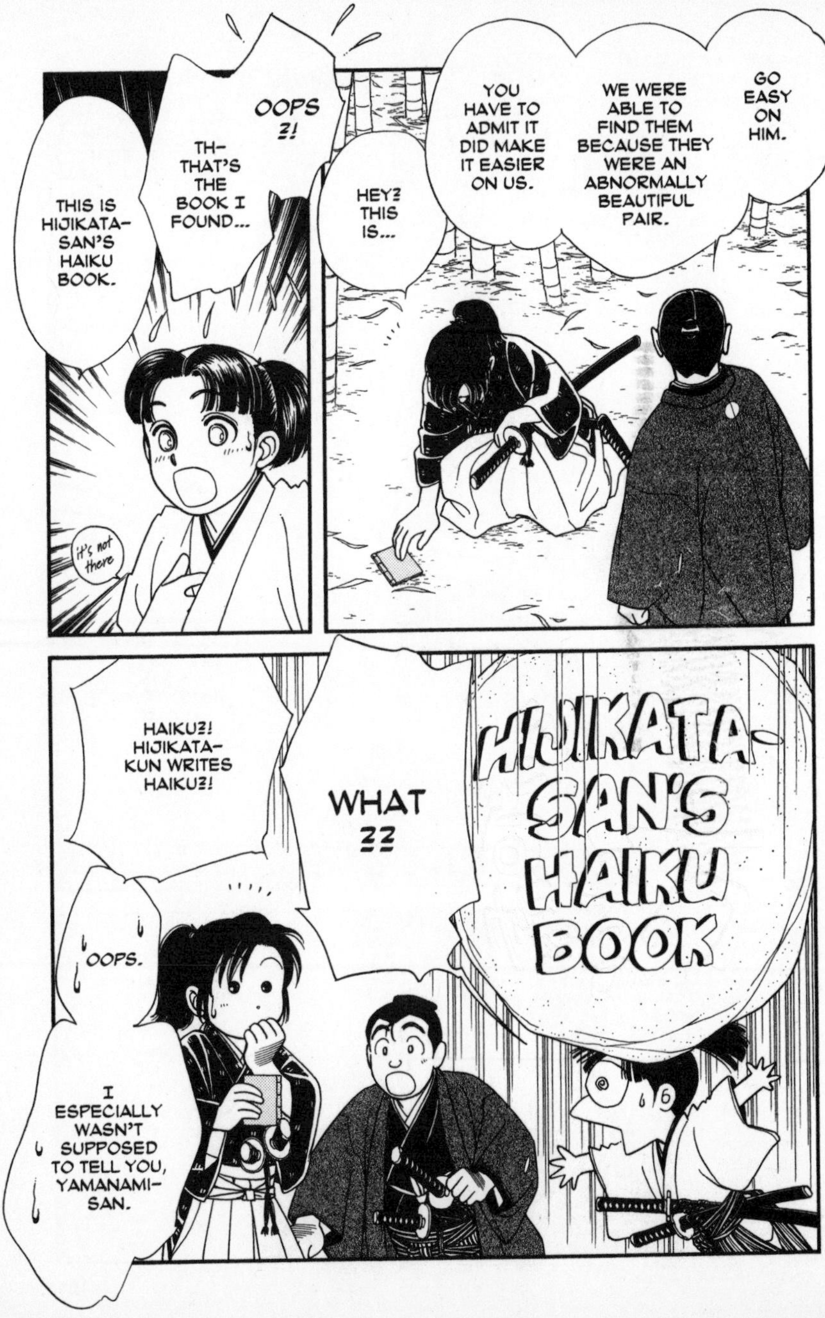
GO EASY ON HIM.
WE WERE ABLE TO FIND THEM BECAUSE THEY WERE AN ABNORMALLY BEAUTIFUL PAIR.
YOU HAVE TO ADMIT IT DID MAKE IT EASIER ON US.
HEY? THIS IS...
OOPS?!
TH-THAT'S THE BOOK I FOUND...
THIS IS HIJIKATA-SAN'S HAIKU BOOK.
it's not there
HIJIKATA-SAN'S HAIKU BOOK
WHAT??
HAIKU?! HIJIKATA-KUN WRITES HAIKU?!
OOPS.
I ESPECIALLY WASN'T SUPPOSED TO TELL YOU, YAMANAMI-SAN.

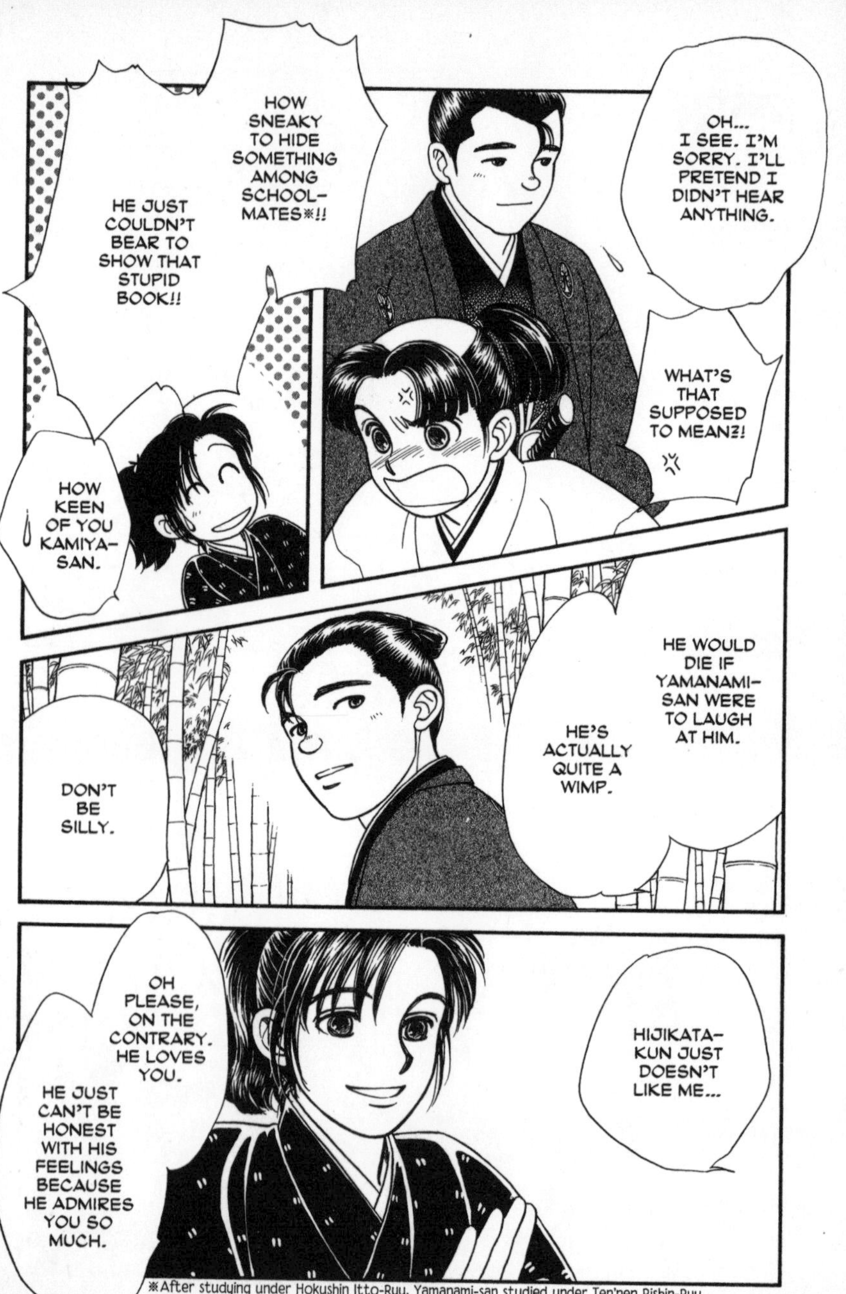
OH... I SEE. I'M SORRY. I'LL PRETEND I DIDN'T HEAR ANYTHING.
WHAT'S THAT SUPPOSED TO MEAN?!
HOW SNEAKY TO HIDE SOMETHING AMONG SCHOOL-MATES※!!
HE JUST COULDN'T BEAR TO SHOW THAT STUPID BOOK!!
HOW KEEN OF YOU KAMIYA-SAN.
HE WOULD DIE IF YAMANAMI-SAN WERE TO LAUGH AT HIM.
HE'S ACTUALLY QUITE A WIMP.
DON'T BE SILLY.
HIJIKATA-KUN JUST DOESN'T LIKE ME...
OH PLEASE, ON THE CONTRARY. HE LOVES YOU.
HE JUST CAN'T BE HONEST WITH HIS FEELINGS BECAUSE HE ADMIRES YOU SO MUCH.

※After studying under Hokushin Itto-Ryu, Yamanami-san studied under Ten'nen Rishin-Ryu.

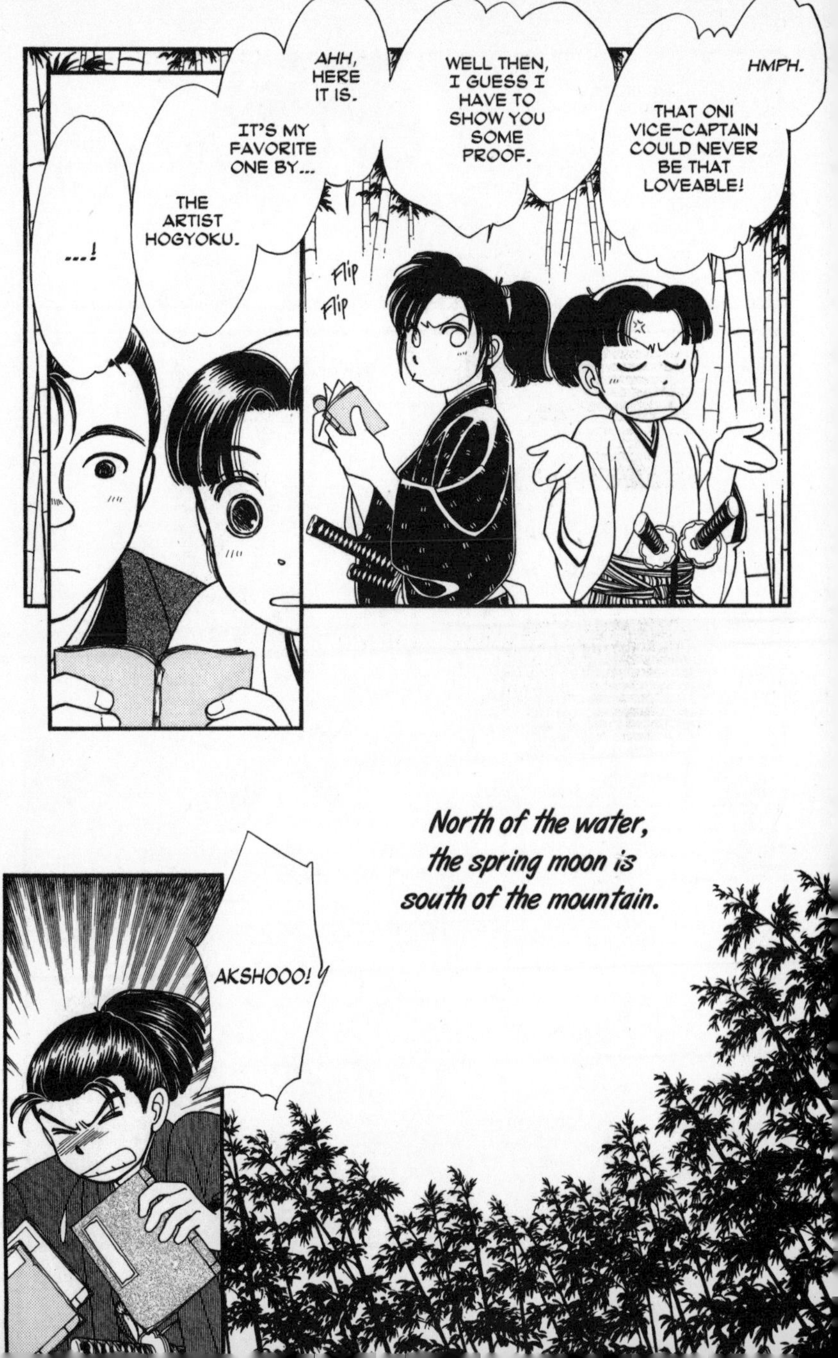
HMPH.
THAT ONI VICE-CAPTAIN COULD NEVER BE THAT LOVEABLE!
WELL THEN, I GUESS I HAVE TO SHOW YOU SOME PROOF.
AHH, HERE IT IS.
Flip Flip
IT'S MY FAVORITE ONE BY...
THE ARTIST HOGYOKU.
...!
North of the water, the spring moon is south of the mountain.
AKSHOOO!

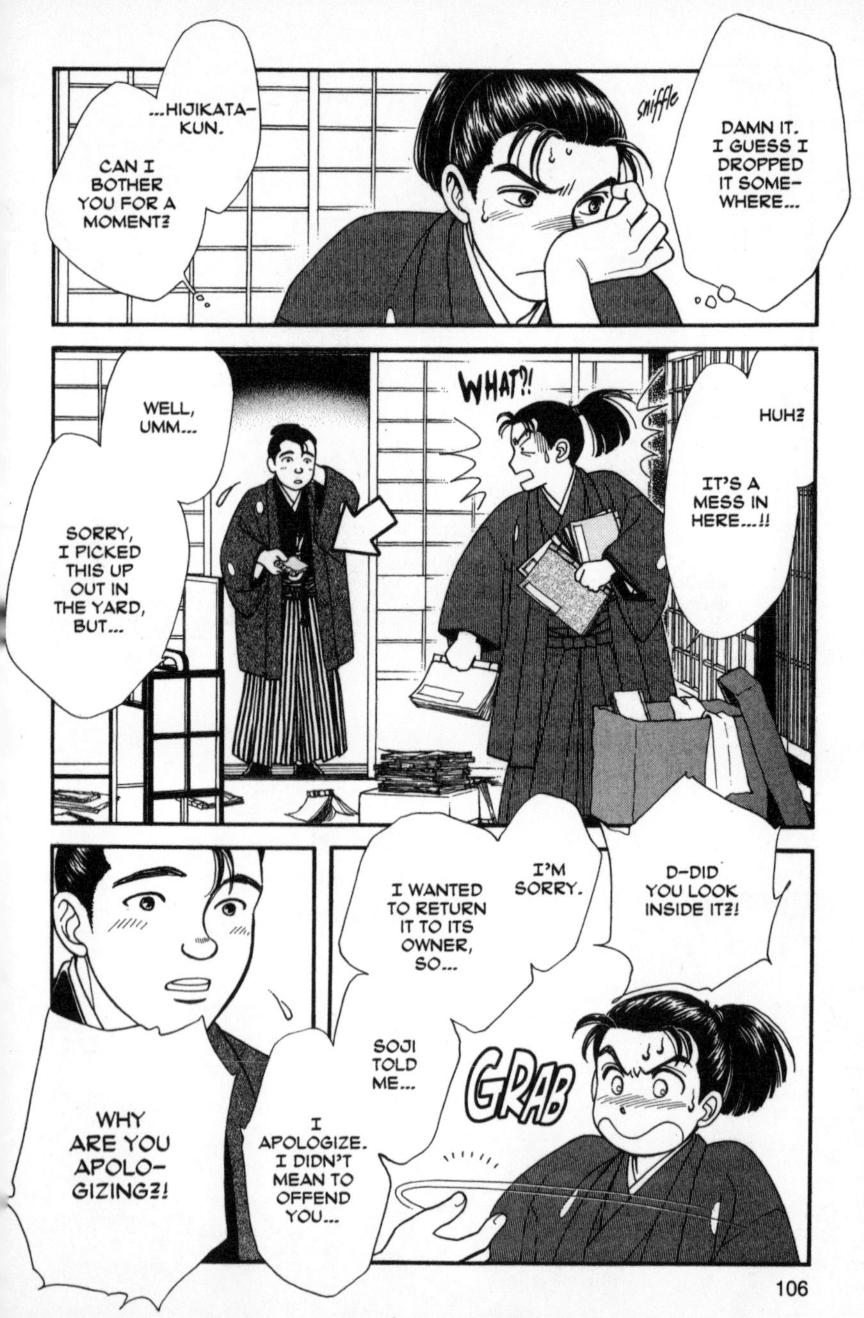
DAMN IT. I GUESS I DROPPED IT SOME-WHERE...
sniffle
...HIJIKATA-KUN.
CAN I BOTHER YOU FOR A MOMENT?
HUH?
IT'S A MESS IN HERE...!!
WHAT?!
WELL, UMM...
SORRY, I PICKED THIS UP OUT IN THE YARD, BUT...
D-DID YOU LOOK INSIDE IT?!
I'M SORRY.
I WANTED TO RETURN IT TO ITS OWNER, SO...
GRAB
SOJI TOLD ME...
I APOLOGIZE. I DIDN'T MEAN TO OFFEND YOU...
WHY ARE YOU APOLO-GIZING?!

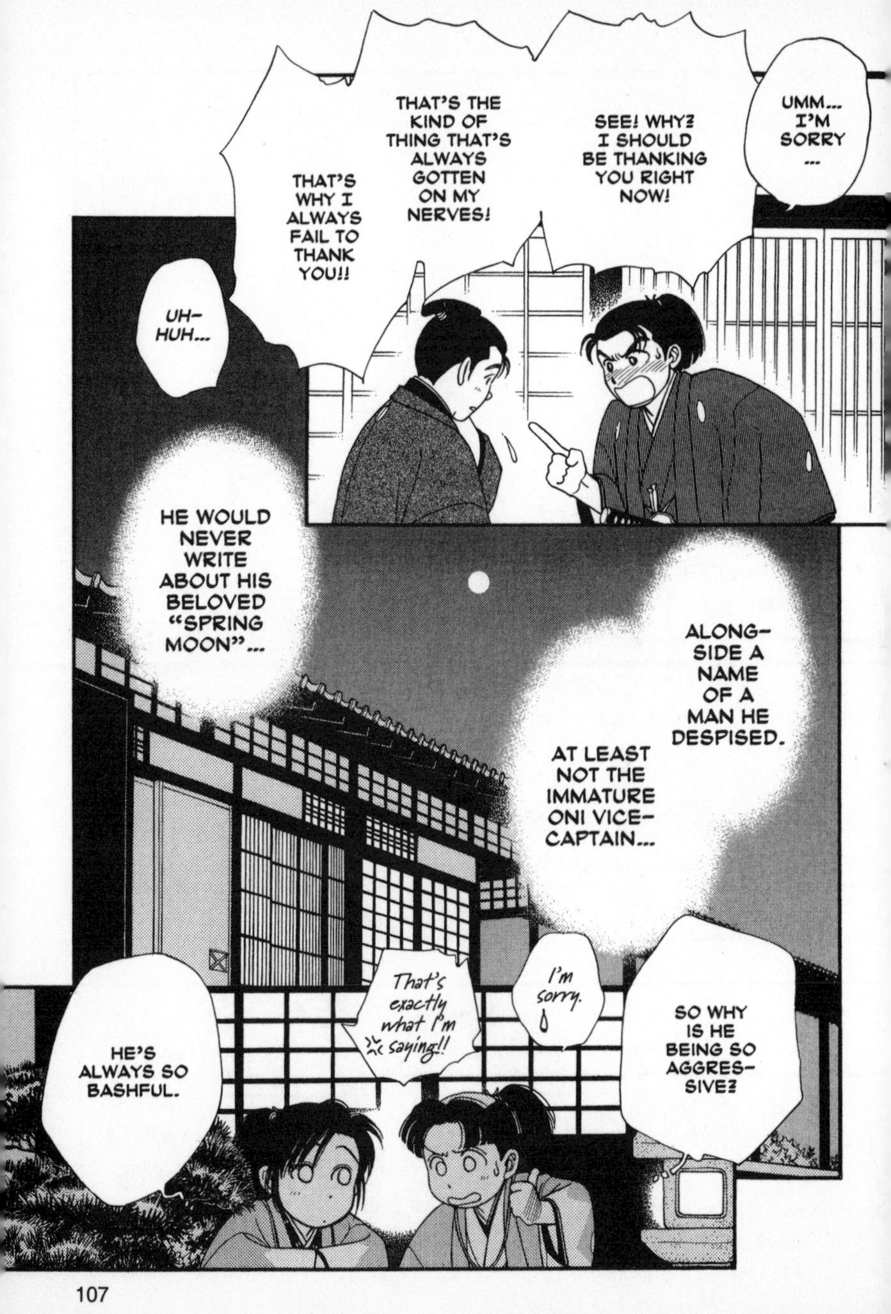
UMM... I'M SORRY ...
SEE! WHY? I SHOULD BE THANKING YOU RIGHT NOW!
THAT'S THE KIND OF THING THAT'S ALWAYS GOTTEN ON MY NERVES!
THAT'S WHY I ALWAYS FAIL TO THANK YOU!!
UH-HUH...
HE WOULD NEVER WRITE ABOUT HIS BELOVED "SPRING MOON"...
ALONG-SIDE A NAME OF A MAN HE DESPISED.
AT LEAST NOT THE IMMATURE ONI VICE-CAPTAIN...
SO WHY IS HE BEING SO AGGRES-SIVE?
I'm sorry.
That's exactly what I'm saying!!
HE'S ALWAYS SO BASHFUL.

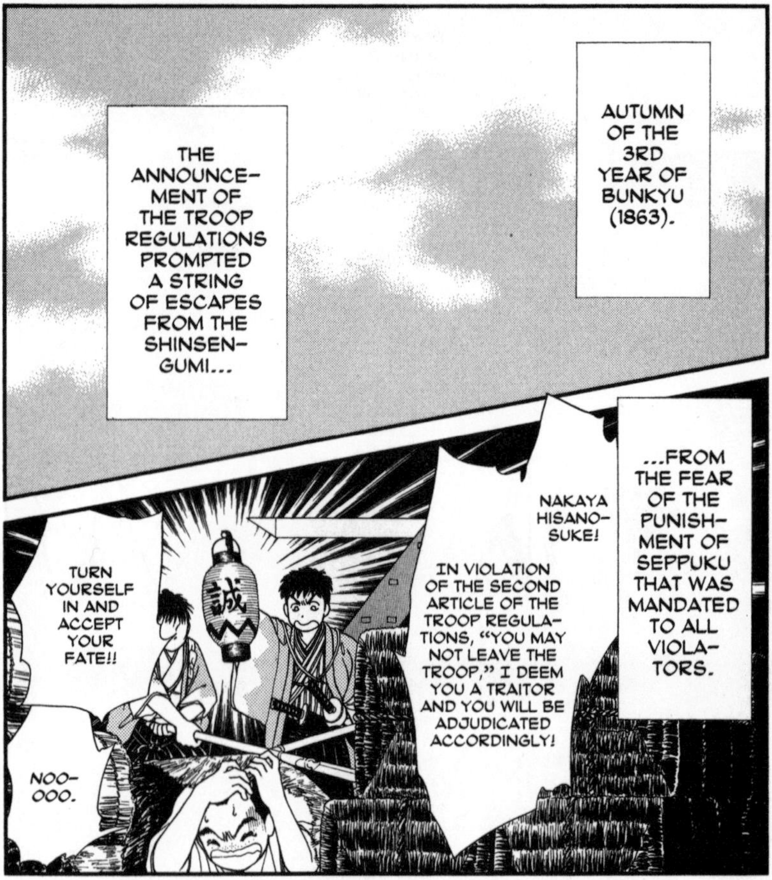
AUTUMN OF THE 3RD YEAR OF BUNKYU (1863).
THE ANNOUNCEMENT OF THE TROOP REGULATIONS PROMPTED A STRING OF ESCAPES FROM THE SHINSENGUMI...
...FROM THE FEAR OF THE PUNISHMENT OF SEPPUKU THAT WAS MANDATED TO ALL VIOLATORS.
NAKAYA HISANOSUKE!
IN VIOLATION OF THE SECOND ARTICLE OF THE TROOP REGULATIONS, "YOU MAY NOT LEAVE THE TROOP," I DEEM YOU A TRAITOR AND YOU WILL BE ADJUDICATED ACCORDINGLY!
誠
TURN YOURSELF IN AND ACCEPT YOUR FATE!!
NOO-OOO.

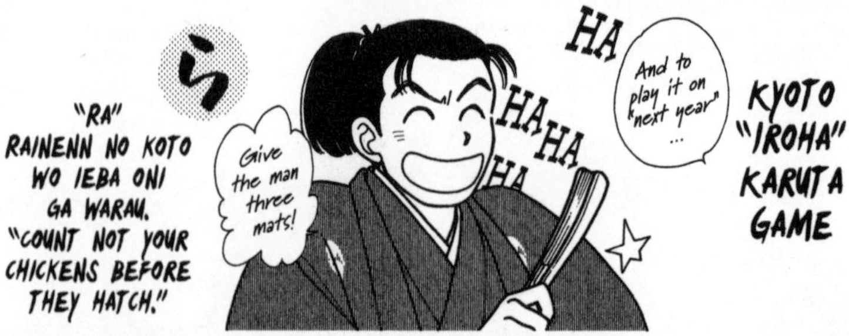
KYOTO "IROHA" KARUTA GAME
And to play it on "next year"...
HA HA HA HA
Give the man three mats!
ら
"RA" RAINENN NO KOTO WO IEBA ONI GA WARAU. "COUNT NOT YOUR CHICKENS BEFORE THEY HATCH."

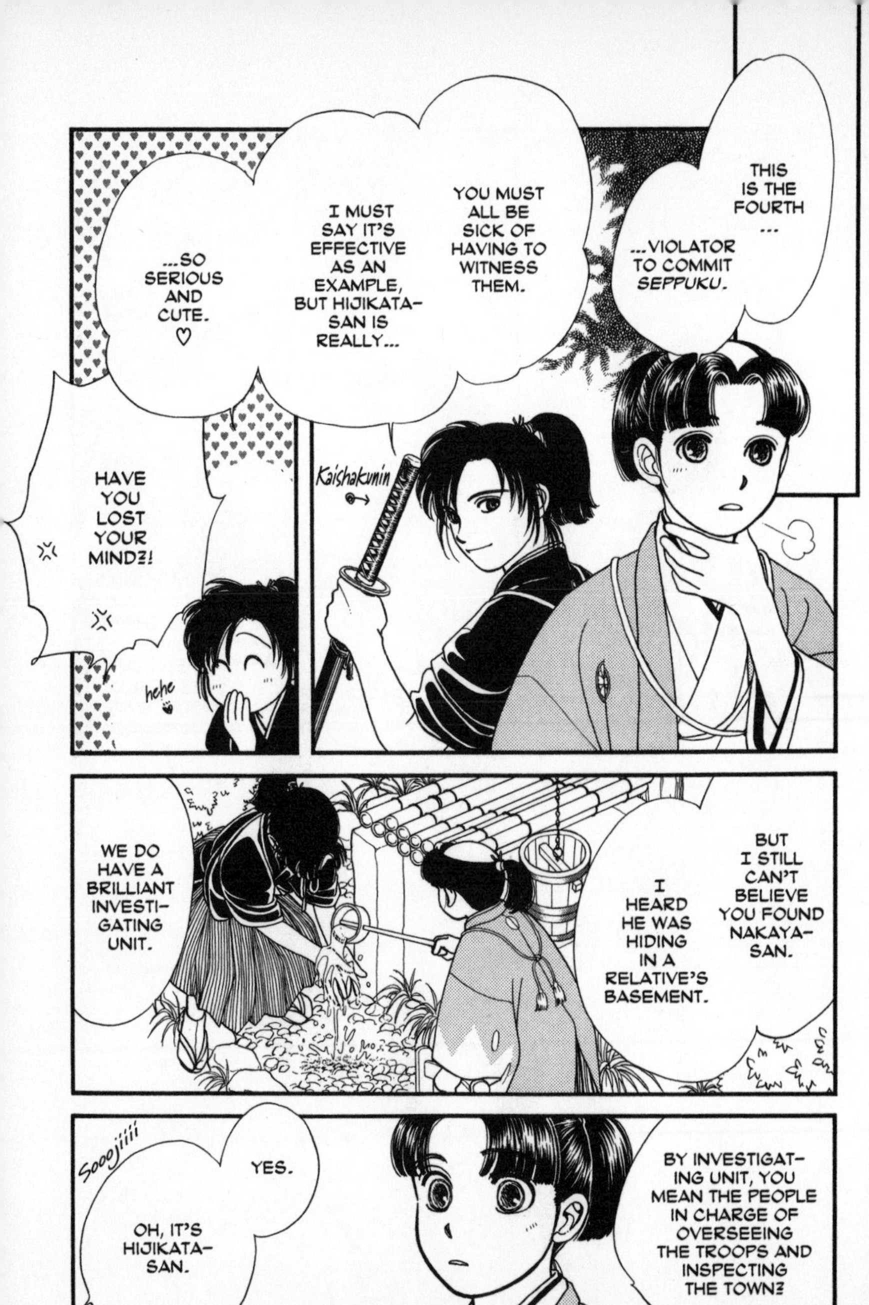
THIS IS THE FOURTH...
...VIOLATOR TO COMMIT *SEPPUKU*.
YOU MUST ALL BE SICK OF HAVING TO WITNESS THEM.
I MUST SAY IT'S EFFECTIVE AS AN EXAMPLE, BUT HIJIKATA-SAN IS REALLY...
Kaishakunin
...SO SERIOUS AND CUTE. ♡
HAVE YOU LOST YOUR MIND?!
hehe
BUT I STILL CAN'T BELIEVE YOU FOUND NAKAYA-SAN.
I HEARD HE WAS HIDING IN A RELATIVE'S BASEMENT.
WE DO HAVE A BRILLIANT INVESTIGATING UNIT.
BY INVESTIGATING UNIT, YOU MEAN THE PEOPLE IN CHARGE OF OVERSEEING THE TROOPS AND INSPECTING THE TOWN?
YES.
OH, IT'S HIJIKATA-SAN.
Sooojiiiii

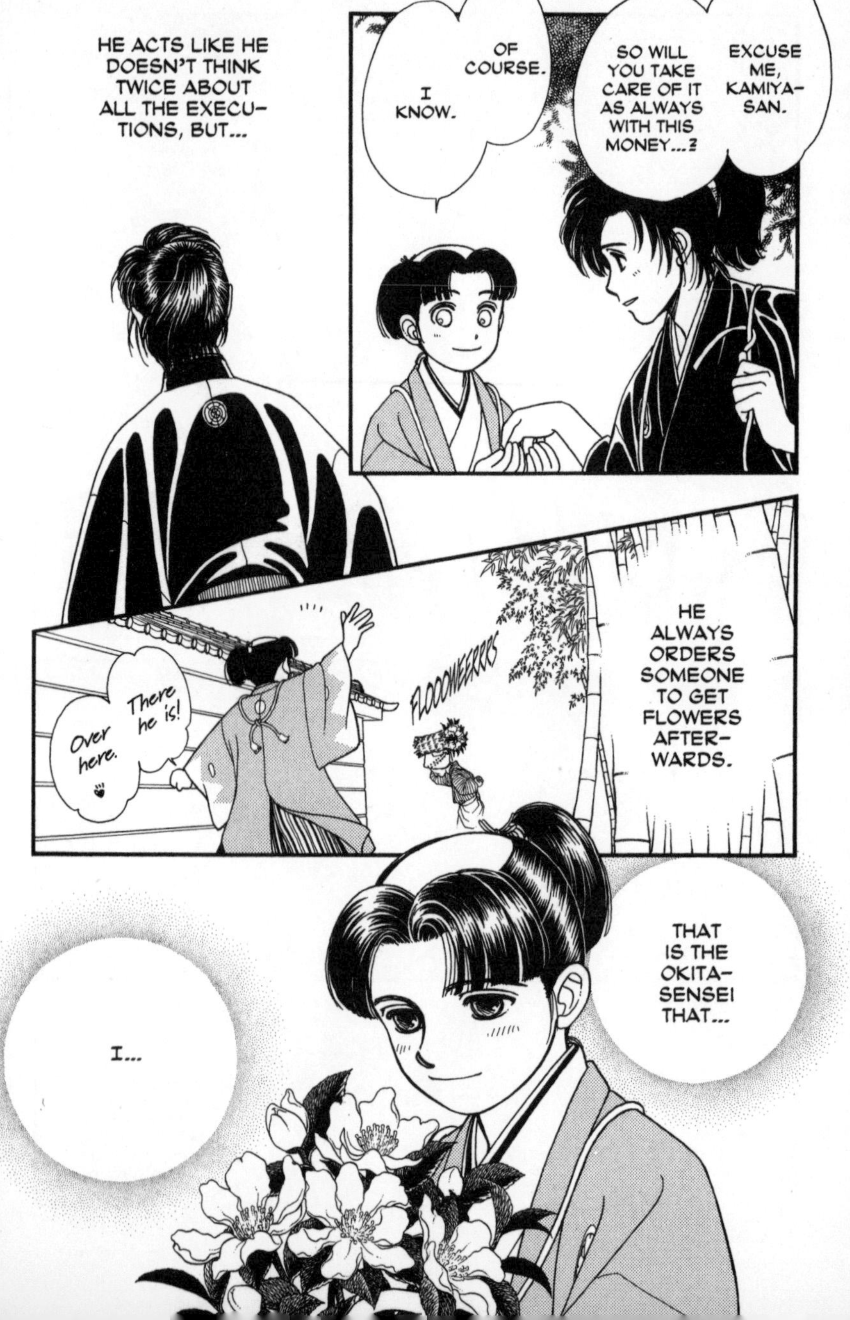
EXCUSE ME, KAMIYA-SAN.
SO WILL YOU TAKE CARE OF IT AS ALWAYS WITH THIS MONEY...?
OF COURSE.
I KNOW.
HE ACTS LIKE HE DOESN'T THINK TWICE ABOUT ALL THE EXECU-TIONS, BUT...
HE ALWAYS ORDERS SOMEONE TO GET FLOWERS AFTER-WARDS.
FLOOOWEERRRS
There he is!
Over here.
THAT IS THE OKITA-SENSEI THAT...
I...

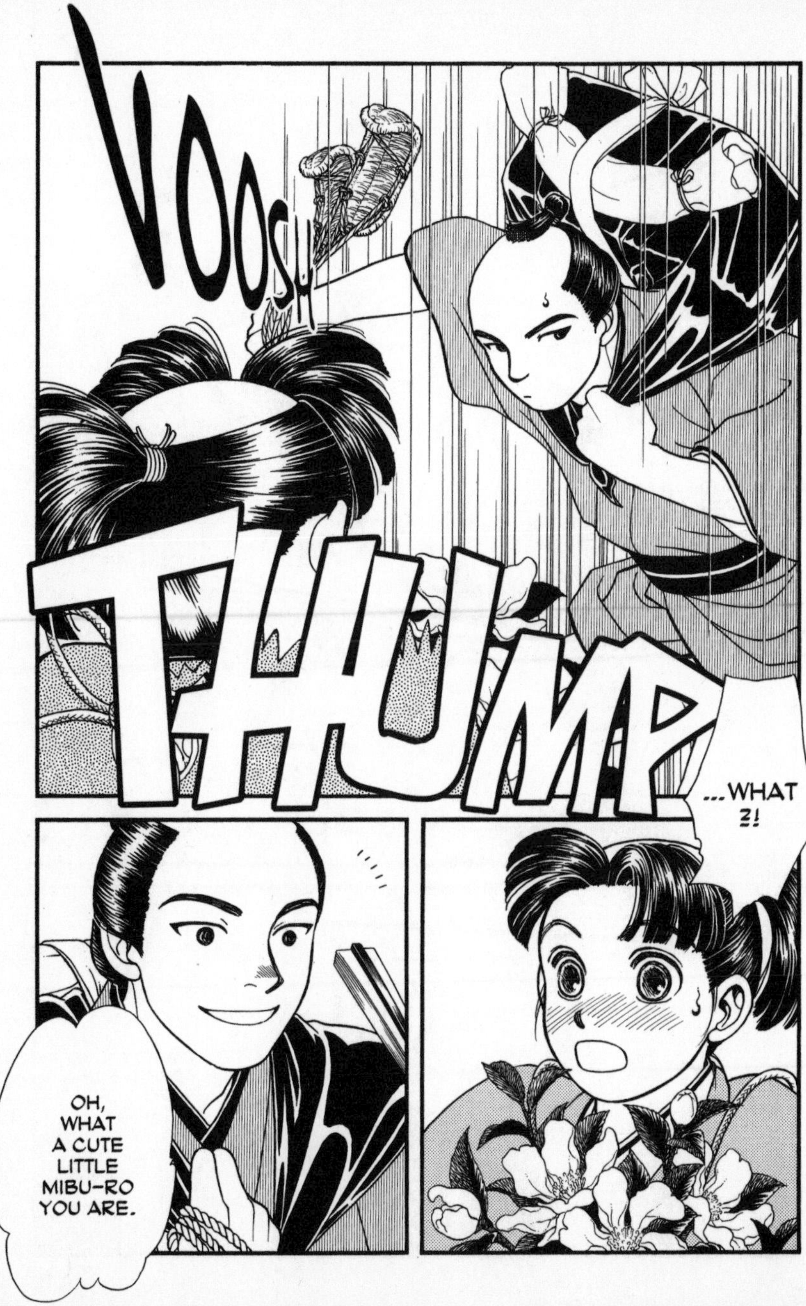
VOOSH
THUMP
...WHAT ?!
OH, WHAT A CUTE LITTLE MIBU-RO YOU ARE.

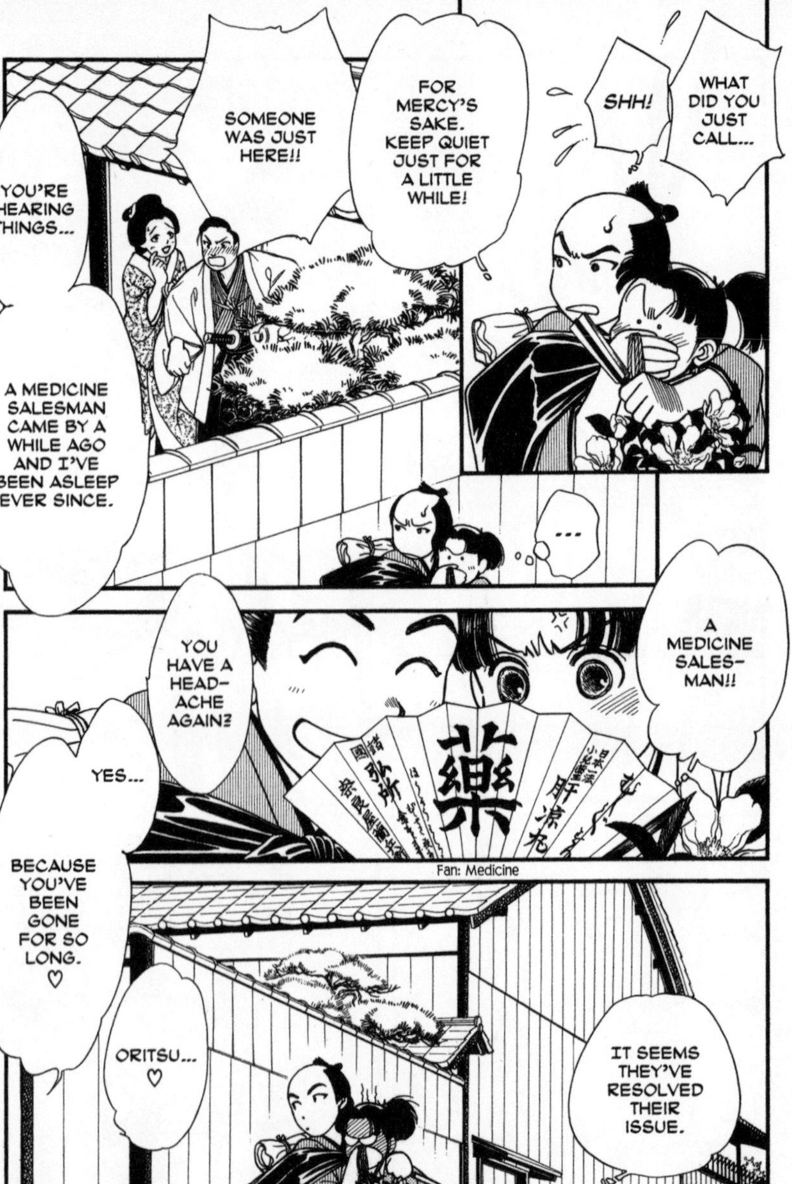
WHAT DID YOU JUST CALL...
SHH!
FOR MERCY'S SAKE. KEEP QUIET JUST FOR A LITTLE WHILE!
SOMEONE WAS JUST HERE!!
YOU'RE HEARING THINGS...
A MEDICINE SALESMAN CAME BY A WHILE AGO AND I'VE BEEN ASLEEP EVER SINCE.
...
A MEDICINE SALES-MAN!!
YOU HAVE A HEAD-ACHE AGAIN?
藥
YES...
BECAUSE YOU'VE BEEN GONE FOR SO LONG. ♡
ORITSU... ♡
IT SEEMS THEY'VE RESOLVED THEIR ISSUE.
Fan: Medicine

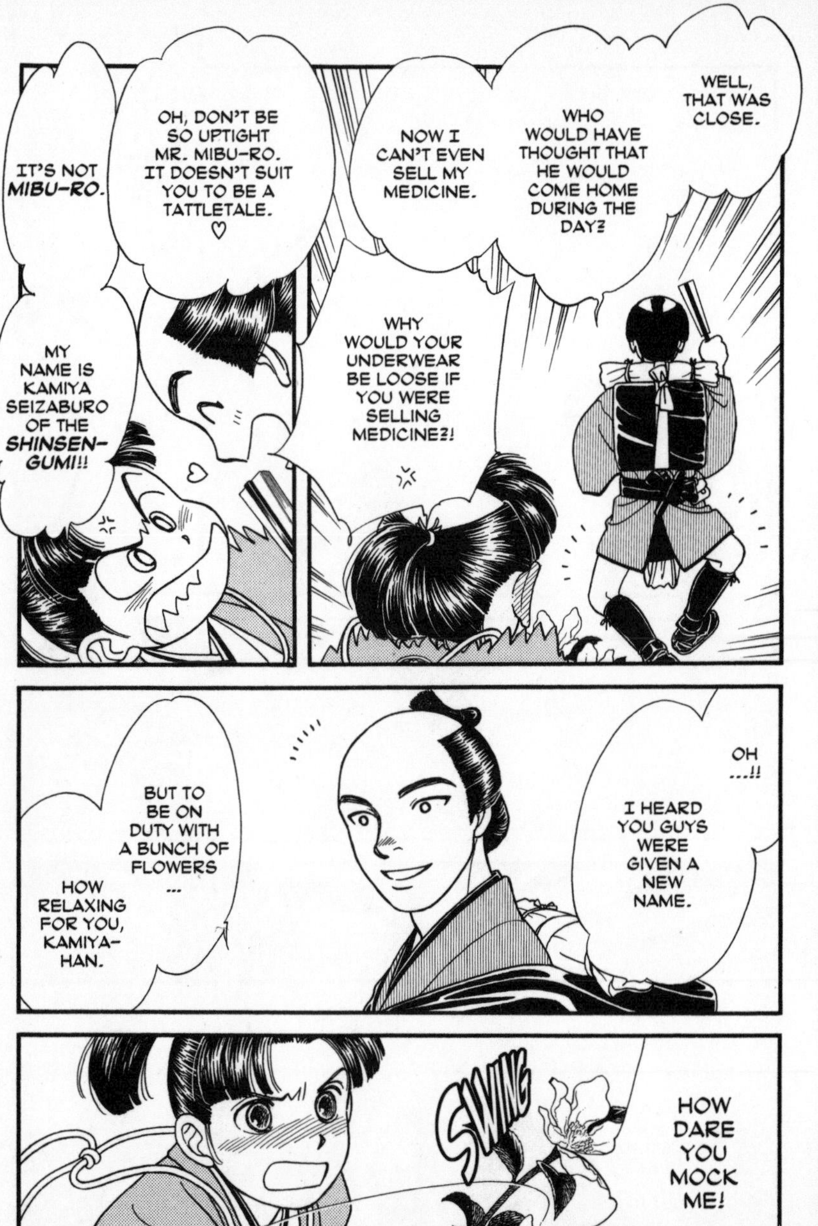
WELL, THAT WAS CLOSE.
WHO WOULD HAVE THOUGHT THAT HE WOULD COME HOME DURING THE DAY?
NOW I CAN'T EVEN SELL MY MEDICINE.
WHY WOULD YOUR UNDERWEAR BE LOOSE IF YOU WERE SELLING MEDICINE?!
OH, DON'T BE SO UPTIGHT MR. MIBU-RO. IT DOESN'T SUIT YOU TO BE A TATTLETALE. ♡
IT'S NOT *MIBU-RO*.
MY NAME IS KAMIYA SEIZABURO OF THE *SHINSEN-GUMI*!!
OH ...!!
I HEARD YOU GUYS WERE GIVEN A NEW NAME.
BUT TO BE ON DUTY WITH A BUNCH OF FLOWERS ...
HOW RELAXING FOR YOU, KAMIYA-HAN.
SWING
HOW DARE YOU MOCK ME!

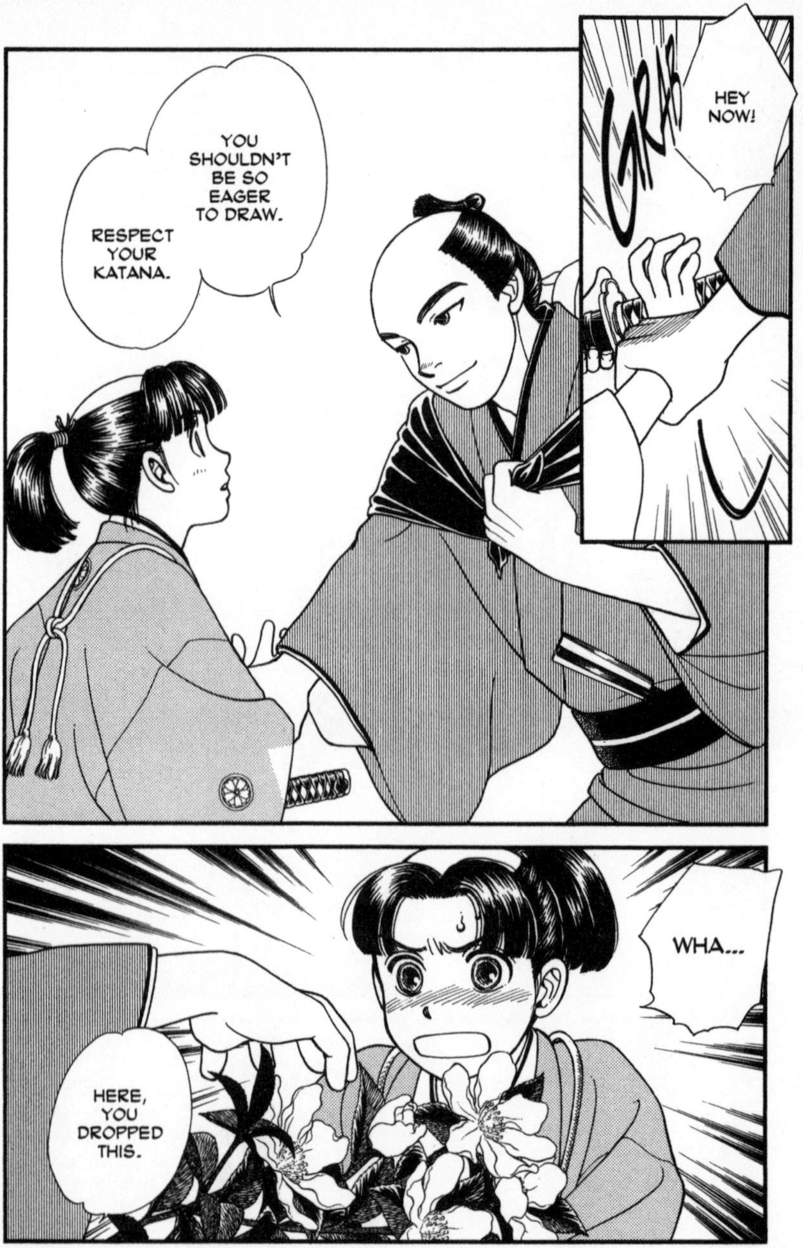
GRAB
HEY NOW!
YOU SHOULDN'T BE SO EAGER TO DRAW.
RESPECT YOUR KATANA.
WHA...
HERE, YOU DROPPED THIS.

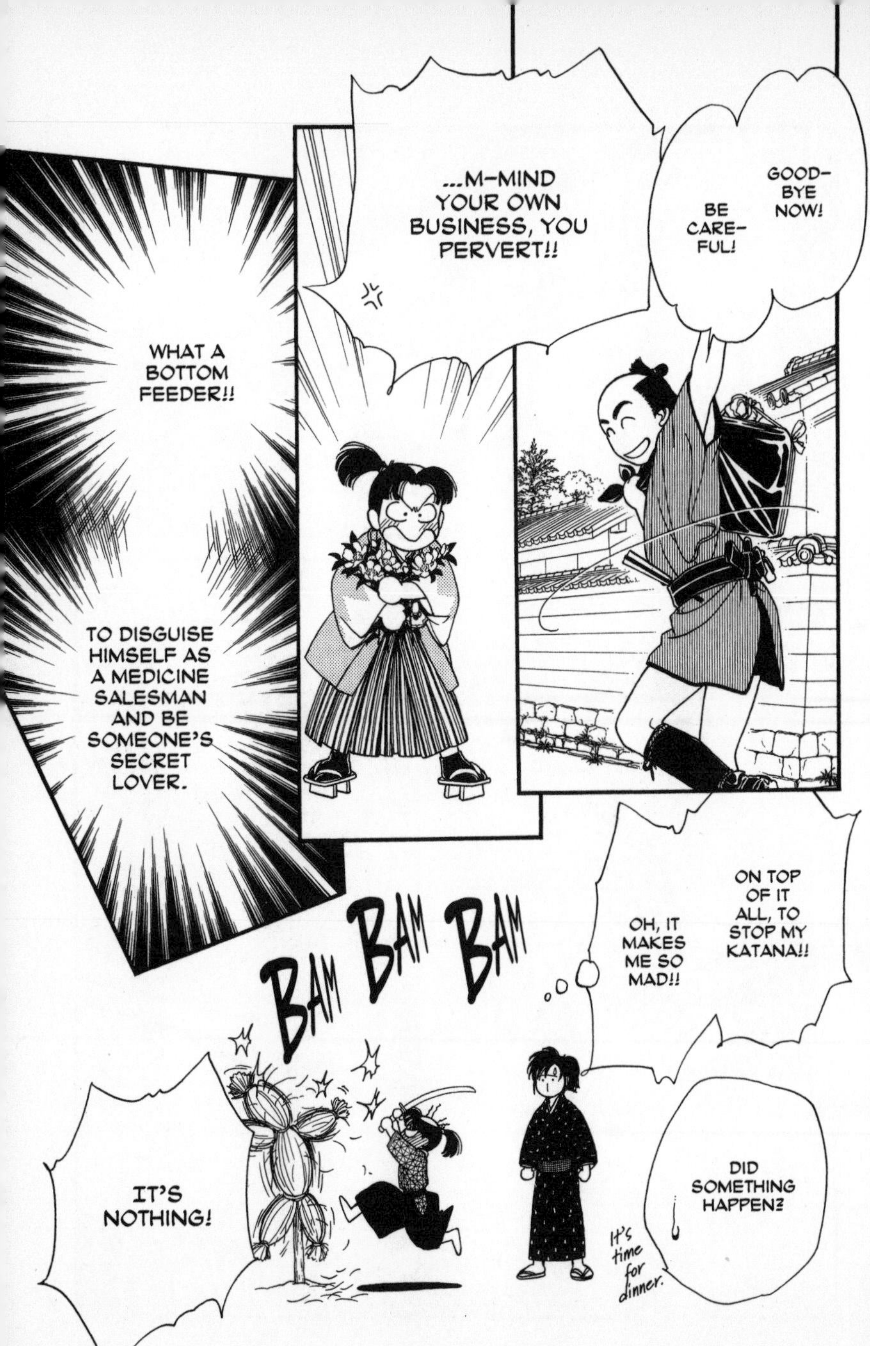
GOOD-BYE NOW!
BE CARE-FUL!
...M-MIND YOUR OWN BUSINESS, YOU PERVERT!!
WHAT A BOTTOM FEEDER!!
TO DISGUISE HIMSELF AS A MEDICINE SALESMAN AND BE SOMEONE'S SECRET LOVER.
ON TOP OF IT ALL, TO STOP MY KATANA!!
OH, IT MAKES ME SO MAD!!
BAM BAM BAM
DID SOMETHING HAPPEN?
It's time for dinner.
IT'S NOTHING!

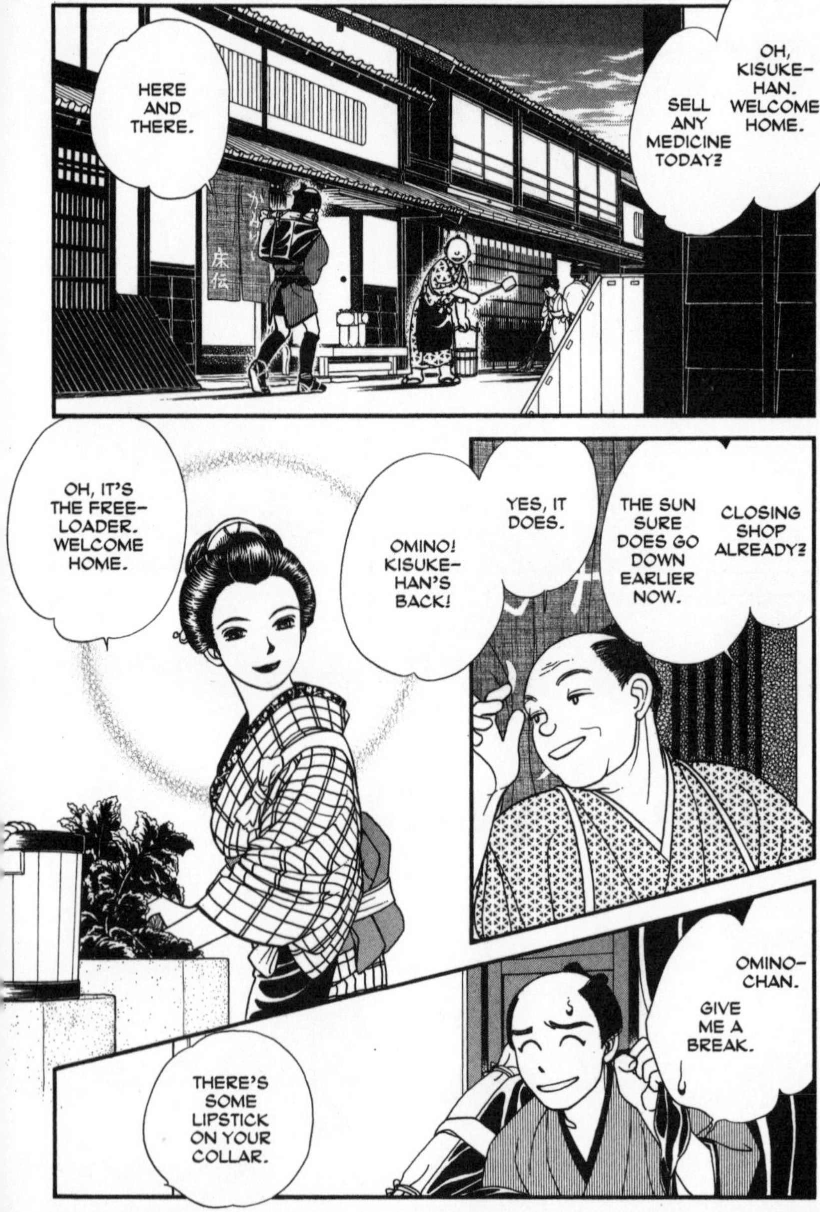
OH, KISUKE-HAN. WELCOME HOME.
SELL ANY MEDICINE TODAY?
HERE AND THERE.
CLOSING SHOP ALREADY?
THE SUN SURE DOES GO DOWN EARLIER NOW.
YES, IT DOES.
OMINO! KISUKE-HAN'S BACK!
OH, IT'S THE FREE-LOADER. WELCOME HOME.
OMINO-CHAN.
GIVE ME A BREAK.
THERE'S SOME LIPSTICK ON YOUR COLLAR.

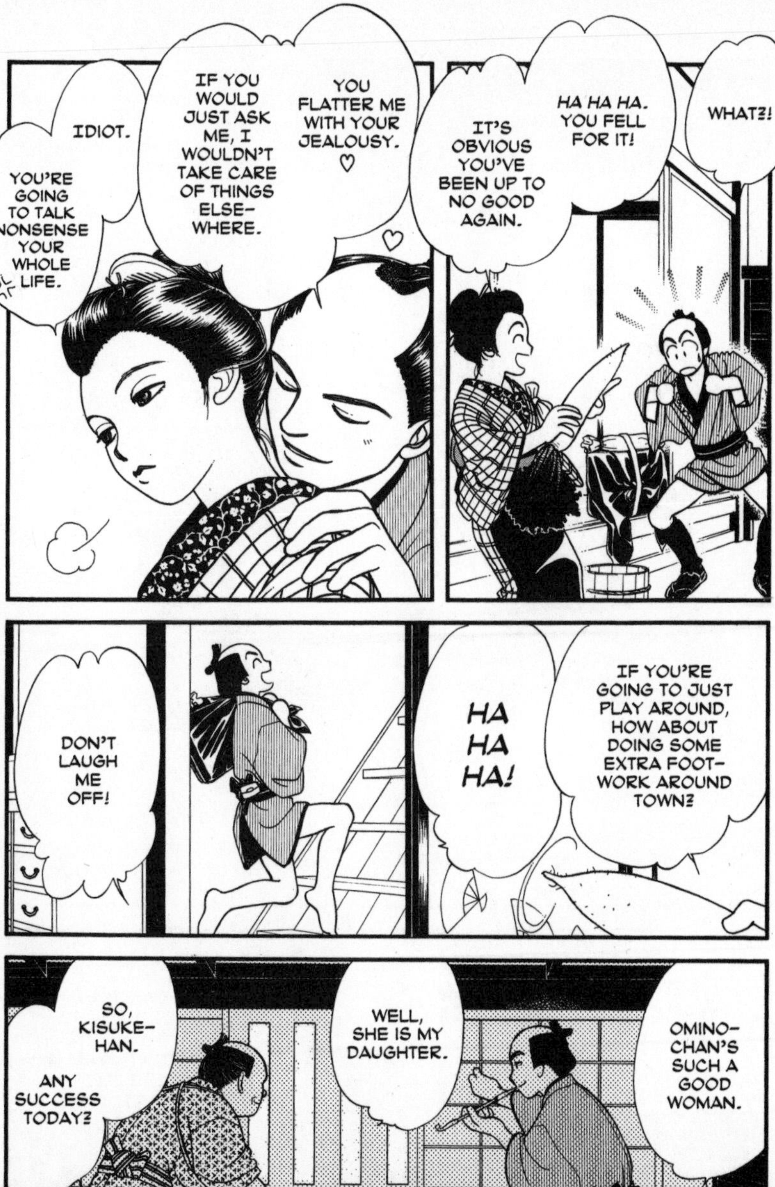
WHAT?!
HA HA HA. YOU FELL FOR IT!
IT'S OBVIOUS YOU'VE BEEN UP TO NO GOOD AGAIN.
YOU FLATTER ME WITH YOUR JEALOUSY. ♡
IF YOU WOULD JUST ASK ME, I WOULDN'T TAKE CARE OF THINGS ELSE-WHERE.
IDIOT.
YOU'RE GOING TO TALK NONSENSE YOUR WHOLE LIFE.
IF YOU'RE GOING TO JUST PLAY AROUND, HOW ABOUT DOING SOME EXTRA FOOT-WORK AROUND TOWN?
HA HA HA!
DON'T LAUGH ME OFF!
OMINO-CHAN'S SUCH A GOOD WOMAN.
WELL, SHE IS MY DAUGHTER.
SO, KISUKE-HAN.
ANY SUCCESS TODAY?

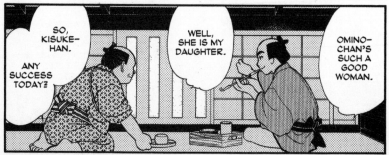

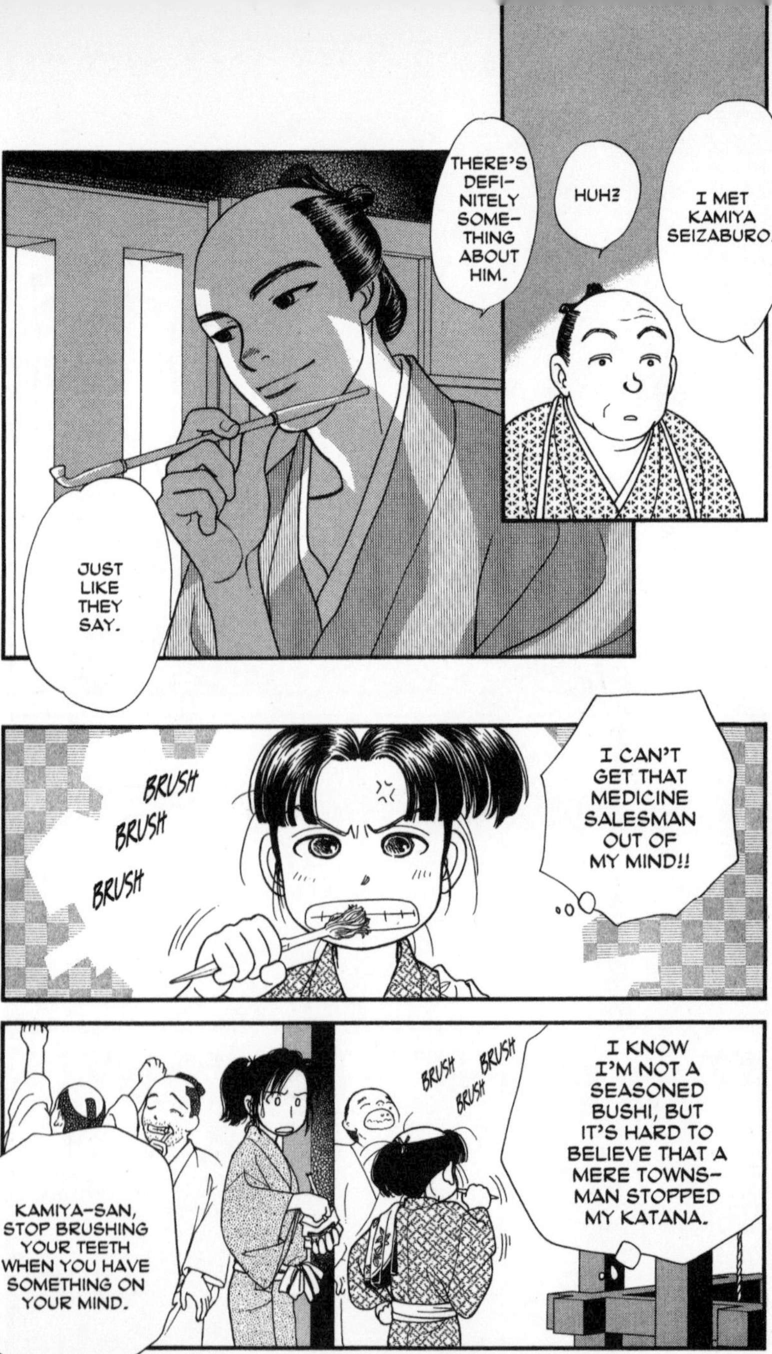
I MET KAMIYA SEIZABURO.
HUH?
THERE'S DEFINITELY SOMETHING ABOUT HIM.
JUST LIKE THEY SAY.
I CAN'T GET THAT MEDICINE SALESMAN OUT OF MY MIND!!
BRUSH
BRUSH
BRUSH
I KNOW I'M NOT A SEASONED BUSHI, BUT IT'S HARD TO BELIEVE THAT A MERE TOWNSMAN STOPPED MY KATANA.
BRUSH
BRUSH
BRUSH
KAMIYA-SAN, STOP BRUSHING YOUR TEETH WHEN YOU HAVE SOMETHING ON YOUR MIND.

You've grown into such a man.♪

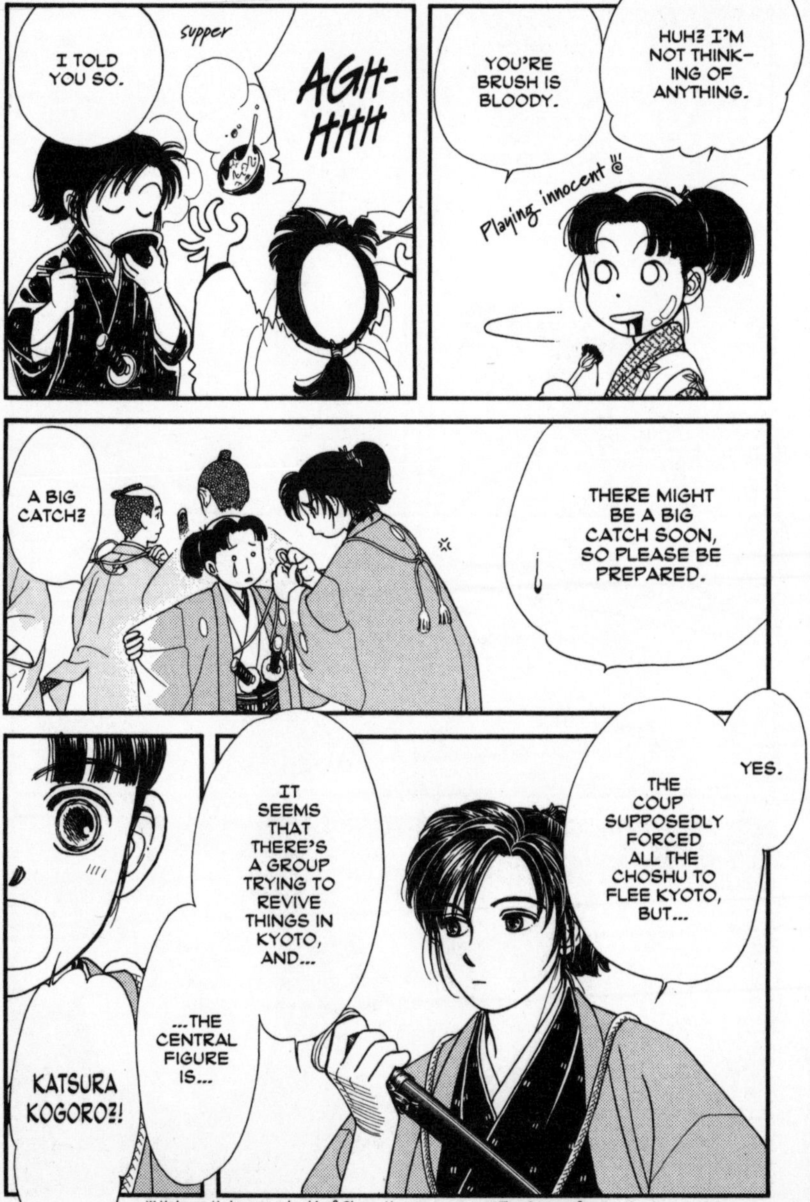
HUH? I'M NOT THINKING OF ANYTHING.
YOU'RE BRUSH IS BLOODY.
Playing innocent!!
AGH-HHH
supper
I TOLD YOU SO.
THERE MIGHT BE A BIG CATCH SOON, SO PLEASE BE PREPARED.
A BIG CATCH?
YES.
THE COUP SUPPOSEDLY FORCED ALL THE CHOSHU TO FLEE KYOTO, BUT...
IT SEEMS THAT THERE'S A GROUP TRYING TO REVIVE THINGS IN KYOTO, AND...
...THE CENTRAL FIGURE IS...
KATSURA KOGORO?!

※ Katsura Koto was a bushi of Chosu. He was a leader-like figure among the Sonjo bushi.

※ The Coup refers to the August 18th Coup.

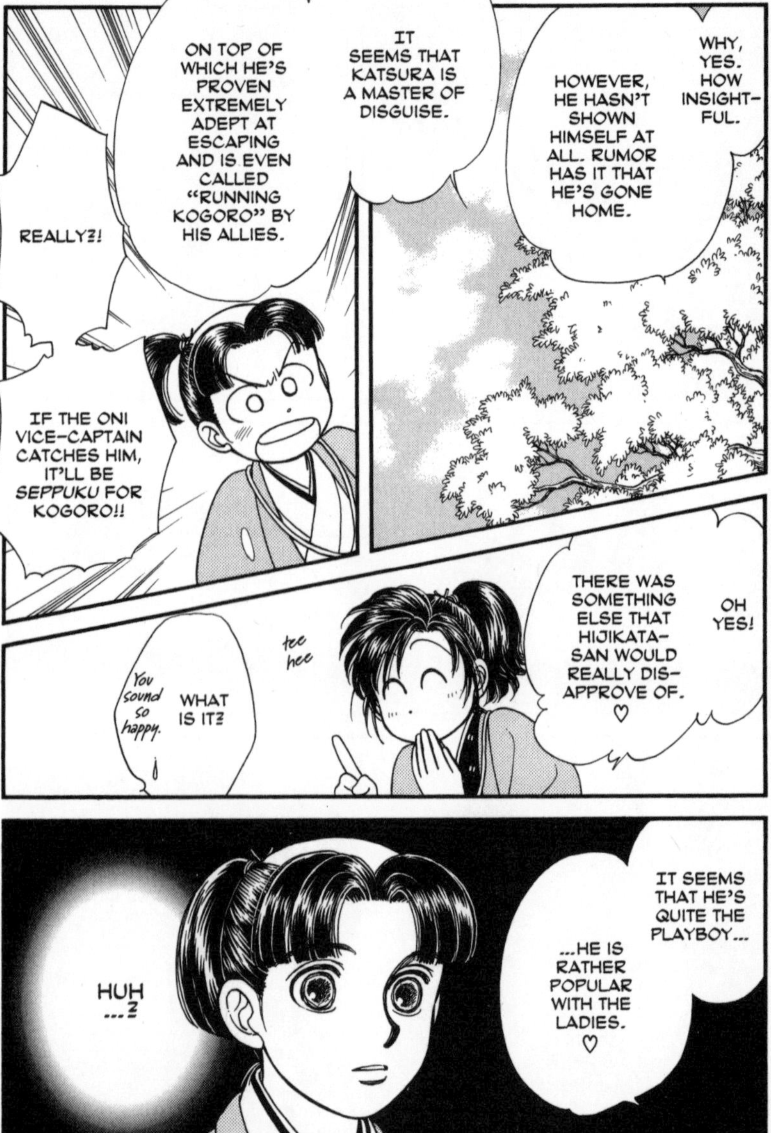
WHY, YES. HOW INSIGHT-FUL.
HOWEVER, HE HASN'T SHOWN HIMSELF AT ALL. RUMOR HAS IT THAT HE'S GONE HOME.
IT SEEMS THAT KATSURA IS A MASTER OF DISGUISE.
ON TOP OF WHICH HE'S PROVEN EXTREMELY ADEPT AT ESCAPING AND IS EVEN CALLED "RUNNING KOGORO" BY HIS ALLIES.
REALLY?!
IF THE ONI VICE-CAPTAIN CATCHES HIM, IT'LL BE *SEPPUKU* FOR KOGORO!!
OH YES!
THERE WAS SOMETHING ELSE THAT HIJIKATA-SAN WOULD REALLY DIS-APPROVE OF. ♡
tee hee
WHAT IS IT?
You sound so happy.
IT SEEMS THAT HE'S QUITE THE PLAYBOY...
...HE IS RATHER POPULAR WITH THE LADIES. ♡
HUH ...?

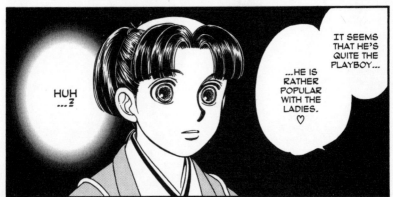

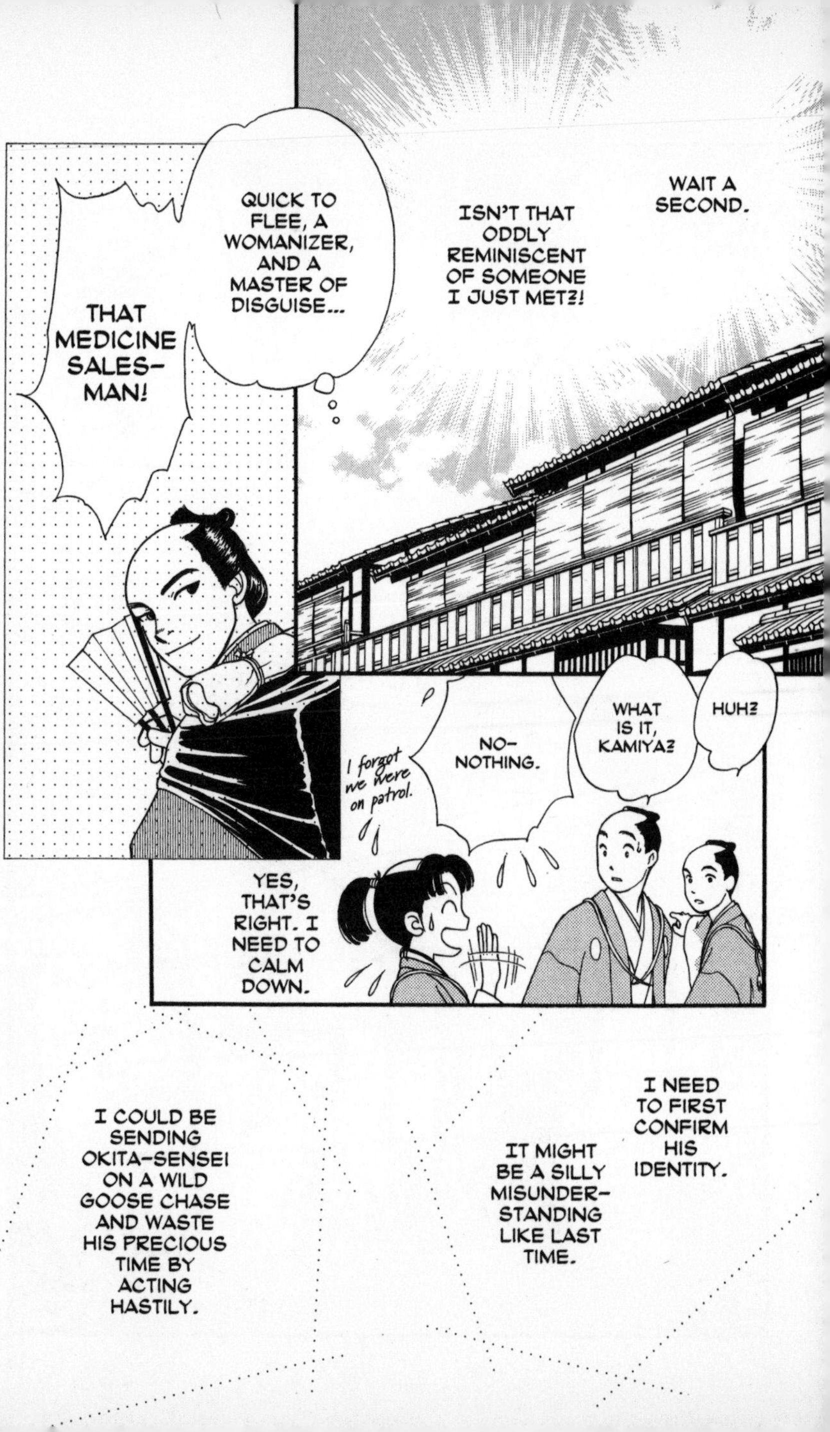
WAIT A SECOND.
ISN'T THAT ODDLY REMINISCENT OF SOMEONE I JUST MET?!
QUICK TO FLEE, A WOMANIZER, AND A MASTER OF DISGUISE...
THAT MEDICINE SALES-MAN!
HUH?
WHAT IS IT, KAMIYA?
NO-NOTHING.
I forgot we were on patrol.
YES, THAT'S RIGHT. I NEED TO CALM DOWN.
I NEED TO FIRST CONFIRM HIS IDENTITY.
IT MIGHT BE A SILLY MISUNDER-STANDING LIKE LAST TIME.
I COULD BE SENDING OKITA-SENSEI ON A WILD GOOSE CHASE AND WASTE HIS PRECIOUS TIME BY ACTING HASTILY.

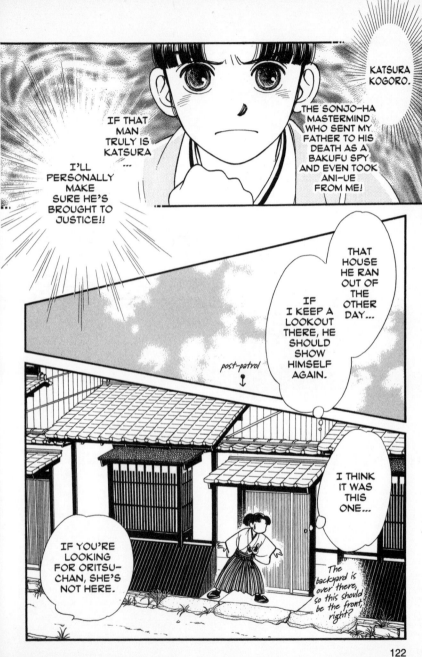

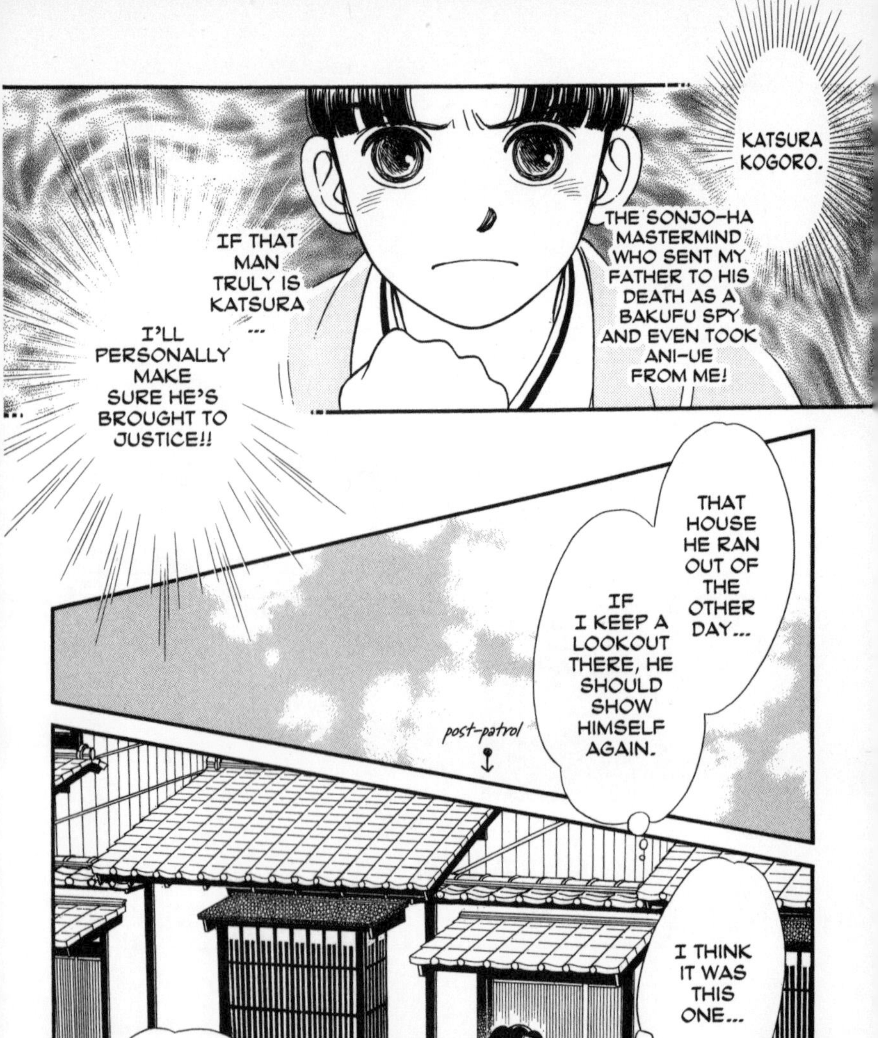
KATSURA KOGORO.
THE SONJO-HA MASTERMIND WHO SENT MY FATHER TO HIS DEATH AS A BAKUFU SPY AND EVEN TOOK ANI-UE FROM ME!
IF THAT MAN TRULY IS KATSURA ...
I'LL PERSONALLY MAKE SURE HE'S BROUGHT TO JUSTICE!!
THAT HOUSE HE RAN OUT OF THE OTHER DAY...
IF I KEEP A LOOKOUT THERE, HE SHOULD SHOW HIMSELF AGAIN.
post-patrol
I THINK IT WAS THIS ONE...
The backyard is over there, so this should be the front, right?
IF YOU'RE LOOKING FOR ORITSU-CHAN, SHE'S NOT HERE.

※A Tea House is the equivalent of a present-day small restaurant which offers not only professional hostesses, but where regular waitresses also work.

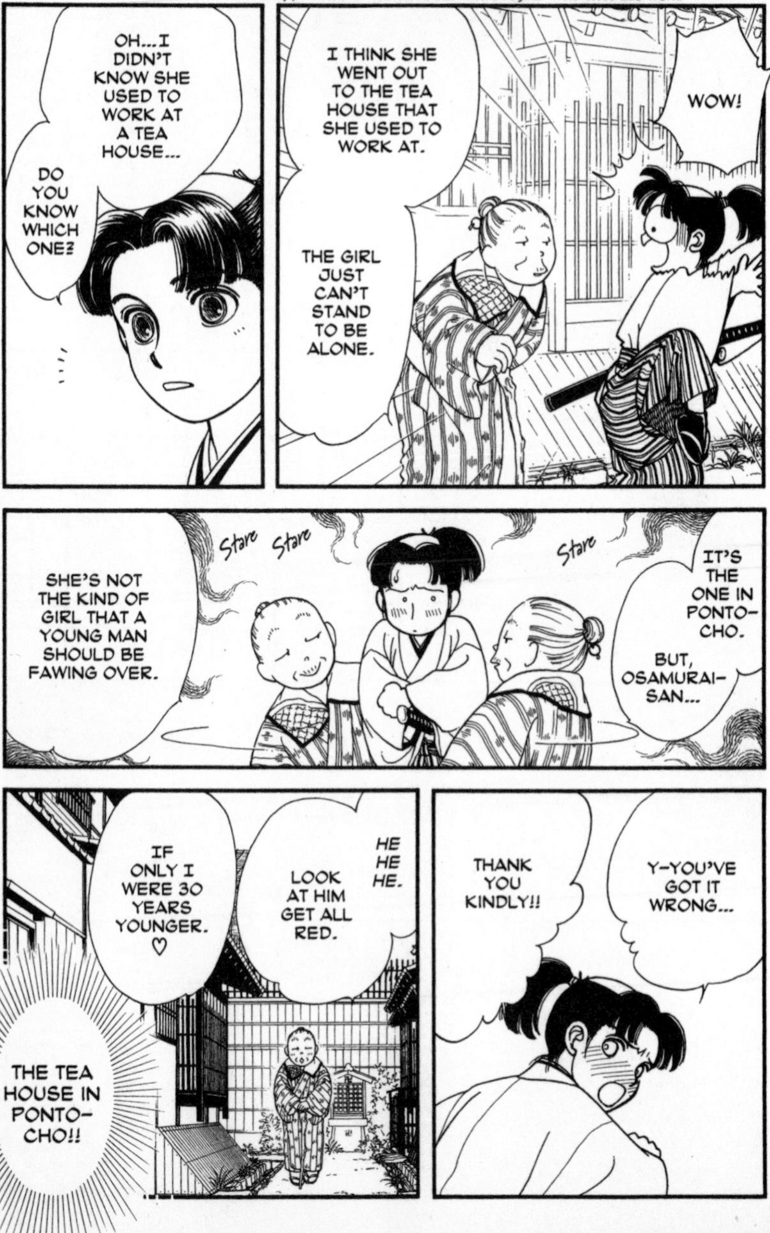
WOW!
I THINK SHE WENT OUT TO THE TEA HOUSE THAT SHE USED TO WORK AT.
THE GIRL JUST CAN'T STAND TO BE ALONE.
OH...I DIDN'T KNOW SHE USED TO WORK AT A TEA HOUSE...
DO YOU KNOW WHICH ONE?
IT'S THE ONE IN PONTO-CHO.
BUT, OSAMURAI-SAN...
Stare
Stare
Stare
SHE'S NOT THE KIND OF GIRL THAT A YOUNG MAN SHOULD BE FAWING OVER.
Y-YOU'VE GOT IT WRONG...
THANK YOU KINDLY!!
HE HE HE.
LOOK AT HIM GET ALL RED.
IF ONLY I WERE 30 YEARS YOUNGER. ♡
THE TEA HOUSE IN PONTO-CHO!!

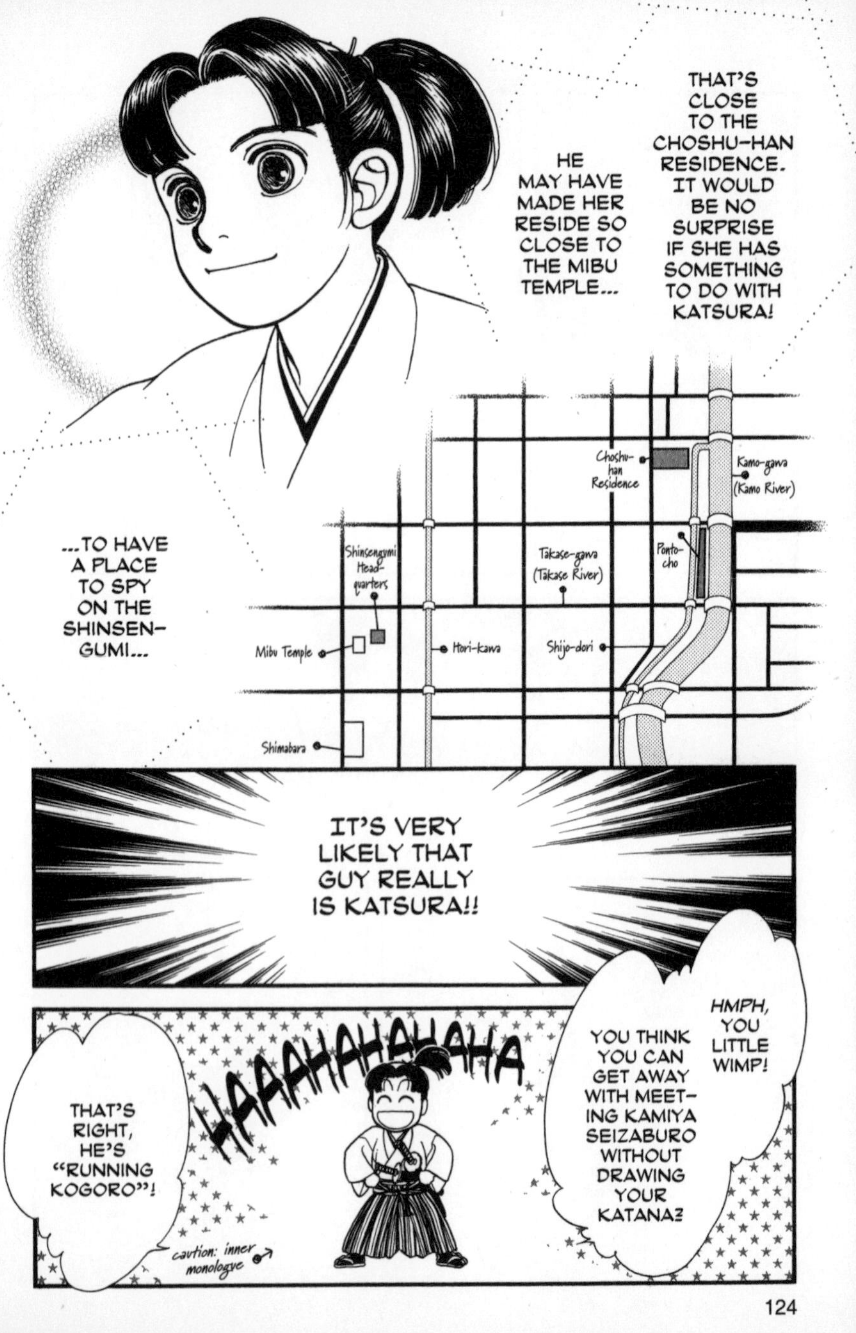
THAT'S CLOSE TO THE CHOSHU-HAN RESIDENCE. IT WOULD BE NO SURPRISE IF SHE HAS SOMETHING TO DO WITH KATSURA!
HE MAY HAVE MADE HER RESIDE SO CLOSE TO THE MIBU TEMPLE...
...TO HAVE A PLACE TO SPY ON THE SHINSEN-GUMI...
Choshu-han Residence
Kamo-gawa (Kamo River)
Ponto-cho
Takase-gawa (Takase River)
Shinsengumi Head-quarters
Mibu Temple
Hori-kawa
Shijo-dori
Shimabara
IT'S VERY LIKELY THAT GUY REALLY IS KATSURA!!
HMPH, YOU LITTLE WIMP!
YOU THINK YOU CAN GET AWAY WITH MEET-ING KAMIYA SEIZABURO WITHOUT DRAWING YOUR KATANA?
HAAAHAHAHAHA
THAT'S RIGHT, HE'S "RUNNING KOGORO"!
caution: inner monologue

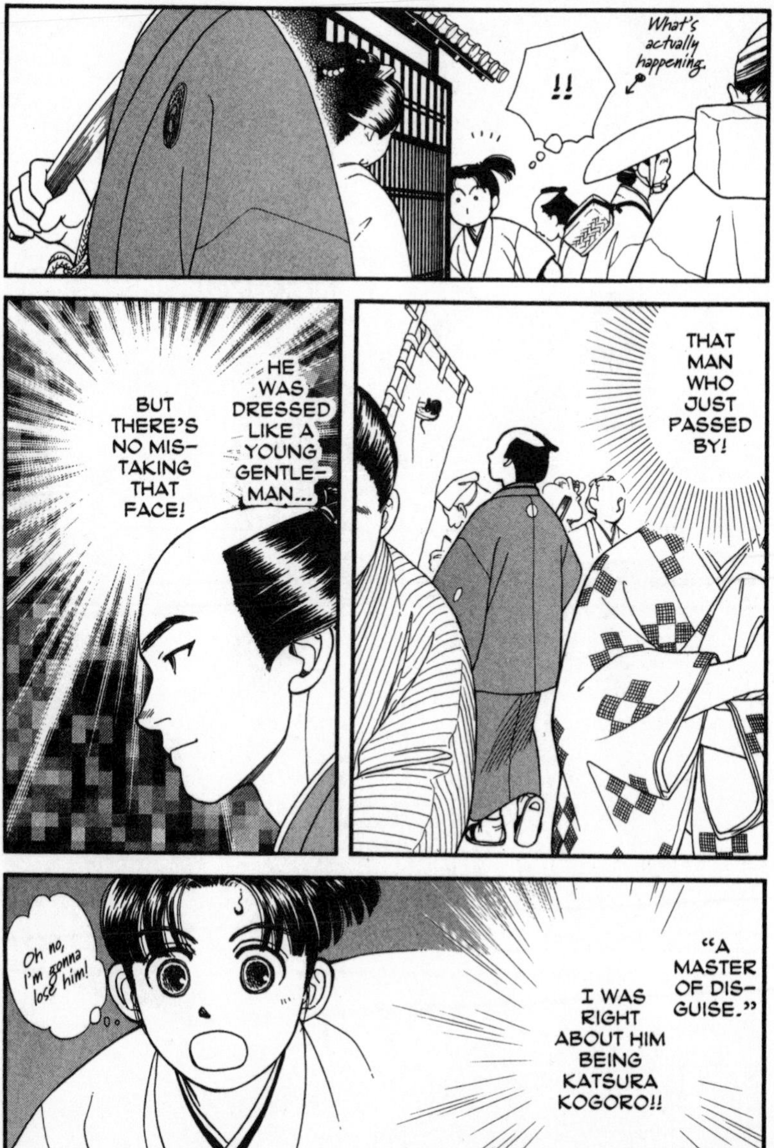
What's actually happening.
!!
THAT MAN WHO JUST PASSED BY!
HE WAS DRESSED LIKE A YOUNG GENTLEMAN...
BUT THERE'S NO MISTAKING THAT FACE!
"A MASTER OF DISGUISE."
I WAS RIGHT ABOUT HIM BEING KATSURA KOGORO!!
Oh no, I'm gonna lose him!

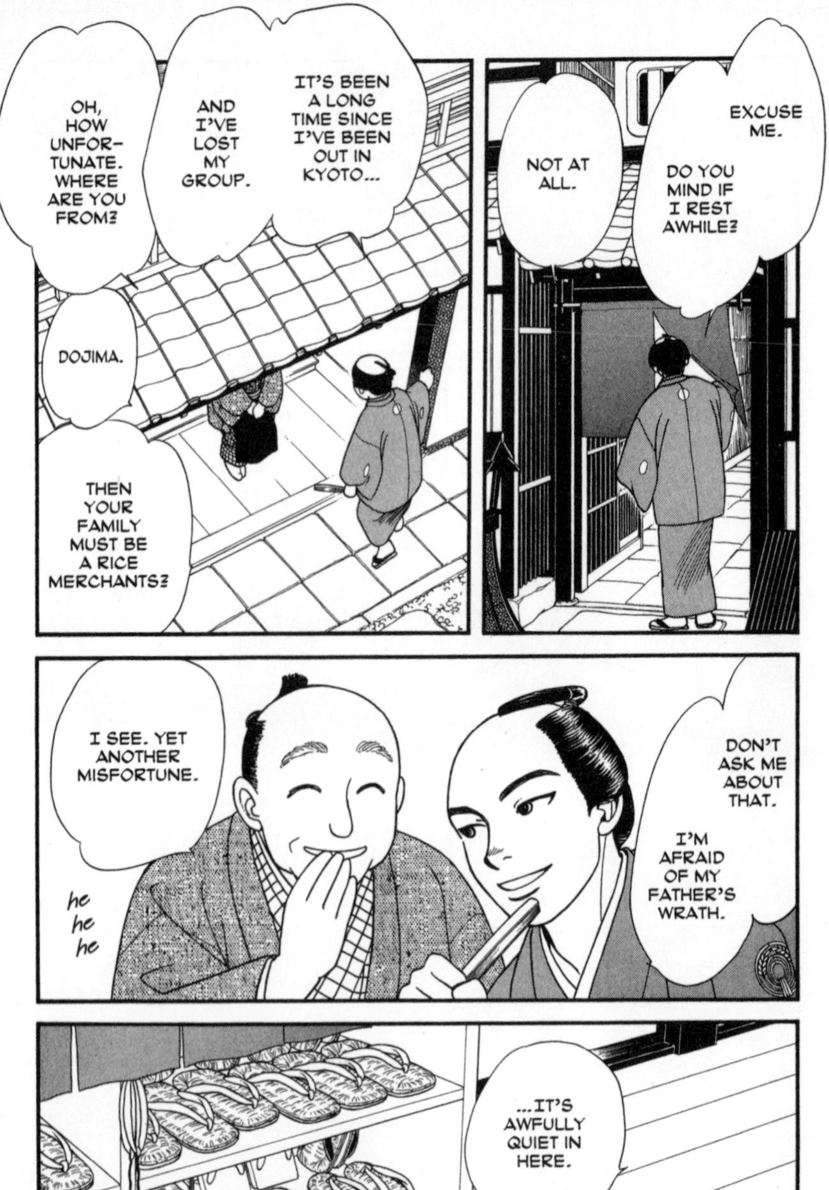
EXCUSE ME.
DO YOU MIND IF I REST AWHILE?
NOT AT ALL.
IT'S BEEN A LONG TIME SINCE I'VE BEEN OUT IN KYOTO...
AND I'VE LOST MY GROUP.
OH, HOW UNFOR-TUNATE. WHERE ARE YOU FROM?
DOJIMA.
THEN YOUR FAMILY MUST BE A RICE MERCHANTS?
DON'T ASK ME ABOUT THAT.
I'M AFRAID OF MY FATHER'S WRATH.
I SEE. YET ANOTHER MISFORTUNE.
he he he
...IT'S AWFULLY QUIET IN HERE.

※ Osaka Dojima had the largest rice market in Japan at that time.

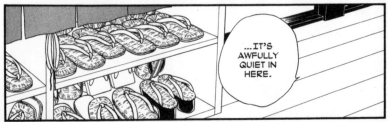

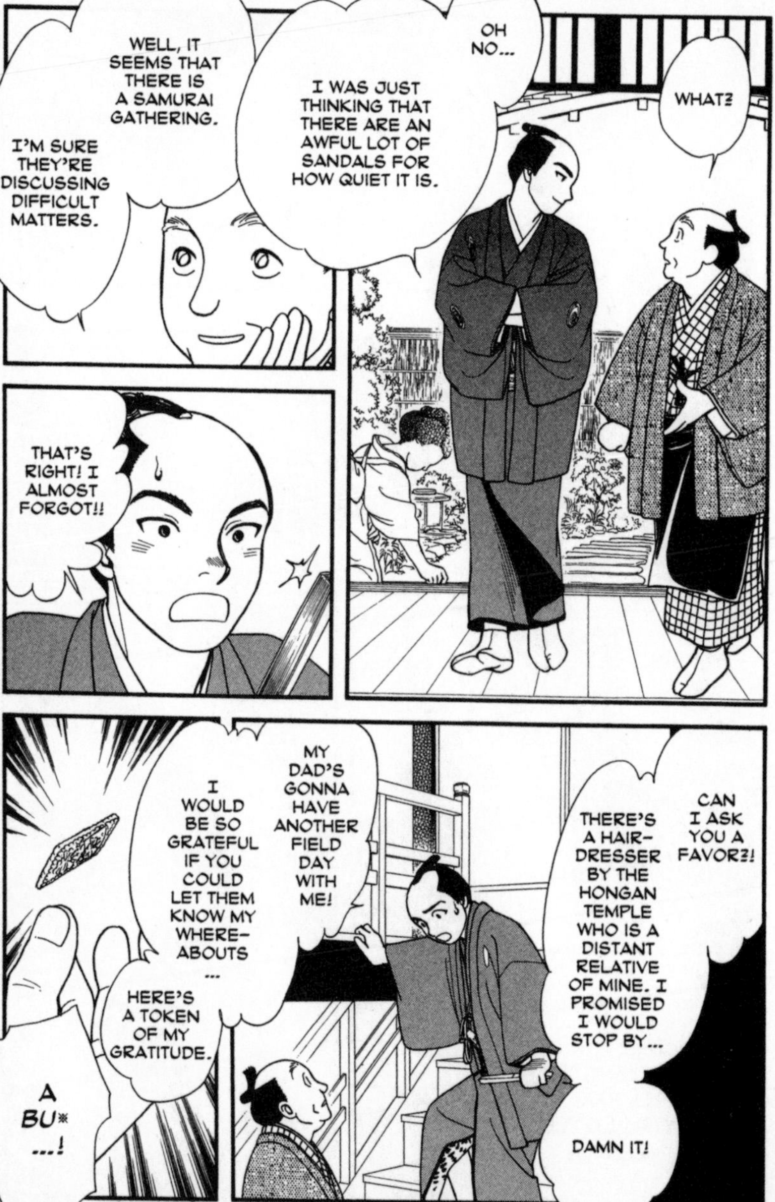
WHAT?
OH NO...
I WAS JUST THINKING THAT THERE ARE AN AWFUL LOT OF SANDALS FOR HOW QUIET IT IS.
WELL, IT SEEMS THAT THERE IS A SAMURAI GATHERING.
I'M SURE THEY'RE DISCUSSING DIFFICULT MATTERS.
THAT'S RIGHT! I ALMOST FORGOT!!
CAN I ASK YOU A FAVOR?!
THERE'S A HAIR-DRESSER BY THE HONGAN TEMPLE WHO IS A DISTANT RELATIVE OF MINE. I PROMISED I WOULD STOP BY...
DAMN IT!
MY DAD'S GONNA HAVE ANOTHER FIELD DAY WITH ME!
I WOULD BE SO GRATEFUL IF YOU COULD LET THEM KNOW MY WHERE-ABOUTS ...
HERE'S A TOKEN OF MY GRATITUDE.
A BU※ ...!

※A quarter of a ryo, which would be the equivalent of 20,000 yen ($200) in the present day.

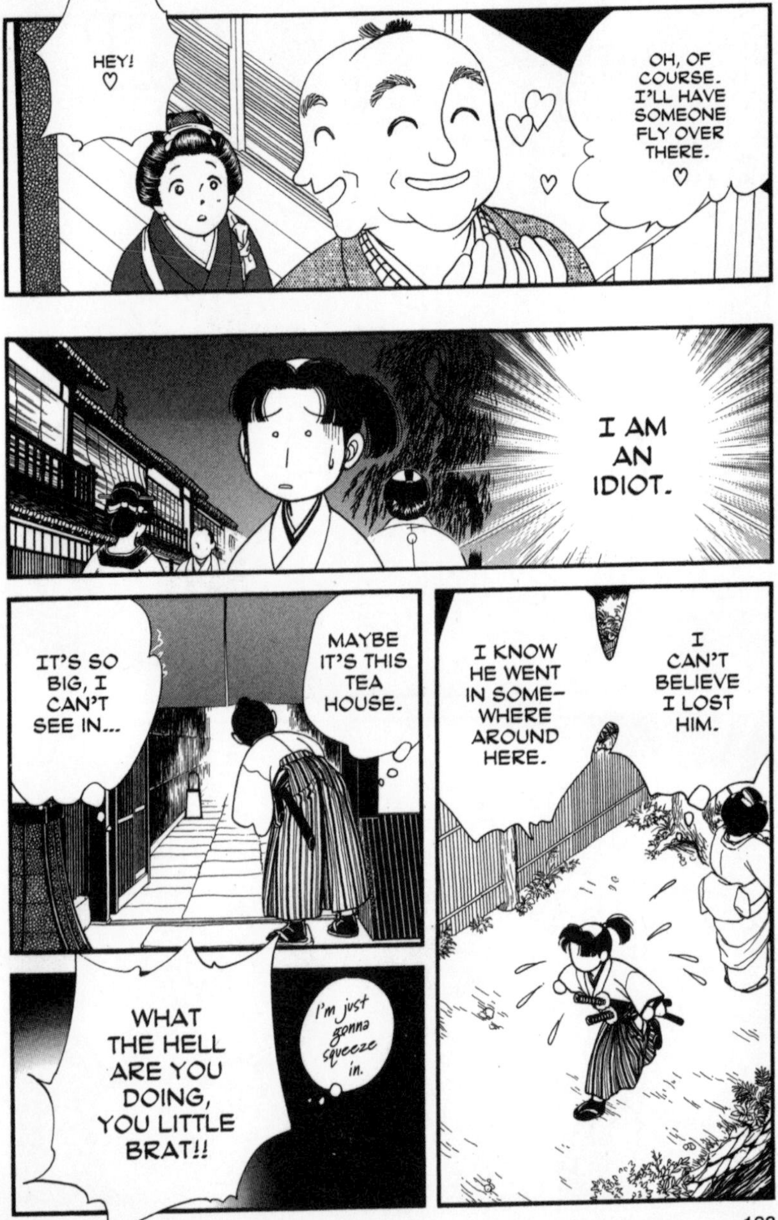
OH, OF COURSE. I'LL HAVE SOMEONE FLY OVER THERE. ♡
HEY! ♡
I AM AN IDIOT.
I CAN'T BELIEVE I LOST HIM.
I KNOW HE WENT IN SOME-WHERE AROUND HERE.
MAYBE IT'S THIS TEA HOUSE.
IT'S SO BIG, I CAN'T SEE IN...
I'm just gonna squeeze in.
WHAT THE HELL ARE YOU DOING, YOU LITTLE BRAT!!

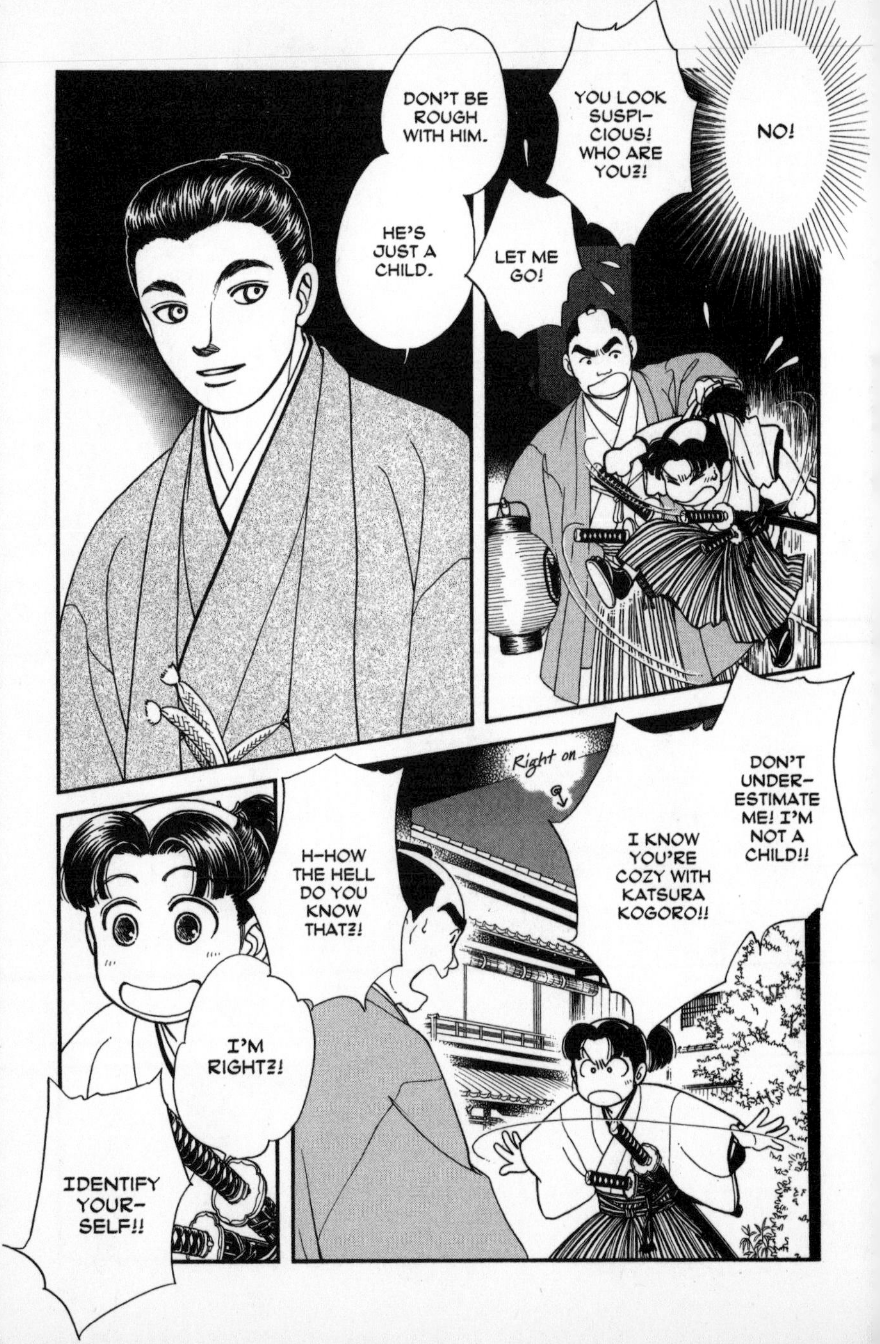
NO!
YOU LOOK SUSPICIOUS! WHO ARE YOU?!
LET ME GO!
DON'T BE ROUGH WITH HIM.
HE'S JUST A CHILD.
DON'T UNDERESTIMATE ME! I'M NOT A CHILD!!
I KNOW YOU'RE COZY WITH KATSURA KOGORO!!
Right on
H-HOW THE HELL DO YOU KNOW THAT?!
I'M RIGHT?!
IDENTIFY YOURSELF!!

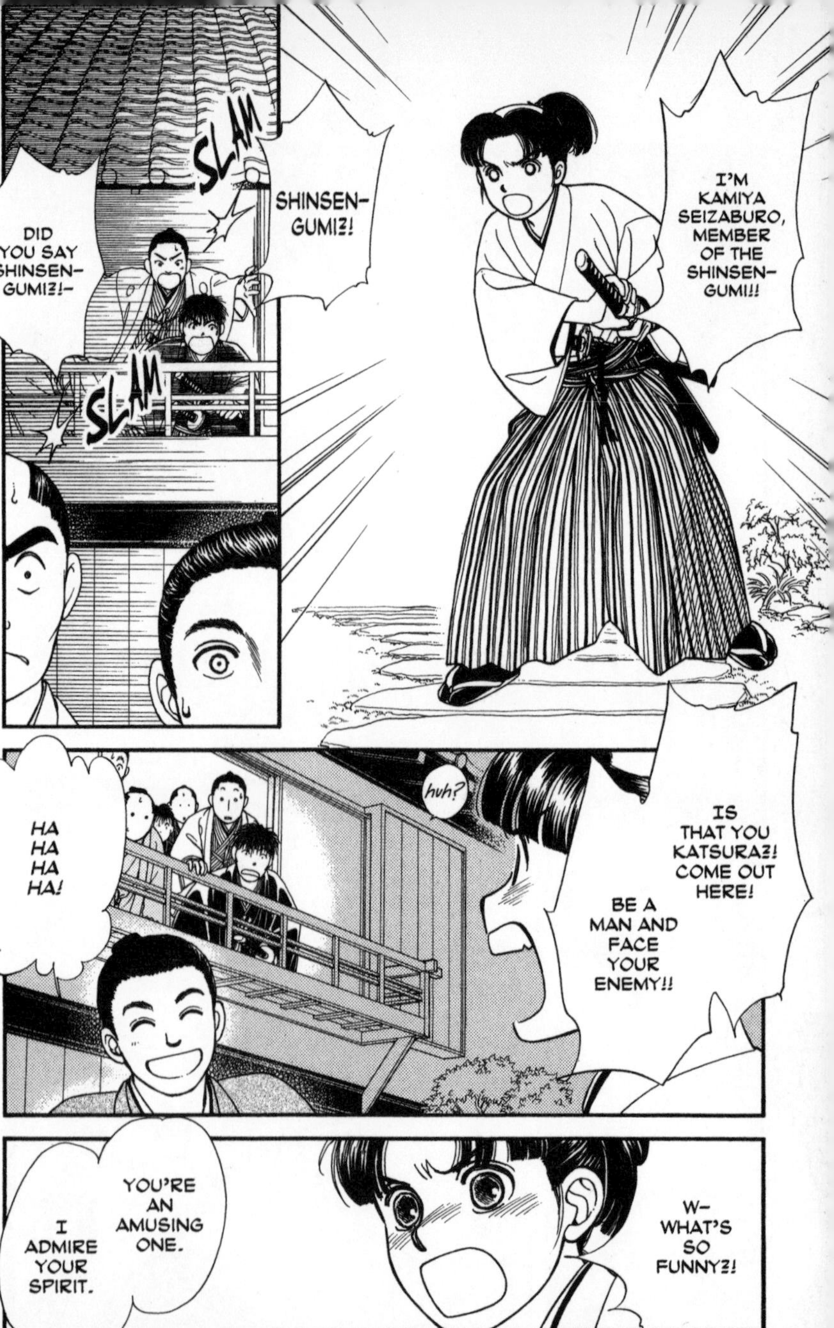

I'M KAMIYA SEIZABURO, MEMBER OF THE SHINSEN-GUMI!!
SLAM
SHINSEN-GUMI!?
DID YOU SAY SHINSEN-GUMI!?–
SLAM
IS THAT YOU KATSURA!? COME OUT HERE!
BE A MAN AND FACE YOUR ENEMY!!
huh?
HA HA HA HA!
W–WHAT'S SO FUNNY!?
YOU'RE AN AMUSING ONE.
I ADMIRE YOUR SPIRIT.

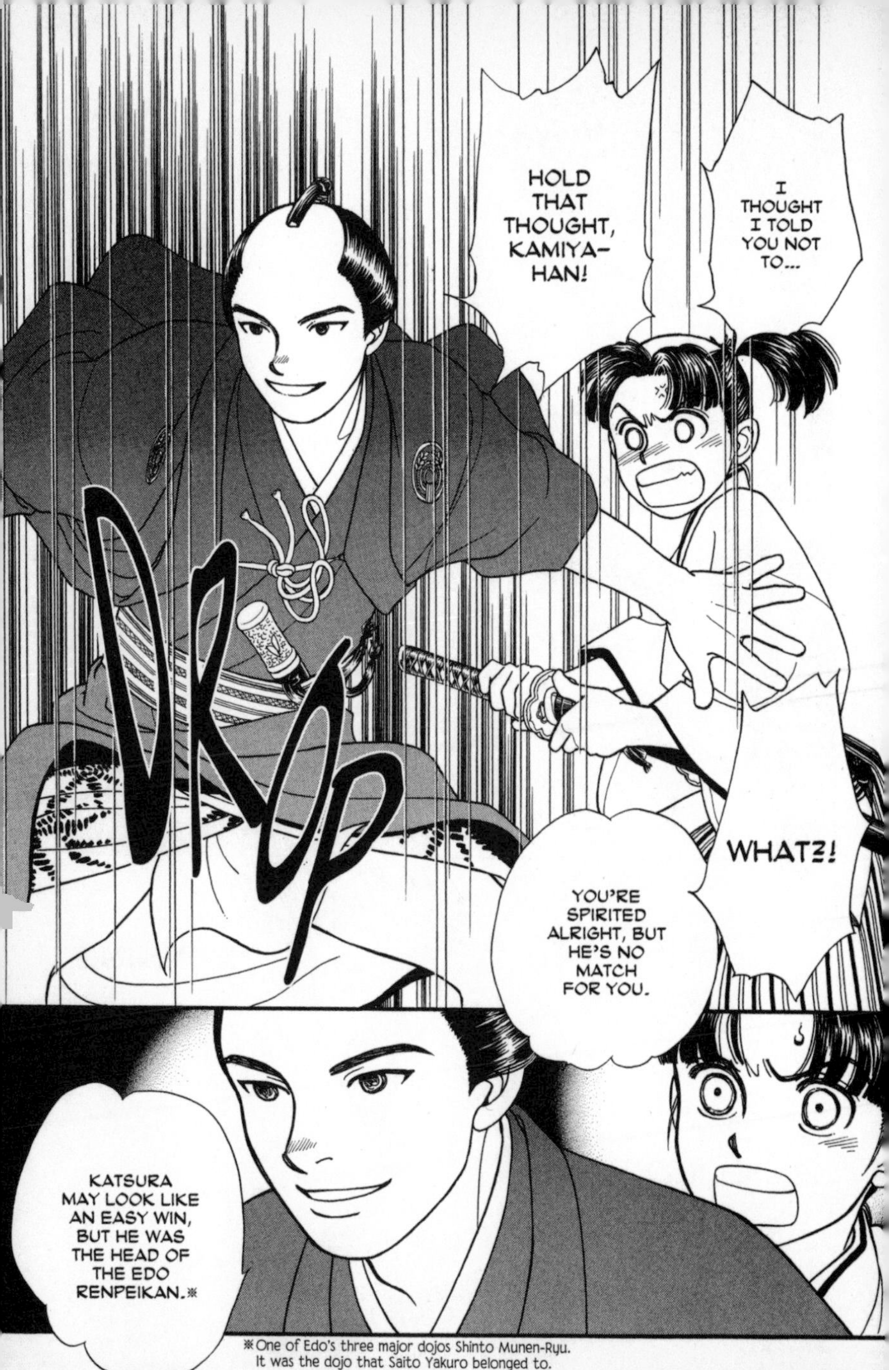
I THOUGHT I TOLD YOU NOT TO...
HOLD THAT THOUGHT, KAMIYA-HAN!
DROP
WHAT?!
YOU'RE SPIRITED ALRIGHT, BUT HE'S NO MATCH FOR YOU.
KATSURA MAY LOOK LIKE AN EASY WIN, BUT HE WAS THE HEAD OF THE EDO RENPEIKAN.※

※One of Edo's three major dojos Shinto Munen-Ryu.
It was the dojo that Saito Yakuro belonged to.

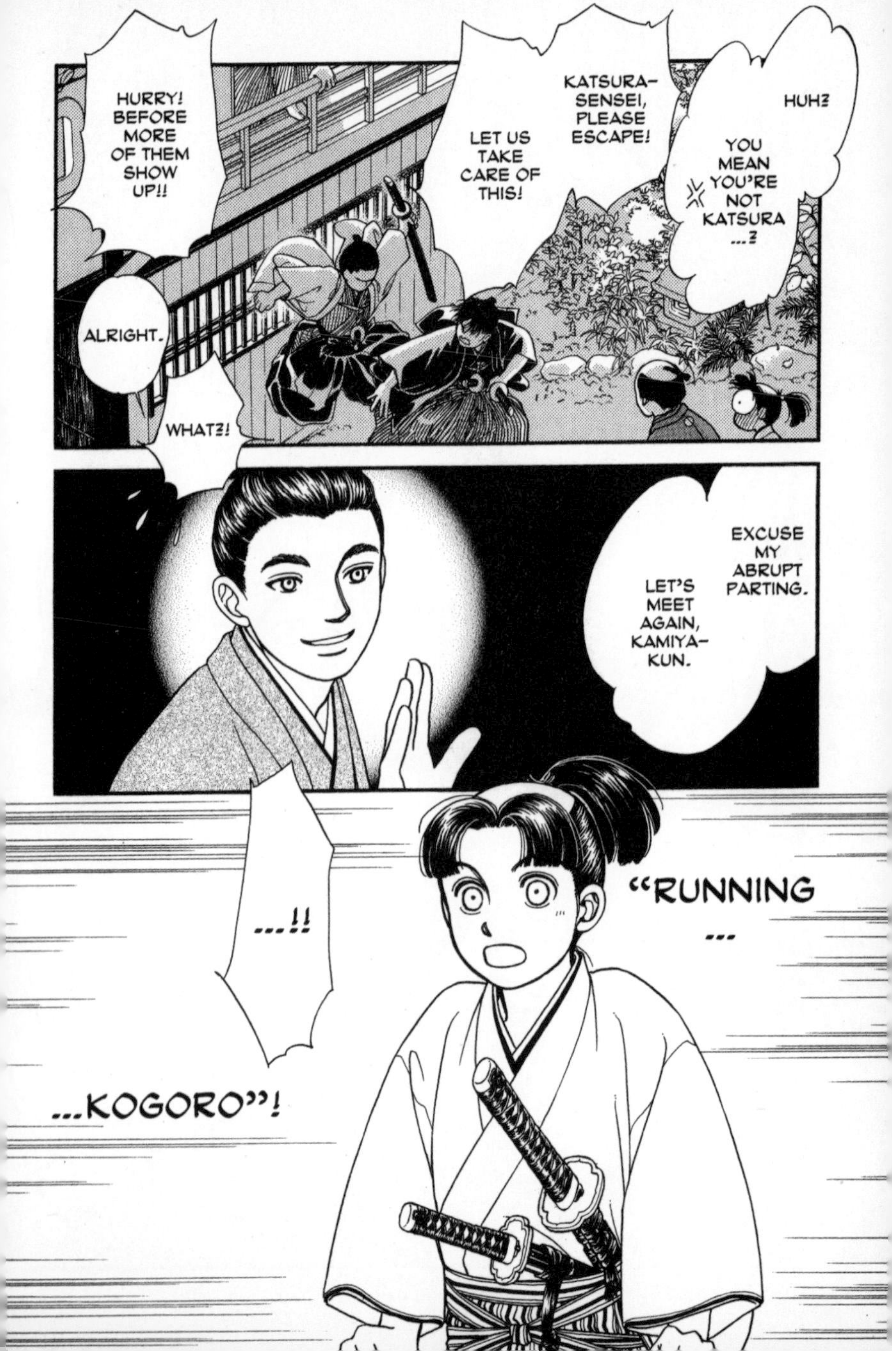
KATSURA-SENSEI, PLEASE ESCAPE!
LET US TAKE CARE OF THIS!
HURRY! BEFORE MORE OF THEM SHOW UP!!
ALRIGHT.
HUH?
YOU MEAN YOU'RE NOT KATSURA ...?
WHAT?!
EXCUSE MY ABRUPT PARTING.
LET'S MEET AGAIN, KAMIYA-KUN.
"RUNNING ...
...!!
...KOGORO"!

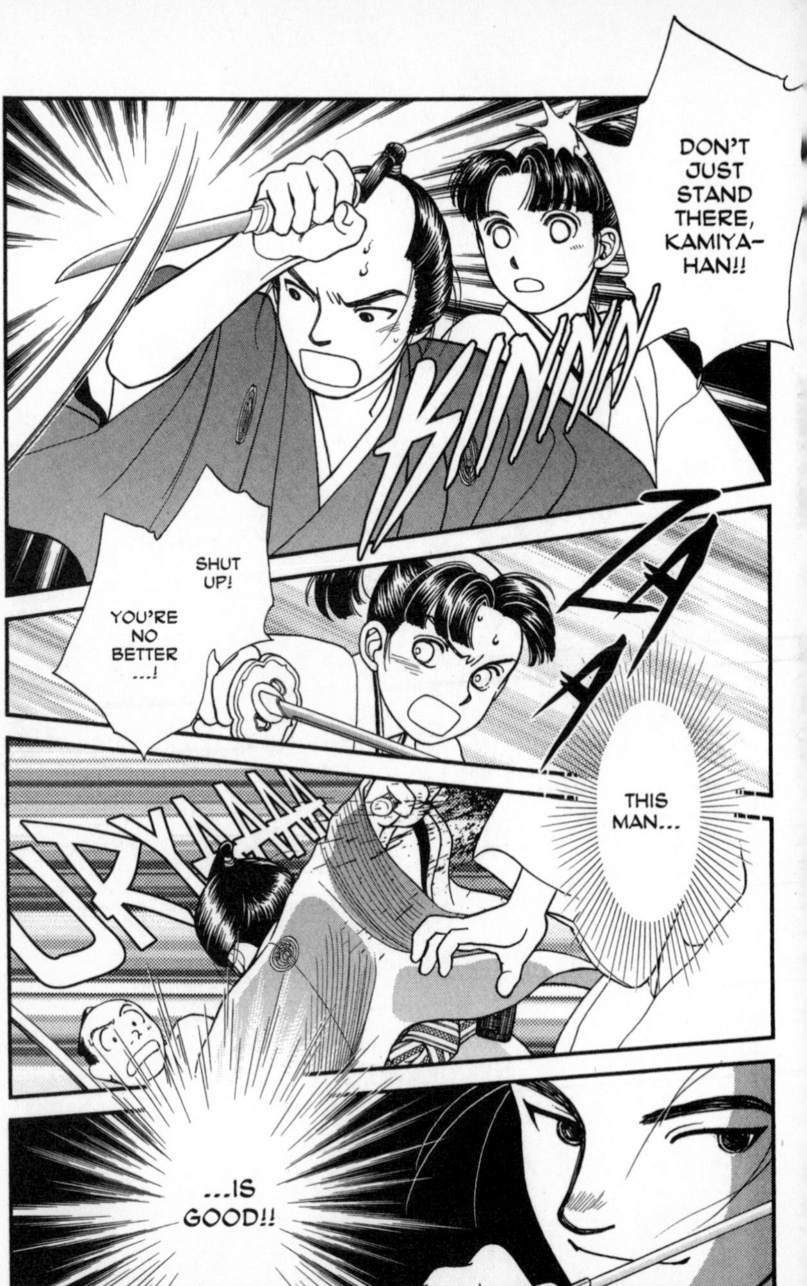
DON'T JUST STAND THERE, KAMIYA-HAN!!
KINNN
SHUT UP!
YOU'RE NO BETTER ...!
ZAA
THIS MAN...
URYAAAH
...IS GOOD!!

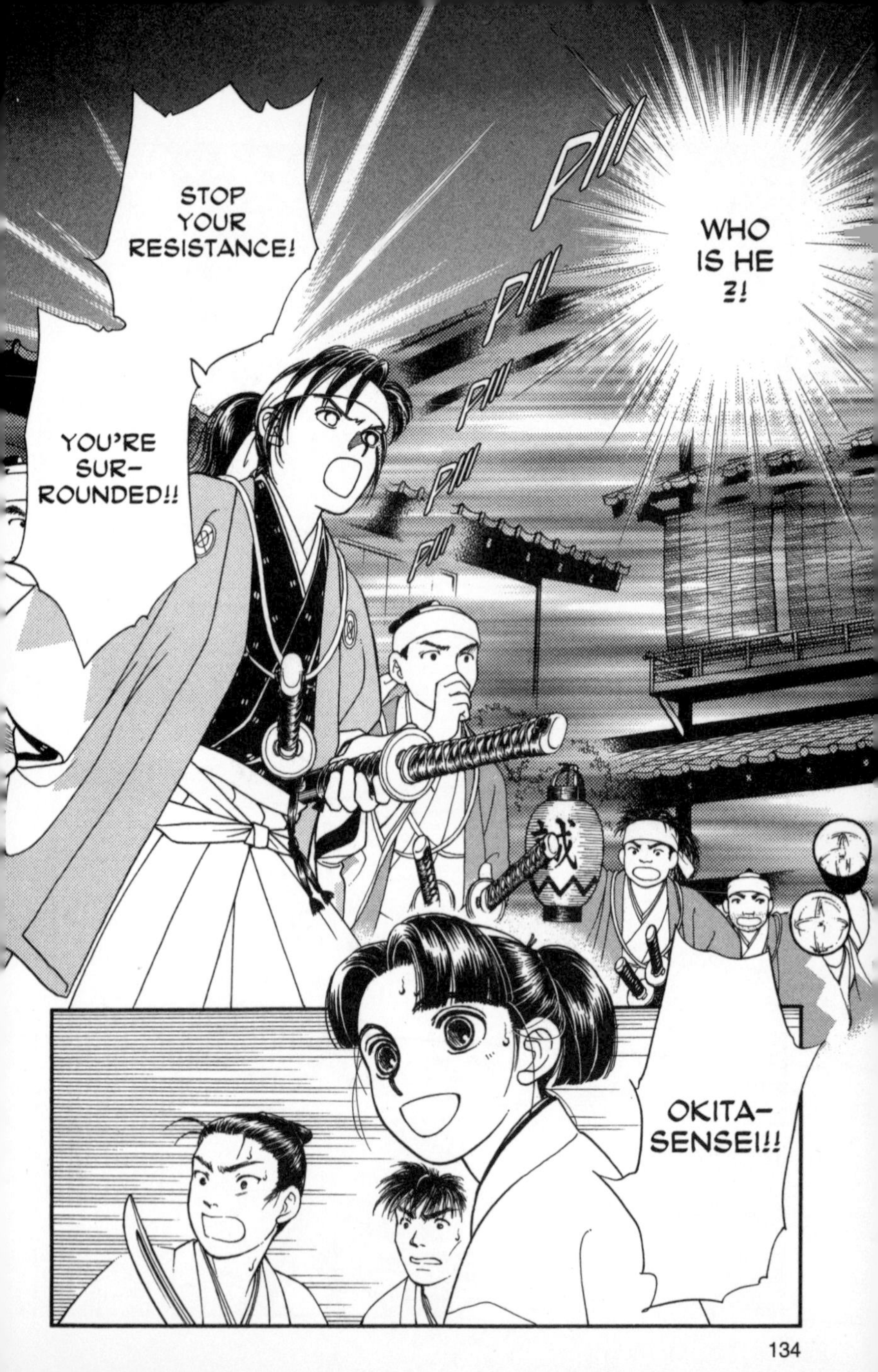
WHO IS HE ?!
STOP YOUR RESISTANCE!
YOU'RE SUR-ROUNDED!!
OKITA-SENSEI!!!

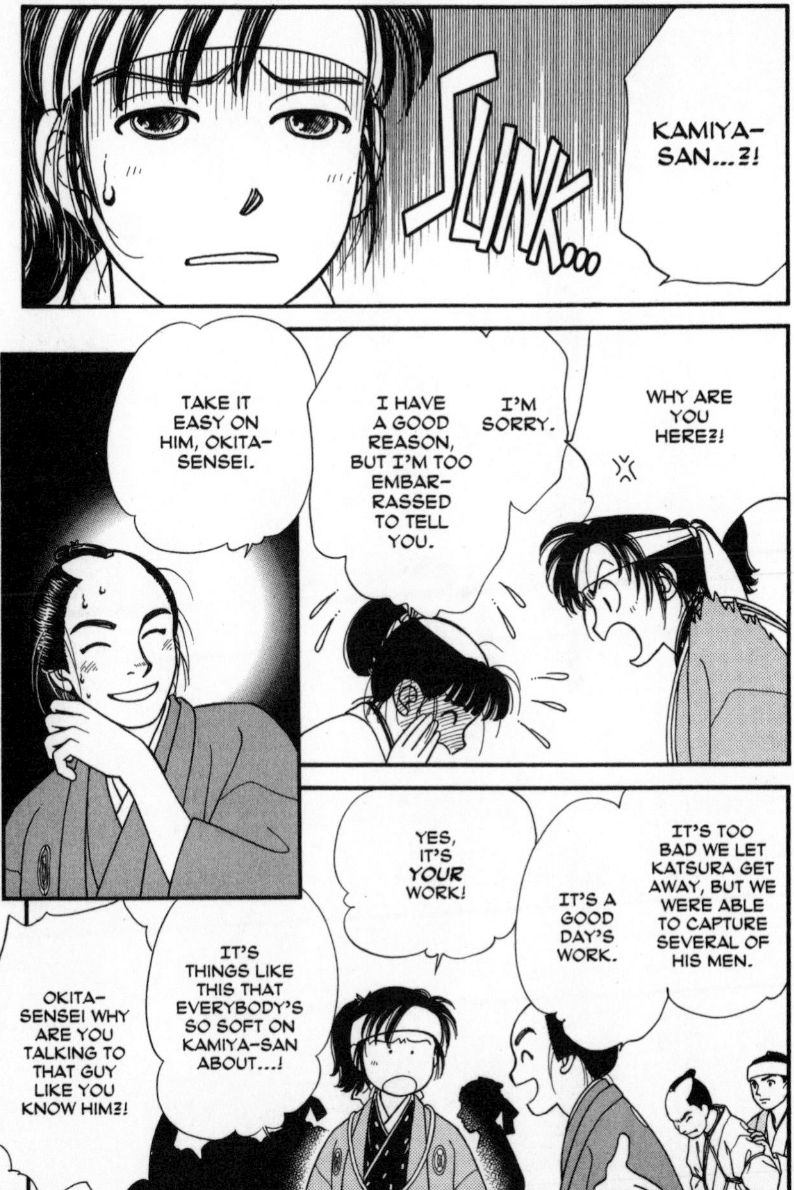
KAMIYA-SAN...?!
SLINK...
WHY ARE YOU HERE?!
I'M SORRY.
I HAVE A GOOD REASON, BUT I'M TOO EMBARRASSED TO TELL YOU.
TAKE IT EASY ON HIM, OKITA-SENSEI.
IT'S TOO BAD WE LET KATSURA GET AWAY, BUT WE WERE ABLE TO CAPTURE SEVERAL OF HIS MEN.
IT'S A GOOD DAY'S WORK.
YES, IT'S *YOUR* WORK!
IT'S THINGS LIKE THIS THAT EVERYBODY'S SO SOFT ON KAMIYA-SAN ABOUT...!
OKITA-SENSEI WHY ARE YOU TALKING TO THAT GUY LIKE YOU KNOW HIM?!

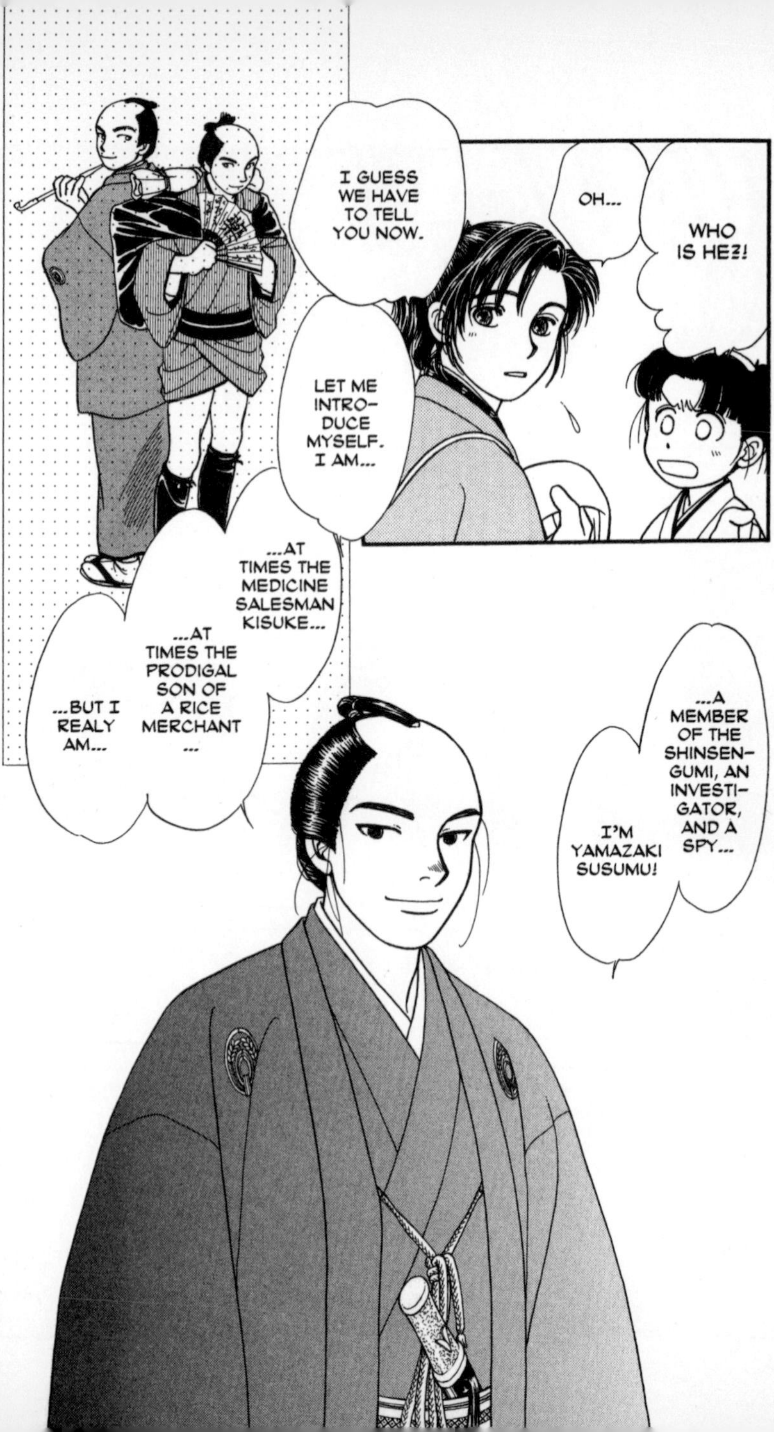
OH...
WHO IS HE?!
I GUESS WE HAVE TO TELL YOU NOW.
LET ME INTRO-DUCE MYSELF. I AM...
...AT TIMES THE MEDICINE SALESMAN KISUKE...
...AT TIMES THE PRODIGAL SON OF A RICE MERCHANT...
...BUT I REALY AM...
...A MEMBER OF THE SHINSEN-GUMI, AN INVESTI-GATOR, AND A SPY...
I'M YAMAZAKI SUSUMU!

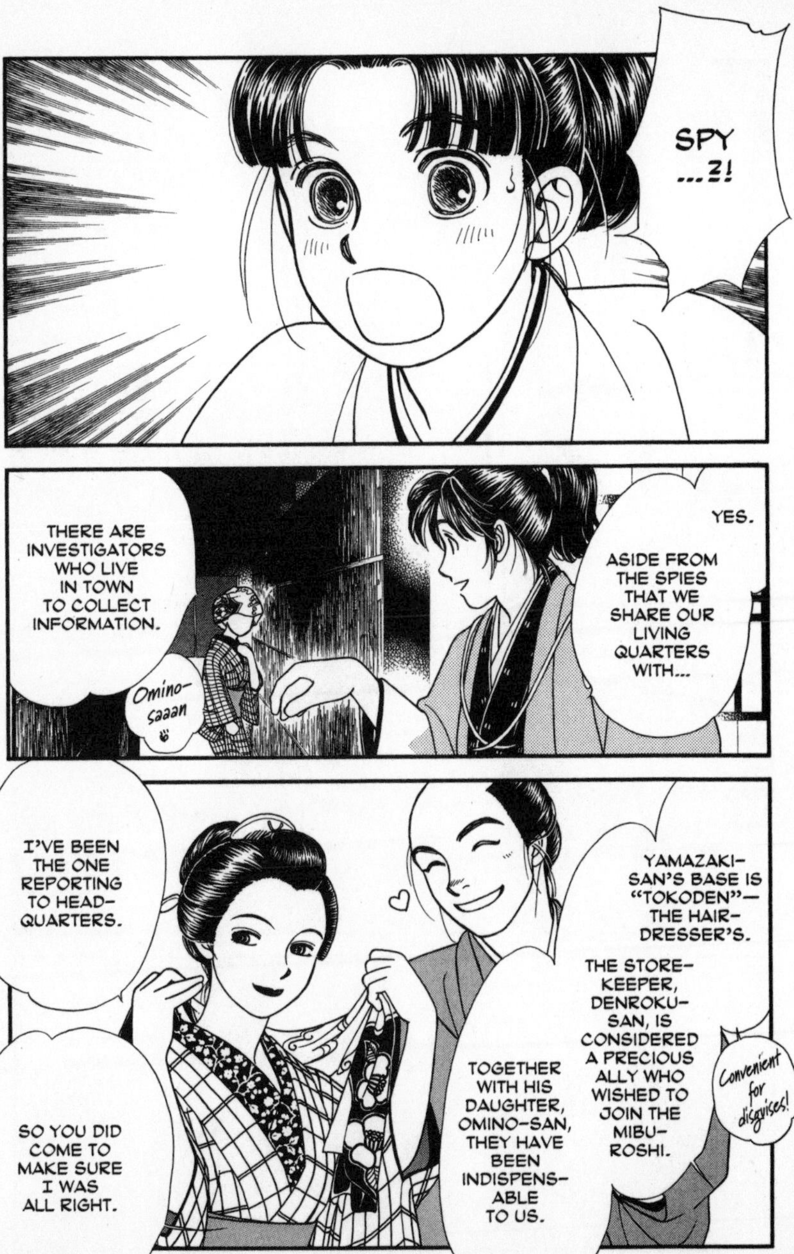
SPY ...?!
YES.
ASIDE FROM THE SPIES THAT WE SHARE OUR LIVING QUARTERS WITH...
THERE ARE INVESTIGATORS WHO LIVE IN TOWN TO COLLECT INFORMATION.
Omino-saaan
YAMAZAKI-SAN'S BASE IS "TOKODEN"—THE HAIR-DRESSER'S.
THE STORE-KEEPER, DENROKU-SAN, IS CONSIDERED A PRECIOUS ALLY WHO WISHED TO JOIN THE MIBU-ROSHI.
TOGETHER WITH HIS DAUGHTER, OMINO-SAN, THEY HAVE BEEN INDISPENS-ABLE TO US.
Convenient for disguises!
I'VE BEEN THE ONE REPORTING TO HEAD-QUARTERS.
SO YOU DID COME TO MAKE SURE I WAS ALL RIGHT.

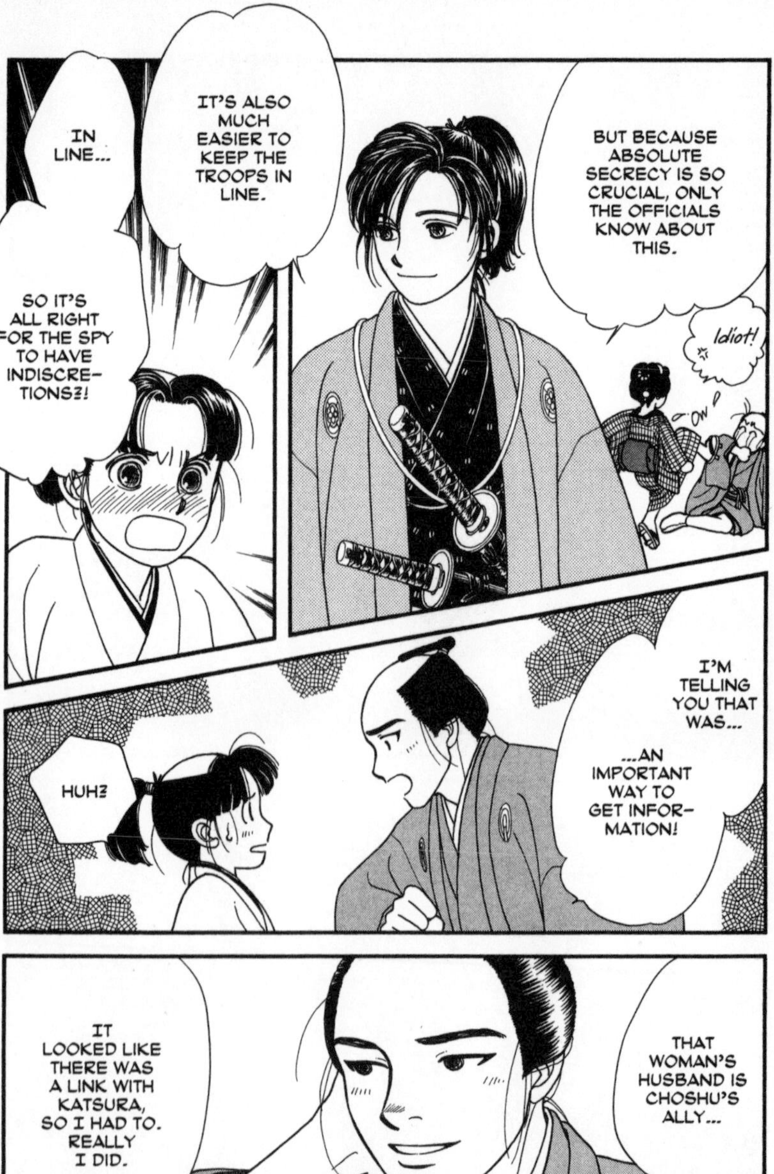
BUT BECAUSE ABSOLUTE SECRECY IS SO CRUCIAL, ONLY THE OFFICIALS KNOW ABOUT THIS.
Idiot!
OW!
IT'S ALSO MUCH EASIER TO KEEP THE TROOPS IN LINE.
IN LINE...
SO IT'S ALL RIGHT FOR THE SPY TO HAVE INDISCRETIONS?!
I'M TELLING YOU THAT WAS...
...AN IMPORTANT WAY TO GET INFORMATION!
HUH?
THAT WOMAN'S HUSBAND IS CHOSHU'S ALLY...
IT LOOKED LIKE THERE WAS A LINK WITH KATSURA, SO I HAD TO. REALLY I DID.

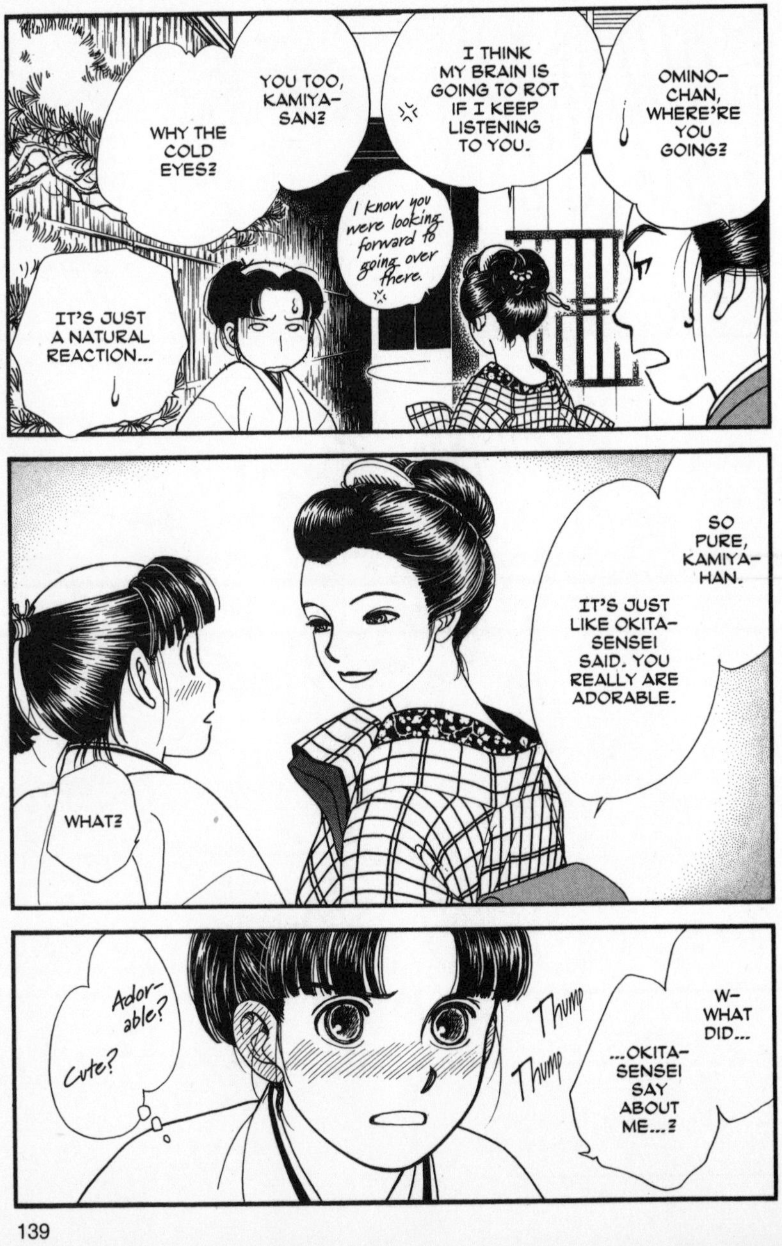
OMINO-CHAN, WHERE'RE YOU GOING?
I THINK MY BRAIN IS GOING TO ROT IF I KEEP LISTENING TO YOU.
I know you were looking forward to going over there.
YOU TOO, KAMIYA-SAN?
WHY THE COLD EYES?
IT'S JUST A NATURAL REACTION...
SO PURE, KAMIYA-HAN.
IT'S JUST LIKE OKITA-SENSEI SAID. YOU REALLY ARE ADORABLE.
WHAT?
W-WHAT DID...
...OKITA-SENSEI SAY ABOUT ME...?
Thump
Thump
Ador-able?
Cute?

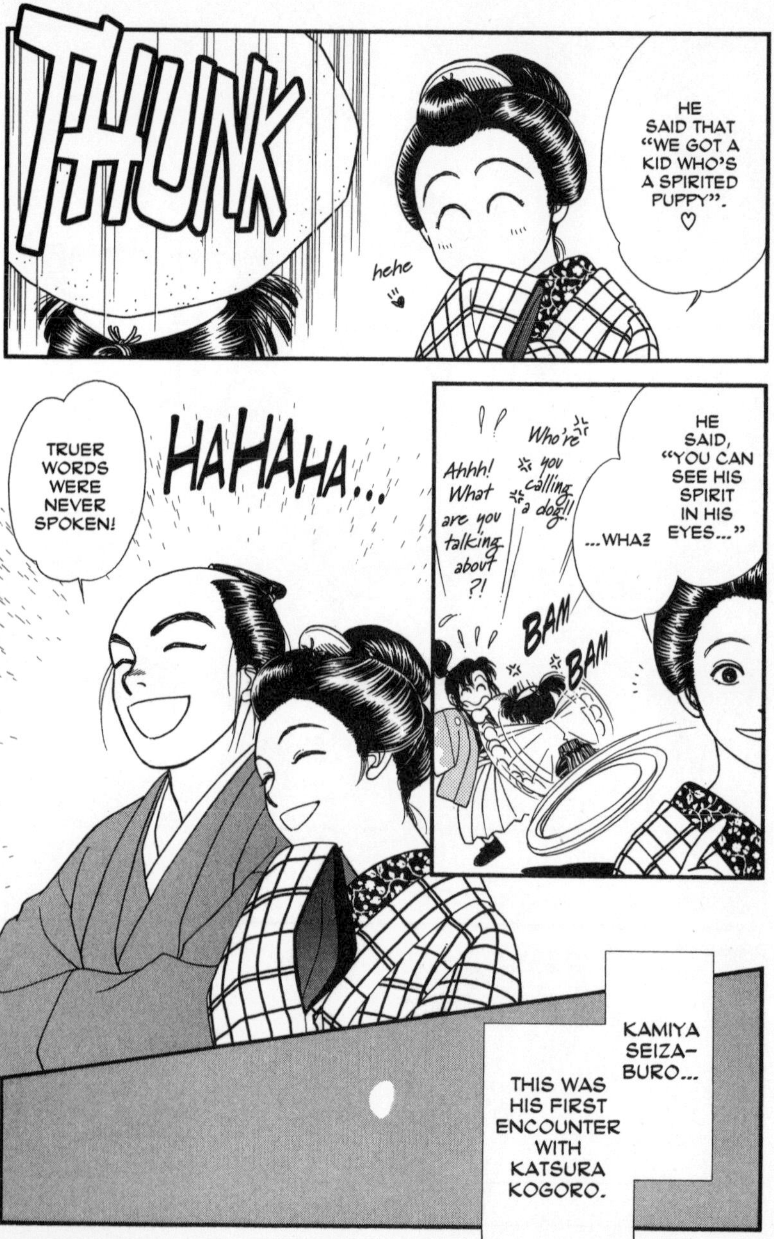
HE SAID THAT "WE GOT A KID WHO'S A SPIRITED PUPPY". ♡
hehe
THUNK
HE SAID, "YOU CAN SEE HIS SPIRIT IN HIS EYES..."
...WHA?
Who're you calling a dog!!
Ahhh! What are you talking about?!
BAM
BAM
HAHAHA...
TRUER WORDS WERE NEVER SPOKEN!
KAMIYA SEIZABURO...
THIS WAS HIS FIRST ENCOUNTER WITH KATSURA KOGORO.

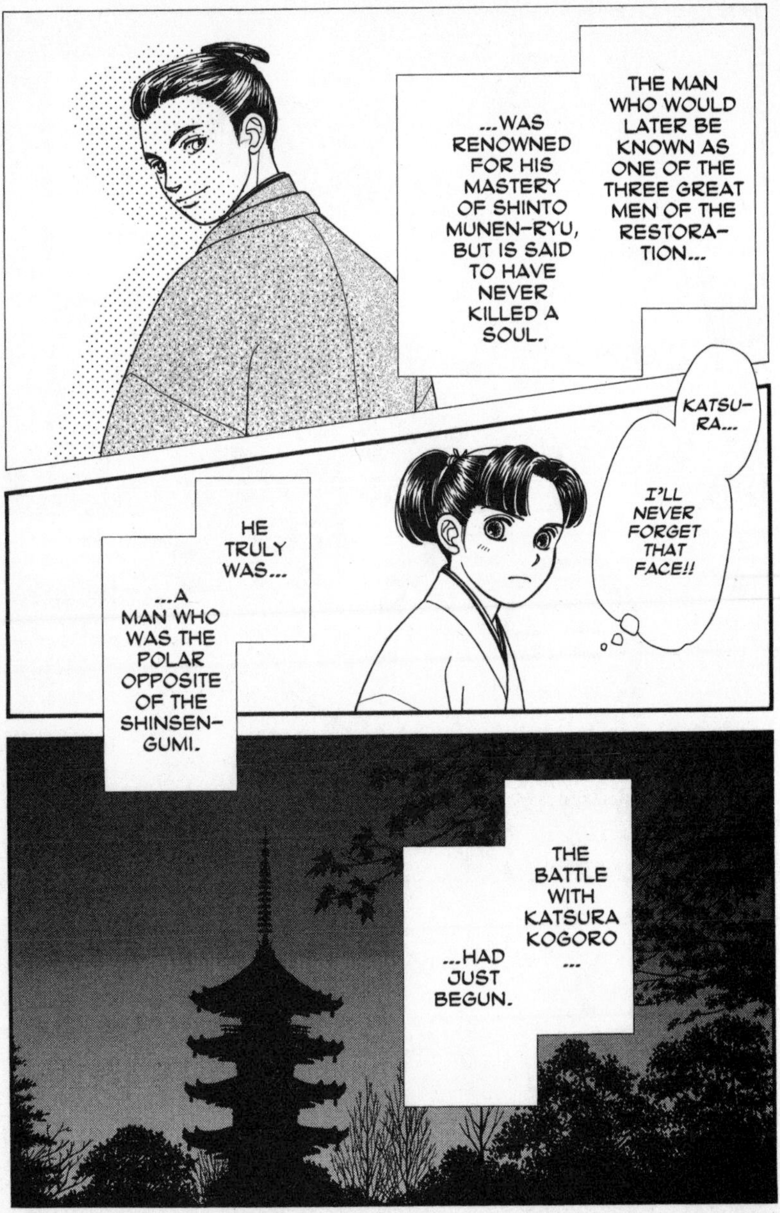
THE MAN WHO WOULD LATER BE KNOWN AS ONE OF THE THREE GREAT MEN OF THE RESTORATION...
...WAS RENOWNED FOR HIS MASTERY OF SHINTO MUNEN-RYU, BUT IS SAID TO HAVE NEVER KILLED A SOUL.
KATSU-RA...
I'LL NEVER FORGET THAT FACE!!
HE TRULY WAS...
...A MAN WHO WAS THE POLAR OPPOSITE OF THE SHINSEN-GUMI.
THE BATTLE WITH KATSURA KOGORO...
...HAD JUST BEGUN.

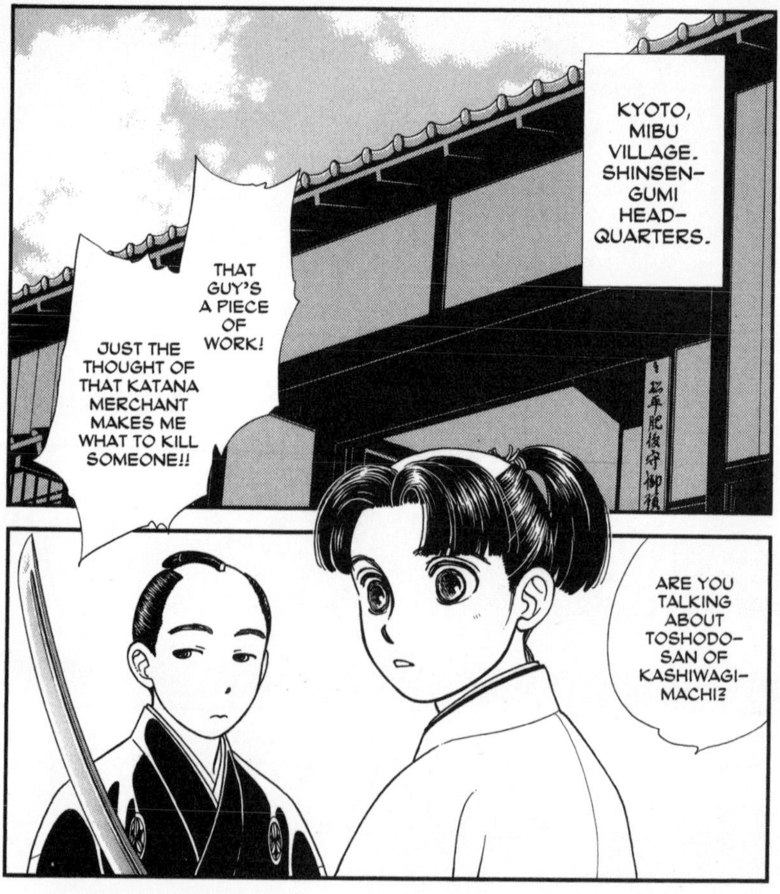
KYOTO, MIBU VILLAGE. SHINSEN-GUMI HEAD-QUARTERS.
THAT GUY'S A PIECE OF WORK!
JUST THE THOUGHT OF THAT KATANA MERCHANT MAKES ME WHAT TO KILL SOMEONE!!
ARE YOU TALKING ABOUT TOSHODO-SAN OF KASHIWAGI-MACHI?

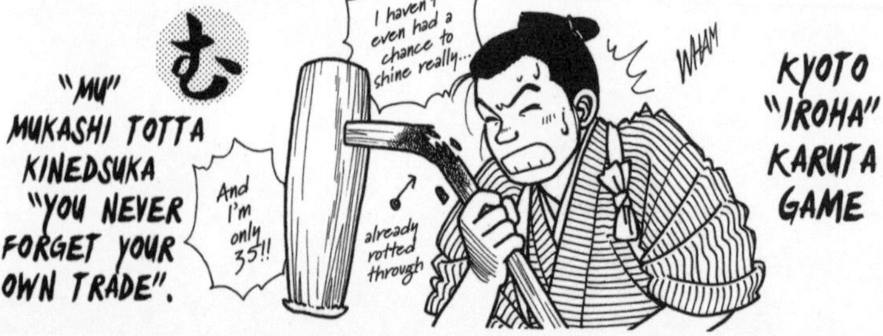
KYOTO "IROHA" KARUTA GAME
I haven't even had a chance to shine really...
WHAM
already rotted through
And I'm only 35!!
む
"MU" MUKASHI TOTTA KINEDSUKA "YOU NEVER FORGET YOUR OWN TRADE".

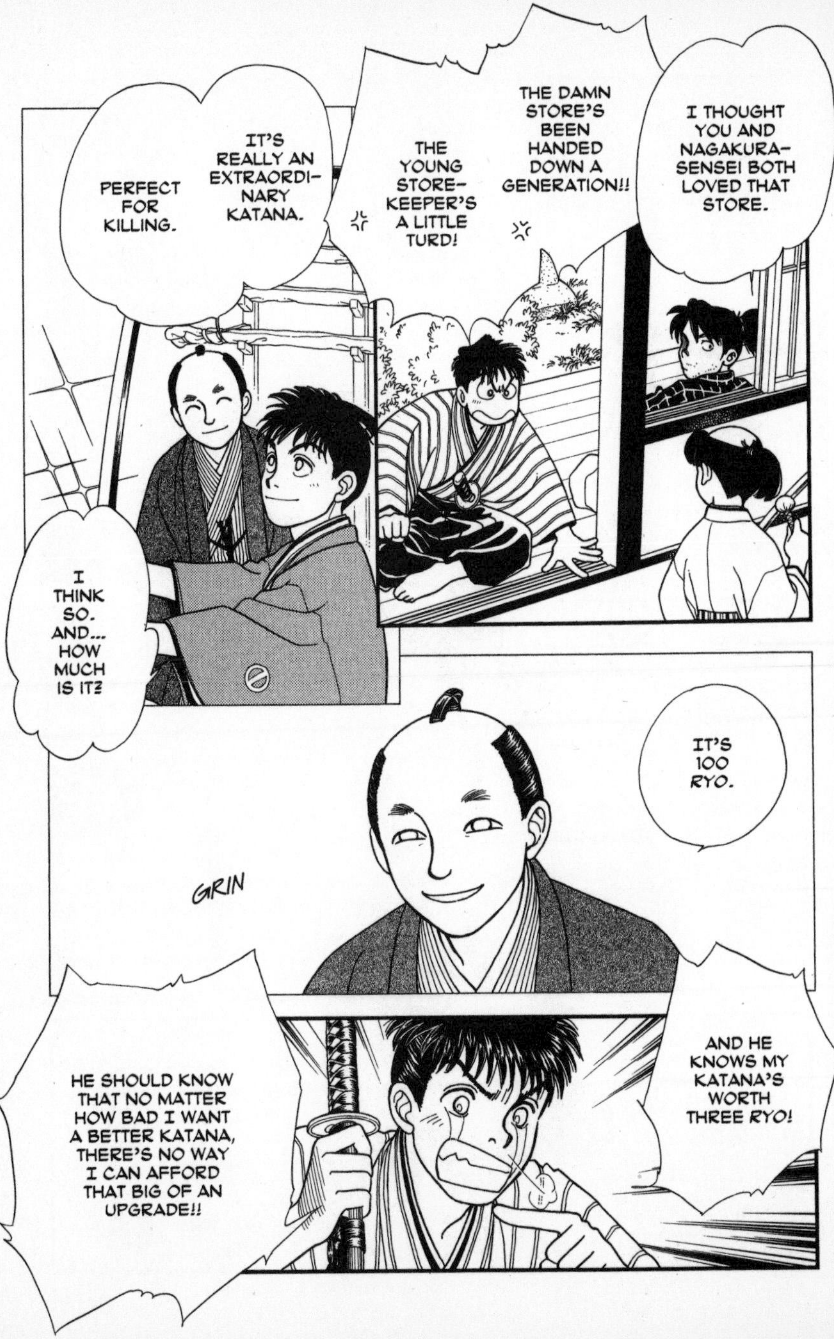
I THOUGHT YOU AND NAGAKURA-SENSEI BOTH LOVED THAT STORE.
THE DAMN STORE'S BEEN HANDED DOWN A GENERATION!!
THE YOUNG STOREKEEPER'S A LITTLE TURD!
IT'S REALLY AN EXTRAORDINARY KATANA.
PERFECT FOR KILLING.
I THINK SO. AND... HOW MUCH IS IT?
IT'S 100 RYO.
GRIN
AND HE KNOWS MY KATANA'S WORTH THREE RYO!
HE SHOULD KNOW THAT NO MATTER HOW BAD I WANT A BETTER KATANA, THERE'S NO WAY I CAN AFFORD THAT BIG OF AN UPGRADE!!

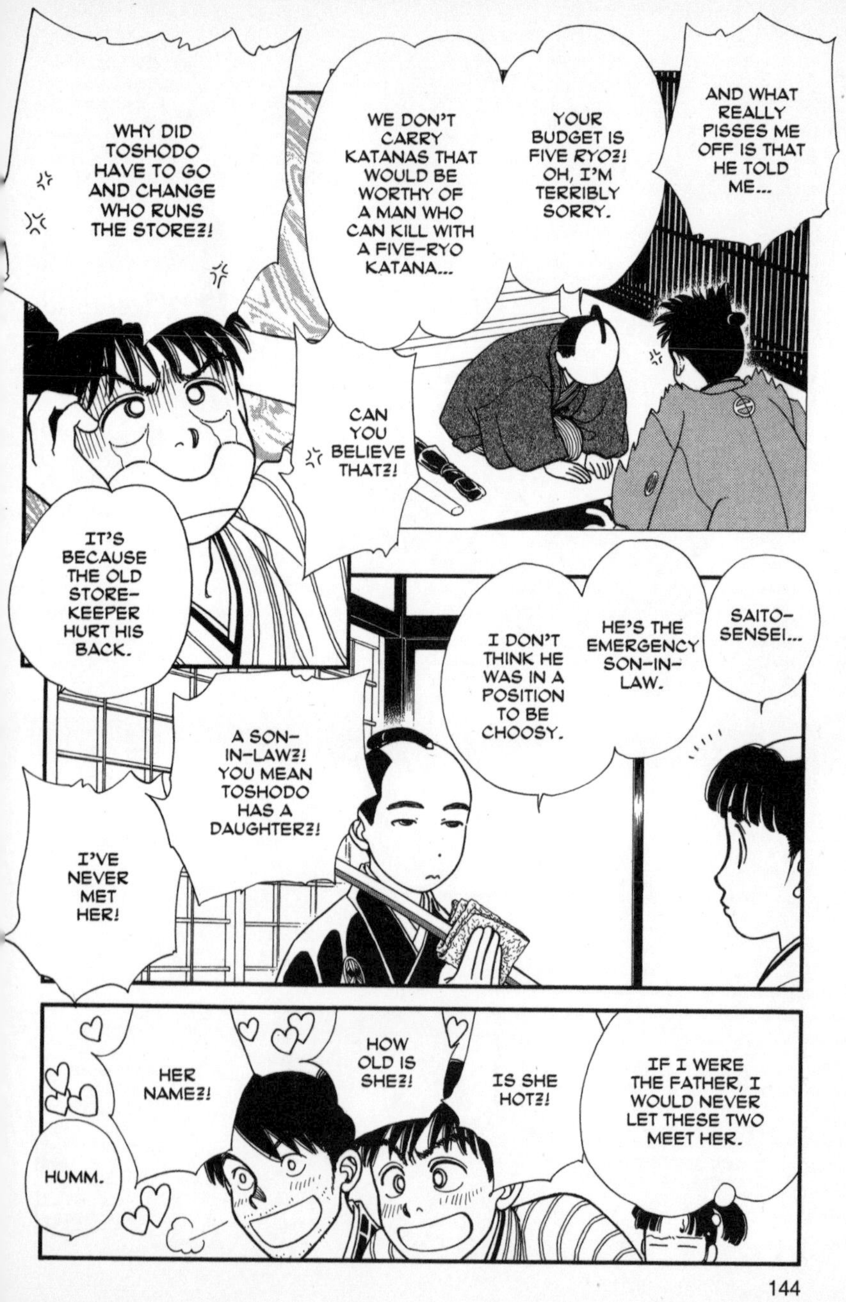

AND WHAT REALLY PISSES ME OFF IS THAT HE TOLD ME...
YOUR BUDGET IS FIVE *RYO*?! OH, I'M TERRIBLY SORRY.
WE DON'T CARRY KATANAS THAT WOULD BE WORTHY OF A MAN WHO CAN KILL WITH A FIVE-RYO KATANA...
CAN YOU BELIEVE THAT?!
WHY DID TOSHODO HAVE TO GO AND CHANGE WHO RUNS THE STORE?!
IT'S BECAUSE THE OLD STORE-KEEPER HURT HIS BACK.
SAITO-SENSEI...
HE'S THE EMERGENCY SON-IN-LAW.
I DON'T THINK HE WAS IN A POSITION TO BE CHOOSY.
A SON-IN-LAW?! YOU MEAN TOSHODO HAS A DAUGHTER?!
I'VE NEVER MET HER!
IF I WERE THE FATHER, I WOULD NEVER LET THESE TWO MEET HER.
IS SHE HOT?!
HOW OLD IS SHE?!
HER NAME?!
HUMM.

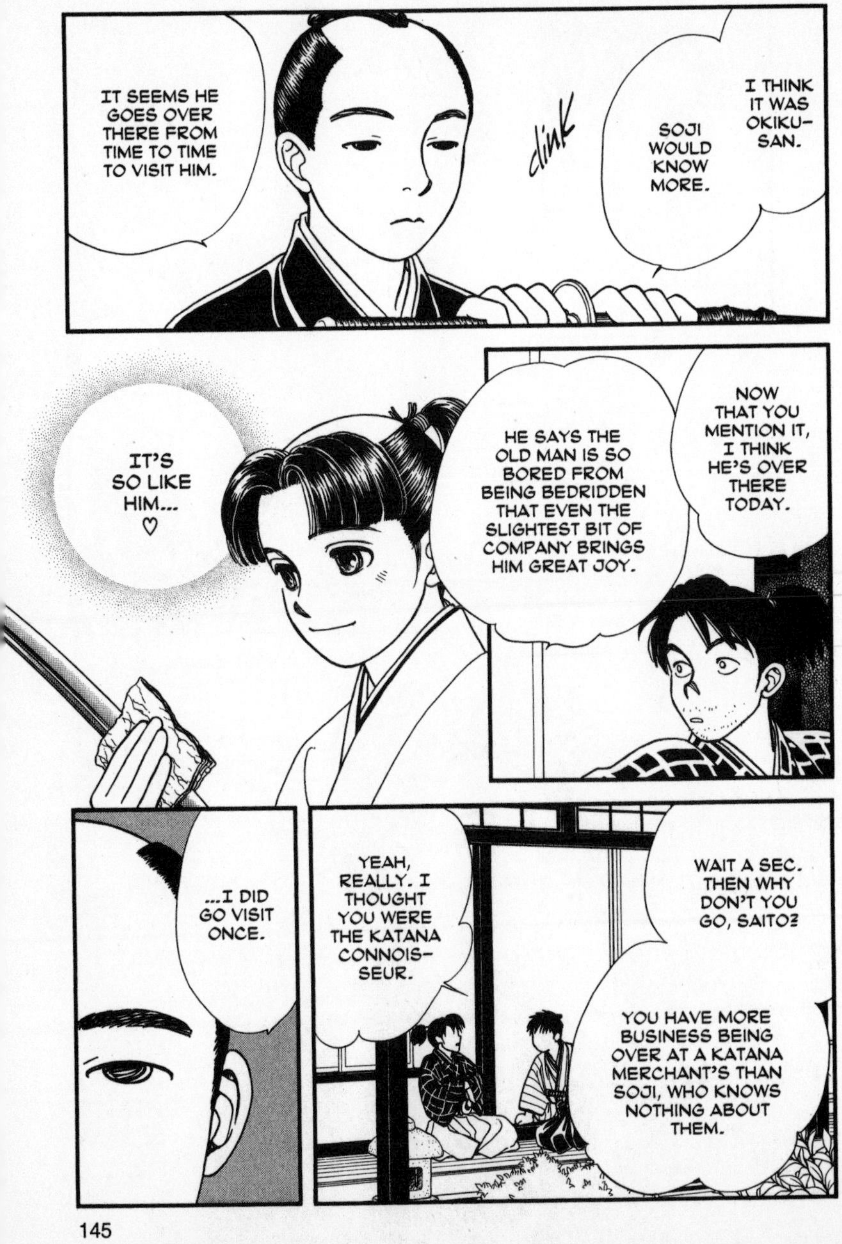
I THINK IT WAS OKIKU-SAN.
SOJI WOULD KNOW MORE.
clink
IT SEEMS HE GOES OVER THERE FROM TIME TO TIME TO VISIT HIM.
NOW THAT YOU MENTION IT, I THINK HE'S OVER THERE TODAY.
HE SAYS THE OLD MAN IS SO BORED FROM BEING BEDRIDDEN THAT EVEN THE SLIGHTEST BIT OF COMPANY BRINGS HIM GREAT JOY.
IT'S SO LIKE HIM... ♡
WAIT A SEC. THEN WHY DON'T YOU GO, SAITO?
YOU HAVE MORE BUSINESS BEING OVER AT A KATANA MERCHANT'S THAN SOJI, WHO KNOWS NOTHING ABOUT THEM.
YEAH, REALLY. I THOUGHT YOU WERE THE KATANA CONNOIS-SEUR.
...I DID GO VISIT ONCE.

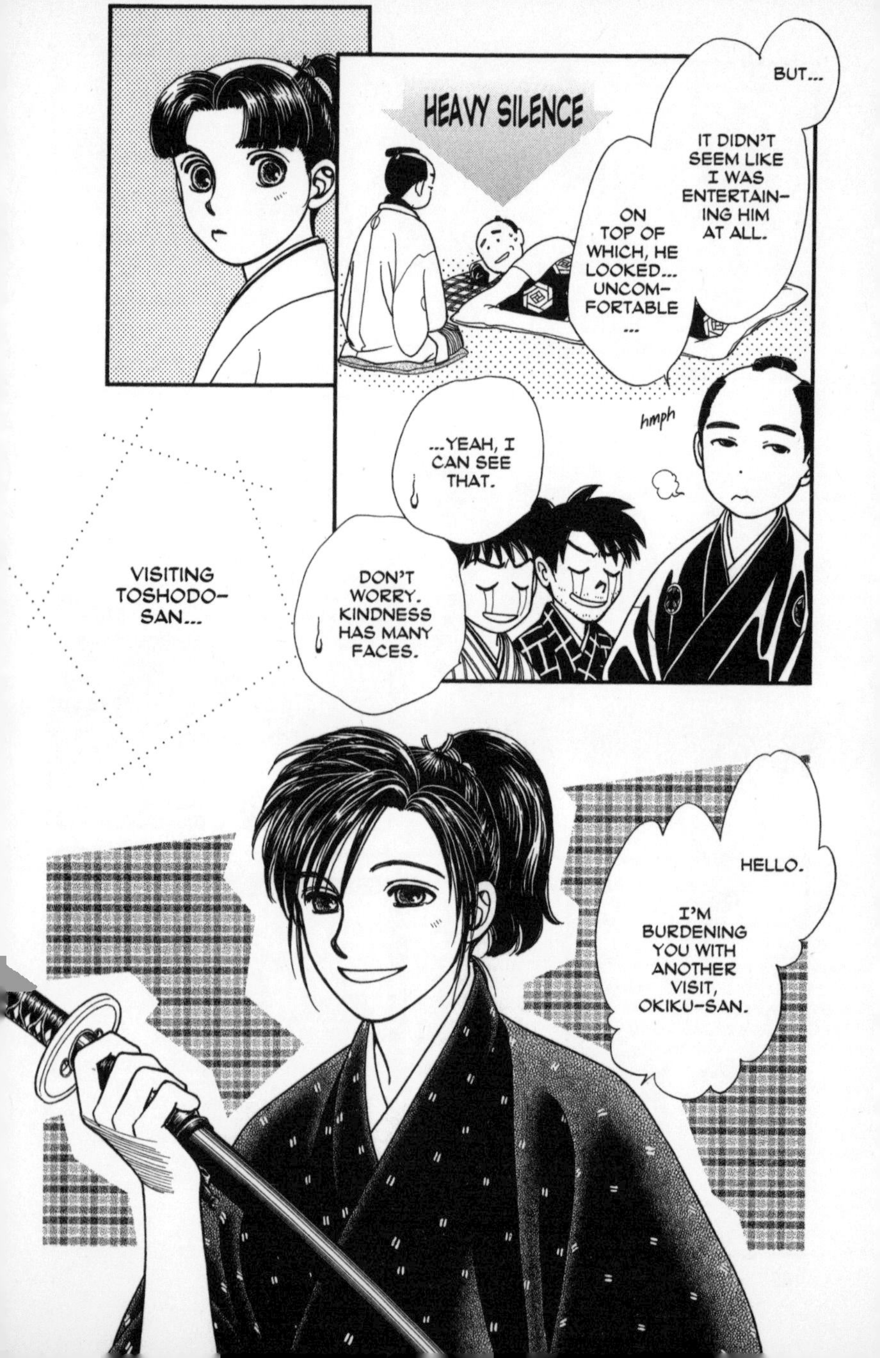
BUT...
IT DIDN'T SEEM LIKE I WAS ENTERTAINING HIM AT ALL.
ON TOP OF WHICH, HE LOOKED... UNCOMFORTABLE ...
HEAVY SILENCE
hmph
...YEAH, I CAN SEE THAT.
DON'T WORRY. KINDNESS HAS MANY FACES.
VISITING TOSHODO-SAN...
HELLO.
I'M BURDENING YOU WITH ANOTHER VISIT, OKIKU-SAN.

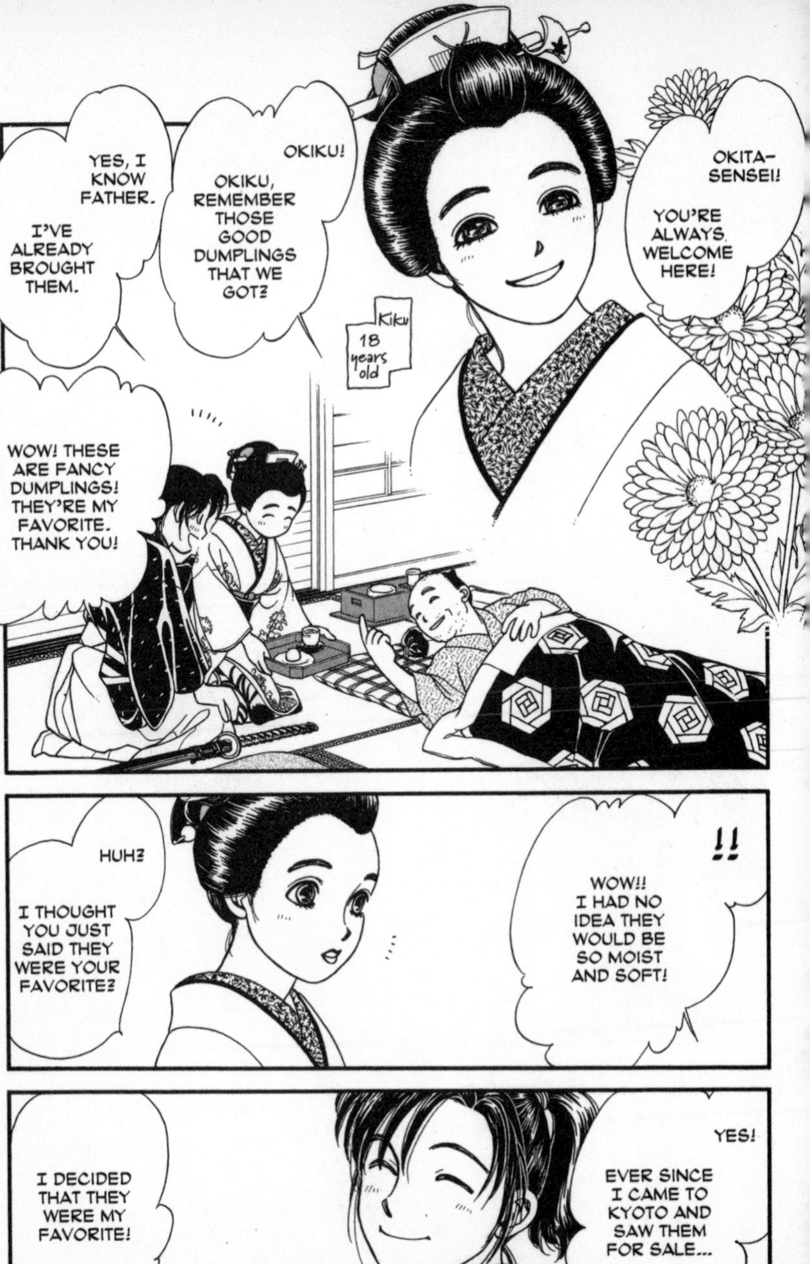
OKITA-SENSEI!
YOU'RE ALWAYS WELCOME HERE!
OKIKU!
OKIKU, REMEMBER THOSE GOOD DUMPLINGS THAT WE GOT?
YES, I KNOW FATHER.
I'VE ALREADY BROUGHT THEM.
Kiku 18 years old
WOW! THESE ARE FANCY DUMPLINGS! THEY'RE MY FAVORITE. THANK YOU!
!!
WOW!! I HAD NO IDEA THEY WOULD BE SO MOIST AND SOFT!
HUH?
I THOUGHT YOU JUST SAID THEY WERE YOUR FAVORITE?
YES!
EVER SINCE I CAME TO KYOTO AND SAW THEM FOR SALE...
I DECIDED THAT THEY WERE MY FAVORITE!

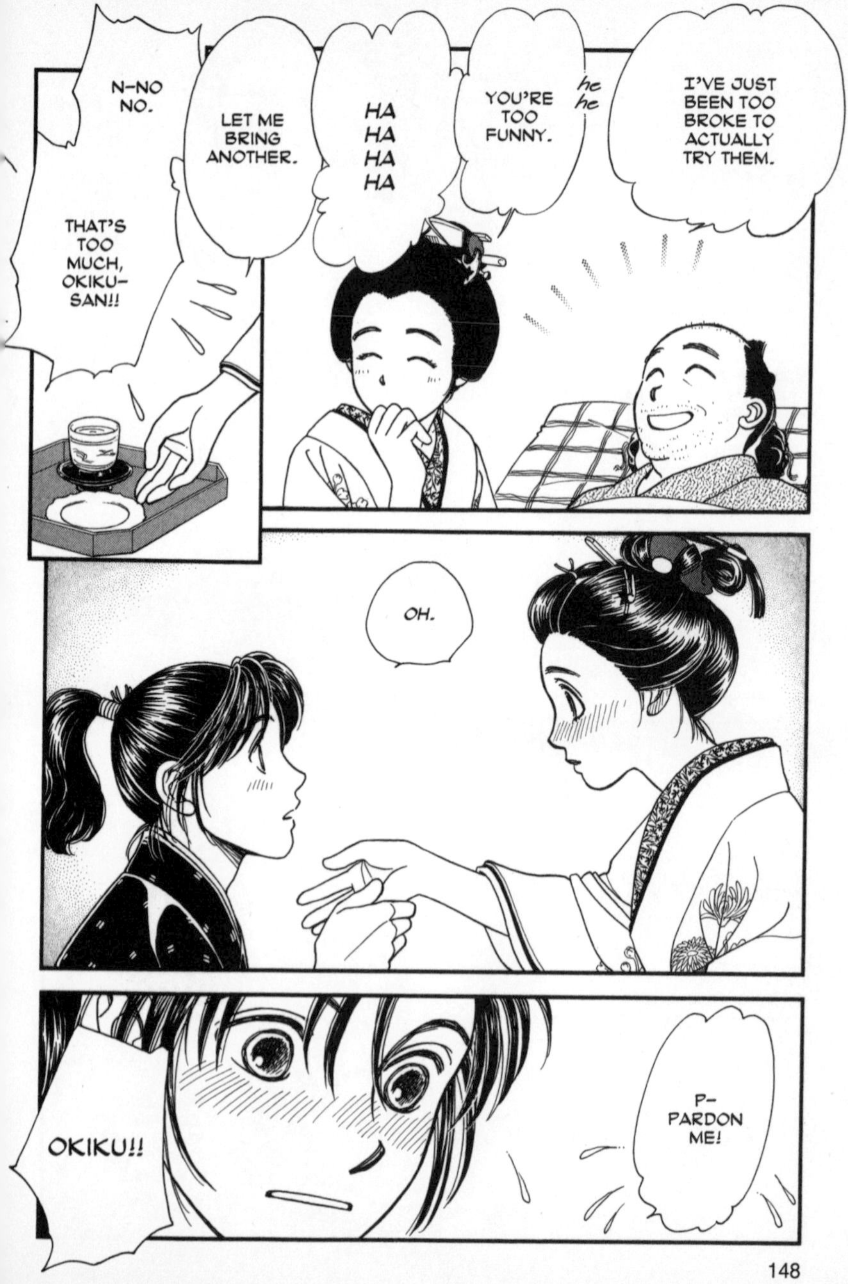
I'VE JUST BEEN TOO BROKE TO ACTUALLY TRY THEM.
he he
YOU'RE TOO FUNNY.
HA HA HA HA
LET ME BRING ANOTHER.
N-NO NO.
THAT'S TOO MUCH, OKIKU-SAN!!
OH.
P-PARDON ME!
OKIKU!!

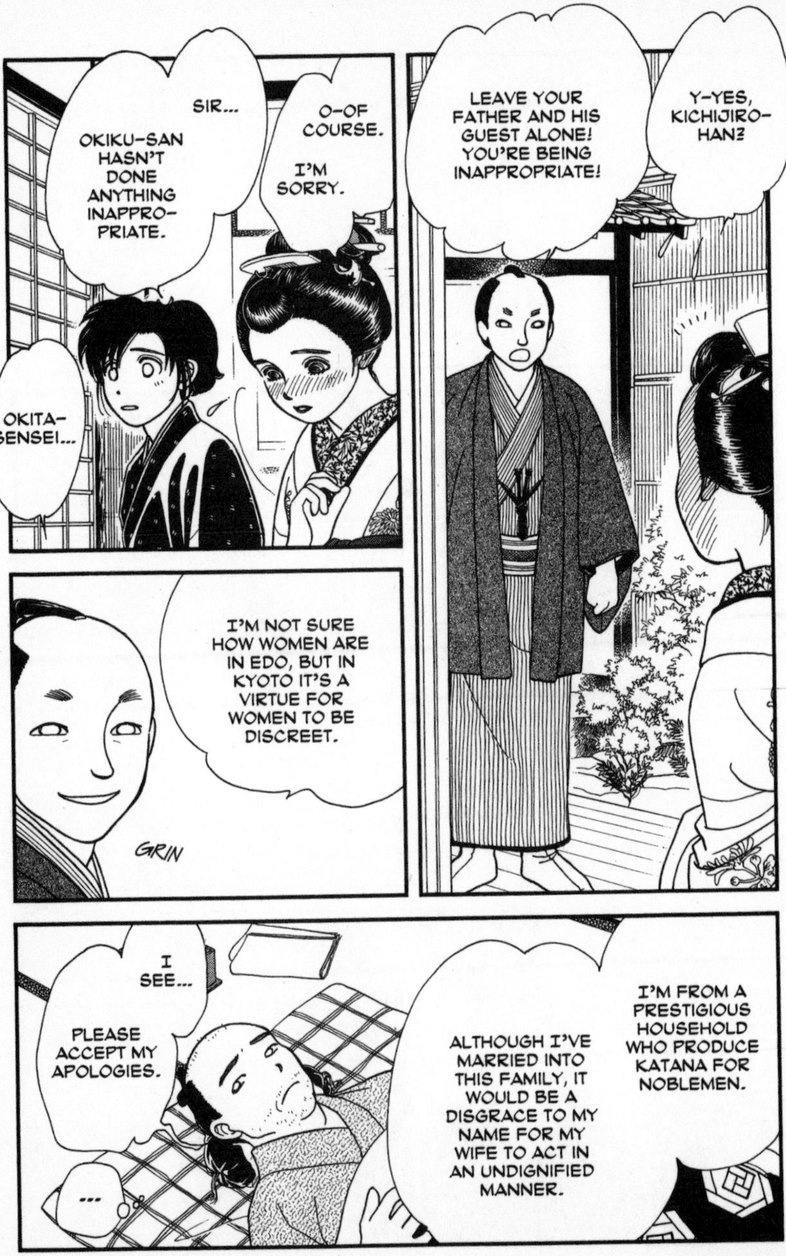
Y-YES, KICHIJIRO-HAN?
LEAVE YOUR FATHER AND HIS GUEST ALONE! YOU'RE BEING INAPPROPRIATE!
O-OF COURSE.
I'M SORRY.
SIR...
OKIKU-SAN HASN'T DONE ANYTHING INAPPROPRIATE.
OKITA-SENSEI...
I'M NOT SURE HOW WOMEN ARE IN EDO, BUT IN KYOTO IT'S A VIRTUE FOR WOMEN TO BE DISCREET.
GRIN
I'M FROM A PRESTIGIOUS HOUSEHOLD WHO PRODUCE KATANA FOR NOBLEMEN.
ALTHOUGH I'VE MARRIED INTO THIS FAMILY, IT WOULD BE A DISGRACE TO MY NAME FOR MY WIFE TO ACT IN AN UNDIGNIFIED MANNER.
I SEE...
PLEASE ACCEPT MY APOLOGIES.
...

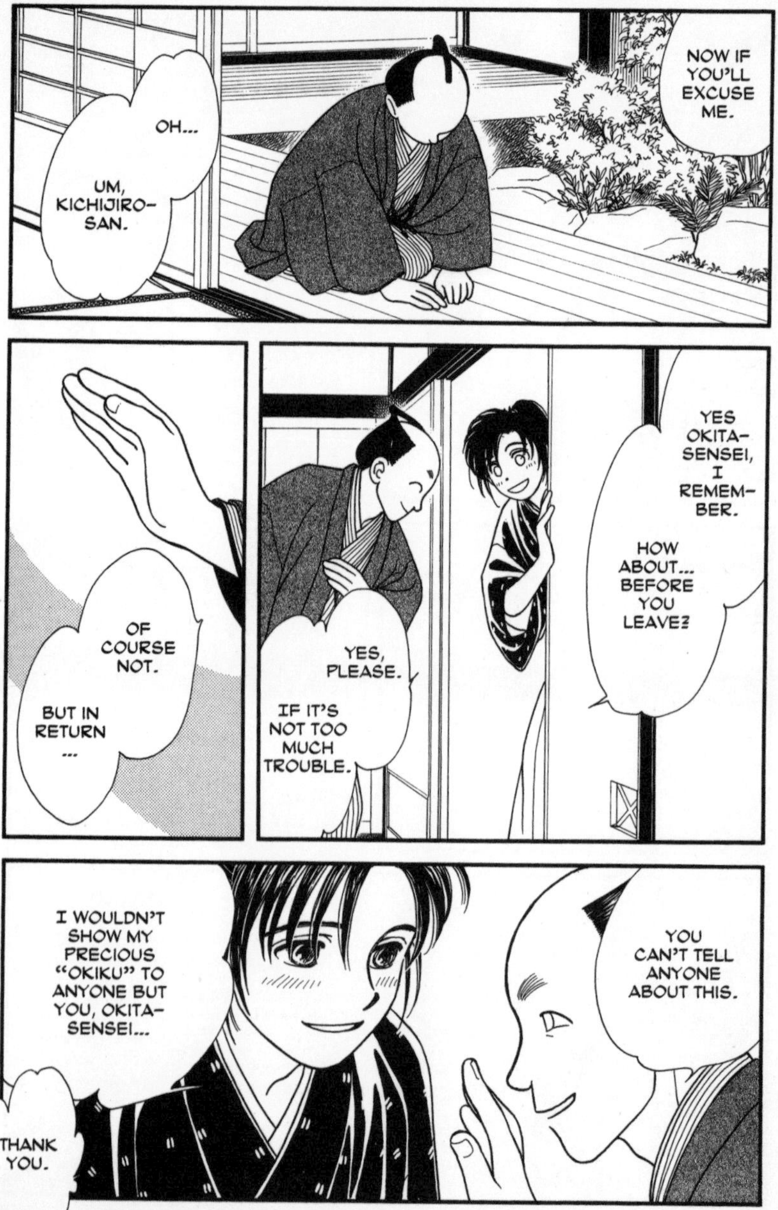
NOW IF YOU'LL EXCUSE ME.
OH...
UM, KICHIJIRO-SAN.
YES OKITA-SENSEI, I REMEMBER.
HOW ABOUT... BEFORE YOU LEAVE?
YES, PLEASE.
IF IT'S NOT TOO MUCH TROUBLE.
OF COURSE NOT.
BUT IN RETURN ...
YOU CAN'T TELL ANYONE ABOUT THIS.
I WOULDN'T SHOW MY PRECIOUS "OKIKU" TO ANYONE BUT YOU, OKITA-SENSEI...
THANK YOU.

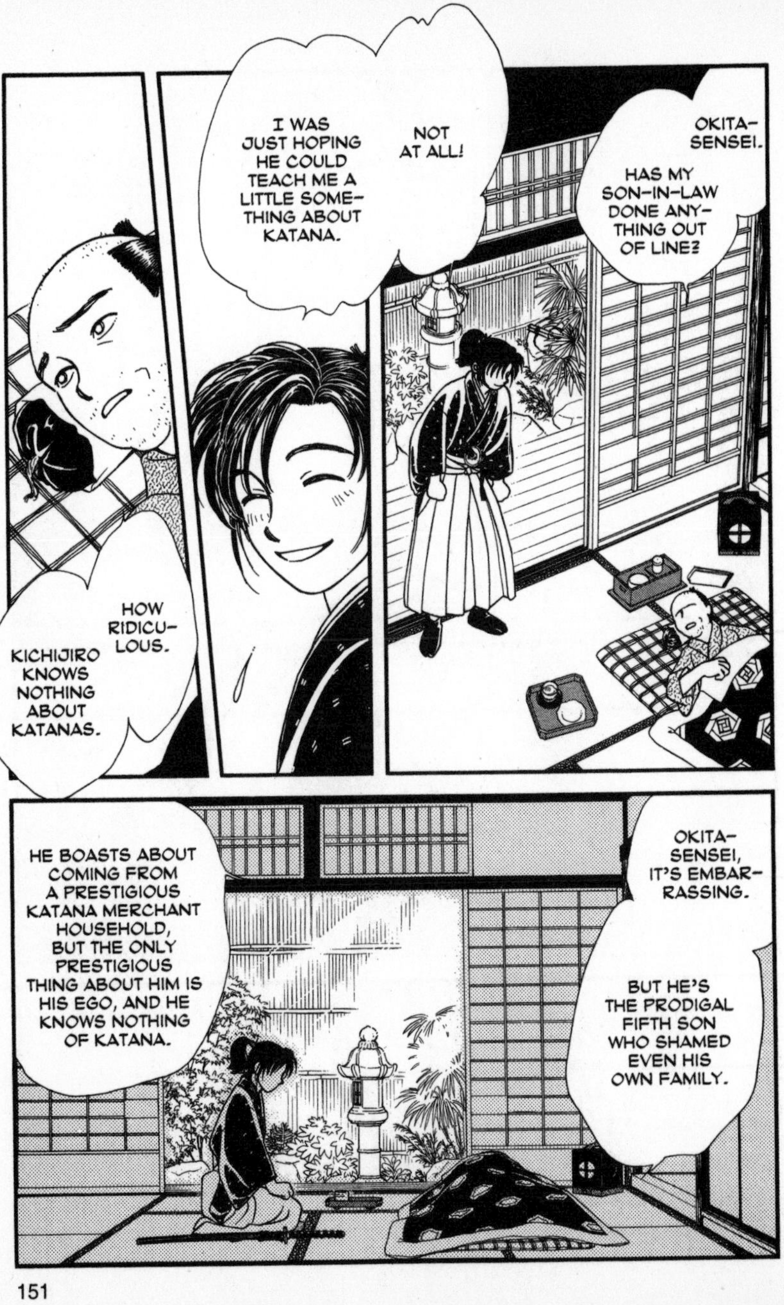
OKITA-SENSEI.
HAS MY SON-IN-LAW DONE ANYTHING OUT OF LINE?
NOT AT ALL!
I WAS JUST HOPING HE COULD TEACH ME A LITTLE SOMETHING ABOUT KATANA.
HOW RIDICULOUS.
KICHIJIRO KNOWS NOTHING ABOUT KATANAS.
OKITA-SENSEI, IT'S EMBARRASSING.
BUT HE'S THE PRODIGAL FIFTH SON WHO SHAMED EVEN HIS OWN FAMILY.
HE BOASTS ABOUT COMING FROM A PRESTIGIOUS KATANA MERCHANT HOUSEHOLD, BUT THE ONLY PRESTIGIOUS THING ABOUT HIM IS HIS EGO, AND HE KNOWS NOTHING OF KATANA.

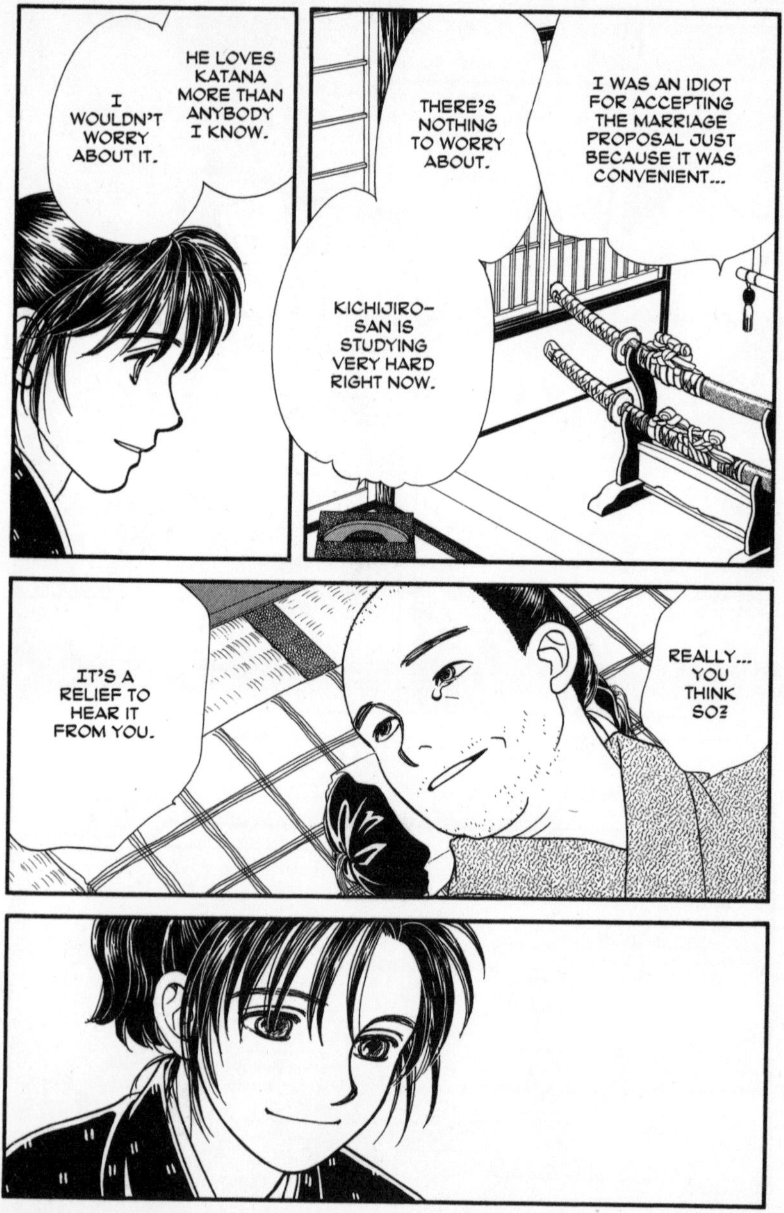
I WAS AN IDIOT FOR ACCEPTING THE MARRIAGE PROPOSAL JUST BECAUSE IT WAS CONVENIENT...
THERE'S NOTHING TO WORRY ABOUT.
KICHIJIRO-SAN IS STUDYING VERY HARD RIGHT NOW.
HE LOVES KATANA MORE THAN ANYBODY I KNOW.
I WOULDN'T WORRY ABOUT IT.
REALLY... YOU THINK SO?
IT'S A RELIEF TO HEAR IT FROM YOU.

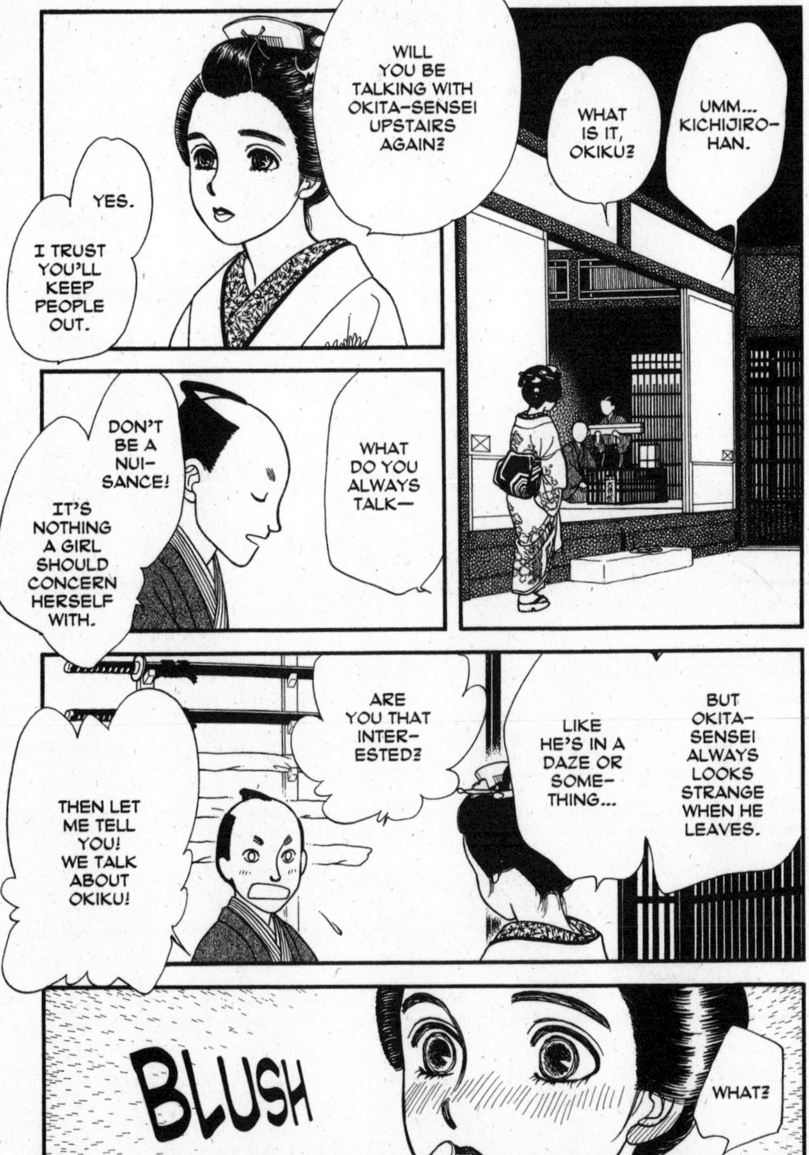
UMM... KICHIJIRO-HAN.
WHAT IS IT, OKIKU?
WILL YOU BE TALKING WITH OKITA-SENSEI UPSTAIRS AGAIN?
YES.
I TRUST YOU'LL KEEP PEOPLE OUT.
WHAT DO YOU ALWAYS TALK—
DON'T BE A NUI-SANCE!
IT'S NOTHING A GIRL SHOULD CONCERN HERSELF WITH.
BUT OKITA-SENSEI ALWAYS LOOKS STRANGE WHEN HE LEAVES.
LIKE HE'S IN A DAZE OR SOME-THING...
ARE YOU THAT INTER-ESTED?
THEN LET ME TELL YOU! WE TALK ABOUT OKIKU!
WHAT?
BLUSH

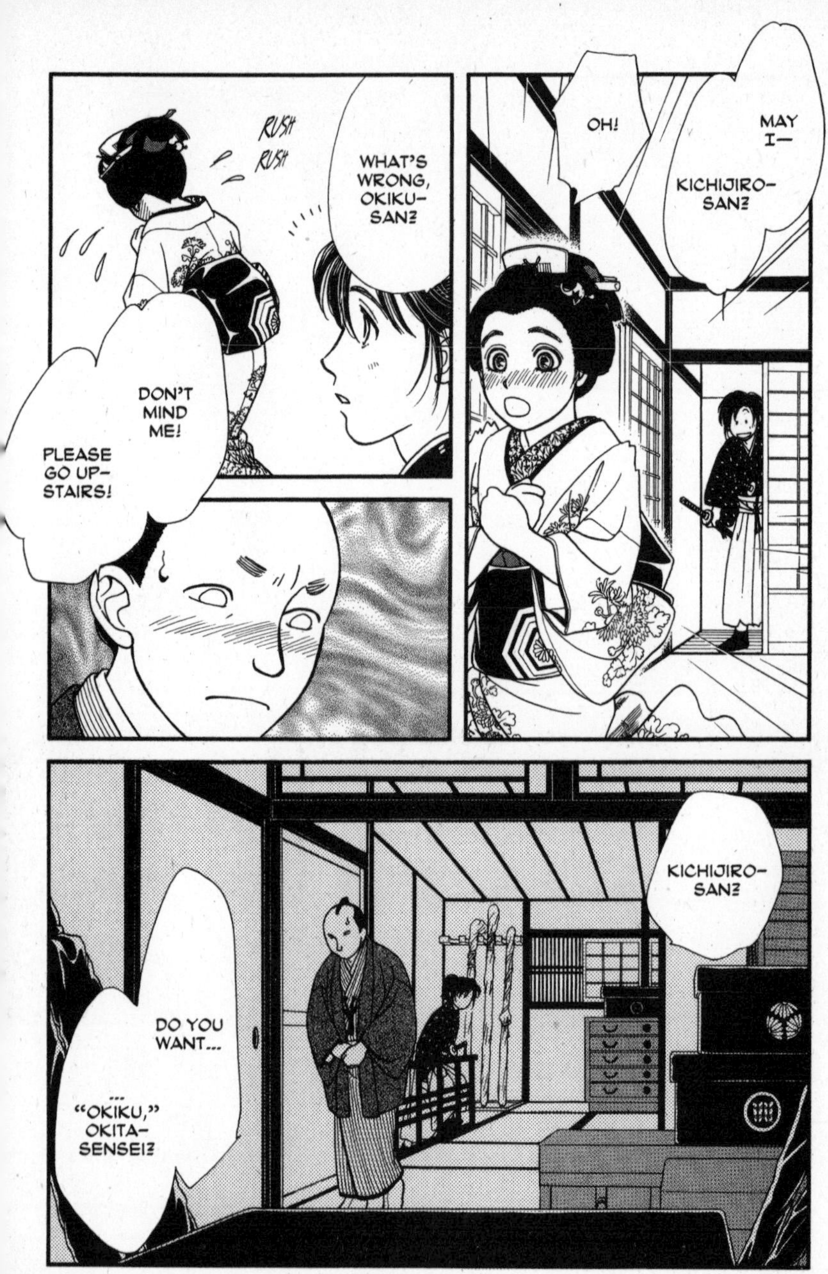
MAY I— KICHIJIRO-SAN?
OH!
WHAT'S WRONG, OKIKU-SAN?
RUSH RUSH
DON'T MIND ME! PLEASE GO UP-STAIRS!
KICHIJIRO-SAN?
DO YOU WANT...
...“OKIKU,” OKITA-SENSEI?

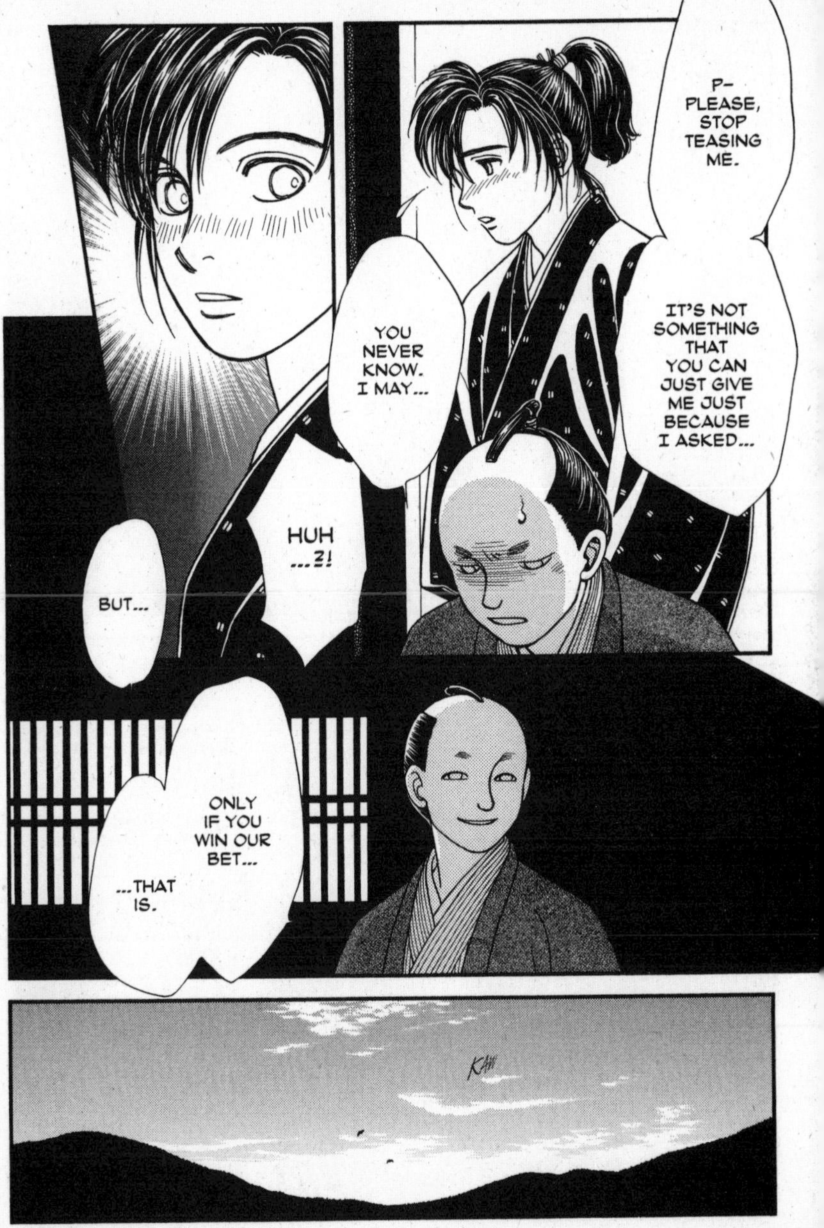
P-PLEASE, STOP TEASING ME.
IT'S NOT SOMETHING THAT YOU CAN JUST GIVE ME JUST BECAUSE I ASKED...
YOU NEVER KNOW. I MAY...
HUH ...?!
BUT...
ONLY IF YOU WIN OUR BET...
...THAT IS.
KAW

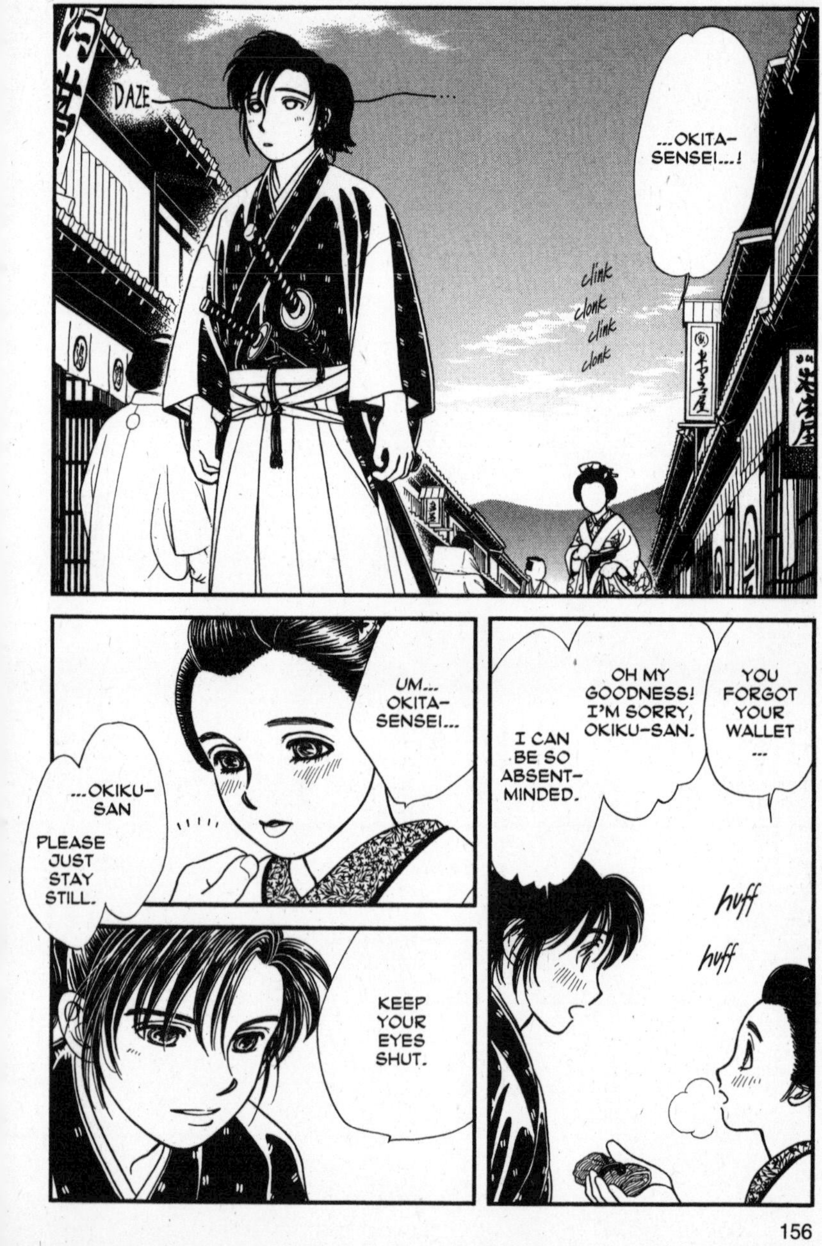
...OKITA-SENSEI...!
clink clonk clink clonk
DAZE—...
YOU FORGOT YOUR WALLET ...
OH MY GOODNESS! I'M SORRY, OKIKU-SAN.
I CAN BE SO ABSENT-MINDED.
huff huff
UM... OKITA-SENSEI...
...OKIKU-SAN
PLEASE JUST STAY STILL.
KEEP YOUR EYES SHUT.

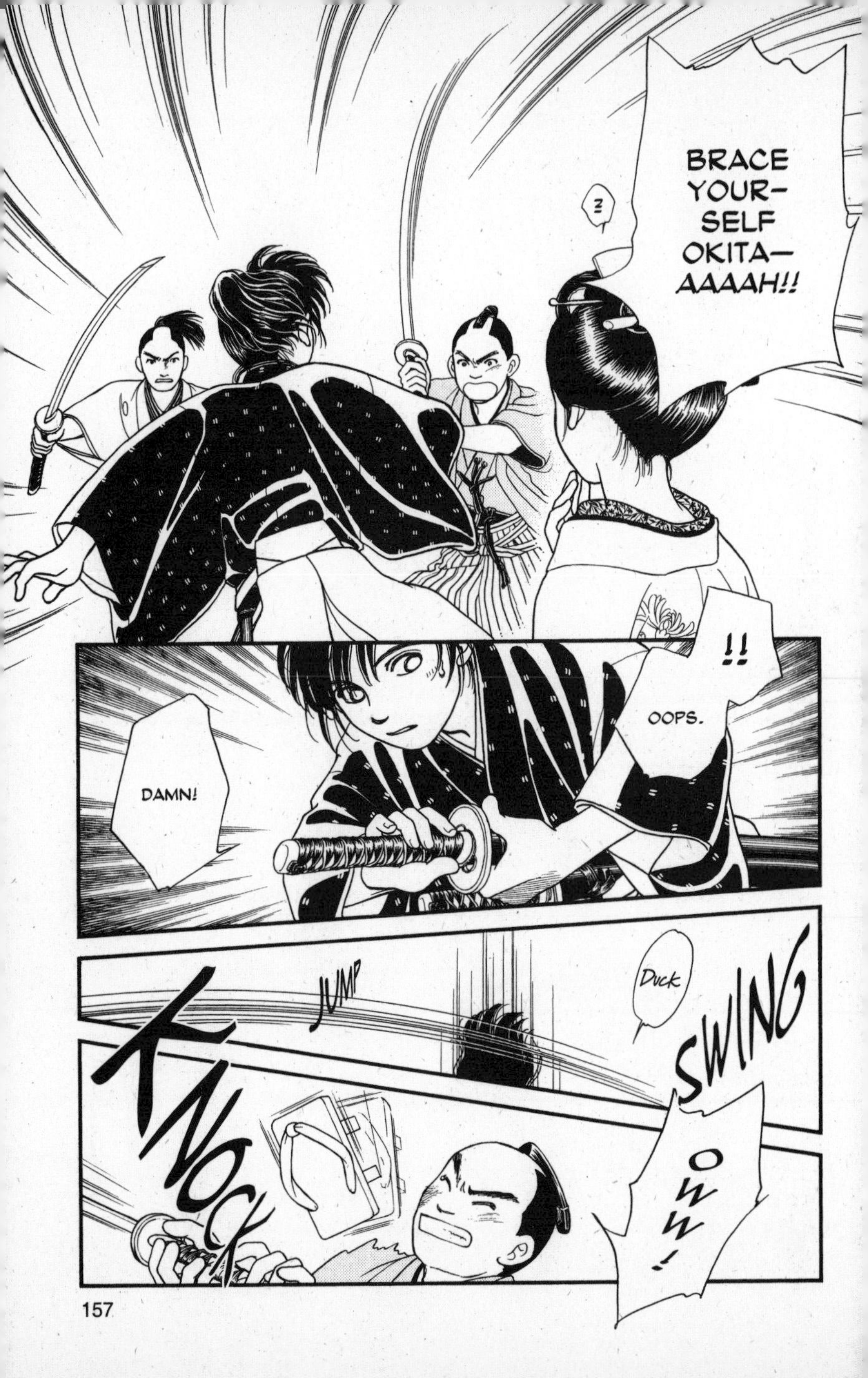
BRACE YOUR-SELF OKITA-AAAAH!!
!!
OOPS.
DAMN!
SWING
Duck
JUMP
OWW!
KNOCK

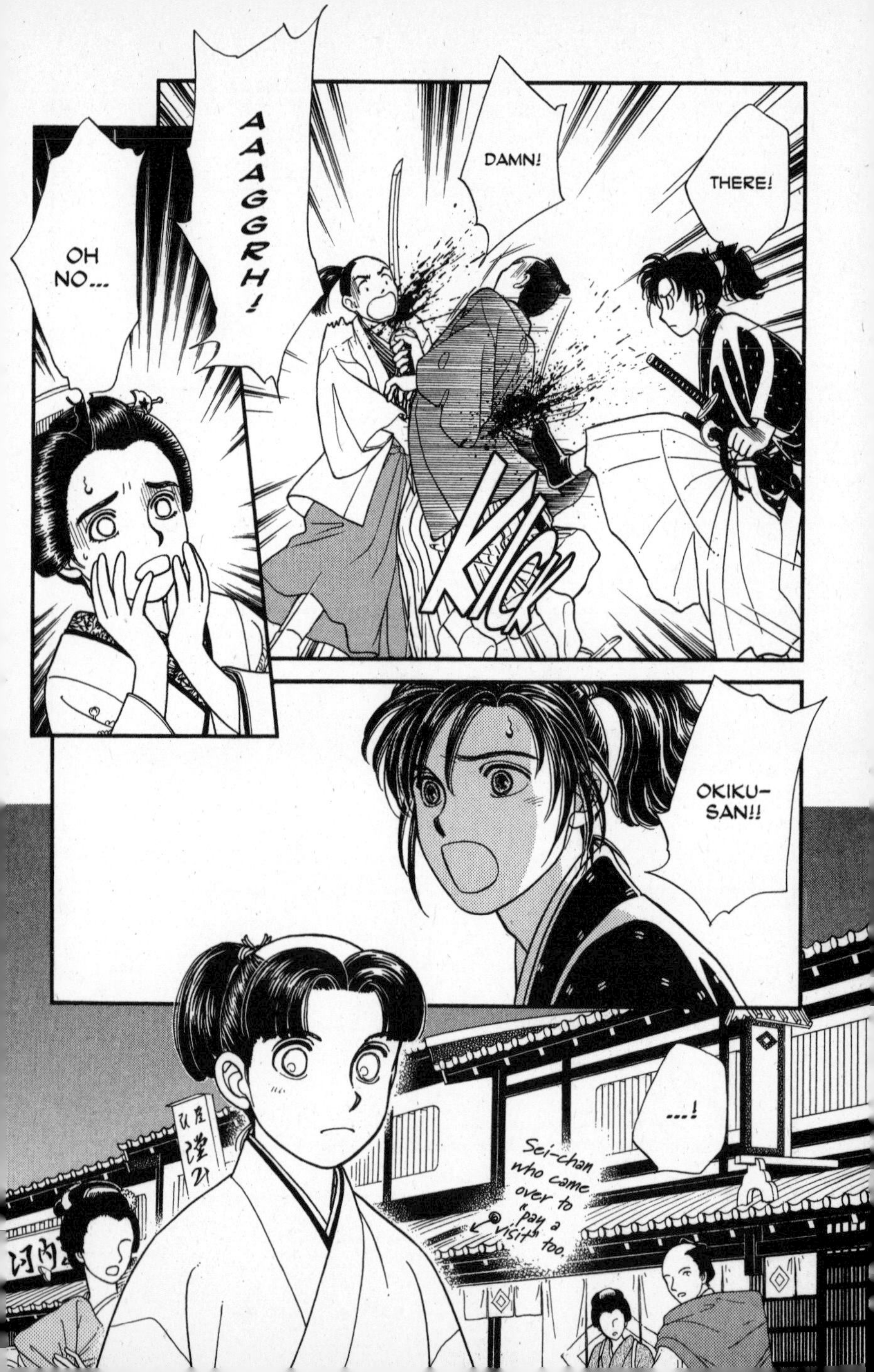
THERE!
DAMN!
AAAGGRH!
OH NO...
OKIKU-SAN!!
...!
Sei-chan who came over to "pay a visit" too.

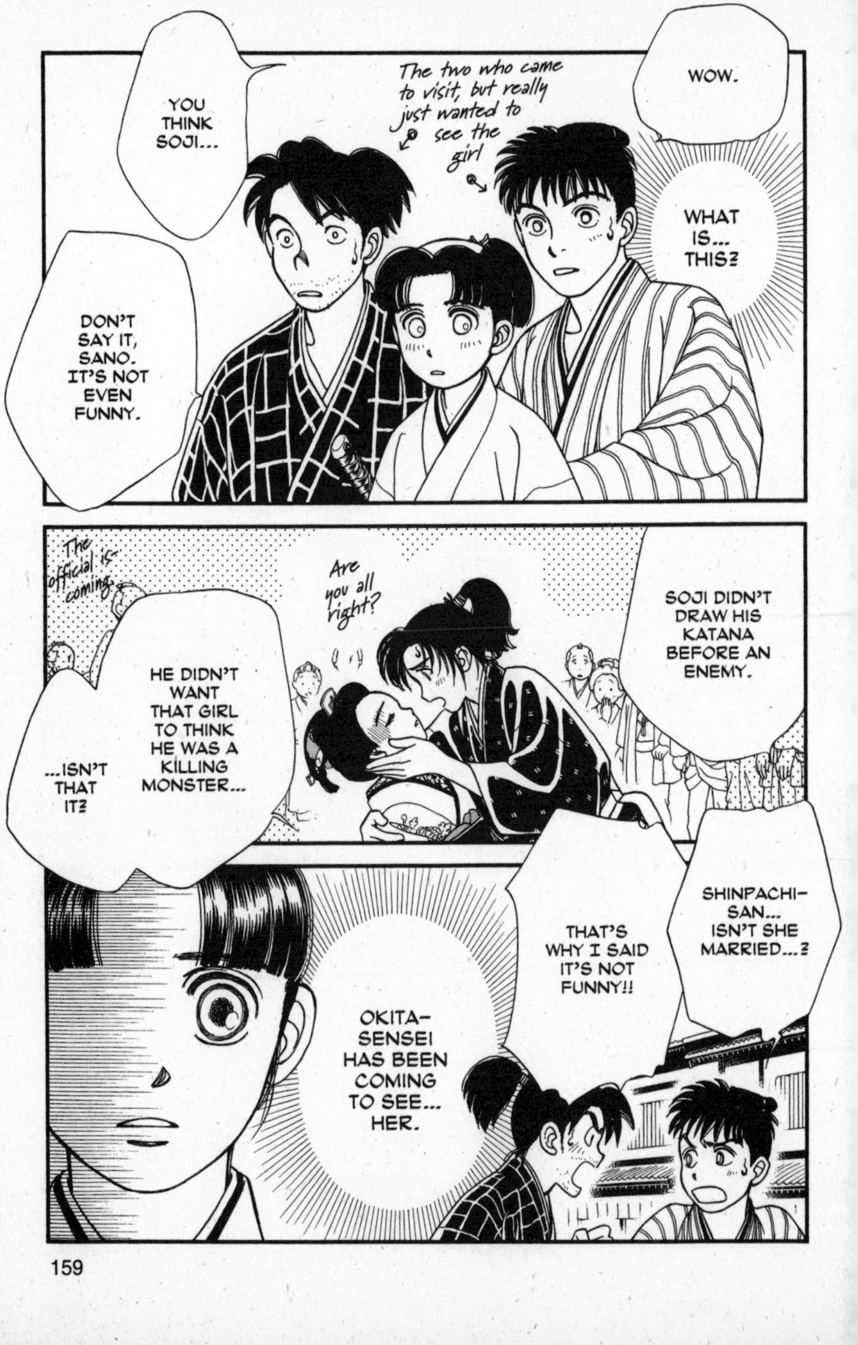
WOW.
WHAT IS... THIS?
The two who came to visit, but really just wanted to see the girl
YOU THINK SOJI...
DON'T SAY IT, SANO. IT'S NOT EVEN FUNNY.
SOJI DIDN'T DRAW HIS KATANA BEFORE AN ENEMY.
Are you all right?
HE DIDN'T WANT THAT GIRL TO THINK HE WAS A KILLING MONSTER...
...ISN'T THAT IT?
The official is coming
SHINPACHI-SAN... ISN'T SHE MARRIED...?
THAT'S WHY I SAID IT'S NOT FUNNY!!
OKITA-SENSEI HAS BEEN COMING TO SEE... HER.

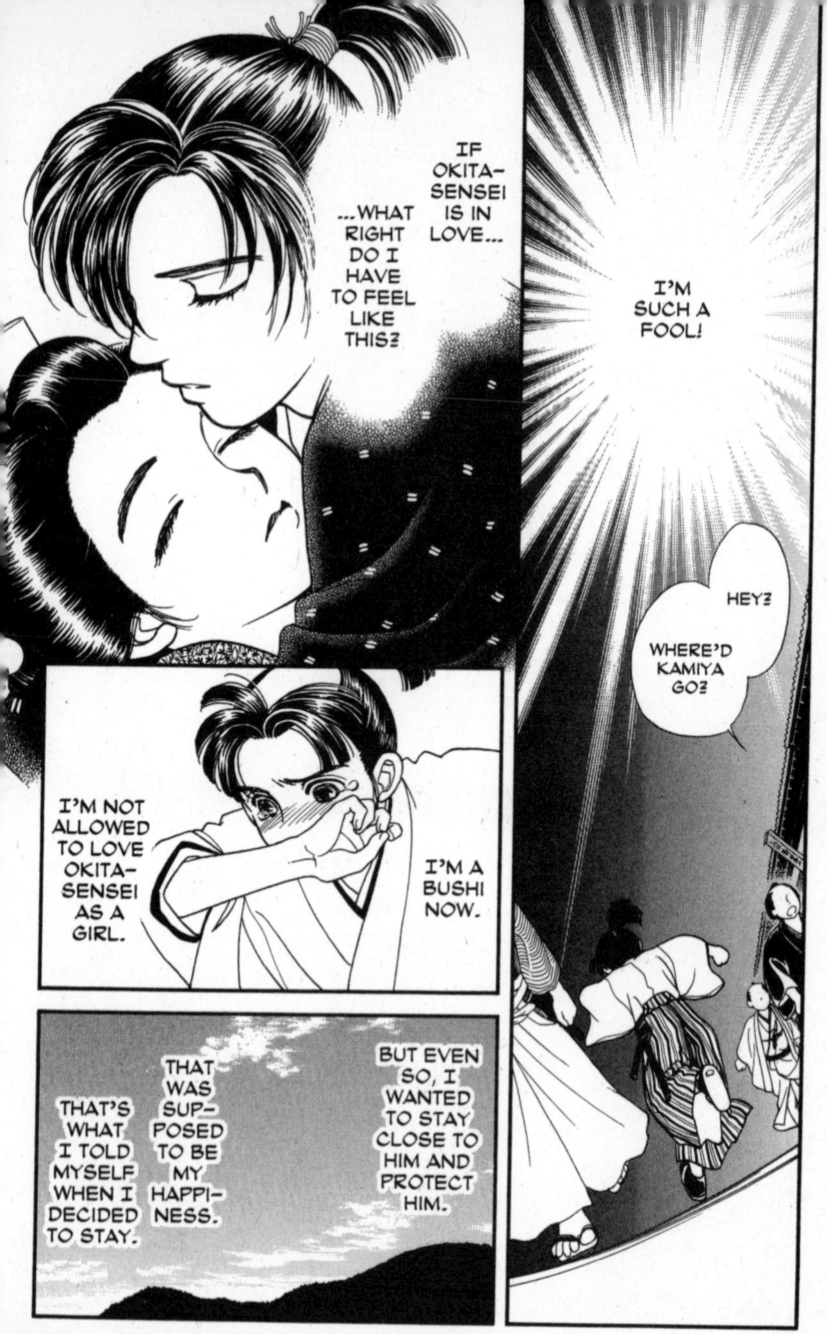
I'M SUCH A FOOL!
HEY?
WHERE'D KAMIYA GO?
IF OKITA-SENSEI IS IN LOVE...
...WHAT RIGHT DO I HAVE TO FEEL LIKE THIS?
I'M A BUSHI NOW.
I'M NOT ALLOWED TO LOVE OKITA-SENSEI AS A GIRL.
BUT EVEN SO, I WANTED TO STAY CLOSE TO HIM AND PROTECT HIM.
THAT WAS SUP-POSED TO BE MY HAPPI-NESS.
THAT'S WHAT I TOLD MYSELF WHEN I DECIDED TO STAY.

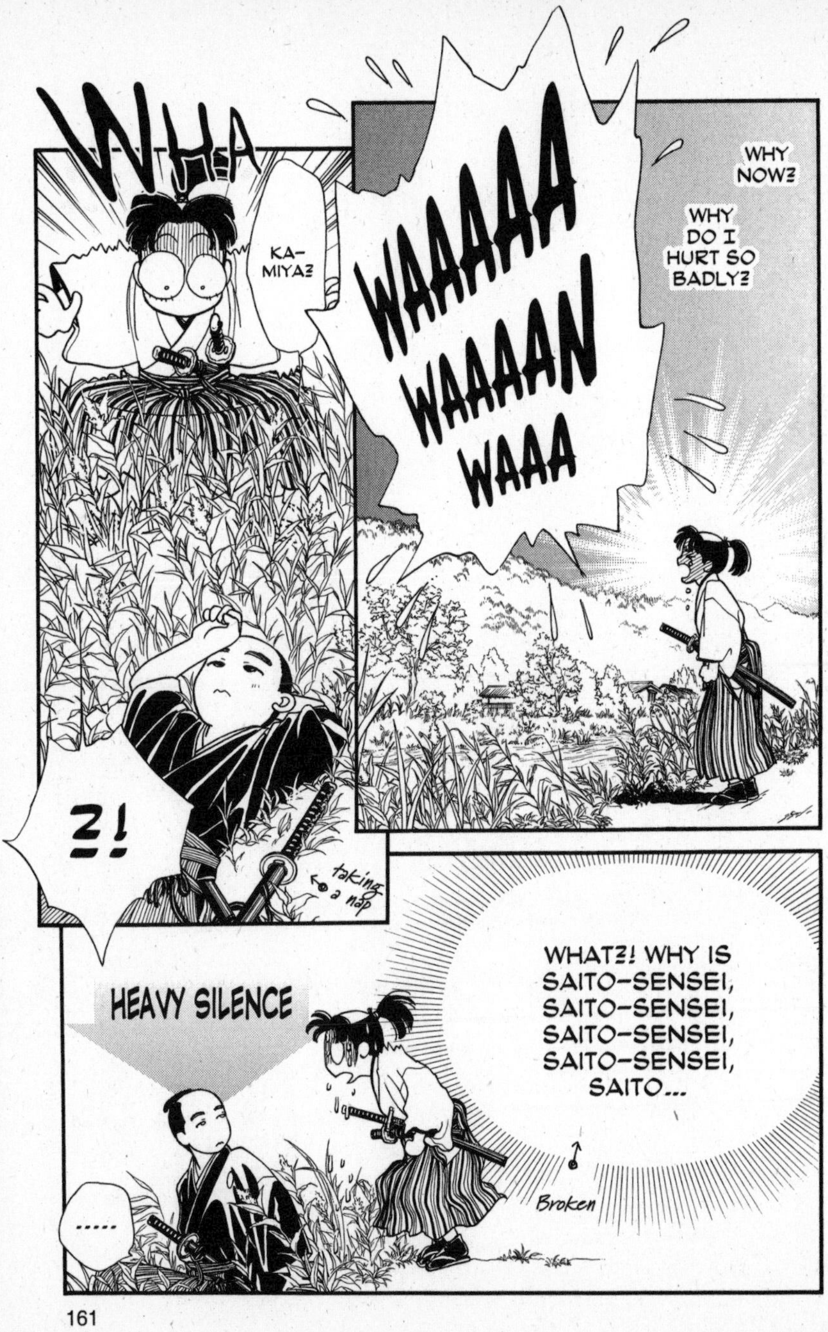
WHY NOW?
WHY DO I HURT SO BADLY?
WAAAAA WAAAAN WAAA
WHA
KA-MIYA?
?!
taking a nap
WHAT?! WHY IS SAITO-SENSEI, SAITO-SENSEI, SAITO-SENSEI, SAITO-SENSEI, SAITO...
Broken
HEAVY SILENCE
......

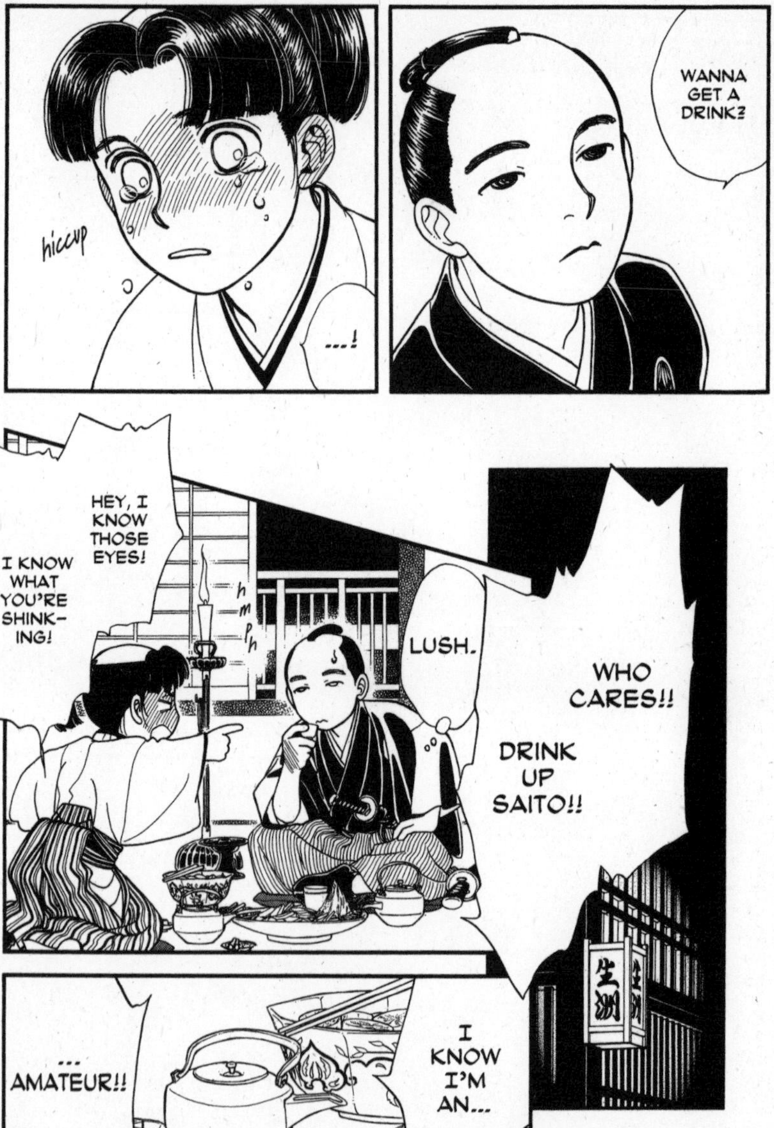
WANNA GET A DRINK?
hiccup
...!
WHO CARES!!
DRINK UP SAITO!!
LUSH.
hmph
HEY, I KNOW THOSE EYES!
I KNOW WHAT YOU'RE SHINK-ING!
生洲
I KNOW I'M AN...
...AMATEUR!!

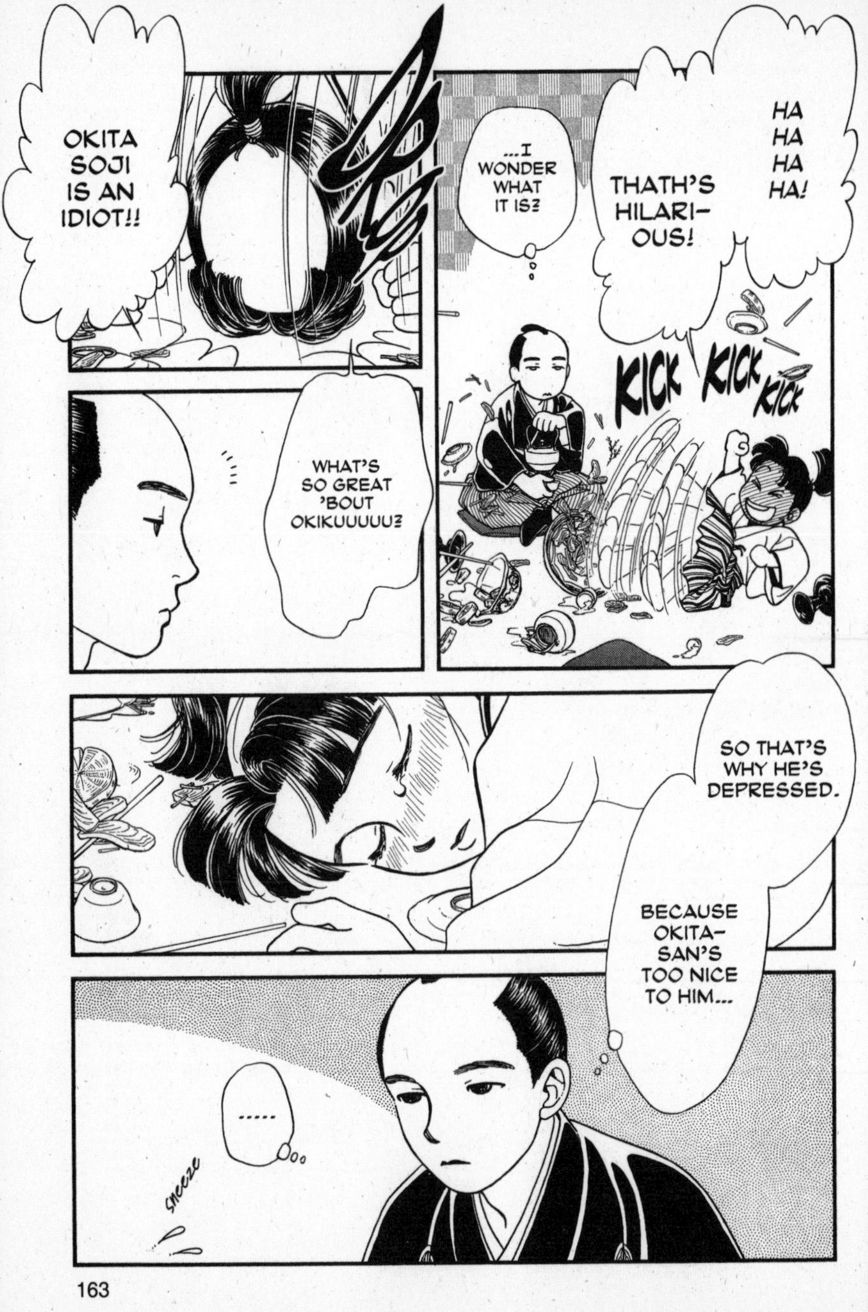
HA HA HA HA!
THATH'S HILARI-OUS!
...I WONDER WHAT IT IS?
KICK KICK KICK
OKITA SOJI IS AN IDIOT!!
WHAT'S SO GREAT 'BOUT OKIKUUUUU?
SO THAT'S WHY HE'S DEPRESSED.
BECAUSE OKITA-SAN'S TOO NICE TO HIM...
.....
sneeze

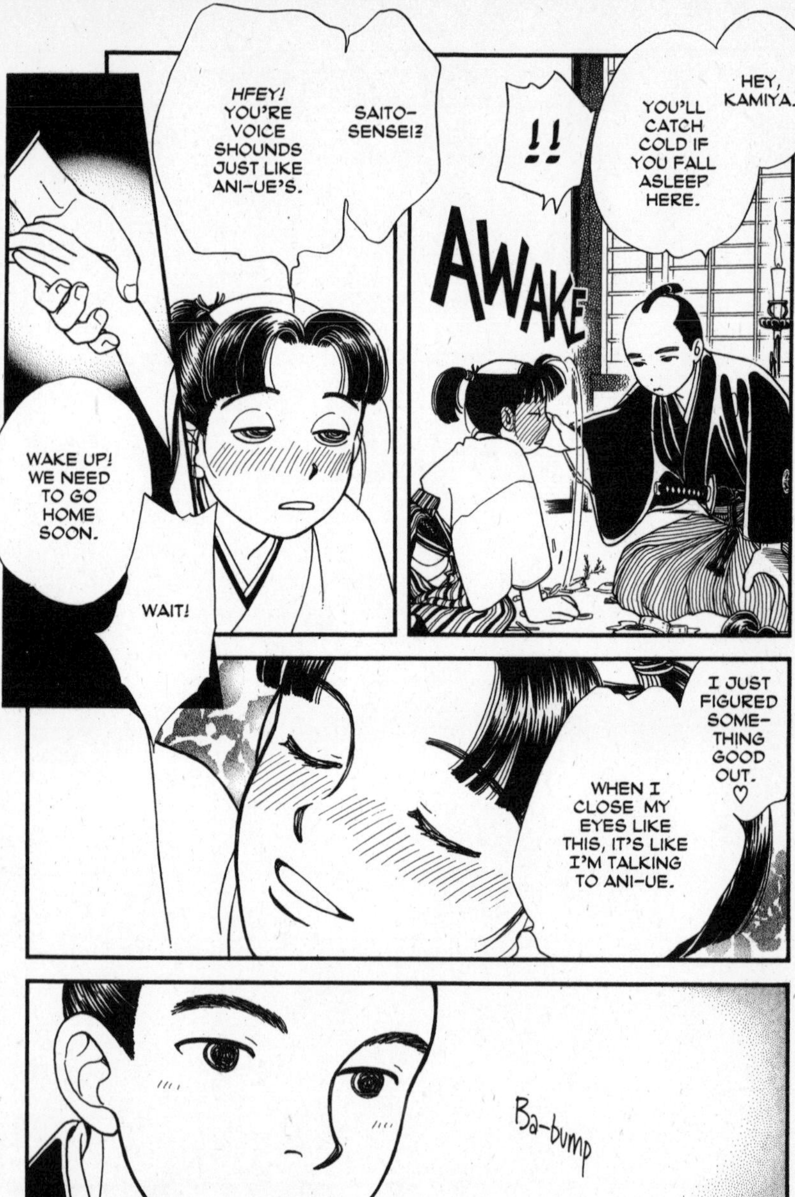
HEY, KAMIYA.
YOU'LL CATCH COLD IF YOU FALL ASLEEP HERE.
!!
AWAKE
SAITO-SENSEI!?
HFEY! YOU'RE VOICE SHOUNDS JUST LIKE ANI-UE'S.
WAKE UP! WE NEED TO GO HOME SOON.
WAIT!
I JUST FIGURED SOME-THING GOOD OUT. ♡
WHEN I CLOSE MY EYES LIKE THIS, IT'S LIKE I'M TALKING TO ANI-UE.
Ba-bump

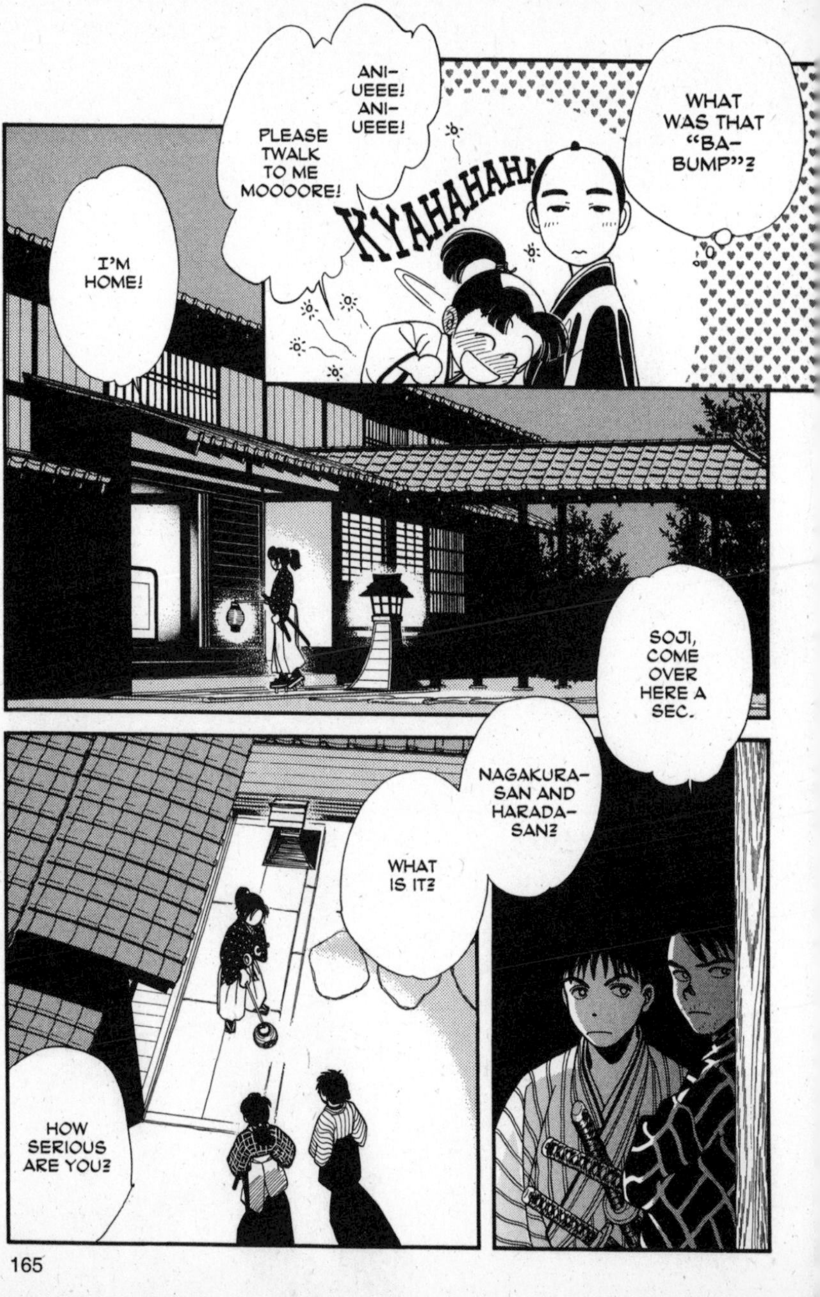
ANI-UEEE! ANI-UEEE!
PLEASE TWALK TO ME MOOOORE!
KYAHAHAHA
WHAT WAS THAT "BA-BUMP"?
I'M HOME!
SOJI, COME OVER HERE A SEC.
NAGAKURA-SAN AND HARADA-SAN?
WHAT IS IT?
HOW SERIOUS ARE YOU?

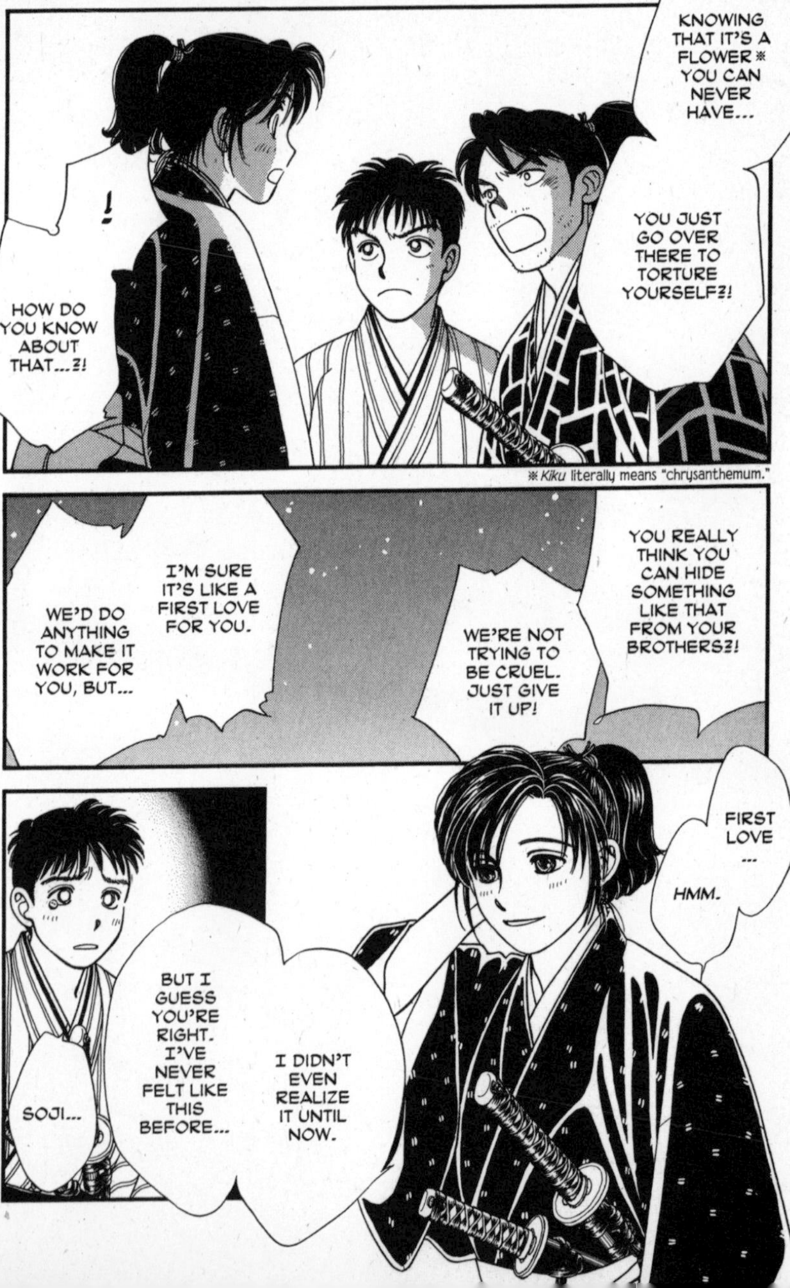
KNOWING THAT IT'S A FLOWER※ YOU CAN NEVER HAVE...
YOU JUST GO OVER THERE TO TORTURE YOURSELF?!
!
HOW DO YOU KNOW ABOUT THAT...?!
YOU REALLY THINK YOU CAN HIDE SOMETHING LIKE THAT FROM YOUR BROTHERS?!
WE'RE NOT TRYING TO BE CRUEL. JUST GIVE IT UP!
I'M SURE IT'S LIKE A FIRST LOVE FOR YOU.
WE'D DO ANYTHING TO MAKE IT WORK FOR YOU, BUT...
FIRST LOVE ...
HMM.
BUT I GUESS YOU'RE RIGHT. I'VE NEVER FELT LIKE THIS BEFORE...
I DIDN'T EVEN REALIZE IT UNTIL NOW.
SOJI...

※*Kiku* literally means "chrysanthemum."

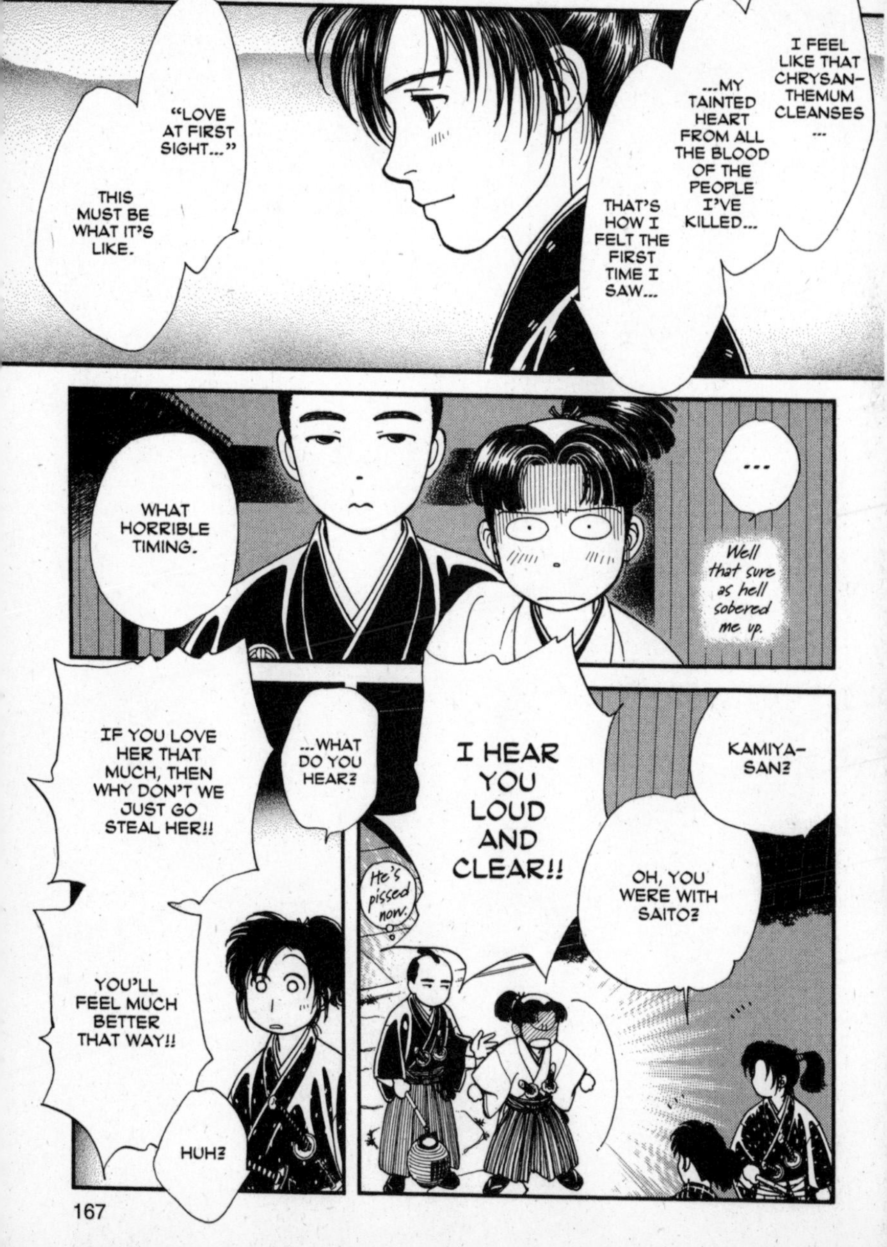

I FEEL LIKE THAT CHRYSANTHEMUM CLEANSES...
...MY TAINTED HEART FROM ALL THE BLOOD OF THE PEOPLE I'VE KILLED...
THAT'S HOW I FELT THE FIRST TIME I SAW...
“LOVE AT FIRST SIGHT...” THIS MUST BE WHAT IT'S LIKE.
...
Well that sure as hell sobered me up.
WHAT HORRIBLE TIMING.
KAMIYA-SAN?
OH, YOU WERE WITH SAITO?
I HEAR YOU LOUD AND CLEAR!!
He's pissed now.
...WHAT DO YOU HEAR?
IF YOU LOVE HER THAT MUCH, THEN WHY DON'T WE JUST GO STEAL HER!!
YOU'LL FEEL MUCH BETTER THAT WAY!!
HUH?

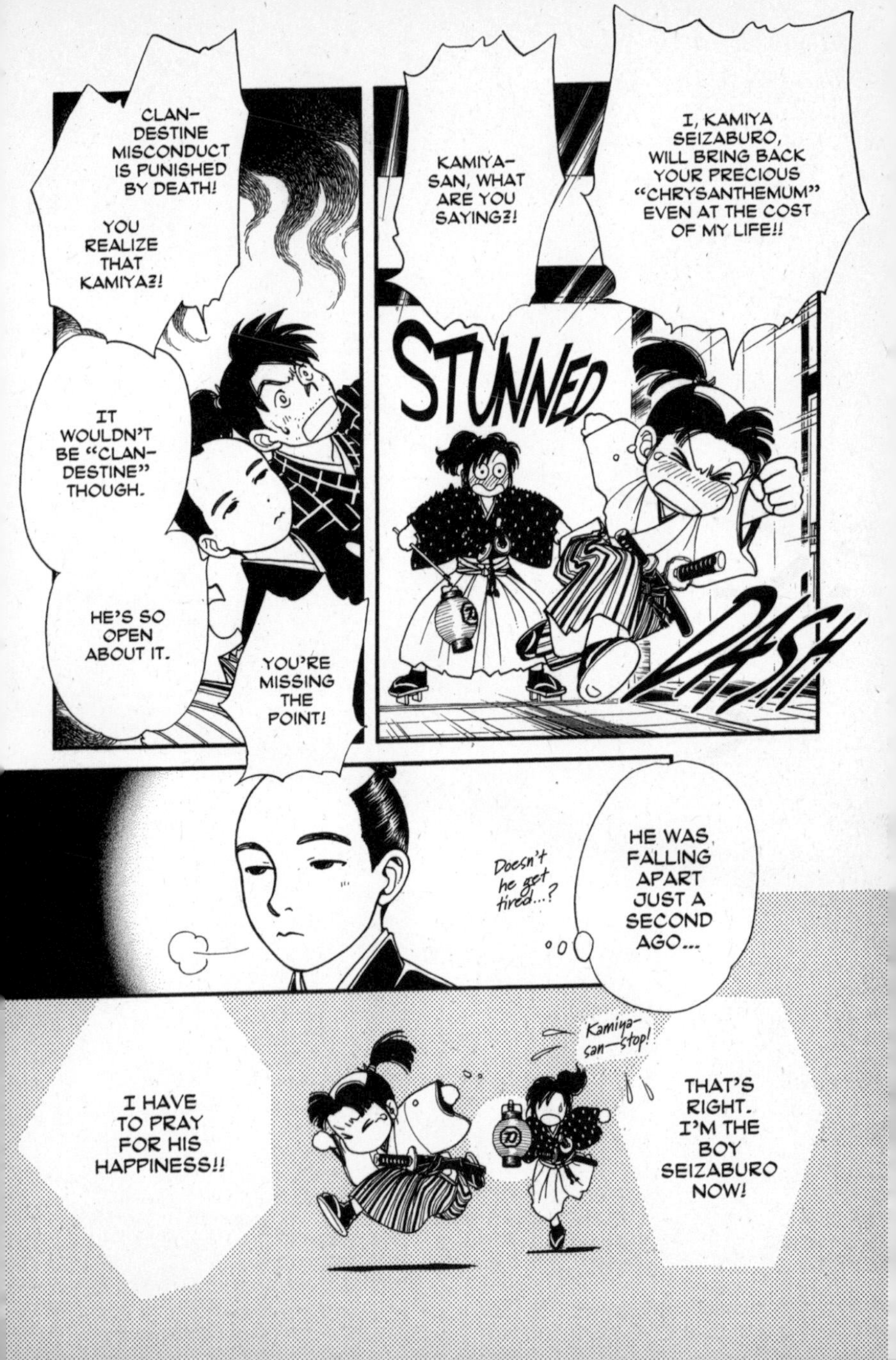
I, KAMIYA SEIZABURO, WILL BRING BACK YOUR PRECIOUS "CHRYSANTHEMUM" EVEN AT THE COST OF MY LIFE!!
KAMIYA-SAN, WHAT ARE YOU SAYING?!
STUNNED
DASH
CLAN-DESTINE MISCONDUCT IS PUNISHED BY DEATH!
YOU REALIZE THAT KAMIYA?!
IT WOULDN'T BE "CLAN-DESTINE" THOUGH.
HE'S SO OPEN ABOUT IT.
YOU'RE MISSING THE POINT!
HE WAS FALLING APART JUST A SECOND AGO...
Doesn't he get tired...?
THAT'S RIGHT. I'M THE BOY SEIZABURO NOW!
Kamiya-san—stop!
I HAVE TO PRAY FOR HIS HAPPINESS!!

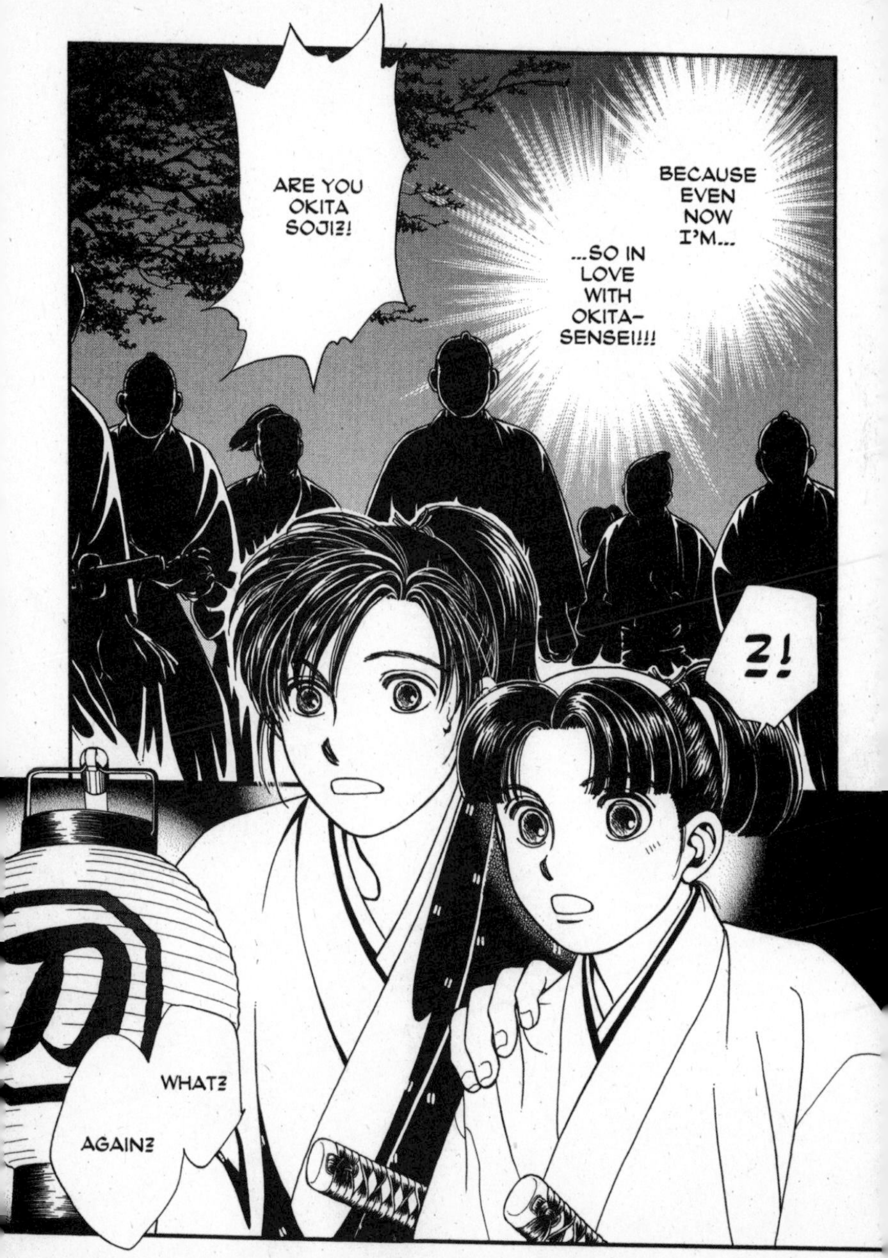
BECAUSE EVEN NOW I'M...
...SO IN LOVE WITH OKITA-SENSEI!!!!
ARE YOU OKITA SOJI?!
?!
WHAT?
AGAIN?

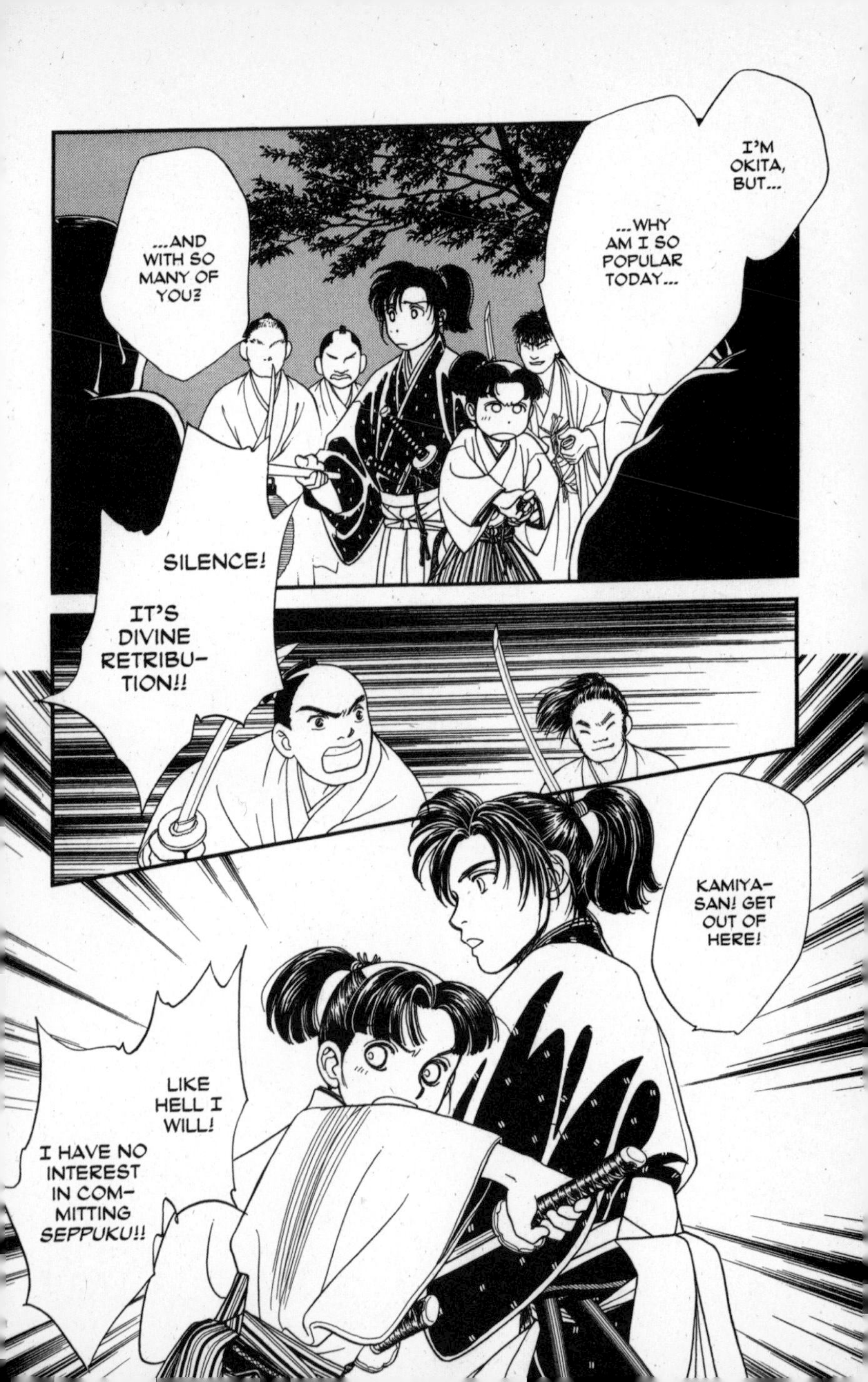
I'M OKITA, BUT...
...WHY AM I SO POPULAR TODAY...
...AND WITH SO MANY OF YOU?
SILENCE!
IT'S DIVINE RETRIBU-TION!!
KAMIYA-SAN! GET OUT OF HERE!
LIKE HELL I WILL!
I HAVE NO INTEREST IN COM-MITTING SEPPUKU!!

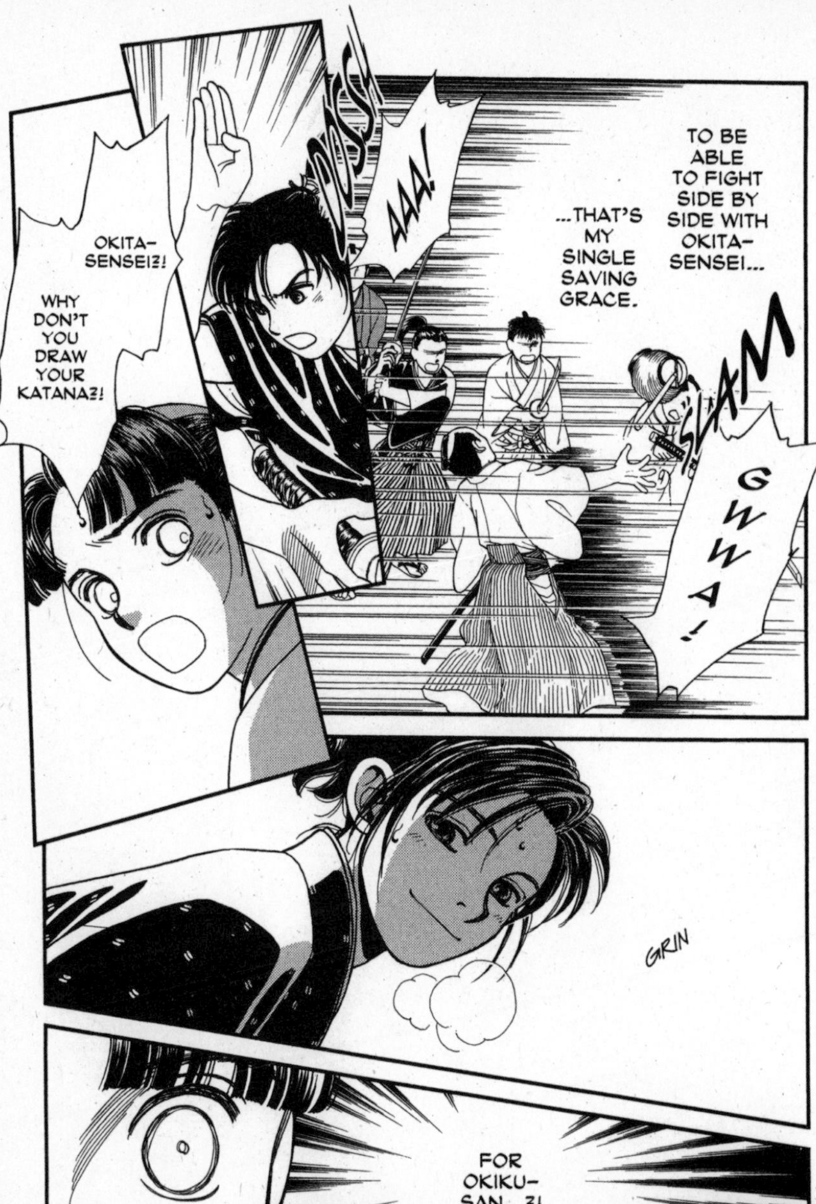
TO BE ABLE TO FIGHT SIDE BY SIDE WITH OKITA-SENSEI...
...THAT'S MY SINGLE SAVING GRACE.
AAA!
SLAM
GWWA!
OKITA-SENSEI?!
WHY DON'T YOU DRAW YOUR KATANA?!
GRIN
FOR OKIKU-SAN...?!

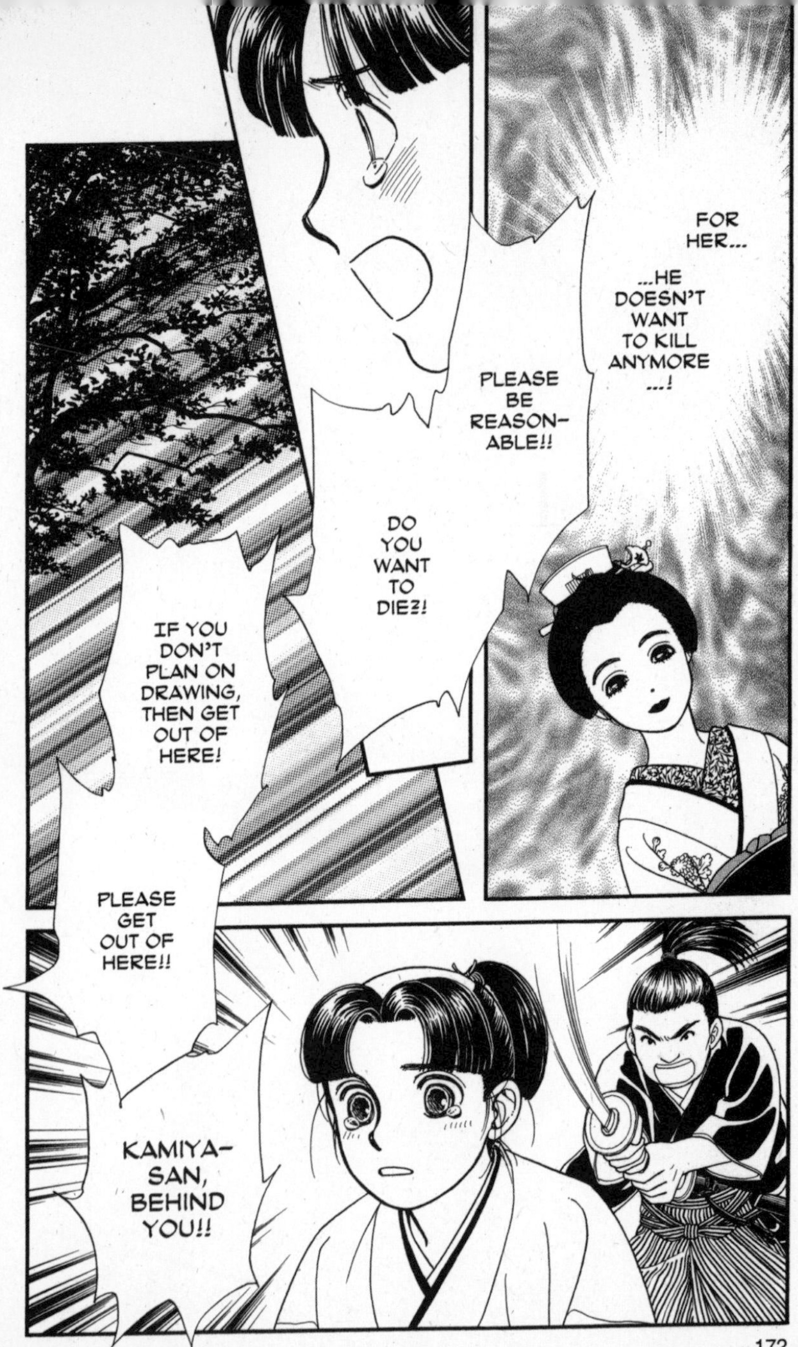
FOR HER...
...HE DOESN'T WANT TO KILL ANYMORE ...!
PLEASE BE REASON-ABLE!!
DO YOU WANT TO DIE?!
IF YOU DON'T PLAN ON DRAWING, THEN GET OUT OF HERE!
PLEASE GET OUT OF HERE!!
KAMIYA-SAN, BEHIND YOU!!

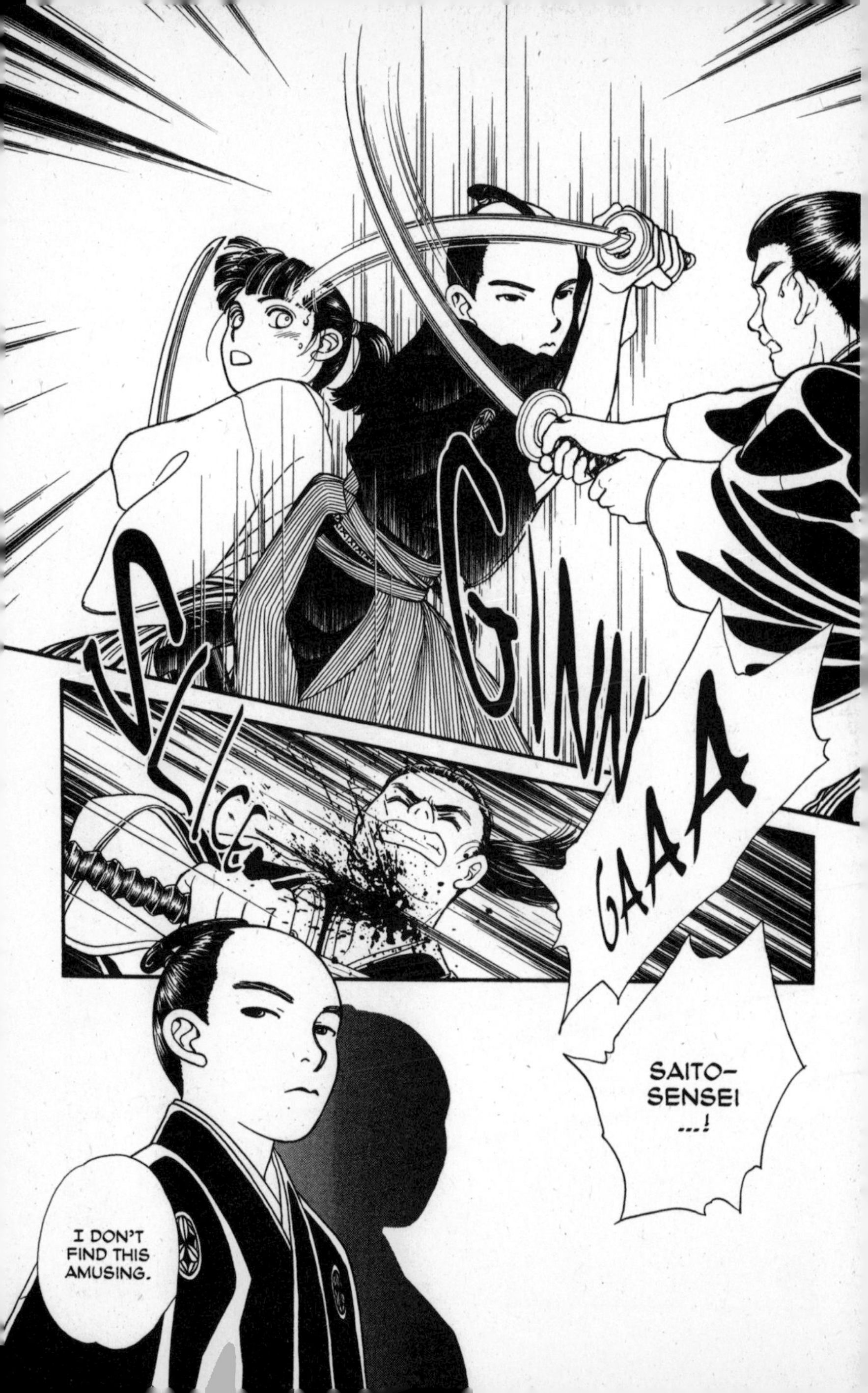
GINN
GAAA
SAITO-SENSEI ...!
I DON'T FIND THIS AMUSING.

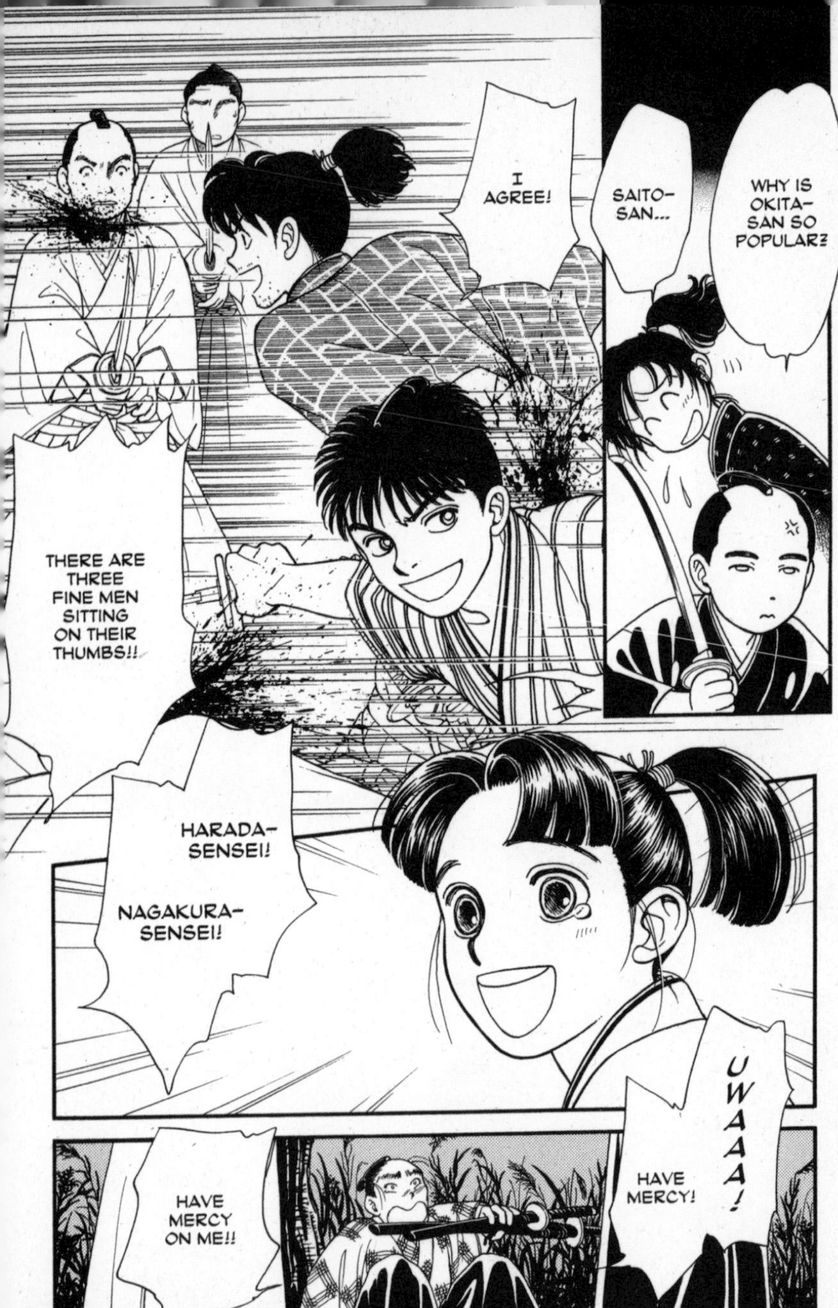
WHY IS OKITA-SAN SO POPULAR?
SAITO-SAN...
I AGREE!
THERE ARE THREE FINE MEN SITTING ON THEIR THUMBS!!
HARADA-SENSEI!
NAGAKURA-SENSEI!
UWAAAA!
HAVE MERCY!
HAVE MERCY ON ME!!

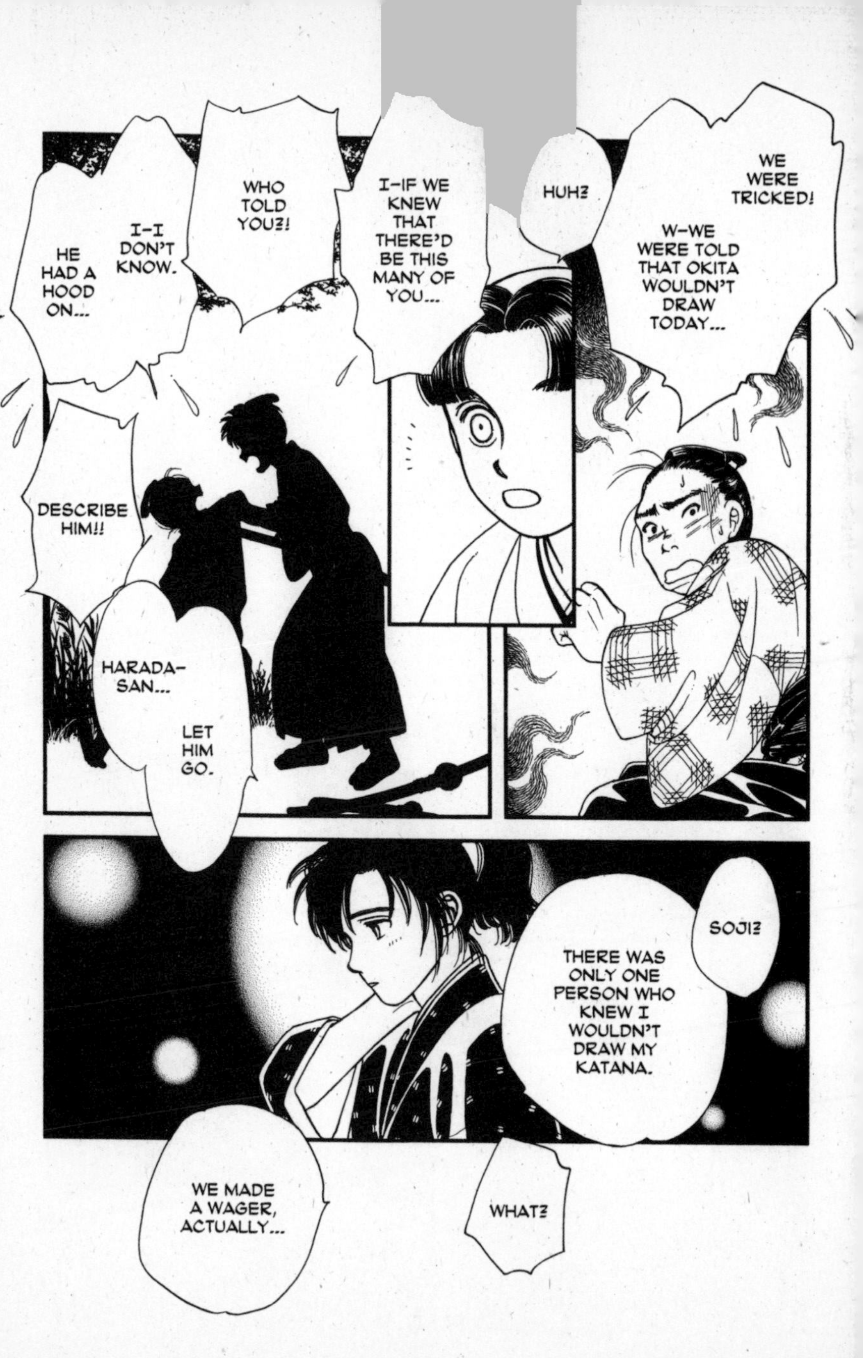
WE WERE TRICKED!
W-WE WERE TOLD THAT OKITA WOULDN'T DRAW TODAY...
HUH?
I-IF WE KNEW THAT THERE'D BE THIS MANY OF YOU...
WHO TOLD YOU?!
I-I DON'T KNOW.
HE HAD A HOOD ON...
DESCRIBE HIM!!
HARADA-SAN...
LET HIM GO.
SOJI?
THERE WAS ONLY ONE PERSON WHO KNEW I WOULDN'T DRAW MY KATANA.
WHAT?
WE MADE A WAGER, ACTUALLY...

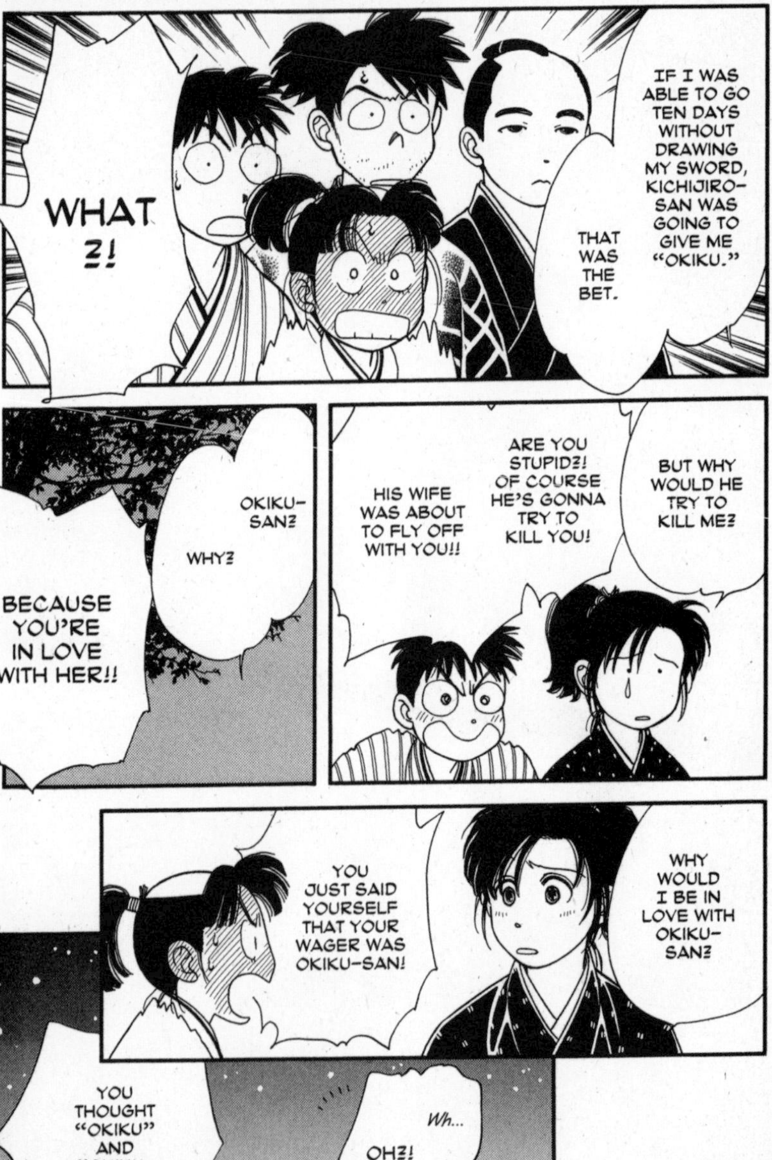
IF I WAS ABLE TO GO TEN DAYS WITHOUT DRAWING MY SWORD, KICHIJIRO-SAN WAS GOING TO GIVE ME "OKIKU."
THAT WAS THE BET.
WHAT ?!
BUT WHY WOULD HE TRY TO KILL ME?
ARE YOU STUPID?! OF COURSE HE'S GONNA TRY TO KILL YOU!
HIS WIFE WAS ABOUT TO FLY OFF WITH YOU!!
OKIKU-SAN?
WHY?
BECAUSE YOU'RE IN LOVE WITH HER!!
WHY WOULD I BE IN LOVE WITH OKIKU-SAN?
YOU JUST SAID YOURSELF THAT YOUR WAGER WAS OKIKU-SAN!
Wh...
OH?!
YOU THOUGHT "OKIKU" AND "OKIKU-SAN"...?!

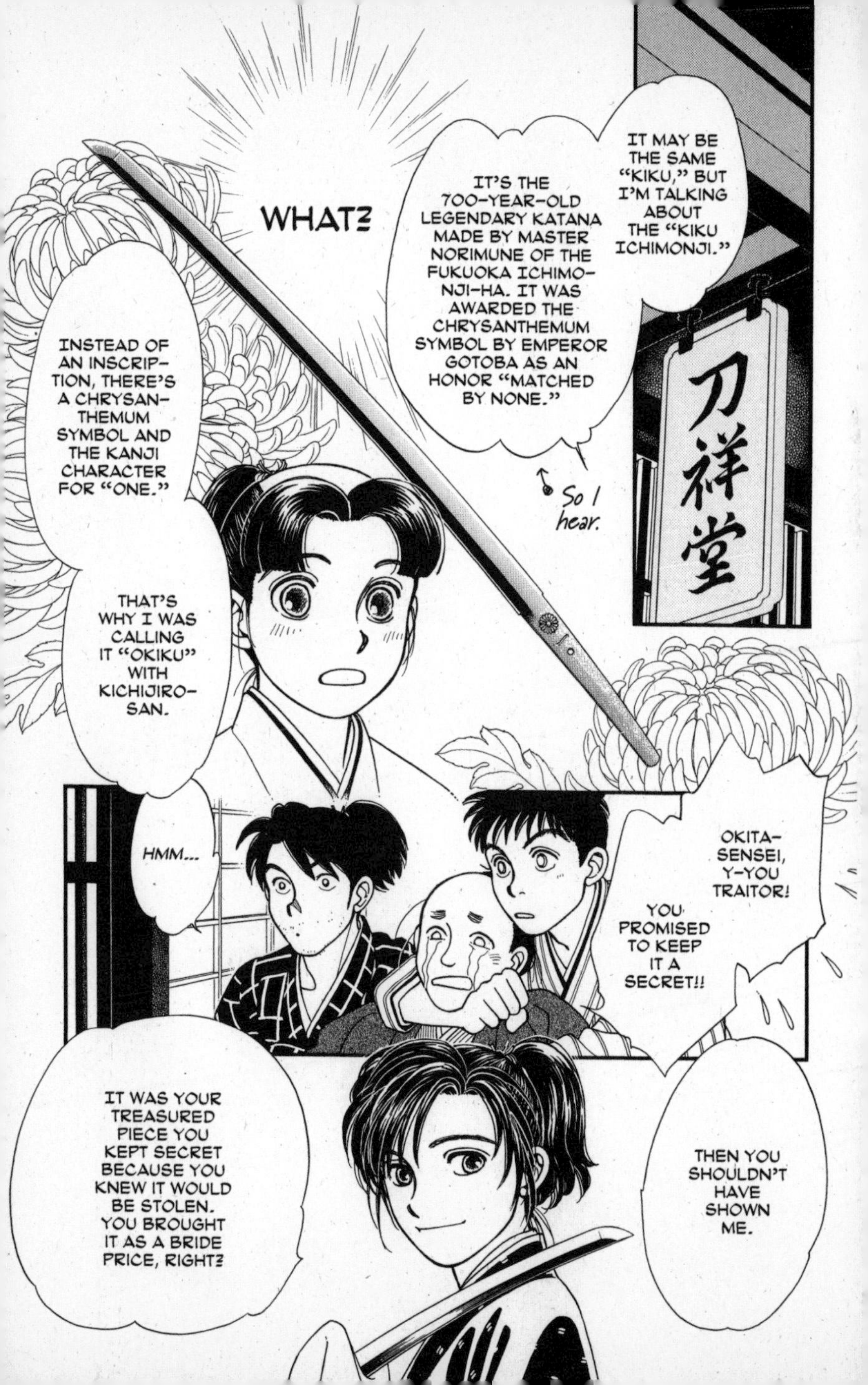
IT MAY BE THE SAME "KIKU," BUT I'M TALKING ABOUT THE "KIKU ICHIMONJI."
IT'S THE 700-YEAR-OLD LEGENDARY KATANA MADE BY MASTER NORIMUNE OF THE FUKUOKA ICHIMONJI-HA. IT WAS AWARDED THE CHRYSANTHEMUM SYMBOL BY EMPEROR GOTOBA AS AN HONOR "MATCHED BY NONE."
So I hear.
刀祥堂
WHAT?
INSTEAD OF AN INSCRIPTION, THERE'S A CHRYSANTHEMUM SYMBOL AND THE KANJI CHARACTER FOR "ONE."
THAT'S WHY I WAS CALLING IT "OKIKU" WITH KICHIJIRO-SAN.
OKITA-SENSEI, Y-YOU TRAITOR!
YOU PROMISED TO KEEP IT A SECRET!!
HMM...
THEN YOU SHOULDN'T HAVE SHOWN ME.
IT WAS YOUR TREASURED PIECE YOU KEPT SECRET BECAUSE YOU KNEW IT WOULD BE STOLEN. YOU BROUGHT IT AS A BRIDE PRICE, RIGHT?

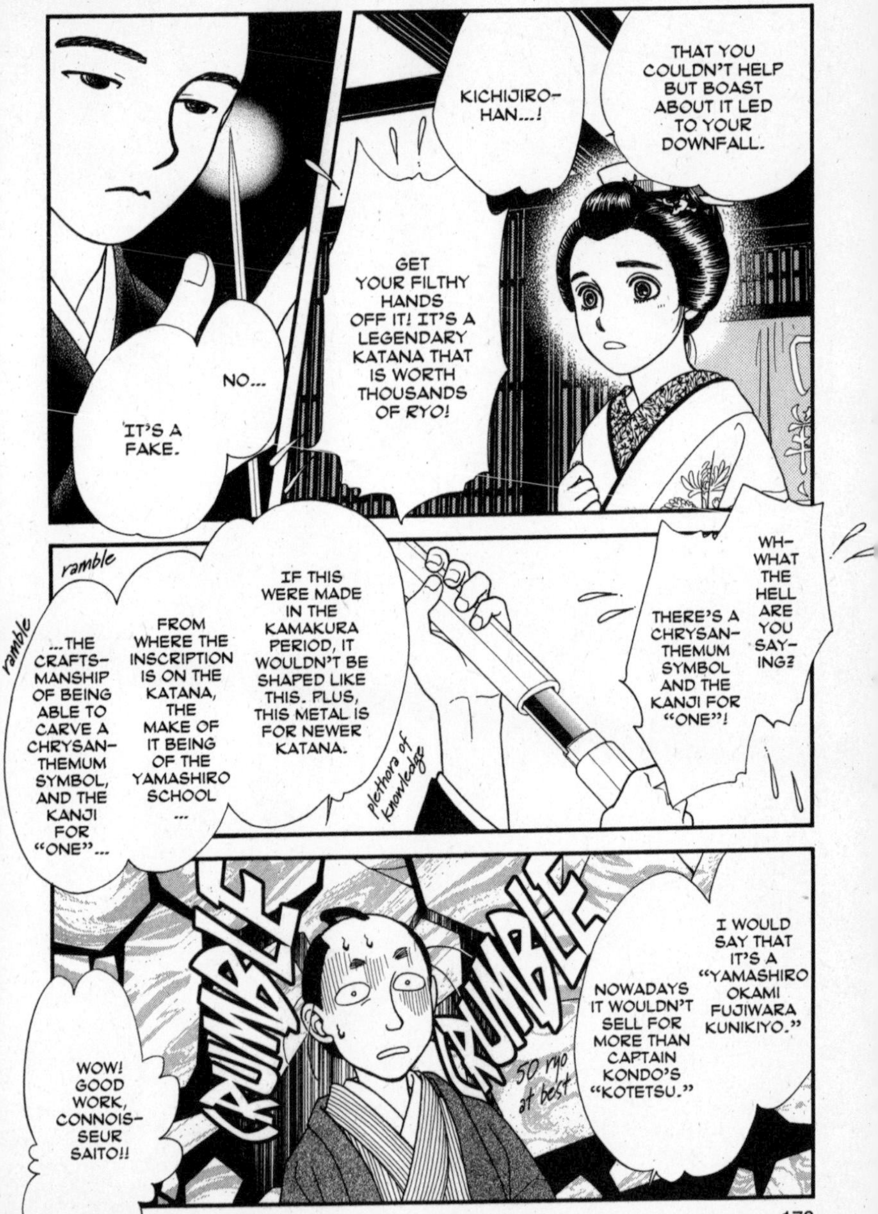
THAT YOU COULDN'T HELP BUT BOAST ABOUT IT LED TO YOUR DOWNFALL.
KICHIJIRO-HAN...!
GET YOUR FILTHY HANDS OFF IT! IT'S A LEGENDARY KATANA THAT IS WORTH THOUSANDS OF RYO!
NO...
IT'S A FAKE.
WH-WHAT THE HELL ARE YOU SAYING?
THERE'S A CHRYSANTHEMUM SYMBOL AND THE KANJI FOR "ONE"!
IF THIS WERE MADE IN THE KAMAKURA PERIOD, IT WOULDN'T BE SHAPED LIKE THIS. PLUS, THIS METAL IS FOR NEWER KATANA.
plethora of knowledge
FROM WHERE THE INSCRIPTION IS ON THE KATANA, THE MAKE OF IT BEING OF THE YAMASHIRO SCHOOL ...
...THE CRAFTSMANSHIP OF BEING ABLE TO CARVE A CHRYSANTHEMUM SYMBOL, AND THE KANJI FOR "ONE"...
ramble
ramble
I WOULD SAY THAT IT'S A "YAMASHIRO OKAMI FUJIWARA KUNIKIYO."
NOWADAYS IT WOULDN'T SELL FOR MORE THAN CAPTAIN KONDO'S "KOTETSU."
50 ryo at best
CRUMBLE
CRUMBLE
WOW! GOOD WORK, CONNOISSEUR SAITO!!

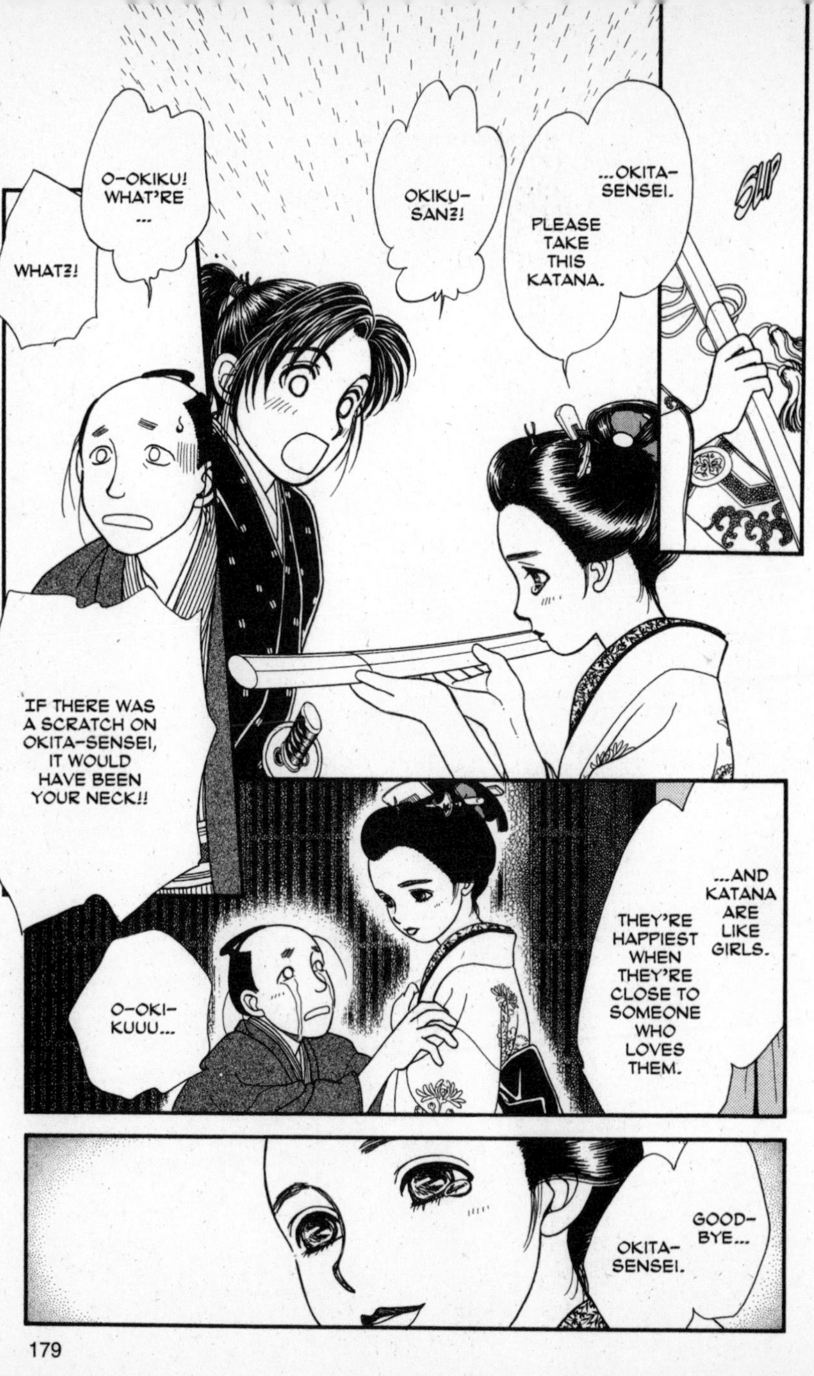
SLIP
...OKITA-SENSEI.
PLEASE TAKE THIS KATANA.
OKIKU-SAN?!
O-OKIKU! WHAT'RE ...
WHAT?!
IF THERE WAS A SCRATCH ON OKITA-SENSEI, IT WOULD HAVE BEEN YOUR NECK!!
...AND KATANA ARE LIKE GIRLS.
THEY'RE HAPPIEST WHEN THEY'RE CLOSE TO SOMEONE WHO LOVES THEM.
O-OKI-KUUU...
GOOD-BYE...
OKITA-SENSEI.

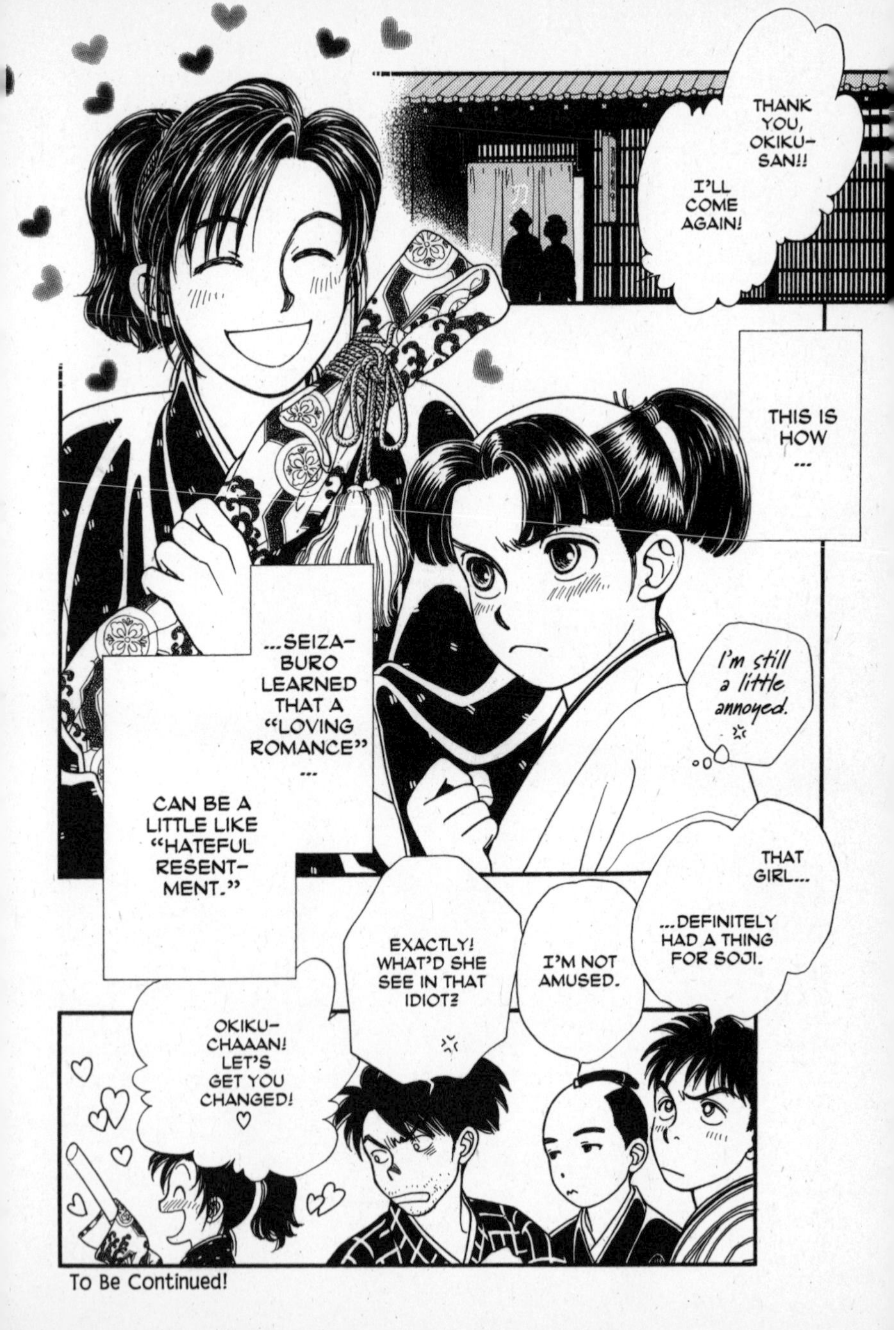
THANK YOU, OKIKU-SAN!!
I'LL COME AGAIN!
THIS IS HOW ...
...SEIZABURO LEARNED THAT A "LOVING ROMANCE"...
CAN BE A LITTLE LIKE "HATEFUL RESENTMENT."
I'm still a little annoyed.
THAT GIRL...
...DEFINITELY HAD A THING FOR SOJI.
I'M NOT AMUSED.
EXACTLY! WHAT'D SHE SEE IN THAT IDIOT?
OKIKU-CHAAAN! LET'S GET YOU CHANGED! ♡

To Be Continued!

TAEKO WATANABE PRESENTS

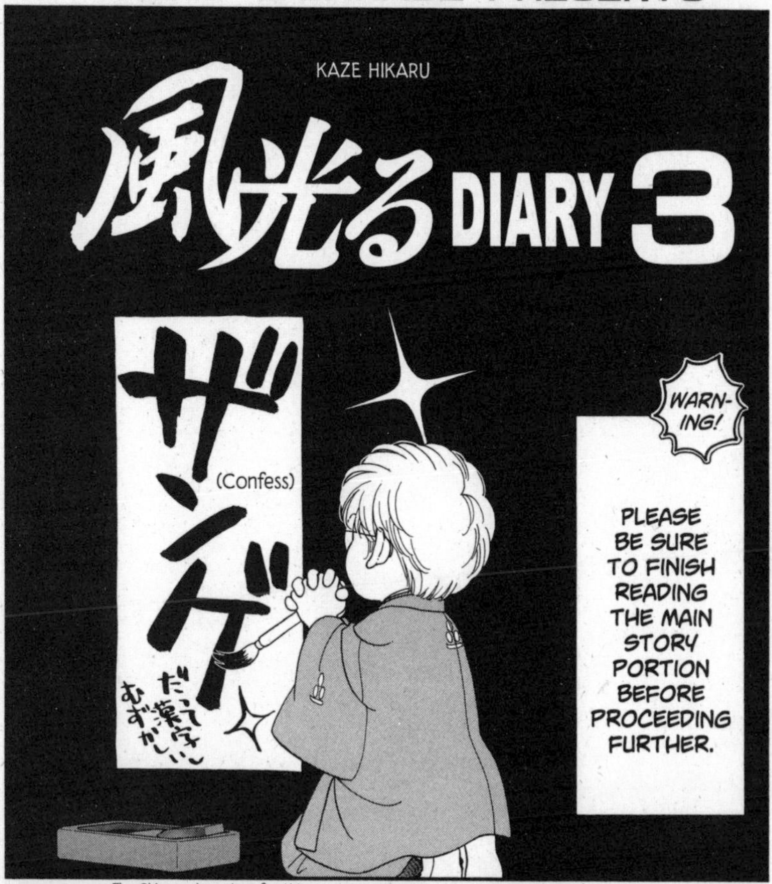
KAZE HIKARU
風光る DIARY 3
WARNING!
PLEASE BE SURE TO FINISH READING THE MAIN STORY PORTION BEFORE PROCEEDING FURTHER.
ザンゲ
(Confess)
だって漢字むずかしい

The Chinese characters for this word are so hard...

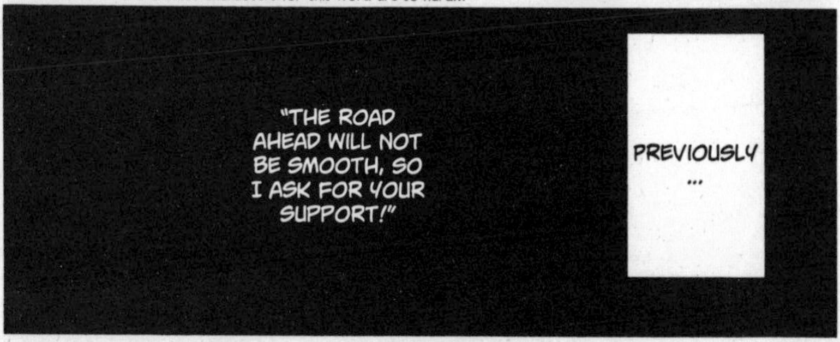
PREVIOUSLY ...
"THE ROAD AHEAD WILL NOT BE SMOOTH, SO I ASK FOR YOUR SUPPORT!"

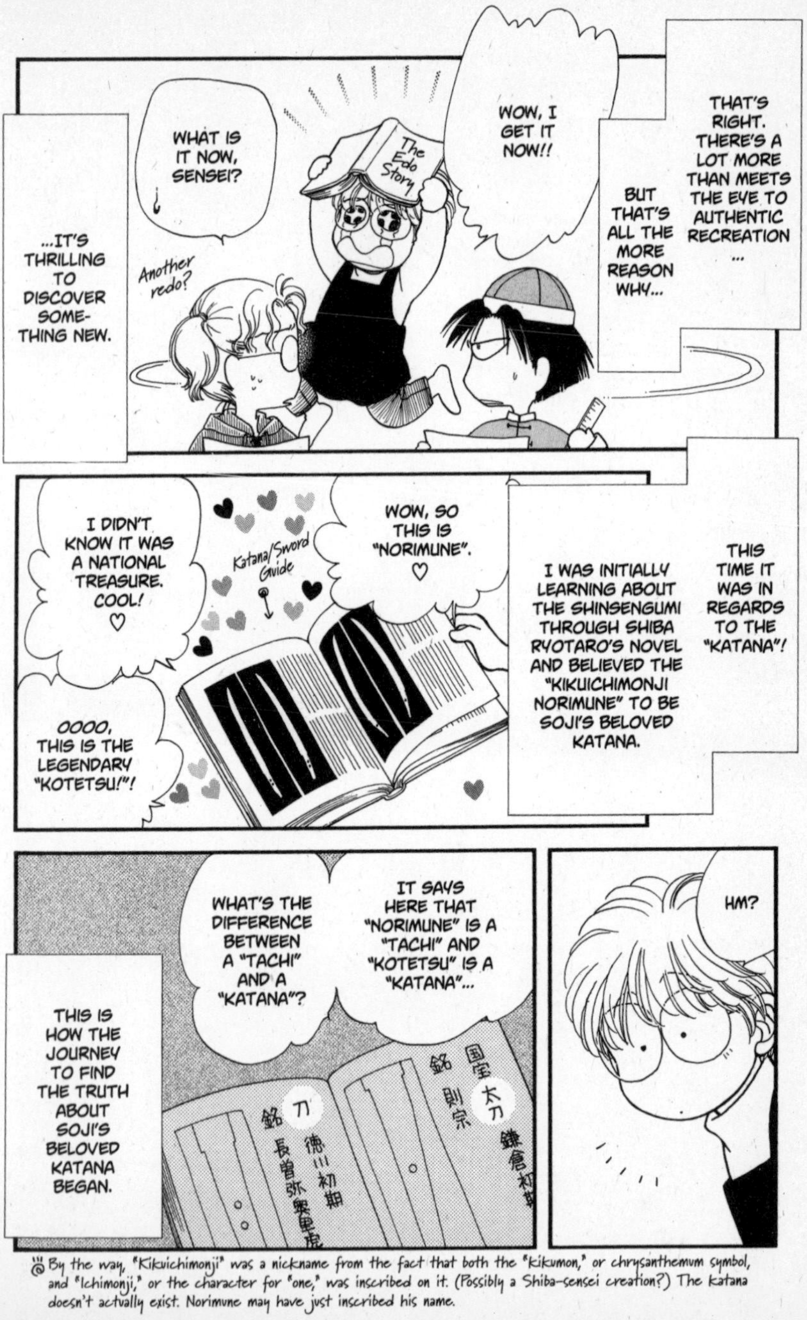
THAT'S RIGHT. THERE'S A LOT MORE THAN MEETS THE EYE TO AUTHENTIC RECREATION ...
BUT THAT'S ALL THE MORE REASON WHY...
WOW, I GET IT NOW!!
The Edo Story
WHAT IS IT NOW, SENSEI?
Another redo?
...IT'S THRILLING TO DISCOVER SOME-THING NEW.
THIS TIME IT WAS IN REGARDS TO THE "KATANA"!
I WAS INITIALLY LEARNING ABOUT THE SHINSENGUMI THROUGH SHIBA RYOTARO'S NOVEL AND BELIEVED THE "KIKUICHIMONJI NORIMUNE" TO BE SOJI'S BELOVED KATANA.
WOW, SO THIS IS "NORIMUNE". ♡
Katana/Sword Guide
I DIDN'T KNOW IT WAS A NATIONAL TREASURE. COOL! ♡
OOOO, THIS IS THE LEGENDARY "KOTETSU!"!
HM?
IT SAYS HERE THAT "NORIMUNE" IS A "TACHI" AND "KOTETSU" IS A "KATANA"...
WHAT'S THE DIFFERENCE BETWEEN A "TACHI" AND A "KATANA"?
国宝
太刀
銘
則宗
鎌倉初期
刀
銘
徳川初期
THIS IS HOW THE JOURNEY TO FIND THE TRUTH ABOUT SOJI'S BELOVED KATANA BEGAN.

By the way, "Kikuichimonji" was a nickname from the fact that both the "kikumon," or chrysanthemum symbol, and "Ichimonji," or the character for "one," was inscribed on it. (Possibly a Shiba-sensei creation?) The katana doesn't actually exist. Norimune may have just inscribed his name.

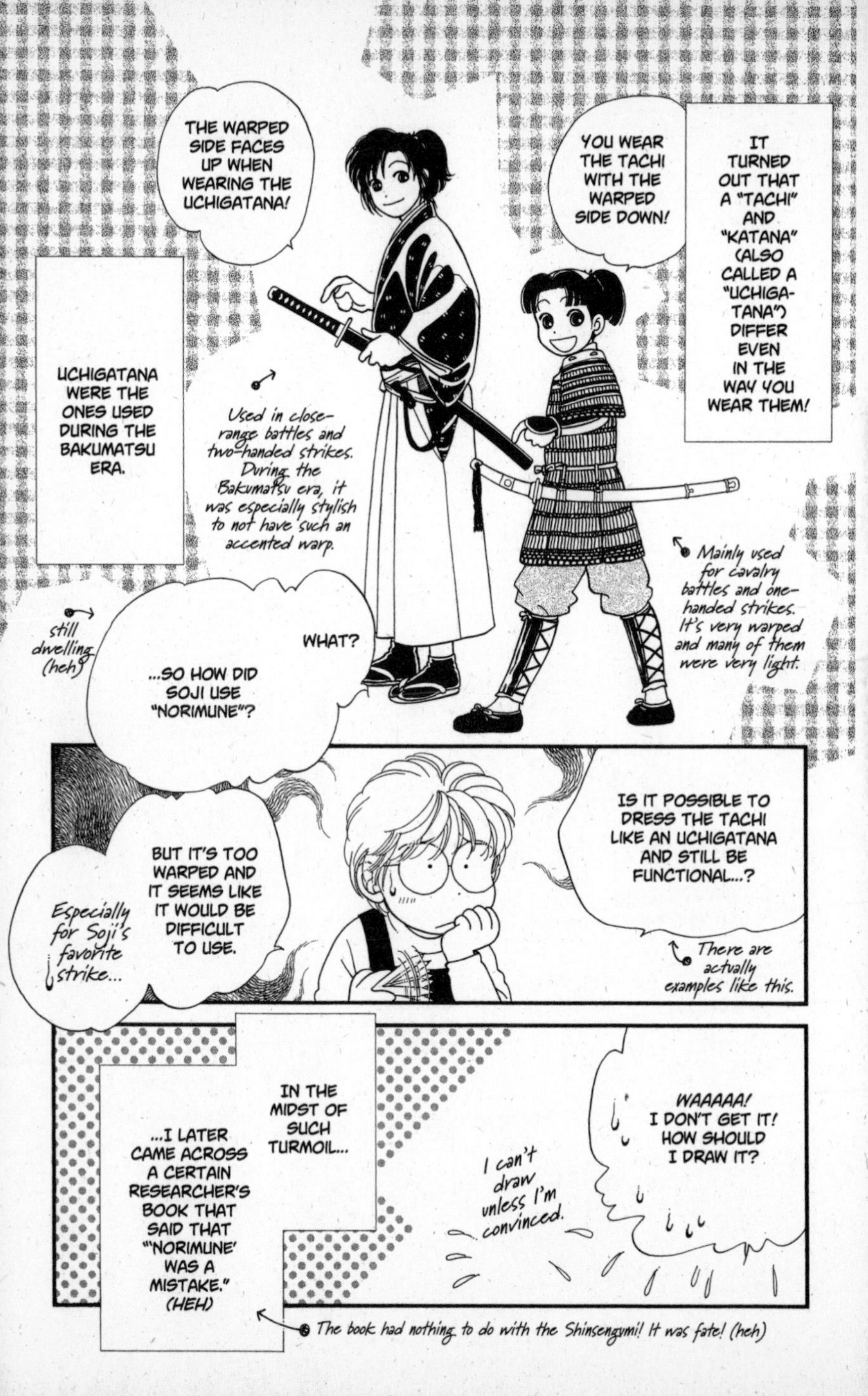
IT TURNED OUT THAT A "TACHI" AND "KATANA" (ALSO CALLED A "UCHIGATANA") DIFFER EVEN IN THE WAY YOU WEAR THEM!
YOU WEAR THE TACHI WITH THE WARPED SIDE DOWN!
THE WARPED SIDE FACES UP WHEN WEARING THE UCHIGATANA!
UCHIGATANA WERE THE ONES USED DURING THE BAKUMATSU ERA.
Mainly used for cavalry battles and one-handed strikes. It's very warped and many of them were very light.
Used in close-range battles and two-handed strikes. During the Bakumatsu era, it was especially stylish to not have such an accented warp.
WHAT?
...SO HOW DID SOJI USE "NORIMUNE"?
still dwelling (heh)
IS IT POSSIBLE TO DRESS THE TACHI LIKE AN UCHIGATANA AND STILL BE FUNCTIONAL...?
There are actually examples like this.
BUT IT'S TOO WARPED AND IT SEEMS LIKE IT WOULD BE DIFFICULT TO USE.
Especially for Soji's favorite strike...
WAAAAA! I DON'T GET IT! HOW SHOULD I DRAW IT?
I can't draw unless I'm convinced.
IN THE MIDST OF SUCH TURMOIL...
...I LATER CAME ACROSS A CERTAIN RESEARCHER'S BOOK THAT SAID THAT "'NORIMUNE' WAS A MISTAKE." (HEH)
The book had nothing to do with the Shinsengumi! It was fate! (heh)

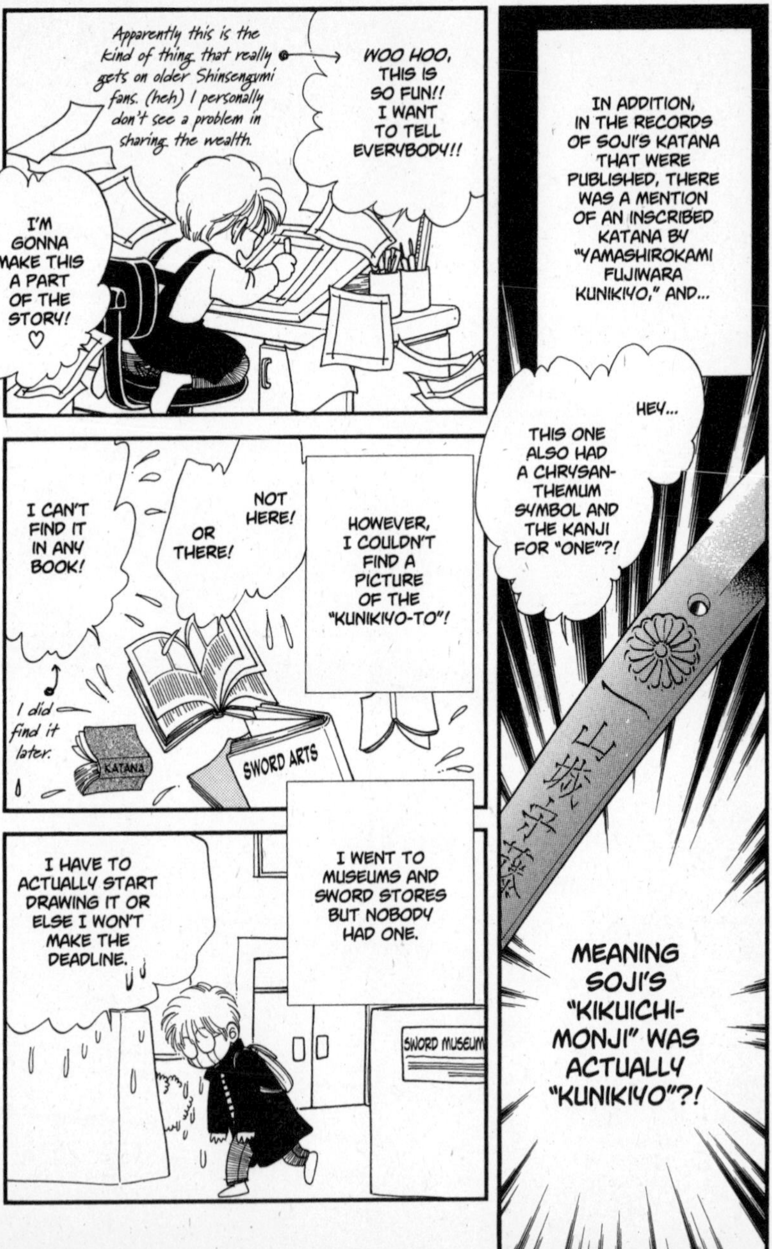
IN ADDITION, IN THE RECORDS OF SOJI'S KATANA THAT WERE PUBLISHED, THERE WAS A MENTION OF AN INSCRIBED KATANA BY "YAMASHIROKAMI FUJIWARA KUNIKIYO," AND...
HEY...
THIS ONE ALSO HAD A CHRYSANTHEMUM SYMBOL AND THE KANJI FOR "ONE"?!
MEANING SOJI'S "KIKUICHI-MONJI" WAS ACTUALLY "KUNIKIYO"?!
WOO HOO, THIS IS SO FUN!! I WANT TO TELL EVERYBODY!!
Apparently this is the kind of thing that really gets on older Shinsengumi fans. (heh) I personally don't see a problem in sharing the wealth.
I'M GONNA MAKE THIS A PART OF THE STORY! ♡
HOWEVER, I COULDN'T FIND A PICTURE OF THE "KUNIKIYO-TO"!
NOT HERE!
OR THERE!
I CAN'T FIND IT IN ANY BOOK!
I did find it later.
SWORD ARTS
KATANA
I WENT TO MUSEUMS AND SWORD STORES BUT NOBODY HAD ONE.
I HAVE TO ACTUALLY START DRAWING IT OR ELSE I WON'T MAKE THE DEADLINE.
SWORD MUSEUM

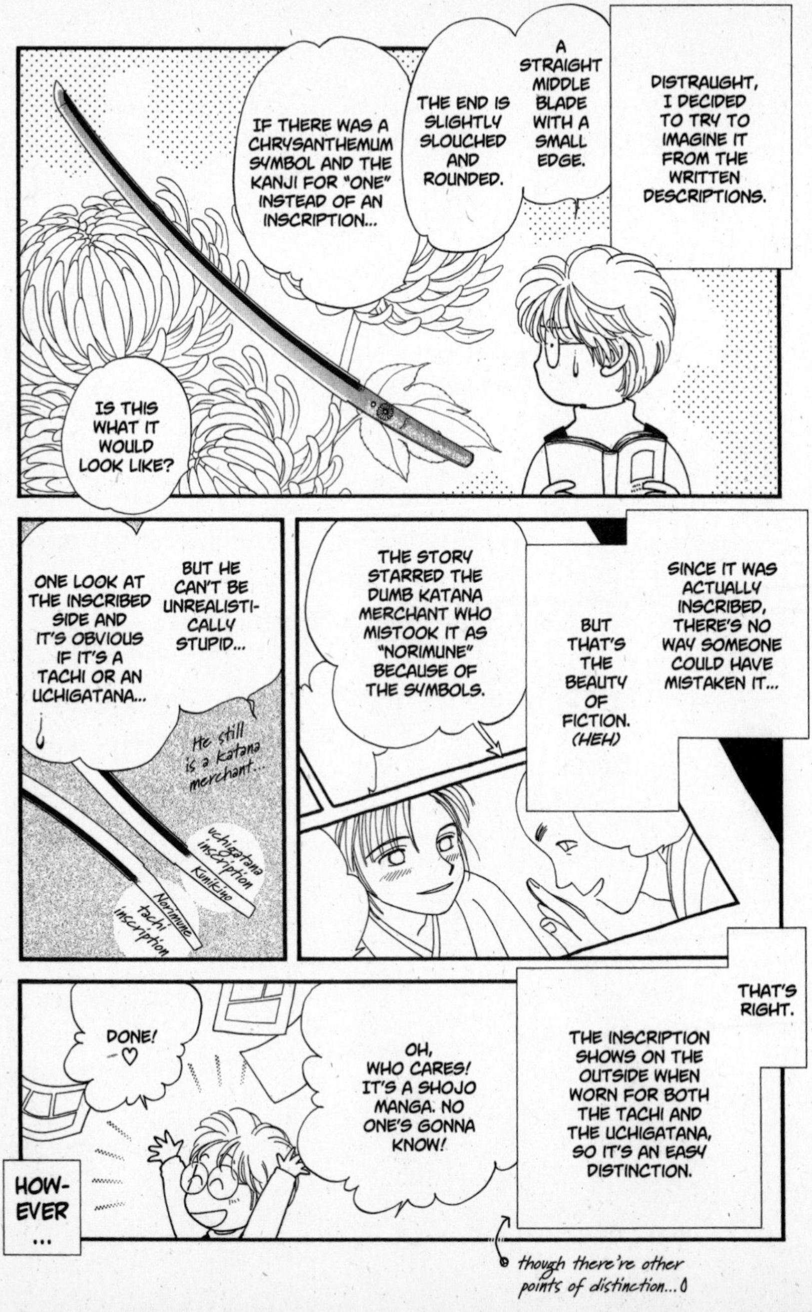
DISTRAUGHT, I DECIDED TO TRY TO IMAGINE IT FROM THE WRITTEN DESCRIPTIONS.
A STRAIGHT MIDDLE BLADE WITH A SMALL EDGE.
THE END IS SLIGHTLY SLOUCHED AND ROUNDED.
IF THERE WAS A CHRYSANTHEMUM SYMBOL AND THE KANJI FOR "ONE" INSTEAD OF AN INSCRIPTION...
IS THIS WHAT IT WOULD LOOK LIKE?
SINCE IT WAS ACTUALLY INSCRIBED, THERE'S NO WAY SOMEONE COULD HAVE MISTAKEN IT...
BUT THAT'S THE BEAUTY OF FICTION. (HEH)
THE STORY STARRED THE DUMB KATANA MERCHANT WHO MISTOOK IT AS "NORIMUNE" BECAUSE OF THE SYMBOLS.
BUT HE CAN'T BE UNREALISTI-CALLY STUPID...
ONE LOOK AT THE INSCRIBED SIDE AND IT'S OBVIOUS IF IT'S A TACHI OR AN UCHIGATANA...
He still is a katana merchant...
uchigatana inscription
Kunikino
Norimune
tachi inscription
THAT'S RIGHT.
THE INSCRIPTION SHOWS ON THE OUTSIDE WHEN WORN FOR BOTH THE TACHI AND THE UCHIGATANA, SO IT'S AN EASY DISTINCTION.
OH, WHO CARES! IT'S A SHOJO MANGA. NO ONE'S GONNA KNOW!
DONE! ♡
HOW-EVER...
though there're other points of distinction...

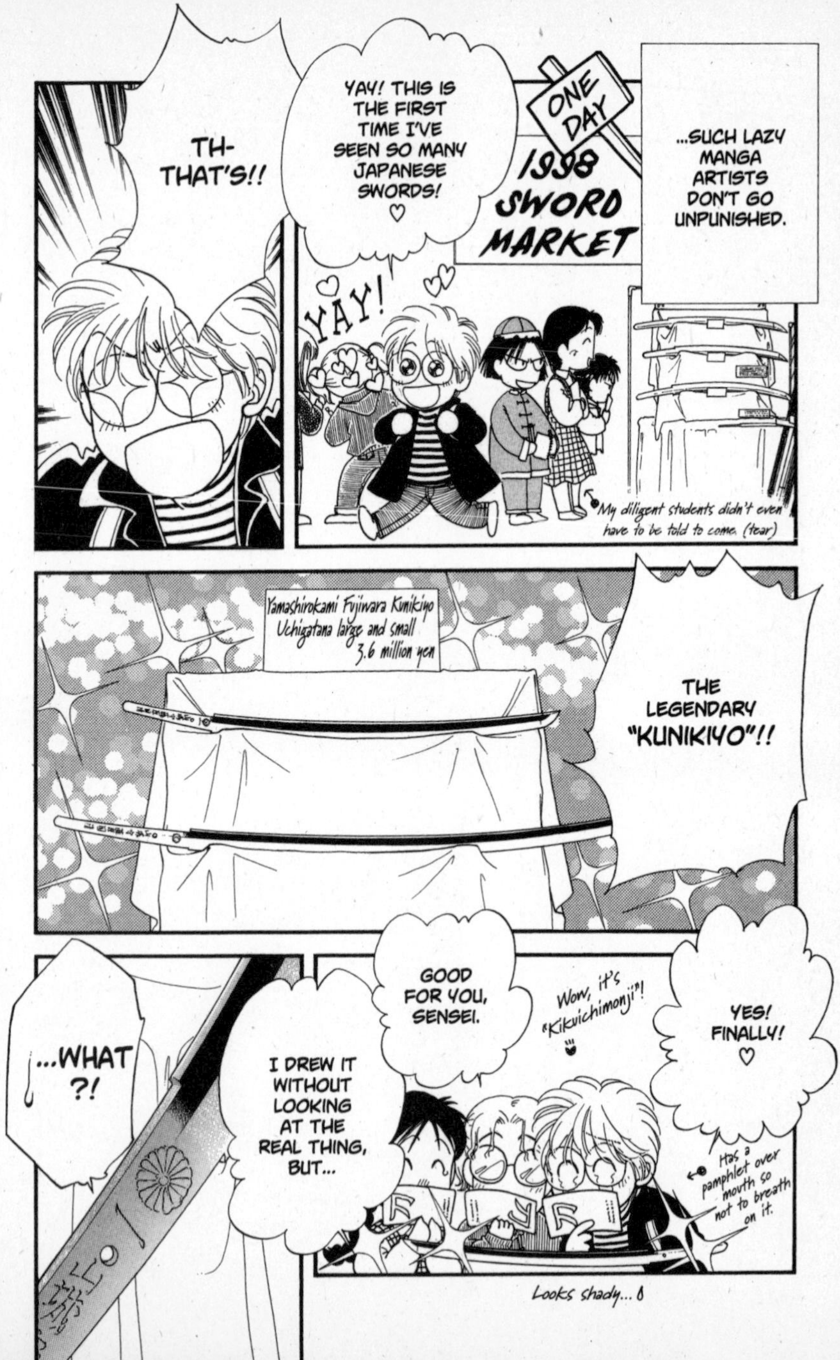
...SUCH LAZY MANGA ARTISTS DON'T GO UNPUNISHED.
ONE DAY
1998 SWORD MARKET
YAY! THIS IS THE FIRST TIME I'VE SEEN SO MANY JAPANESE SWORDS! ♡
YAY!
My diligent students didn't even have to be told to come. (tear)
TH- THAT'S!!
THE LEGENDARY "KUNIKIYO"!!
Yamashirokami Fujiwara Kunikiyo Uchigatana large and small 3.6 million yen
YES! FINALLY! ♡
Wow, it's "Kikuichimonji"!
GOOD FOR YOU, SENSEI.
I DREW IT WITHOUT LOOKING AT THE REAL THING, BUT...
Has a pamphlet over mouth so not to breath on it.
Looks shady...
...WHAT?!

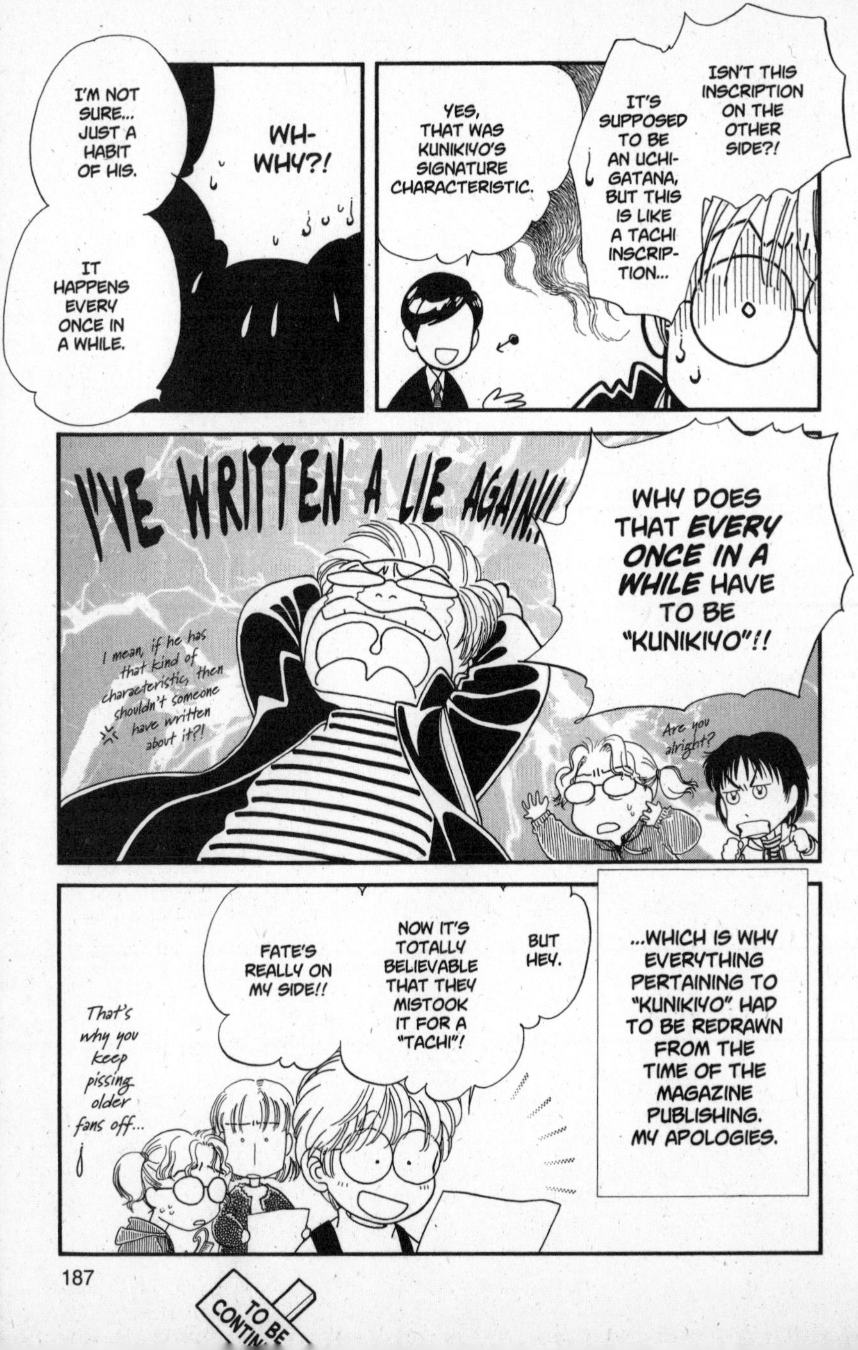
ISN'T THIS INSCRIPTION ON THE OTHER SIDE?!
IT'S SUPPOSED TO BE AN UCHI-GATANA, BUT THIS IS LIKE A TACHI INSCRIP-TION...
YES, THAT WAS KUNIKIYO'S SIGNATURE CHARACTERISTIC.
WH- WHY?!
I'M NOT SURE... JUST A HABIT OF HIS.
IT HAPPENS EVERY ONCE IN A WHILE.
WHY DOES THAT EVERY ONCE IN A WHILE HAVE TO BE "KUNIKIYO"!!
I'VE WRITTEN A LIE AGAIN!!!
Are you alright?
I mean, if he has that kind of characteristic, then shouldn't someone have written about it?!
...WHICH IS WHY EVERYTHING PERTAINING TO "KUNIKIYO" HAD TO BE REDRAWN FROM THE TIME OF THE MAGAZINE PUBLISHING. MY APOLOGIES.
BUT HEY.
NOW IT'S TOTALLY BELIEVABLE THAT THEY MISTOOK IT FOR A "TACHI"!
FATE'S REALLY ON MY SIDE!!
That's why you keep pissing older fans off...
TO BE CONTIN

Decoding Kaze Hikaru

Kaze Hikaru is a historical drama based in 19th century Japan and thus contains some fairly mystifying terminology. In this glossary we'll break down archaic phrases, terms, and other linguistic curiosities for you so that you can move through life with the smug assurance that you are indeed a know-it-all.

First and foremost, because *Kaze Hikaru* is a period story, we kept all character names in their traditional Japanese form—that is, family name followed by first name. For example, the character Okita Soji's family name is Okita and his personal name is Soji.

AKO-ROSHI:
The ronin (samurai) of Ako; featured in the immortal Kabuki play *Chushingura* (Loyalty), aka *47 Samurai*.

ANI-UE:
Literally, "brother above"; an honorific for an elder male sibling.

BAKUFU:
Literally, "tent government." It is the shogunate—the feudal, military government that dominated Japan for more than 200 years.

BUSHI:
A samurai or warrior (part of the compound word *bushido*, which means "way of the samurai").

CHICHI-UE:
An honorific meaning "father above."

DO:
In kendo (a Japanese fencing sport that uses bamboo swords), this is a short way of describing the offensive single-hit strike to the stomach.

-HAN:

The same as the honorific –SAN, pronounced in the dialect of southern Japan.

-KUN:

An honorific suffix that indicates a difference in rank and title. The use of *kun* is also a way of indicating familiarity and friendliness between students or compatriots.

MEN:

In the context of *Kaze Hikaru*, *men* refers to one of the "points" in kendo. It is a strike to the forehead and is considered a basic move.

MIBU-ROSHI:

A group of warriors who support the Bakufu.

NE'E-SAN:

Can mean "older sister," "ma'am," or "miss."

NI'I-CHAN:

Short for oni'isan or oni'i-chan, meaning older brother.

OKU-SAMA:

This is a polite way to refer to someone's wife. *Oku* means "deep" or "further back," and comes from the fact that wives (in affluent families) stayed hidden away in the back rooms of the house.

ONI:

Literally means "ogre." This is Sei's nickname for Vice Captain Hijikata.

RANPO:

Medical science derived from the Dutch.

RONIN:
Masterless samurai.

RYO:
At the time, one *ryo* and two *bu* (four *bu* equaled roughly one *ryo*) were enough currency to support a family of five for an entire month.

-SAN:
An honorific suffix that carries the meaning of "Mr." or "Ms."

SENSEI:
A teacher, master or instructor.

SEPPUKU:
A ritualistic suicide by disembowlment that was considered a privilege of the nobility and samurai elite.

SONJO-HA:
Those loyal to the emperor and dedicated to the expulsion of foreigners from the country.

TAMEBO:
A short version of the name Tamesaburo.

YUBO:
A short version of the name Yunosuke.

Thanks to the flu I caught early this year, the release of this volume was delayed a month. My sincerest apologies to the fans who patiently awaited its release!

I'm sure there are many of you who can vouch for me as to how intense the flu was this year. I've never even had a cold during work and I can't remember ever having a fever over 100 degrees!! Really, I think the only thing you can do when you feel that sick is to psych yourself out. Like, "I feel this crappy but how tough of me to keep working without going to the doctor..." (laugh) But I guess if I were tough, I wouldn't get sick in the first place. Note to self...I must reflect upon my own actions!

Taeko Watanabe debuted as a manga artist in 1979 with her story *Waka-chan no Netsuai Jidai* (Love Struck Days of Waka). *Kaze Hikaru* is her longest-running series, but she has created a number of other popular series. Watanabe is a two-time winner of the prestigious Shogakukan Manga Award in the girls category—her manga *Hajime-chan ga Ichiban!* (Hajime-chan Is Number One!) claimed the award in 1991 and *Kaze Hikaru* took it in 2003.

Watanabe read hundreds of historical sources to create *Kaze Hikaru*. She is from Tokyo.

KAZE HIKARU VOL. 4
The Shojo Beat Manga Edition

STORY AND ART BY
TAEKO WATANABE

Translation & English Adaptation/Mai Ihara
Touch-up Art & Lettering/Gia Cam Luc
Design/Courtney Utt
Editor/Nancy Thistlethwaite

Managing Editor/Megan Bates
Editorial Director/Elizabeth Kawasaki
VP & Editor in Chief/Yumi Hoashi
Sr. Director of Acquisitions/Rika Inouye
Sr. VP of Marketing/Liza Coppola
Exec. VP of Sales & Marketing/John Easum
Publisher/Hyoe Narita

© 1997 Taeko WATANABE/Shogakukan Inc. First published by Shogakukan Inc.
in Japan as "Kaze Hikaru." New and adapted artwork and text © 2007 VIZ Media, LLC.
The KAZE HIKARU logo is a trademark of VIZ Media, LLC. All rights reserved.
The stories, characters and incidents mentioned in this publication are entirely fictional.

Printed in Canada

Published by VIZ Media, LLC.
P.O. Box 77010
San Francisco, CA 94107

Shojo Beat Manga Edition
10 9 8 7 6 5 4 3 2 1
First printing, February 2007

www.viz.com

store.viz.com

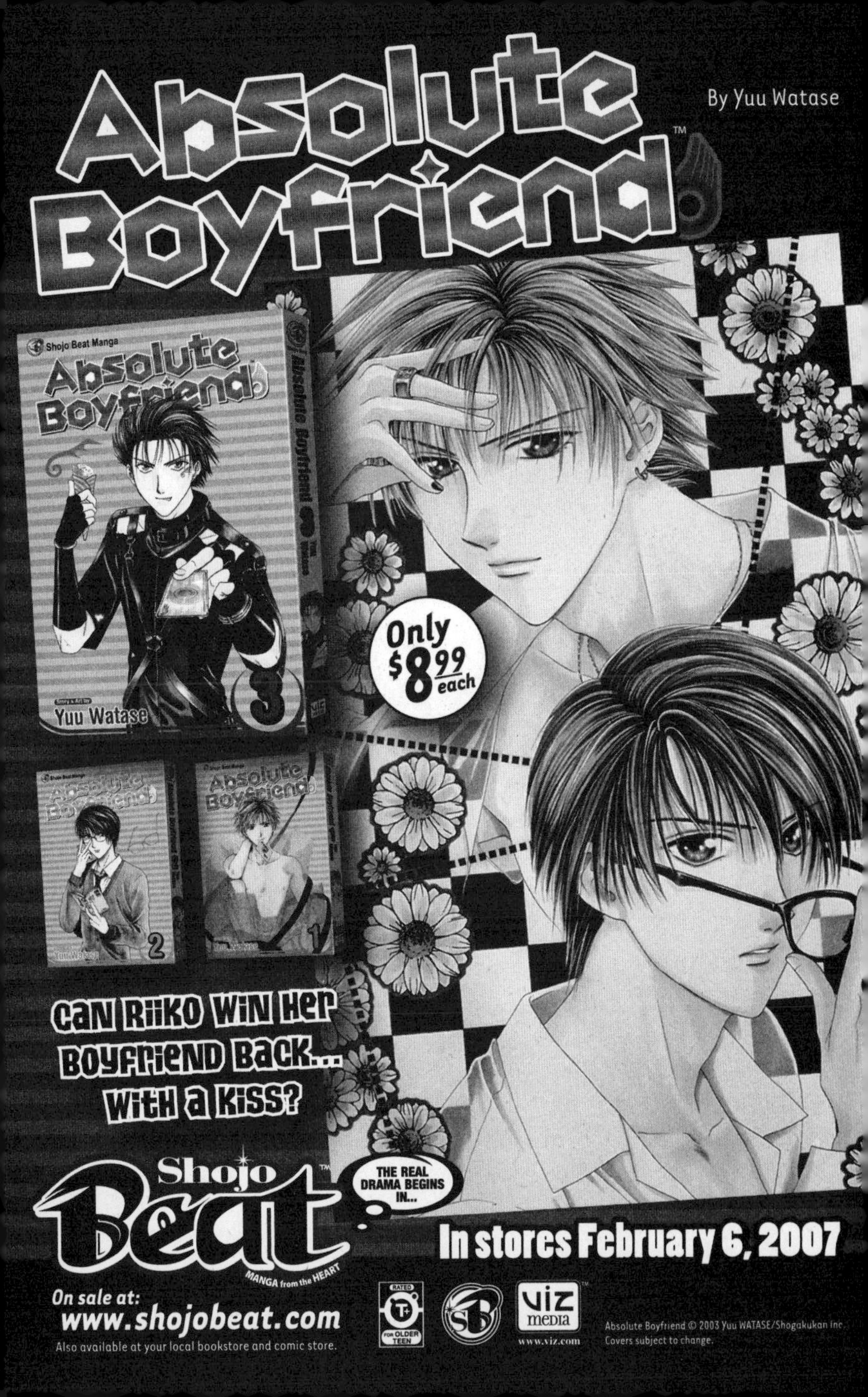

Absolute Boyfriend™
By Yuu Watase
Only $8.99 each
CAN RIIKO WIN HER BOYFRIEND BACK... WITH A KISS?
Shojo Beat™
MANGA from the HEART
THE REAL DRAMA BEGINS IN...
In stores February 6, 2007
On sale at:
www.shojobeat.com
Also available at your local bookstore and comic store.
www.viz.com
Absolute Boyfriend © 2003 Yuu WATASE/Shogakukan Inc.
Covers subject to change.

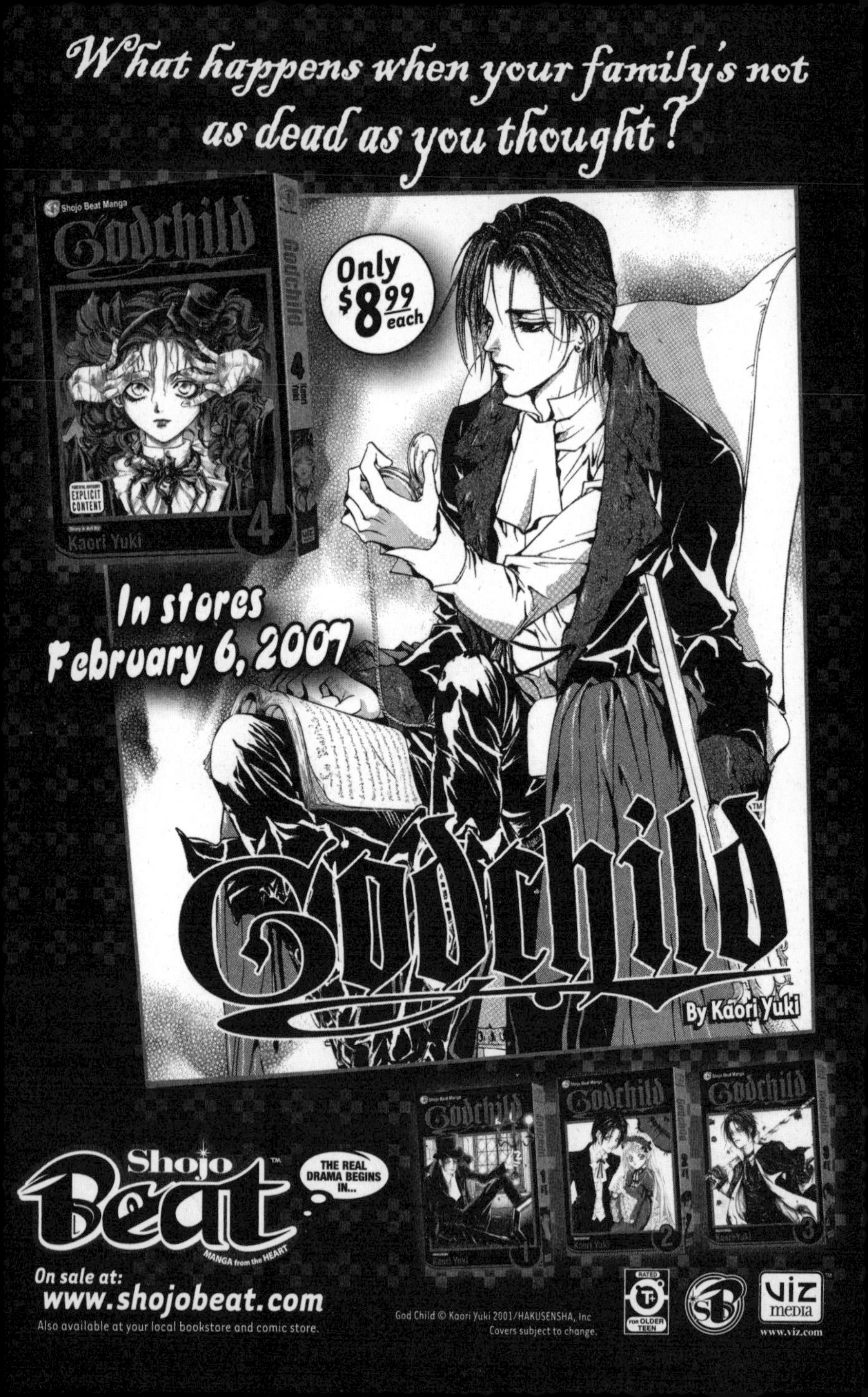

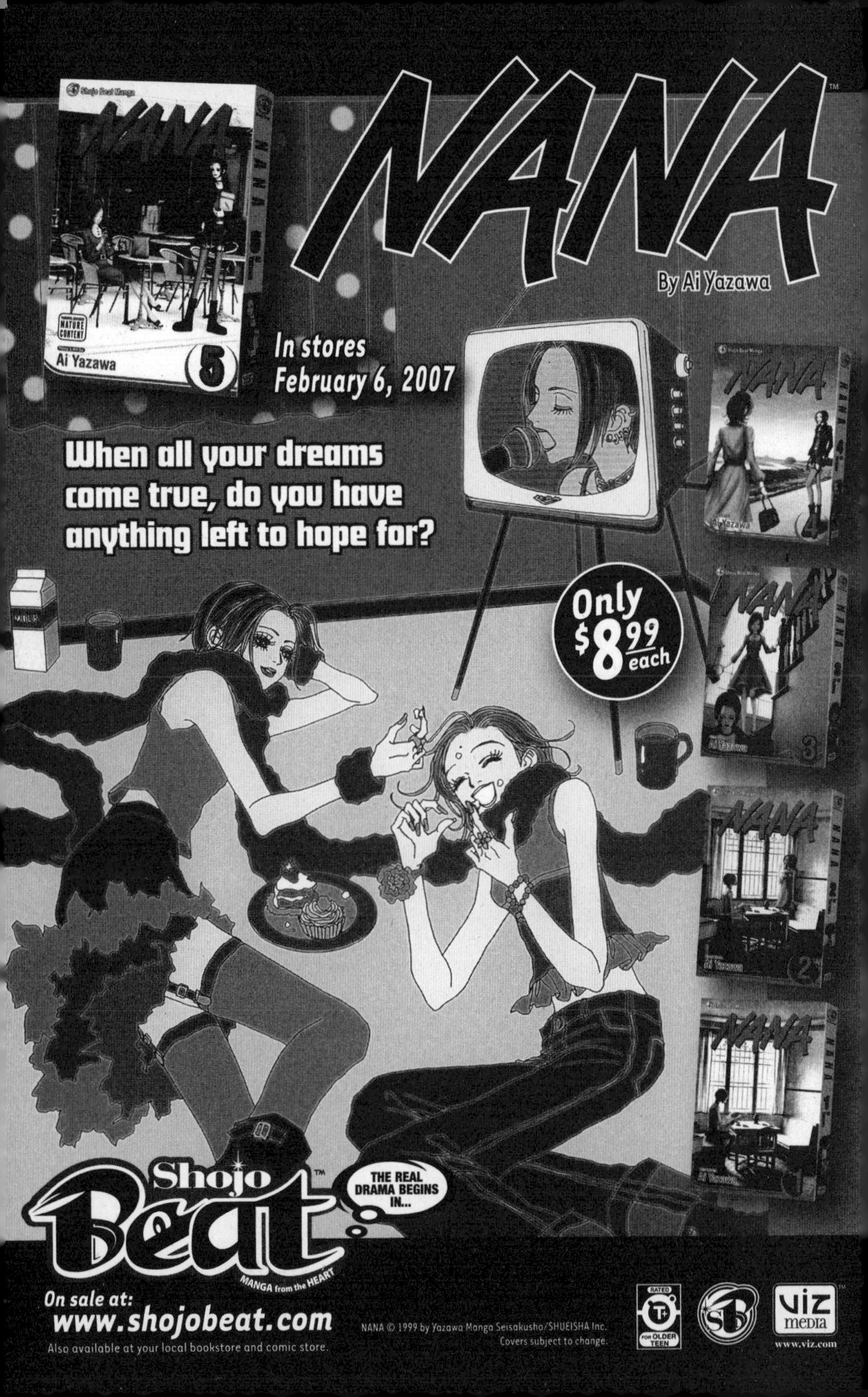

NANA™
By Ai Yazawa
In stores
February 6, 2007
When all your dreams come true, do you have anything left to hope for?
Only $8.99 each
Ai Yazawa
Shojo Beat™
THE REAL DRAMA BEGINS IN...
MANGA from the HEART
On sale at:
www.shojobeat.com
Also available at your local bookstore and comic store.
NANA © 1999 by Yazawa Manga Seisakusho/SHUEISHA Inc.
Covers subject to change.
RATED T+ FOR OLDER TEEN
viz media
www.viz.com

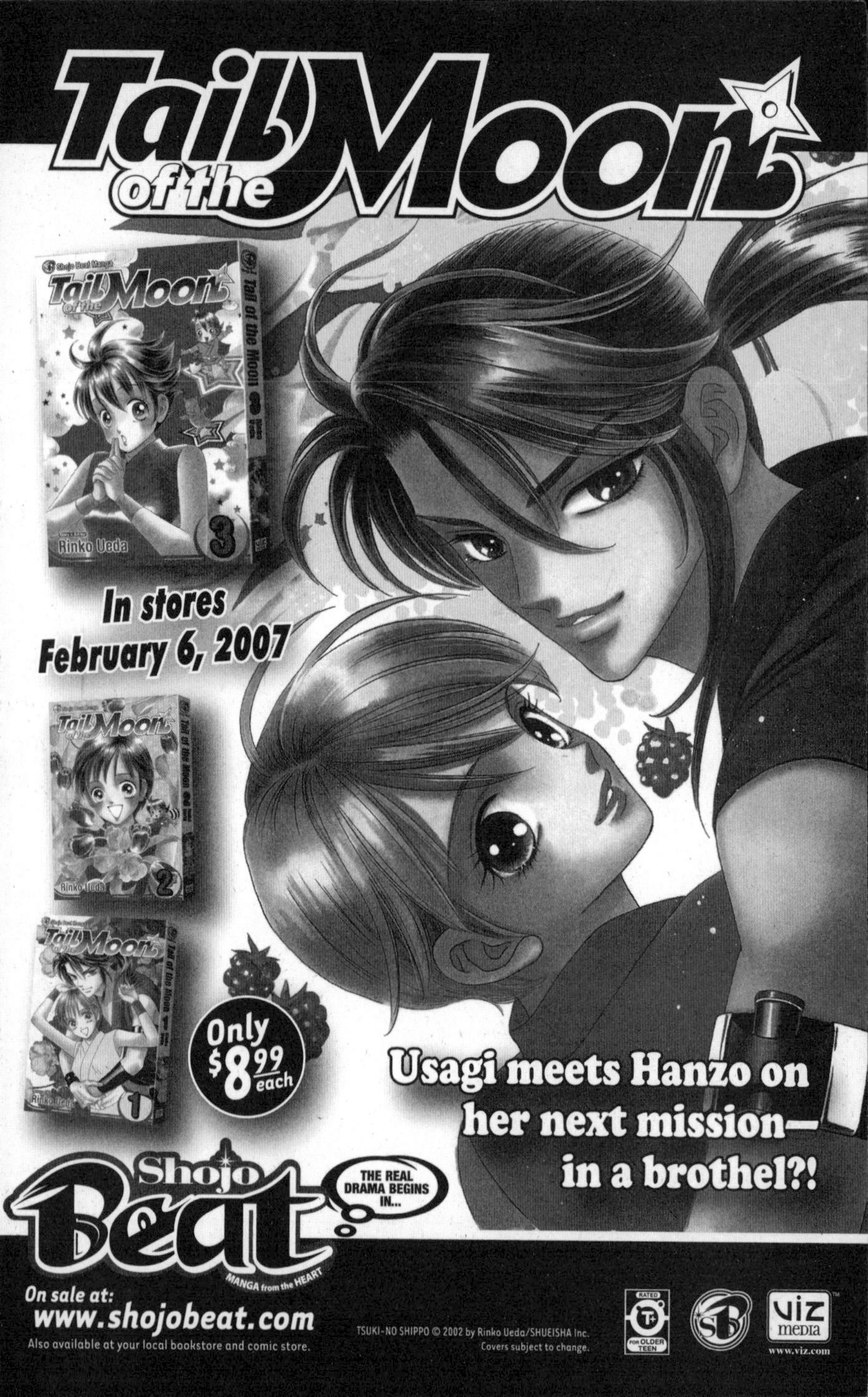
Tail of the Moon
Tail of the Moon 3
Rinko Ueda
In stores
February 6, 2007
Tail of the Moon 2
Rinko Ueda
Tail of the Moon 1
Rinko Ueda
Only $8.99 each
Usagi meets Hanzo on
her next mission—
in a brothel?!
Shojo Beat
THE REAL DRAMA BEGINS IN...
MANGA from the HEART
On sale at:
www.shojobeat.com
Also available at your local bookstore and comic store.
TSUKI-NO SHIPPO © 2002 by Rinko Ueda/SHUEISHA Inc.
Covers subject to change.
RATED T+ FOR OLDER TEEN
viz media
www.viz.com